Intensive
CARING

Intensive CARING

NEW HOPE FOR HIGH-RISK PREGNANCY

Dianne Hales and Timothy R.B. Johnson, M.D.

CROWN PUBLISHERS, INC., NEW YORK

Grateful acknowledgment is made to the following for permission to reprint previously published and unpublished material:

"Guarding the Quarterback" by Scott Penniman was excerpted with his permission from *Intensive Caring Unlimited* May/June 1986, a bimonthly newsletter published by a Philadelphia support group of the same name.

Phyllis DiFelice quote, from *Intensive Caring Unlimited*, a bimonthly newsletter published by a Philadelphia support group of the same name.

The chart on "Common Discomforts of Pregnancy and What to Do About Them" was reprinted from *New Hope for Problem Pregnancies*, by Dianne Hales and Robert K. Creasy, M.D. (Harper and Row, 1983). Reprinted by permission of Dianne Hales

"Do You Need Preconception Counseling", in Chapter 2, and "Fetal Movement Chart," in Chapter 5, were developed by Johns Hopkins Hospital Department of Gynecology and Obstetrics.

Bed and Bored, a pamphlet written by Susan Schwartz and Sponsored by Birthways

"Defusing Stress: A Relaxation Exercise," in Chapter 6, developed by Lenette Moses of Intensive Caring Unlimited.

Sections of Chapter 7 were adapted from "Bed—and Bored," by Susan Schwartz (distributed by Birthways, Oakland, CA.)

"What is Bedrest?", a questionaire in Chapter 7, was developed by Lenette Moses and first appeared in *Intensive Caring Unlimited,* the group's bimonthly newsletter.

"National Perinatal Centers," a listing in the appendix, was compiled and distributed by the National Perinatal Information Center, 668 Eddy St., One Blackstone Place; Providence, R.I. 02903

A photograph of Kelsey Whitney Clayburgh, by permission of her parents Wayne and Rae Jean Clayburgh. They would like to thank Dr. Johnson for all his support and caring.

Published by Crown Publishers, Inc., 201 East 50th Street, New York, New York 10022

CROWN is a trademark of Crown Publishers, Inc.

Manufactured in the United States of America

Library of Congress Cataloging-in-Publication Data

Hales, Dianne R.
   Intensive caring : new hope for high-risk pregnancy / by Dianne Hales and Timothy R. B. Johnson—1st ed.
       p.   cm.
     1. Pregnancy, Complications of.   2. Labor, Complicated.
I. Johnson, Timothy R. B.   II. Title.
RG571.H28   1989
618.3—dc20   89-9832
                                                                    CIP

ISBN 0-517-57477-2

10 9 8 7 6 5 4 3 2 1

Design by Lauren Dong

First Edition

To our parents,
Henry and Lucille Plucinnik and Tim and Myra Johnson;
our partners, Bob and Jo;
and our children, Julia, Bradley, Clark, and Anna.
With our love, always,
and to the mothers whose caring and courage inspire us all,
With our admiration.

CONTENTS

IN APPRECIATION

We wish to express our appreciation to the physicians, staff members, and patients of Johns Hopkins Hospital who contributed their time, expertise, and experience to this book. We are especially grateful to: Drs. Edward Wallach, Marilee Allen, Karin Blakemore, Ed Goldberg, Emily Haller, Michelle Petri, John Repke, Frank Witter, and Rhonda Zuckerman; Cindy Bell, Ginny Corson, Lilli Kazazian, Lisa Paine, Rae Jean Claybaugh, Deborah Cohn, Rebecca Copeland, Ruth Faden, Maryann Hylander, Barbara Jackson, Janet Jonah, Nancy and Robert Kay, Barbara Maczis, and Ellen Goldberg.

Our title was inspired by Page Talbott Gould, Ph.D., a cofounder with Lenette Moses of a Philadelphia-based support group for parents called Intensive Caring Unlimited. We also are thankful to Intensive Caring Unlimited and Birthways of Oakland, California, for their generosity in sharing materials with us.

This book owes its life to Barbara Grossman of Crown, whose own intensive caring as an editor (as well as a high-risk mother) we appreciate and admire. We also thank Lynn Seligman, our agent, for serving as midwife to this book and JoAnn Rodgers for her literary match-making.

FOREWORD

"You're pregnant."

You hear the words, and a thousand dreams are born. Someone new to love. Someone to cuddle and cherish. Someone like you and your partner. Someone special. Then—often without warning—you discover that your pregnancy may not be perfect, that conditions or circumstances beyond your control have put you and your baby "at risk."

All of a sudden, you don't know how to feel—excited or anxious, hopeful or apprehensive. Part of you wants to find out everything you can about what could go wrong; part of you doesn't want to know.

Yet the questions keep bubbling up inside: What's going to happen over the next few months? Why is your baby in jeopardy? What can medical science do to help? What can't it do? Will your baby be normal? What about your plans to work, travel, take childbirth classes? What should you tell your worried family? And how can you deal with the bewildering blitz of emotions sweeping over you?

A generation ago you might have had to keep such questions to yourself. "Don't think about it," relatives and friends might have said. "You're better off not knowing." Often there was little even the obstetricians could say. They, too, had more questions than answers.

Of course, the answer that you, like very expectant mother, really want to hear is that you and your baby are going to be fine. And with proper care, the overwhelming odds are that you will be. Yet, while we'd like to offer you complete reassurance, we can't. No one can guarantee any pregnant woman that her pregnancy will be problem-free or her baby will be perfect. Ultimately, there is no such thing as a no-risk pregnancy.

But we can tell you that the prospects for having a healthy baby are brighter than ever before. Never before has medical science been able to offer so much help—and hope—to mothers and their babies. Prenatal tests are more precise; technology, more sophisticated; treatments, more effective. There never has been a better time to have a baby—whether or not you're at risk.

But as you watch the monitors, listen to the specialists, and marvel at the technology, you might worry that your own importance will diminish. However, in a high-risk pregnancy, the mother's role is more crucial than ever, if only because her unborn baby needs her more.

For every pregnant woman, there comes a moment when the life within her body becomes real, when she begins acting and reacting like a mother. For a woman in a high-risk pregnancy, that moment comes earlier than usual. Long before you can see, touch, or hold your child, you will find yourself responding to its needs as only you can—as a mother.

As you, your family, and your caregivers make a commitment to a person you've never seen or held, a person who needs care and caring more now than he or she ever will again, *Intensive Caring: New Hope for the High-Risk Pregnancy* can help. While it is not a substitute for discussing your concerns with your medical caregivers, it can answer your questions simply, directly, and honestly.

We have presented the latest information on the medical advances that are helping babies before they're born. In easy-to-understand language, we have described the tests, treatments, and options available for high-risk mothers and their babies. And we've covered every type of risk—from the mother's medical history, to problems that develop without warning in a pregnancy, to special circumstances like carrying twins or becoming pregnant after losing a baby. We've also included the stories of women, much like you, who struggled against the odds to have healthy babies.

But the focus of this book is *you:* what you can expect, what you should know, what you can do, what you may feel or fear, how you can cope. Just as important as intensive care is intensive caring—just as our title states. Your intensive caring can make the crucial difference in the months before your baby is born—as well as through all the years thereafter.

Intensive CARING

CHAPTER 1

The High-Risk Pregnancy

"Birth is a metaphor for life. How we plan for it, how we experience it, how we feel about it afterward are all part of who we are."

Rahima Baldwin and Terra Palmarini, *Pregnant Feelings*

• Rebecca's son, born far too soon, spent months in a newborn intensive care nursery, desperately struggling for a chance at life. He survived but suffered lifelong disabilities. Her second child, born even earlier and smaller, lived only for a day. Rebecca longed for another baby, but feared that it, too, might not have the time needed to mature within her womb. Could her next child have a better chance?

• By the time she reached the hospital, Janet had lost so much blood she was in danger of dying. An ectopic pregnancy—a misplaced fetus and amniotic sac—had burst inside one of her fallopian tubes. Emergency surgery to remove the tube saved Janet's life. Months later a second pregnancy lodged within her remaining fallopian tube. Could doctors remove it without removing her last hope for a child?

• Barbara's firstborn son—rosy with perfection at birth—died suddenly after just a few months of life. Her second child, a daughter, developed the same fatal genetic disorder. Barbara's arms ached for a baby to hold, but she couldn't face the agony of watching another child die. Could prenatal tests reveal the fate of her next baby before its birth?

Today these women—all former high-risk pregnancy patients at Johns Hopkins—are the mothers of healthy, normal children. While all babies are precious, theirs are especially so. Just a few years ago, these miracle babies might have had little, if any, hope of survival. They owe their lives and their futures to major advances that med-

"What we'd been thinking
of, dreaming of, planning
for was a baby. Instead we
got a pregnancy—and a
complicated one at that."

icine has made on one of its most exciting frontiers: the long-mysterious months before birth.

What Is a High-Risk Pregnancy?

Each year about four million women in this country give birth. While most of their pregnancies are uncomplicated, the process of forming a new human being is so complex that hundreds of different things can and—more often than most people realize—do go wrong.

While pregnancy and childbearing have never been safer, mothers-to-be still face very real—and very distressing—risks. More than two hundred fifty thousand to three hundred thousand babies are born prematurely each year. The incidence of miscarriages and ectopic pregnancies has soared in the past decade. Despite great progress in neonatology—the care of high-risk newborns—forty thousand babies die before their first birthdays, and the United States ranks sixteenth in infant survival rates, lagging far behind most industrialized countries.

In general, about one in every four to five pregnancies becomes "high risk." This doesn't mean a problem *will* jeopardize a mother and her baby, but that the possibility of complications is greater. A high-risk pregnancy is, quite simply, one in which a mother and her unborn child need special care and caring. By various estimates, the total number of "risk" pregnancies each year ranges from seven hundred fifty thousand to more than a million.

A great many factors can put a mother or unborn baby at risk: chronic illnesses, like diabetes; unexpected complications, like bleeding; previous miscarriages; labor that begins too soon. Some risks start long before pregnancy begins with genetic defects passed from generation to generation in certain families and ethnic groups. Because of their age, weight, health, and habits, some women are especially likely to encounter problems in pregnancy. However, even young, healthy, conscientious women can find themselves or their babies at risk.

The first step to overcoming any risk is recognizing that it exists—and the sooner the better. The American College of Obstetricians and Gynecologists urges all women considering pregnancy to undergo "prepregnancy" exams that can detect potential problems before pregnancy even begins. Often changes in behavior (like cutting out alcohol) or medical treatment (such as surgery to repair a malformed uterus) can eliminate or minimize a potential threat to an unborn child.

Windows into the Womb

Not very long ago, once a pregnancy began, all that parents or doctors could do was guess about the unborn: whether there was more than one baby, whether the child was normal or deformed, if he or she was healthy or at risk. Nothing has revolutionized obstetrics more than the development of sophisticated methods for peering into the womb and watching a fetus as it grows.

The use of sound waves that bounce off the structures of the womb to create an image called a sonogram provided the first glimpse of life before birth. As sonograms have become more precise and technicians more skilled, their usefulness has multiplied. Today perinatologists (specialists in high-risk pregnancies) use ultrasound to "watch" a baby breathe, assess its muscle tone, monitor its blood flow, scan every part of its body—including the tiny chambers of the heart—for defects.

Advances in technology and technique also have made it possible to test for genetic defects months earlier than in the past. Chorionic villus sampling (CVS) tells parents at nine or ten weeks into a pregnancy what they once had to wait months to find out: whether their child has a genetic disorder. Still-experimental refinements of this test can detect many hereditary problems as early as six weeks into a pregnancy.

Another breakthrough technique—PUBS (percutaneous umbilical blood sampling)—allows obstetricians to remove a sample of blood from the fetal umbilical cord, revealing blood diseases, such as anemia or hemophilia, and difficult-to-detect infections, such as toxoplasmosis. Late in pregnancy, other testing techniques can give an unborn baby a checkup in the womb, alerting doctors to any ominous changes in the baby's condition before its survival is jeopardized.

Helping Babies Before They're Born

Throughout pregnancy, such careful monitoring is the cornerstone of high-risk care—and, along with intensive caring, the only difference a high-risk mother may encounter as she awaits her baby's birth. But when a baby is in trouble, high-risk women and a team of specialists have to work closely together to treat complications as quickly and effectively as possible.

For women with chronic health problems, such as diabetes or high blood pressure, the months before pregnancy are as crucial as those before birth. If, for example, a diabetic woman establishes good blood-sugar control *before* conceiving, her chances of having a

> "The history of the nine months preceding . . . birth would probably be far more interesting and contain events of greater moment than all the three score and ten years that follow it."
>
> **Samuel Taylor Coleridge**

baby with a birth defect are no greater than any other woman's. (Without good early control, the risks can be three to four times higher.)

For women whose pregnancies unexpectedly become complicated, early recognition of what's wrong often can prevent further problems. A mother-to-be who learns she's at risk of having a premature baby, for example, can rely on home monitoring and regular checkups to detect the first signs of labor—soon enough to get treatment to buy her baby more time in the womb.

But sometimes treating a mother is not enough, and the unborn baby itself becomes the "patient." The first fetal treatment consisted of transfusions of blood for babies with Rh factor whose own blood cells were being destroyed by their mothers' antibodies. Once such babies had only a 30 percent chance of survival; now, with PUBS sending blood directly into the umbilical cord of the fetus, 85 percent survive. Perinatologists also can administer medication—such as digitalis for a fetus with a too-rapid heart rate—directly into the umbilical cord or, in rare cases, insert hollow tubes to drain off dangerous buildups of fluid within a baby's kidneys or abdomen.

The majority of high-risk pregnancies do not require such elaborate interventions. In fact, most women discover that a high-risk pregnancy is much like any other. All mothers-to-be worry about the babies growing within their bodies. They hope for the best, fear the worst, wonder about the unknowns.

High-risk mothers also worry, and hope, and fear, and wonder—just more intensely. But while a high-risk pregnancy brings its share of the tears and fears every mother eventually comes to know, it also brings some special rewards, including the satisfaction of doing everything possible for a baby, right from the start. That is the most precious gift any mother can give her unborn child.

Are You at Risk?

"I'd rather know that I'm high-risk and deal with the potential for problems right from the start than start off assuming everything's just fine and then have the sky fall in on me."

Life is a risky business. Almost everything you do, from crossing the street to flying cross-country, involves some element of potential harm. Every day, without even thinking, you take steps to minimize such risks. As soon as pregnancy is a possibility, you should do the same. After all, the stakes are undeniably higher, for at least two lives can be profoundly changed by what happens during the crucial nine months before a birth.

The more you know about what can jeopardize a pregnancy, the sooner you can recognize whether you're at risk. And that realization is the all-important first step to assuring that you and your unborn baby get the care you may need.

Usually the problems that put a pregnancy at risk affect both mother and child, although in different ways. In some high-risk pregnancies, the primary concern is the mother's condition, generally because of a preexisting illness that jeopardizes her well-being and, indirectly, her baby's. Other problems, such as a blood-type incompatibility, are a danger only to the unborn child.

WHAT MAKES A PREGNANCY HIGH RISK?

Risk factors take many forms. Some are part of a woman's genetic legacy; others are the result of a chronic illness. Some can be identified before conception. Others appear without warning late in pregnancy. Their impact also varies, from relatively minor to potentially life-threatening.

"My doctor started ticking off my various risk factors—my age, my blood pressure, the abortions I'd had way back when—and I was aghast. It never occurred to me that any of those things could affect not just me but my child."

Personal Characteristics

Weight. Women who weigh 10 percent more than their ideal weights are at greater risk of high blood pressure and a type of diabetes that can develop during pregnancy. Some reports have suggested that very heavy women have longer labors with more delays and complications. A cesarean delivery is not more likely, but if it should be necessary, extra fat can increase the likelihood of problems related to anesthesia, bleeding, infection, and healing. (Heavy women should *not* diet during pregnancy because they must meet their babies' nutritional needs.)

Women who weigh 10 percent less than their ideal weight prior to conception have an increased risk of preterm labor; their babies are more likely to have low birth weights. A weight gain of thirty pounds during pregnancy can minimize these risks.

Height. Women who are less than five feet tall are at somewhat greater risk of preterm delivery. While height usually has little impact on a pregnancy, a short woman may have more difficulty if she is carrying twins or triplets.

Age. From a purely physiologic point of view, the prime time for a woman to have a baby is between the ages of twenty to thirty. All organ systems are fully mature. The woman's heart is strong. The risk of a genetic defect is low.

Women under age fifteen or over age thirty-five are statistically at greater risk. Teenagers, often emotionally unprepared to cope with a pregnancy, also may be poorly nourished, smoke, use and abuse drugs, or be infected with a sexually transmitted disease (often without realizing they are). Women at the opposite end of the reproductive span—those over thirty-five—are at greater risk of conceiving a child with a chromosomal defect, such as Down syndrome. They also are more likely to have chronic illnesses, such as hypertension and diabetes, which can complicate pregnancy.

Socioeconomic. Women with less than a grade-school education who live in poverty are more likely to develop complications in pregnancy. While education and affluence can not protect a woman from all possible risks, they can eliminate or minimize some very basic dangers, such as lack of prenatal care or malnutrition.

Chronic Medical Disorders

A family history of a medical problem, such as high blood pressure, diabetes, seizures, or bleeding disorders, heightens your risk even though you may have no symptoms yourself. Any chronic illness or condition that affects you may affect your baby. Among the problems that can put a pregnancy at risk are:

High blood pressure (hypertension). This common condition increases the risk of heart attack, cardiovascular accident (stroke), and kidney damage, whether or not a woman is pregnant. If she is, she's also at higher risk of developing specific hypertensive disorders of pregnancy (preeclampsia and eclampsia) and seizures. The baby, who may not receive adequate blood and nutrients, is at risk of growth retardation, preterm birth, and stillbirth.

Diabetes mellitus. A woman with this metabolic disorder is more likely to experience episodes of high and low blood-sugar levels, which can harm a developing fetus, to develop hypertension or preeclampsia (a hypertensive disorder of pregnancy), and to undergo a cesarean delivery. The baby may be small or very large for its gestational age and is at greater risk of congenital abnormalities. After birth, the newborn may have very low blood-sugar levels and be more vulnerable to respiratory distress syndrome, a dangerous, sometimes deadly breathing problem.

Heart disease. Depending on the severity of her heart problem, the mother-to-be may feel greater strain, and her heart may not be able to function as well as it did before pregnancy. Pregnancy in a woman with advanced heart disease can jeopardize her life. Her baby also is at increased risk of dying before, during, or after birth.

Anemia. Women with iron-deficiency anemia have decreased oxygen in their blood and low energy levels. Their babies are in greater danger of growth retardation, premature birth, and even death in utero.

Thyroid disorder. Women with hypothyroidism (too little thyroid hormone) tend to be infertile. If they do conceive and are not treated, their babies face increased risk of miscarriage, birth defects, goiter, and, if born with low thyroid levels that are not corrected after delivery, severe mental retardation. Women with hyperthyroidism (excessive thyroid hormone production) are more likely to develop preeclampsia (a serious disorder related to high blood pressure and kidney problems) and to bleed excessively after delivery. Their babies are at greater risk of preterm birth.

Kidney disease. If they have moderate to severe impairment, women are at greater risk of kidney failure. Their babies face a greater likelihood of growth retardation and preterm delivery.

Epilepsy. Women with seizure disorders may experience more seizures during pregnancy. The greatest danger to their babies is a cutoff of oxygen during seizures, increasing the risk of miscarriage.

Asthma. Depending on their severity, respiratory problems like asthma can interfere with the oxygen supply of both mother and baby during pregnancy. An attack can temporarily cut off the normal flow of oxygen to the baby; the more severe and prolonged the attack, the greater the danger becomes.

Phenylketonuria (PKU). One baby of every twelve thousand is born with this hereditary deficiency of the liver enzyme needed to convert the amino acid phenylalanine into its usable form. Routine screening, which began in the 1960s, identifies babies with this problem so parents can put them on a special diet of synthetic protein that prevents the mental retardation that can occur with PKU.

As women with PKU reach adulthood, many abandon dietary restrictions. However, their high phenylalanine levels can be extremely dangerous for an unborn child, causing mental retardation, heart defects, and other problems. To prevent these consequences, women must resume the diet before conceiving. Because of the risk of unintentional pregnancy, doctors now advise all PKU women to stay on the diet throughout the childbearing years. (The appendix includes a number for women with PKU to call for more information.)

Gynecologic Disorders

Often women aren't aware of gynecologic risk factors, such as a uterine abnormality, until they become pregnant and miscarry or go into preterm labor. Among the problems that can put a pregnancy at risk are:

DES exposure. Women whose mothers took DES (diethylstilbesterol) during their pregnancies are at greater risk for miscarriages, often because of an incompetent cervix and other structural abnormalities. Their babies face increased chances of preterm birth.

Uterine anomalies. A woman with an abnormally shaped, divided, or double uterus and her baby are at greater risk of miscarriage and preterm labor.

Fibroids or myomas. Depending on their location and size, these benign growths can lead to infertility or miscarriage. They may also play a role in problems involving the placenta and could interfere with a vaginal delivery.

Reproductive History

Any previous pregnancy—whatever its outcome—may influence the course of future pregnancies. The following occurrences increase the risk:

Two or more early miscarriages. The mother-to-be and her child are at greater risk of another miscarriage. She almost certainly will be under increased psychological stress.

Two or more midtrimester elective abortions. Several second-trimester abortions increase the danger of preterm labor; first-trimester abortions usually have no effect on risk. (While obstetricians use the term *abortion* to refer to both miscarriage, or spontaneous abortion, and elective abortion, we are using *abortion* only to designate voluntary termination of pregnancy.)

Preterm labor. A woman who developed preterm labor once faces a 25 percent chance of another preterm birth. The risks to the baby depend on its gestational age at the time of delivery.

Rh or blood group sensitization. While the health of an Rh-negative mother is not threatened, her Rh-positive baby faces greater risks of a potentially fatal disease called hydrops fetalis, severe jaundice, and other serious problems after birth, including low blood-sugar levels and anemia.

Placenta previa (abnormal location of the placenta in the lower part of the uterus, partially or completely blocking the cervix) or **abruptio placenta** (partial or complete separation of the placenta from the wall of the uterus). These placenta problems can recur in subsequent pregnancies, increasing the mother-to-be's risk of hemorrhage and possible hospitalization and the baby's risk of anemia, bleeding, and death before, during, or after birth.

Preeclampsia/eclampsia (major complications of pregnancy involving high blood pressure, fluid retention, and changes in kidney function). Women who've developed either of these problems in one pregnancy are more susceptible to the same problems, especially preeclampsia, in subsequent pregnancies. Their babies are at increased risk of inadequate placental blood supply and low birth weight.

Stillbirth. A woman who's suffered the death of a baby before birth faces great psychological stress in a subsequent pregnancy. The baby is at risk of growth retardation and preterm delivery, but the risk of another stillbirth is low.

Infertility. About one in every five couples has difficulty conceiving a child in a year of trying. Many spend years seeking help, taking medications, and undergoing often-experimental procedures in the hope of having a baby. According to the best medical estimates, about 70 percent succeed.

For these happy, relieved couples, pregnancy is a dream come true. Usually the months preceding their child's birth are uncomplicated and happy. However, the same risk factors that occur in other pregnancies can occur in once-infertile women. And sometimes the same problems that caused infertility, such as fibroids, malformations of the uterus, or DES exposure, can increase the risks during pregnancy.

In addition, the pioneering treatments that make pregnancy possible sometimes create complications. The use of fertility drugs, such as Clomid and Pergonal, and of in-vitro fertilization (IVF) or gamete intra-fallopian transfer (GIFT) (both of which involve the implantation of several eggs within the uterus) multiply the odds of conceiving multiples. Surgery on the uterus to remove fibroids or to correct a malformation can cause scarring that increases the risk of miscarriage or preterm labor.

Current Pregnancy

A woman with no preexisting risk factors may suddenly find herself at risk because of a condition that occurs during her pregnancy. Among such complications are:

Twins, triplets, or larger groups. Except for a slightly increased risk of heavy bleeding after delivery, the well-being of a healthy woman carrying more than one baby usually is not in jeopardy. However, she is more likely to miscarry or go into preterm labor, and the babies are at greater risk of developing problems before and after birth.

Spontaneous premature rupture of the membranes. Once a woman's amniotic sac ruptures, she is at increased risk of developing a potentially serious uterine infection, while her baby faces the dangers of being born prematurely as well as of infection.

German measles (rubella). The child of a woman infected in the first trimester may develop congenital heart disease, cataracts, deafness, and bone lesions. If the mother was infected in the second trimester, the primary risks to the unborn child are hepatitis and blood abnormalities. Infection in the final trimester does not produce defects.

Cytomegalovirus (CMV). A mild disease in adults, this infection increases the risk of growth retardation and brain damage in unborn children.

Pelvic inflammatory disease. Women who have used an intrauterine device (IUD), which increases the likelihood of pelvic infection and scarring, or who have a history of sexually transmitted diseases, including chlamydia and gonorrhea, are more likely to give birth prematurely.

Genital herpes. Women with active lesions may suffer discomfort and may be more likely to undergo a cesarean delivery. If infected at birth, babies can suffer neurologic abnormalities, hepatitis, jaundice, and infection.

Behavior and Life-style

Your habits, before and after you get pregnant, can affect your baby's health. Among the most dangerous are:

Smoking. According to some studies, smoking may be linked to eye malformations and cleft palate. It definitely jeopardizes a baby's well-being by increasing carbon monoxide and decreasing oxygen in the blood. The result: the fetus receives less oxygen and grows poorly. You should stop smoking before or as soon as you become pregnant.

Alcohol. Heavy drinking can interfere with good nutrition in the mother and cause damage to her liver. In the fetus it can produce a characteristic cluster of birth defects called fetal alcohol syndrome. No one knows at what level alcohol consumption in pregnancy becomes dangerous. All women should stop drinking before or as soon as they become pregnant.

Drug use. Marijuana smokers tend to have smaller, sicker babies and higher chances of stillbirths. Cocaine, an especially hazardous drug, releases adrenalinelike chemicals that constrict blood vessels. If blood vessels in the uterus tighten, they can cut off oxygen, which may account for the increased rate of stillbirths and malformations among babies of drug users. Women who've used hard drugs should seek help in breaking their habit and delay conception until they've been drug-free for several months.

Environmental Conditions

High altitude. Women who live at extremely high altitudes may have less oxygen in their blood. Their babies are at greater risk of growth problems and prematurity.

Exposure to a teratogen. A teratogen is an agent—radiation, drugs, chemicals, infection—that adversely affects a developing embryo. The extent of damage a teratogen can do depends on its particular characteristics, the dosage, fetal age, the genetic makeup of the mother and fetus, and exposure to other agents. Sometimes teratogens trigger miscarriages; in other cases they cause abnormalities that range from trivial to life-threatening.

Occupational risks. Many toxic substances used at work sites may increase the danger to a fetus. Among the most dangerous are:

Pesticides. Women exposed through work with tobacco or cotton picking are at increased risk of miscarriage, stillbirths, premature birth, and some degree of mental retardation in their children.

Anesthetic gases. Work in operating rooms has been associated with lower fertility, an increase in miscarriages, and low-birth-weight babies. However, new methods for minimizing gas exposure have lowered these risks.

Lead. In a Finnish study of thirty-five thousand women, female factory workers exposed to lead had a higher miscarriage rate.

VDTs. Women who work at video display terminals (VDTs) may be at greater risk of miscarriage than those who don't. However, no conclusive studies have documented a definite risk.

Psychological Factors

Pregnancy does not bring a moratorium on other worries and woes. A loved one may die or become seriously ill. A business may collapse. A marriage may crumble. In addition to the psychological impact of such problems, stress can trigger a surge of adrenaline, which tightens blood vessels and may jeopardize a fetus. In animal studies, the heart rates and oxygen intakes of monkey fetuses dropped when their mothers underwent stress.

Ironically, the women who most need protection from stress are high-risk mothers, who usually feel greater anxiety because of the probability of a problem. While nothing can eliminate normal fears and worries, the love and support of friends and family can help buffer their effects.

Women who are taking medication for a psychiatric disorder,

such as lithium for manic-depression, antianxiety drugs, or antidepressants, should talk with their therapist and an obstetrician before conception. Some psychotropic (mood-altering) drugs have been linked to birth defects and problems in pregnancy.

GENETIC RISKS

Normally the nucleus of a cell contains forty-six chromosomes, the microscopic structures that carry genes. At conception, twenty-three chromosomes from the mother's egg and twenty-three from the father's sperm join to form the forty-six chromosomes of the baby. One pair consists of the sex chromosomes—an X (female) sex chromosome from the egg and either an X or a Y (male) sex chromosome from the sperm. An XY combination produces a male; an XX, a female. The other twenty-two pairs are called autosomes.

Just as parents pass on their red hair or green eyes to their offspring, they also can transmit genetic defects. From 2 to 4 percent of all babies are born with a genetic disorder. These problems fall into three main categories: single-gene, chromosomal, and polygenic or multifactorial. Some are biochemical disorders and typically involve the faulty production of a hormone or enzyme. Others are structural defects, such as heart and brain anomalies.

Single-Gene Diseases

An abnormal gene may be located on the autosomes or the sex chromosomes. "Dominant" genes cause certain traits to appear regardless of the other member of its chromosome pair. "Recessive" genes have an impact only if they are paired with another recessive gene. About one in every one hundred infants is born with a single-gene disorder.

Single-gene defects can be passed on in three ways:

• by a dominant gene carried by either parent. One parent has the disorder and a 50 percent chance of transmitting it to each of his or her children. A few autosomal-dominant disorders, such as Huntington chorea, a progressive degenerative disease of the nervous system, do not produce symptoms until adulthood. There is no way of predicting the severity of an autosomal-dominant problem. A parent with mild symptoms may have an extremely ill child, or vice versa. Dominant genetic disorders also can result from a spontaneous abnormal change or mutation within the cells of a child whose parents do not have any disorder.

• by a pair of recessive abnormal genes. Since we have so many genes within each cell, each one of us carries some defective recessive genes. Usually no defect appears because a dominant normal gene overrules the defective one. When both parents carry the same abnormal recessive gene, the chances of having an affected child are one in four for every pregnancy; the odds of having a normal, unaffected child are also one in four. The probability that the child will be a carrier is one in two. Recessive diseases, such as cystic fibrosis (a disorder that disrupts the sweat glands and the mucus in the lungs), usually develop shortly after birth or early in childhood.

• by an abnormal gene on the X chromosome. In an X-linked disease, the mutant gene is located on one of the two X chromosomes in a woman or the single X chromosome in a man. An affected father never transmits the disease to a son, who inherits only a Y chromosome, but always passes it on to a daughter. If the mother's gene for the same trait is healthy and dominant, the girl becomes a carrier but develops no symptoms herself. Women who are carriers of recessive X-linked disorders, such as hemophilia (a bleeding disorder), usually do not suffer any symptoms. Their sons have a 50 percent chance of being affected because there is no normal material on their single X chromosome. Their daughters, who inherit a normal X chromosome from the father, have a 50 percent chance of becoming carriers.

Chromosomal Abnormalities

About one in every 160 babies is born with a chromosomal abnormality. Some of these disorders are inherited, but most are caused by an error in the development of the egg or the sperm. These defects, which involve a chromosome and hundreds of genes, are usually severe; many affected babies do not survive until birth. Chromosomal abnormalities trigger an estimated 50 to 60 percent of first-trimester miscarriages and may be responsible for at least 5 percent of stillbirths.

The most common types involve an extra chromosome (the best known is Down syndrome, the result of an extra number 21 chromosome), a missing chromosome (such as Turner syndrome, in which a girl has only one X chromosome), or the transfer of part of one chromosome to another chromosome.

Usually chromosomal abnormalities cause multiple malformations and almost always shorten the lifespan of an affected baby. Mental retardation, ranging from mild to severe, is common.

No one knows precisely why chromosomal abnormalities occur.

Sometimes there is an error in cell division in the formation of the egg or the sperm. The risk increases along with maternal age. Exposure to radiation and viral infections also add to the likelihood of a chromosomal defect.

Polygenic Problems

These disorders are determined by several genes and influenced by environmental factors. Some forms of cancer, diabetes, hypertension, mental illness, and coronary heart disease fall into this group. The only ones that can be detected before birth are neural tube defects, which are described later in this chapter.

The Birth Defects Parents Fear Most

For the last two decades (as long as anyone's been keeping track), the incidence of birth defects has remained the same: about 3 percent. But while various toxic threats have not set off an epidemic of defects, they have created an epidemic of fear. Today's parents, more aware that drugs, radiation, and environmental pollutants can harm unborn children, worry more about the possibility of a problem.

The most common birth defects (occuring more often than in one birth out of a thousand) are relatively minor: cleft lip and palate (abnormalities in the development of the roof of the mouth) and club foot (a defect involving the muscles and anatomy of the foot). They can be corrected after birth, and children born with these problems can live full, healthy, normal lives. The defects that cause more concern have a more profound impact on a baby's health and future. The two best known are Down syndrome and neural tube defects.

Down Syndrome

Down syndrome, or Trisomy 21 (three number 21 chromosomes instead of the usual two), is the leading cause of mental retardation in this country and occurs in about one of every six hundred to one thousand live births.

Children with Down syndrome have characteristic physical features: smaller than normal heads, oval-shaped eyes, flat noses, small ears, slightly protruding lips, tongues that seem too big for the mouth, short necks, dry skin, loose joints, short hands and feet, and short stature. They often have congenital heart abnormalities and increased susceptibility to colds and respiratory infections. Their overall life expectancy is less than the general population's, and by forty years of age, some begin to suffer diseases commonly seen in older individuals.

Most children with Down syndrome are cheerful, friendly, outgoing, and active. They have varying degrees of intellectual capacity. Generally, their IQs range from the 30s to the 60s, and most can learn to do basic tasks, although they may never master reading or simple arithmetic. A stimulating environment, beginning at a very young age, can maximize the potential of children with Down syndrome. Unlike in the past, when youngsters with Down syndrome were often institutionalized, many are growing up at home and attending either special or mainstream schools.

Neural Tube Defects

Neural tube defects are abnormalities in the development of the skull, brain, and spinal column that usually occur in the fourth week after conception. At that time, the embryo's nervous system, which began as a flat, platelike structure, folds over to form the neural tube. If it does not close properly, the results can be:

• *Anencephaly,* a lethal condition in which the brain does not develop fully and the skull is partially or completely missing. About half of fetuses with this defect miscarry; others are stillborn or die within a few hours of birth.

• *Encephalocele,* which occurs when the brain and its covering protrude through the skull, usually at the back of the head. Infants may survive but suffer severe mental retardation.

• *Spina bifida,* the most common neural tube defect, occurs when the spinal cord, along with its nerves and their coverings, protrudes from a region of the spine. There are varying degrees of severity, depending on the nature of the defect. Some involve an associated malformation at the base of the brain that usually causes hydrocephalus, or excessive fluid within the skull. Some affected infants have severe neurological disabilities; others have none. Ultrasound can provide valuable information on how severe a neural tube defect is.

Neural tube defects are more likely to occur in families with a history of these defects. The risk is highest if a woman has had one or two affected children or has an affected parent, uncle, or aunt. Neural tube defects are more common in Britain, Northern Ireland, and South Wales. In the United States, there are about one to two cases for each one thousand newborns or three thousand to six thousand new cases each year. Vitamin deficiency prior to conception may increase the risk; vitamin supplements may decrease it.

Should You Seek Genetic Counseling?

Some genetic defects happen randomly, but much more often there is a pattern to their occurrence. Those at highest risk of having a child with a genetic problem are:

• women in their mid-thirties or older. For years, thirty-five was the age at which women were advised to undergo genetic testing. At about this age, the chance of conceiving a child with Down syndrome becomes statistically greater than the small but real risk of miscarrying after undergoing the test. But the risks at age thirty-four or thirty-three are only slightly less than at thirty-five, and many medical centers, including Johns Hopkins, offer testing to all women thirty-three or older.

• parents who've had a child with a physical or mental impairment or a neural tube defect

• women who've had three or more miscarriages

• couples with a family history of Down syndrome, neural tube defects, hemophilia, mental retardation, or blood disorders such as sickle cell anemia

• women who may be carriers of diseases carried on the X chromosome, like hemophilia, that are passed on only to sons

• couples whose ethnic backgrounds put them at greater risk (see chart page 17)

Some Genetic Risks for Certain Ethnic Groups

Group	Increased Risk
Blacks	Sickle cell anemia (potentially disabling or deadly disorder of red blood cells related to their odd crescent, or sickle, shape)
Chinese	Lactase deficiency (lack of enzyme necessary for digestion of milk products)
English, Irish, Scotch	Neural tube defects
Greek, Italian	Beta-thalassemia, a blood disorder that may cause liver, spleen, and gall bladder problems and death by age thirty
Jewish, Eastern European	Gaucher's (potentially fatal enzyme deficiency) Tay-Sachs (deadly disorder that can cause paralysis, blindness, mental deterioration, and death in very early childhood

"It's not a pretty story," Barbara begins, her brave smile fading quickly as she looks back on nine years of hope and heartache. "All we ever wanted was a baby to love. We never dreamed it would be like this. At times we felt the whole world was against us."

When Barbara, a hospital laboratory technician, and her husband, Dave, a police officer, married in 1976, they talked about a family—someday. Her first pregnancy came as a surprise in 1978 and ended in an early miscarriage: "The loss made us realize how much we wanted a baby, and I got pregnant again the next year."

Born on August 31, 1979, their son Samuel—seven pounds six ounces, strong and healthy—immediately became the light and delight of their lives. "We were thrilled, just as happy as could be," Barbara recalls. Then at a routine checkup at two and a half months, the pediatrician noticed that Sammy's liver and spleen were enlarged and ordered blood tests. Something was wrong—very, very wrong.

The stunned couple took their son to the hospital. "At first, the doctors thought it was leukemia; then they ruled that out," Barbara says. "I was with Sammy almost constantly, but they just couldn't save him." Nine days after he entered the hospital, little Sam died of liver and kidney failure.

The young parents listened to all the things friends and family say when an infant dies: "You'll have another." "You're young." "You'll get over it." Barbara and Dave tried to find out what had gone wrong. No one had any answers. "It was a fluke, a one-in-a-million tragedy," the doctors assured them, encouraging them to have another baby. "It can't happen again."

Two years and countless tears later, Barbara felt strong enough to try for another child. "I was scared to death but happy during the whole pregnancy," she says. On November 24, 1981, she gave birth to a nine-pound girl, Laura, "a big fat Gerber's baby. We were on cloud nine. It was a wonderful time. She was a super baby, sleeping through the night at four weeks, always happy."

But when Laura was four months old, Barbara noticed an odd bump on her ankle. "At first the pediatrician didn't think it was anything, and even I felt I was probably being a little paranoid. Then Laura starting having respiratory problems, and we took her to the hospital." Her symptoms, including the nodules on her ankles, fit the classic pattern of Farber's disease, a rare and fatal genetic disease caused by a missing enzyme. Tests of tissue samples from her brother Sam revealed the same deadly flaw.

Farber's is a recessive hereditary disease, which means that both parents must carry the same defective gene to conceive a child with the illness. "There are only a few known cases in the world, and the odds that both of us would carry the gene for Farber's are astronomical," says Barbara. "Even when both parents are carriers, in every pregnancy there's only a one-in-four chance that we'll both pass on that one bad gene. Yet that's what happened with Sammy and with Laura. It was like being struck by lightning twice."

Devoted to a child they knew could not be saved, Barbara and Dave brought Laura home. When the doctors suggested a bone marrow transplant as a long-shot possibility, every single person in their families volunteered for blood tests to see who might be the best donor. But they ran out of time. Laura died at five and a half months. "We watched her suffer for weeks, and in a way, her death was a relief," says Barbara. "I wanted her to be at peace. But the grief of losing a second child was doubly hard."

The only ray of hope came from Ginny Corson, the genetics counselor at Johns Hopkins, who told Barbara and Dave that amniocentesis could reveal before its birth whether any child they might conceive had Farber's disease. "We knew we'd never have to watch another child suffer and die," says Barbara. "And at least that was something. I got pregnant right away, without planning to. I was frightened, but I had amniocentesis and everyone was very upbeat. They kept saying the odds were with us. I'll never forget the phone call telling me the results were positive and the baby had Farber's."

With aching heart, Barbara arranged an abortion. "I couldn't put another child through the kind of suffering Laura and Sammy went through. Our families were wonderfully supportive, our minister was fantastic, but it was so hard. After that, it took me a while to get up the courage to try again."

Two years later and pregnant, Barbara learned of a still-experimental genetic diagnostic test, chorionic villus sampling (CVS), that could detect Farber's and other problems as early as the ninth week of pregnancy. "I thought that if this baby turned out to have Farber's, an earlier abortion might be easier. I went to Philadelphia, to the doctors with the most experience with CVS. I kept thinking that this was going to be it, that this baby had to be okay."

Two days later the happy news came: The baby was a healthy, normal girl. Dave and Barbara were ecstatic, but their joy was short-lived. The very next day Barbara began spotting and miscarried. "No one could believe it. The risk of miscarrying after CVS is only one in two hundred. I felt so guilty, as if I were responsible. I kept wondering why I had the test, why I hadn't just waited for an amniocentesis. Chances are that I might have miscarried anyway, but I couldn't stop blaming myself."

The next few months were bleak. "Why me?" Barbara would

sob. She felt angry, frustrated, confused. "Dave was more content with being childless than I was. We talked about adopting, but then I turned thirty and I wanted to try again. I would stare at women with babies and feel jealous. I couldn't think of anything but having a child. It was something I *had* to do."

But Barbara couldn't get pregnant. For two years she and her husband tried everything, including fertility drugs. Nothing worked. "One doctor said it could be stress-related, but no one ever figured out exactly what was wrong. It broke our hearts."

One night Barbara suddenly developed severe abdominal pain and was rushed to the emergency room. Tests revealed that the problem was a ruptured ovarian cyst—and that Barbara was pregnant at last. "The first thing we did was arrange for amniocentesis at sixteen weeks. But there were problems with the sample of cells from the test, and the lab couldn't interpret the results." The only option for diagnosis in the first half of pregnancy was an experimental test, percutaneous umbilical blood sampling, or PUBS, in which doctors insert a needle directly into the umbilical cord to remove blood cells and analyze their genetic makeup. The miscarriage risk is higher than with amniocentesis or CVS, but results are available within hours.

"I knew it was risky, but I couldn't face the thought of having another baby die of Farber's, so we went ahead," says Barbara. "PUBS was so new that the room was filled with people who wanted to watch, all with their eyes on my belly. It hurt like a son-of-a-gun because the baby kept moving around and it took a while to get the needle into the umbilical cord."

Two days later Barbara and Dave got the unbelievable results: another Farber's baby. And another harrowing second-trimester abortion. "It was a terrible, terrible time, and it left me with bad feelings about doctors and medical technology," Barbara says softly. Always brave, always optimistic with others, she would stand in the shower and weep uncontrollably.

"I didn't know anyone could cry so much," she says. But few people have had so much reason to cry. In all, Barbara lost six children—unborn babies she'd never seen, as well as a little boy and girl she'd held and nursed. "The pain is never the same, but it's always devastating. And it doesn't ever go away completely."

Despite her grief, something inside her refused to give up. "I kept thinking, 'I don't want this to be it; I don't want all these years to end like this.'" Barbara and Dave went to Johns Hopkins for pre-pregnancy counseling. "I needed to give it one last try. I knew I would be considered high risk, but I felt that at Hopkins I had finally found where I belonged. If there was a problem, I knew the perinatologists could do the tests and whatever else was needed."

Before conceiving, Barbara, who had spotted through all her pregnancies, started taking vitamin and progesterone supplements. Within a few months, she discovered she was pregnant. "We didn't tell anybody. I was happy, but I kept wondering for how long. We had an ultrasound, then an amniocentesis. When we were waiting for the results, I wouldn't answer the phone. Either Dave did, or I'd leave the answering machine on."

When Ginny, the genetics counselor, called, Dave summoned Barbara to the phone. "Ginny was crying. I started crying, and Dave had two hysterical women on his hands." But this time the tears were for joy. Their baby—a boy—was normal. "They were the most wonderful words we ever heard," says Barbara.

On June 2, 1988, Stephen Robert—eight pounds, six ounces and twenty-one inches long—entered the world. The genetics counselor was in the delivery room "because we wanted Ginny to share something happy with us," says Barbara. "And the doctor and nurses just about burst into applause."

Holding her brand-new son, Barbara smiled through her tears. "I couldn't believe it. After all those years, he was actually here. When I looked at him, I didn't see a baby. I saw a miracle."

"At first I resented the label 'high-risk.' It made it sound like at any moment I was going to do something dangerous, like crawl onto a window ledge. But as the pregnancy wore on and things got a little dicey, I would call the doctor's office and the first thing I'd say is, 'I'm high-risk.' I wanted to be sure to get their attention right away."

Most university-based or large hospitals have genetic counselors on staff. In choosing a counselor, look for someone who is very experienced, who does genetic counseling as a full-time job, and who has passed—or is eligible to take—the exam offered by the American Board of Medical Genetics. The usual fee for genetic counseling is about one hundred dollars, exclusive of tests.

Chapter 5 provides descriptions of the two testing methods that can detect many genetic problems before birth: chorionic villus sampling (CVS) and amniocentesis. As many as one hundred fifty thousand of these procedures are performed each year; they reveal a defect in about 1 to 3 percent of pregnancies.

When a genetic test does reveal a problem, counselors cannot tell a couple what is the right decision about continuing the pregnancy. However, they can provide the information and perspective to help would-be parents feel comfortable with the decision they do make.

REDUCING RISKS BEFORE PREGNANCY

The best time to start reducing potential risks is *before* conception. Women who get into top shape before becoming pregnant and who prevent harmful exposures in the first weeks of pregnancy are most likely to have full-term, full-size, healthy babies. Those who start a pregnancy poorly nourished, too thin or too fat, suffering from an unrecognized infection, smoking, drinking, or taking drugs (either medicinal or recreational) have a strike against them and their unborn babies.

In addition, women who are unaware that they're pregnant may be exposed to harmful substances in the early, crucial stages of fetal development. One of the most critical periods begins just seventeen days after conception—before many women suspect they're pregnant—and continues for about five and a half weeks. During this time, the tiny embryo grows 2.5 million times in size. The cells that will become eyes and hands and feet and internal organs differentiate and move to their assigned positions. Exposure to many drugs, alcohol, radiation, or other hazards at this stage can have a devastating impact on a baby's normal development and, sometimes, on its survival.

Who Needs Prepregnancy Counseling?

Many couples who've postponed childbearing to their late thirties seek counseling before pregnancy because they want to know if they've waited too long. Others are concerned about their medical history or exposure to toxic chemicals. Yet every pair of prospective parents—regardless of their age, occupation, and medical history—could benefit from prepregnancy testing.

Women at risk have the most to gain. For example, a woman with diabetes—whose baby may be three or four times more likely to have birth defects—can drastically reduce the potential danger by bringing her blood-sugar levels under tight control before concep-

---

Should You Get Prepregnancy Counseling?

To determine if you might benefit from preconception counseling, ask yourself the following questions:

- Do you have a major medical problem, such as diabetes, asthma, anemia, or high blood pressure?
- Do you know of any family members who've had a child with a birth defect or mental retardation?
- Have you had a child with a birth defect or mental retardation?
- Are you concerned about inherited diseases, such as Tay-Sachs, sickle cell anemia, hemophilia, or thalassemia?
- Do you smoke, drink alcohol, or take illicit drugs?
- Do you take prescription or over-the-counter medications regularly?
- Do you use birth control pills?
- Do you have a cat?
- Are you a strict vegetarian?
- Are you dieting or fasting for any reason?
- Do you run long distances or exercise strenuously?
- Does your job expose you to chemicals, toxic substances, radiation, or anesthesia?
- Do you suspect that you or your partner may have a sexually transmitted disease?
- Have you had German measles (rubella) or a German measles vaccination?
- Have you ever had a miscarriage, ectopic pregnancy, stillbirth, or complicated pregnancy?
- Have you recently traveled outside the United States?

If your answer to any of these questions is yes, contact your caregiver before you become pregnant. Even if you don't have any of these risk factors, a prepregnancy check is probably still worthwhile. By taking a history, examining you, and performing basic tests, your caregiver can assure you that there is no reason to delay pregnancy or advise you on special preparations that may minimize your risks or your baby's.

This chart is adapted from a questionnaire developed by Johns Hopkins Hospital.

tion. For women with phenylketonuria (PKU), a low-phenylal-anine diet is essential prior to conception and during pregnancy. If a mother does not begin treatment before conception, her baby has an increased risk of mental retardation, microencephaly (small brain), congenital heart defects, and growth retardation. Even with good control, babies may be mildly retarded.

Women with other chronic conditions can also learn what steps to take to prepare for the physiological and nutritional demands of pregnancy, so that, once they conceive, pregnancy will be easier on their bodies and minds.

Prepregnancy Testing

A woman and her partner should go together to a prepregnancy consultation with an obstetrician, nurse-midwife, or family physician. Such sessions generally consist of a thorough check of both partners' health, family, and reproductive history, diet, exercise, stress levels, and use of cigarettes, alcohol, and drugs. Here's what you might expect:

• A complete physical to evaluate overall health. Physicians will pay special attention to a woman's vital signs, such as blood pressure and heart function, so they have a baseline for comparison with pregnancy-induced changes. They also will look for problems that might have an impact on pregnancy, such as DES-induced changes in the cervix, polyps, cysts, or fibroids. And they will evaluate health conditions, such as mitral valve prolapse (an abnormality of the heart valves), that might be affected by pregnancy.

• Rubella titer. If a woman doesn't know if she's ever had rubella (German measles), a blood test can determine exposure. If she hasn't been exposed, she should get a vaccination at least three months before trying to conceive.

• Screening tests for sexually transmitted diseases (STDs), including chlamydia, cytomegalovirus, syphilis, and gonorrhea. Many physicians also test for toxoplasmosis.

• Testing of a urine sample for protein and glucose (indicators of how well your metabolism and kidneys are working).

• In women with a history of thyroid disease, testing of the blood to measure thyroid hormone levels.

• For women with seizure disorders who are taking anticonvulsants, a complete history to determine if therapy is necessary and blood-level studies to determine adequacy of medication.

• For women with PKU, development of a low-phenylalanine diet and avoidance of the artificial sweetener Aspartame (Nutra-

Sweet) because its metabolites (chemicals produced when it's broken down in the body) may harm their babies.

What You Can Do

After many physical exams, you leave your doctor's office with a prescription. After a prepregnancy physical, the prescription is more likely to be for behavioral changes than medications. Here are some of the most common recommendations for getting ready to get pregnant:

• Prepare to start eating for two, even though there's still just one of you. In the period between the time you decide to get pregnant and the time you actually conceive, you can build up the nutritional reserves that you will draw on throughout pregnancy and, later, when breastfeeding. In particular, increase your intake of crucial nutrients, such as iron, zinc, calcium, and folic acid. (The chart on page 27 lists good dietary sources.)

• Establish good eating habits. If your typical breakfast consists of coffee and a doughnut and you often skip lunch, get into the habit of eating three nutritious meals a day. Your baby will depend entirely on you to get the nutrients it needs, and regular meals are essential to its healthy development.

• Avoid an extreme weight-loss diet. Women whose body fat falls below 10 percent of their body weight often stop ovulating (normal is 19 to 24 percent). Even if you do get pregnant after drastic dieting, you may not have adequate stores of crucial vitamins and minerals.

• Take your vitamins. Many caregivers suggest starting prenatal vitamin-mineral supplements three months before you try conceiving. Multivitamins may help prevent neural tube defects, which occur when the fetal nervous system is still a tube of embryonic cells and can cause crippling, mental retardation, and death. Researchers from the U.S. Centers for Disease Control in Atlanta have reported that women who took multivitamins before and at the time of conception had a 60 percent lower risk of having an infant with a neural tube defect.

• Shape up. Get in the exercise habit. Start off slowly, choosing an aerobic exercise you genuinely enjoy: swimming, cycling, jogging. If you aren't already fit, brisk walking is an ideal way to launch an exercise regimen. You might want to choose a sport you can continue throughout pregnancy, like tennis or golf, rather than a riskier one, such as downhill skiing or scuba diving. The benefits of exercise—improved muscle tone, circulation, respiration, and stamina—can make pregnancy more comfortable and easier on your body.

• Check with your physician if any risk factors might interfere with safe exercising. And don't overdo. Vigorous workouts in hot, humid weather can boost body temperature to dangerously high levels. Don't launch a long-distance running program, which demands considerable amounts of oxygen.

• Play it cool. According to animal research and some retrospective studies that looked back at possible causes of birth defects in babies, heat may damage a developing embryo in the first trimester of pregnancy. If you're trying to get pregnant, stay out of saunas or hot tubs. Keep bath water below one hundred degrees and limit soak time. High internal temperatures can interfere with normal early development.

• Quit smoking. Cigarettes endanger the life and well-being of a fetus. Babies who develop in smoke-filled wombs may not get an adequate supply of oxygen and are at increased risk of growth retardation, miscarriage, stillbirth, low birth weight, and heart defects. If you've been puffing away for years, you may need help—and time—to break the habit.

• Don't drink. During pregnancy, heavy drinking can cause a constellation of serious symptoms called fetal alcohol syndrome. And alcohol may be especially hazardous early in pregnancy. When researchers at the University of North Carolina injected pregnant mice with large doses of alcohol during the equivalent of a baby's third, fourth, and fifth weeks of gestation, the mice were born with brain and heart defects and abnormal limbs. A recent study of almost five hundred women in the first two months of pregnancy—often before they realized they were pregnant—found that moderate drinking (a daily average of one to three cocktails, glasses of wine, or bottles of beer) sometimes impaired their children's intellectual ability and school performance.

• Take a time-out after the pill. The standard advice is to wait at least two cycles before trying to conceive. Going off the pill can lead to a surge in reproductive hormones, which may increase the likelihood that more than a single egg will be released. Although some obstetricians remain unconvinced, studies at Harvard and Yale universities found a significantly higher rate of multiples—mainly twins—in women who had conceived after going off the pill. The miscarriage rate also is higher.

Birth control pills can cause subtle nutritional deficiences. Some experts believe—though the jury is still out—that the pill interferes with your body's ability to absorb or metabolize folic acid, a nutrient that helps cells divide and that is particularly important in the first weeks of pregnancy. Liver and leafy vegetables are good dietary sources of folic acid.

• Get a complete dental exam. Pregnancy is a bad time for extensive dental work. Try to get any necessary x rays and treatments taken care of before you conceive. Having a healthy mouth will pay

Foods That Provide What You and Your Baby Need Most

Protein (RDA: 74 grams). Provides essential building blocks for the baby's overall growth, muscles, hair, skin, and nails.

Sources:
- Meat
- Cheese
- Dried beans
- Yogurt

Iron (RDA: 30–60 milligrams). Carries oxygen in the blood, fosters growth, and promotes resistance to infection.

Sources:
- Liver
- Red meats
- Oysters
- Lima beans
- Dried beans

Calcium (RDA: 1,200 milligrams). Builds healthy bones and teeth, also needed for blood clotting and proper functioning of the heart, muscles, and nerves.

Sources:
- Milk and other dairy products
- Oysters
- Broccoli
- Collard greens
- Spinach

Folic Acid (RDA: 800 micrograms). Helps form the baby's organs and develop normal red blood cells.

Sources:
- Asparagus
- Melons
- Orange juice
- Wheat germ
- Liver
- Fortified cereals
- Lima beans
- Leafy green vegetables (spinach, romaine lettuce)

"I'm an information freak. The more I know, the better I feel, even when there's not much I can do with the information. That's why I shopped around until I found a doctor who never made me feel bad about asking questions."

off during pregnancy, when susceptibility to gum infections increases.

● Double-check your prescriptions. If you're taking any prescription medication, ask your doctor about its possible effects in pregnancy. Accutane, a widely used acne medication, can cause heart defects and deafness. You should discontinue its use at least a month *before* trying to conceive. If you have a medical condition requiring treatment (such as epilepsy) or must take medications to prevent certain problems (such as clotting in women with artificial heart valves), talk with your primary doctor and your obstetrician about the safest possible drugs.

● Be cautious about over-the-counter (OTC) medications. You may pop a painkiller or reach for the cough syrup without thinking twice about what's in the medicine you're taking. Many nonprescription drugs contain substances you should avoid before and during pregnancy, including alcohol and caffeine. Read labels carefully, and if you're not sure, call your doctor.

● If you have a cat, keep it in the house and have someone else change the litter box. Cats that roam outdoors have a greater chance of developing an infection called toxoplasmosis, which is not a danger to healthy adults but can affect a fetus, and of passing it on to those who change their litter boxes.

What Fathers Can Do

No one yet knows how great an impact a father's risk factors may have on pregnancy. However, some common-sense precautions can eliminate potential dangers:

● Snuff out cigarettes. There's no proof that a father's smoking harms a fetus, but passive smoking during pregnancy may have some effect. And scientists have linked heavy smoking to high numbers of abnormal sperm.

● Drink less. Heavy drinking reduces the number of sperm and interferes with their ability to move. Some evidence suggests that a man's alcohol intake may affect his child's birth weight. In a study of 377 infants, those whose fathers had at least two drinks a day (or five or more in one sitting) in the months before conception averaged 6.5 ounces lighter than the others, regardless of whether the mothers drank.

● Check out dangers at work. Exposure to certain toxins, such as heavy metals, vinyl chloride, and chloroprene (a liquid used to manufacture neoprene rubber), has been linked to higher miscarriage rates in workers' wives.

IDENTIFYING RISKS DURING PREGNANCY

Risk status can change throughout pregnancy. A woman who learns that her heavy smoking is a serious risk factor before she becomes pregnant can quit and eliminate the threat. A woman classified as low risk before or early in pregnancy may suddenly become high risk when she starts bleeding in her seventh month. Another woman with a history of early miscarriages may start out at very high risk and "risk-down" once she enters her last trimester. That's why it's important to see your caregivers regularly before and throughout pregnancy.

Your First Prenatal Visit

Probably the single most important examination of your pregnancy is your first one, which you should schedule as soon as you suspect you're pregnant. Obstetricians review the same information covered at a prepregnancy exam: height, weight, blood pressure, laboratory tests for urinary tract infections, sexually transmitted diseases, anemia, etc. In addition, they check certain factors related to pregnancy, such as pelvic capacity and the size of your expanding uterus.

If you haven't been tested before pregnancy, your caregivers will take a blood sample to identify blood type, irregular antibodies, Rh factor, hemoglobin level (concentration of the molecule that carries oxygen in the blood), and hematocrit (percentage of blood present as blood cells) to detect anemia. Screening for hepatitis B antigens is often performed routinely. It is definitely done if a woman is at risk.

Another key determination is estimating your delivery date. Usually doctors "date" a pregnancy by the first day of your last menstrual cycle. One standard method is Nagele's rule, which takes the date of the last menstrual period, subtracts three months and adds seven days. For example:

First date of last menstrual period:	9/15 (September 15)
minus	3 months
	6/15
plus	7 days
Estimated date of delivery:	6/22 (June 22)

A gestational calculator or wheel (you'll inevitably see your doctor or midwife using one) eliminates the need to do the mathematics yourself. If you do not know the date of your last menstrual period or if your cycle is irregular, your caregiver may recommend an ultrasound scan, or sonogram, which can pinpoint a baby's gestational age. This information, important in any pregnancy, may be crucial in a high-risk pregnancy, when problems may develop and you may need special testing or early delivery.

While most women think of pregnancy in terms of months, your caregivers use weeks for greater precision. A full-term pregnancy of 280 days is the equivalent of forty weeks. You, too, should begin thinking of your pregnancy and your baby's development in terms of weeks.

Recognizing Risks Later in Pregnancy

Since a woman's risk status can change suddenly and unexpectedly throughout pregnancy, it's important to know the early warning signals of some potentially serious problems. You should notify your doctor immediately if you develop any of the following symptoms:

Vaginal bleeding. About 20 to 25 percent of pregnant women spot or bleed lightly in the first months of pregnancy, particularly during the times they would have been menstruating. Continued, heavy bleeding in the first half of pregnancy could be a sign of an impending miscarriage. In the second or third trimesters, bleeding could indicate that the placenta is covering the opening of the uterus (placenta previa) or that the placenta is separating from the uterine wall before delivery (a placental abruption).

Abdominal pain. Early in pregnancy, cramplike pain can be a sign of miscarriage. In the second half of pregnancy, it may indicate preterm labor or a placental abruption.

Nausea and vomiting. Almost half of pregnant women experience some digestive discomfort—in the morning or at any time of day—during their first trimester. However, severe nausea and vomiting may require medical treatment.

Unusual thirst. This is a classic sign of diabetes, and your doctor will want to make sure that you are not developing gestational diabetes.

Chills or fever (above 101 degrees). Both are signs of an infectious disease that may require treatment.

Change in urination. Decreased urine output or pain and

burning on urination can signal a kidney problem or a urinary tract infection.

Swelling of face or fingers. While many pregnant women develop some swelling during pregnancy, you should report any swelling of your face or fingers because it may be a sign of blood-pressure or kidney problems.

Severe or continuous headaches. You may develop headaches about as often as you did before pregnancy, but a persistent or particularly painful headache could signal a blood-pressure problem.

Blurring or dimming of vision. This symptom could indicate that your blood pressure is rising and that you need immediate treatment.

Fluid from your vagina. A sudden gush of fluid early in pregnancy may indicate a miscarriage. Later in pregnancy it could mean that the membrane of your amniotic sac has ruptured and you may begin premature labor.

IF YOU ARE HIGH-RISK

Being at risk may change some aspects of your life, but it doesn't change you. At times you may feel distressingly out of control of your body, but you can still ask questions. You can—and should—participate in decisions. You can express fears and doubts. You also can do a great deal to overcome risks—on your own and by working closely with your caregivers. While they make a diagnosis and management plan, you are the one responsible for following it—for your sake, and for your baby's. And, with state-of-the-art care, you can be assured that your baby will get the best possible start in life.

CHAPTER 3

If You're over Thirty-five

"My mother was twenty-nine when she had her first child, and everyone thought she was old. It's so much better today. I was thirty-seven when I got pregnant, and I was almost a 'youngster' in my doctor's practice."

At thirty-nine, Anne had done it all: finished graduate school, climbed to top management ranks in a major investment firm, traveled to four continents and dozens of countries, bought and decorated a downtown condominium. Her first, brief marriage ended when she was thirty-one. Since remarrying at thirty-six, she and her second husband had created a life they loved.

Yet when Anne's husband asked what the woman who had everything wanted before she turned forty, she answered without hesitating: a baby. While they had talked about starting a family, never before had Anne felt so ready. "Suddenly a baby made sense," she says. "And as soon as I realized that, I wanted to get pregnant immediately. I didn't feel I had a moment to lose."

Anne is one of a new breed of mothers—women in their thirties and forties who, as she puts it, "got their first gray hairs before their first babies." The number of women becoming pregnant for the first time after age thirty-five has quadrupled in the last decade. Mothers over thirty now account for about one-third of births. And with huge numbers of still-childless baby boomers entering their late thirties, the number of older mothers should continue to soar in the coming years.

For women nervously mindful of their ticking biological clocks, the sheer number of midlife mothers can be comforting—at least to a certain extent. "I no longer worry that I'll be the 'old lady' of Lamaze," says one forty-year-old. "But that doesn't mean I don't worry. It's great to know that celebrities and other women have healthy babies later in life, but what concerns me is *my* body and *my* baby, not theirs."

Of course, every woman's risks, at any age, are different. The likelihood of problems in pregnancy always depends more on fitness, overall health, medical problems, and reproductive history than on age alone. But while age in itself does not jeopardize a pregnancy, it does increase the likelihood of other risk factors. Most obstetricians pay special attention to women over thirty-five but generally consider them high-risk only if they have other risk factors or develop complications.

THE NEW "OLD" MOTHERS

Not too long ago first-time mothers over age thirty automatically were dubbed "elderly primiparas," a less-than-flattering medical term for first-time mothers of a certain age. Compared to other mothers of the 1950s or 1960s, who tended to marry young and start their families immediately, the thirtysomething pregnant woman was undeniably older, even though far from truly old.

The post–pill generation has rewritten the timetable for reproduction. Able to control fertility more effectively than ever before, women today are marrying later—and dissolving early marriages to remarry again in their thirties or forties. Single women in their thirties are having babies even if no man is available to share the responsibilities of parenthood. And some women who had children in their early twenties are starting all over again so they can savor the sweetness of motherhood in their maturity.

In most aspects of these women's lives, age doesn't matter—or, at least, doesn't matter much. Those who've been eating nutritiously and exercising regularly don't feel any older at thirty-five or forty than they did at twenty-five or thirty. "I've gotten better as I've gotten older," says a woman of thirty-eight. "When I was in my twenties, I felt I could get away with eating junk foods, drinking a little too much, even smoking. Now I've cut out cigarettes and alcohol and watch what I eat. I'm sure I'm in better condition to have a child than I was ten or twenty years ago."

AGING EGGS: THE GENETIC RISKS

While many risks associated with aging can be overcome by healthful eating, exercise, and good habits, one can not: the increased likelihood of bearing a child with a chromosomal abnormality. For

Down Syndrome and Age

Mother's Age	Risk of Down Syndrome
20	1/1667
21	1/1667
22	1/1429
23	1/1429
24	1/1250
25	1/1250
26	1/1176
27	1/1111
28	1/1053
29	1/1000
30	1/952
31	1/909
32	1/769
33	1/625
34	1/500
35	1/385
36	1/294
37	1/227
38	1/175
39	1/137
40	1/106
41	1/82
42	1/64
43	1/50
44	1/38
45	1/30
46	1/23
47	1/18
48	1/14
49	1/11

unknown reasons, the genetic material within the egg is more likely to be defective as a woman grows older. The egg may contribute an extra chromosome or there may be incomplete chromosomal material because of faulty cell division or breakage.

As the chart on page 34 illustrates, the risk of all chromosomal abnormalities increases dramatically over time, from 1 in 204 at age thirty-five to 1 in 20 at age forty-five. The most common of these disorders are Trisomy 21 (caused by an extra number 21 chromosome), better known as Down syndrome (see chapter 2). Two other trisomies, involving chromosomes 13 and 18, also occur more often with age. Babies with these defects may survive pregnancy, but they're more likely to develop fetal distress during labor, increasing the likelihood of a cesarean section, and they inevitably die a short time after birth.

The standard tests for genetic defects are chorionic villus sampling (CVS) and amniocentesis (both are described in chapter 5). According to the most recent research data, both are about equally safe, triggering miscarriages in only about half a percent of the women undergoing the procedures.

In deciding between the two tests, some women (and their doctors) feel more comfortable with amniocentesis, which has been used longer and much more extensively. However, many favor CVS because it can be performed more than a month earlier, usually at about nine weeks, and the results are available within a few days to two weeks. Amniocentesis, performed in the fourteenth to sixteenth week, may not yield results until the twentieth week.

Maternal age is the most common reason for undergoing genetic testing. In metropolitan centers in the United States, at least 40 percent of women over thirty-five are tested; in 97 percent of the cases, the results are normal. Yet genetic testing can raise unexpected dilemmas and emotions.

Intellectually, older couples may feel that genetic testing—whether with CVS or amniocentesis—is the wisest course. Emotionally, however, the decision to undergo testing may stir up deep issues. Couples who strongly oppose abortion may prefer not to consider testing. Others will proceed with the tests because they feel that, if the results are abnormal, they will have more time to prepare for the birth of a child with a genetic defect.

But if the tests do indeed reveal an abnormality, the couple may rethink their ability to care for a child with a serious disorder because of their age. How will they cope as they grow older? What will happen to their child as an adult? How will he or she cope after their deaths? Sometimes tests reveal other problems, with uncertain potential impacts on a child's life, making the decisions even harder.

The answers are never clear, and the ultimate choice can be wrenching. Even when couples do not oppose abortion and believe that terminating a pregnancy for genetic reasons is the best possible course, they may feel great grief if they have to face the prospect of losing a deeply wished-for child.

Simply waiting for the results of testing—whether it's a matter of days for CVS or weeks for amniocentesis—also can cloud a pregnancy. Parents may feel that the pregnancy, along with their entire future, is "on hold," pending the results. And unlike younger couples, older partners can not comfort each other with reassurances that time is on their side and that, whatever the fate of this pregnancy, there can always be another.

THE BODY IN QUESTION

Women "of a certain age" aren't the girls they used to be (nor would most of them want to be)—and their bodies, however fit, have had to endure the wear and tear of several decades of living. They're a bit less flexible, more easily fatigued, and somewhat less adaptable. They're also less fertile.

Beginning in her late thirties, a woman may not release eggs as regularly as before. In some cycles, she may not ovulate at all. An older woman is also more likely to have the gynecologic disorders that interfere with conception: pelvic infection and damage to the fallopian tubes because of sexually transmitted diseases or IUD use, fibroid tumors, and endometriosis. If she becomes pregnant, a history of infertility can become an additional risk factor.

Most women over age thirty-five do not have age-related chronic illnesses, but those who do definitely need extra monitoring and care. Generally these conditions can be treated successfully, but they occasionally become dangerous for older women. Fewer than one in every ten thousand women die in pregnancy, but those from ages thirty-five to thirty-nine face five times the mortality risk of women in their early twenties.

In addition, many women approaching middle age have a complicated reproductive history. Some have undergone extensive treatments, including surgery, for infertility or gynecologic problems. Some have had first- or second-trimester abortions. Others have had miscarriages or pregnancies that ended in stillbirths or the premature birth of a baby, increasing the statistical odds that these sad events will occur again.

Certain complications of pregnancy also occur more often when mothers-to-be are over thirty-five. They include:

Twins. The peak age for women to conceive twins is the thirties, with twin rates peaking in thirty-five to thirty-nine-year-olds. No one knows precisely why, although some speculate that, as women near the end of their reproductive years, they sometimes release more than one egg per menstrual cycle. After age forty, the odds go down again.

Pregnancy-induced hypertension. Most women whose blood pressure rises during pregnancy had normal readings prior to pregnancy; some have a family history of hypertension. Women who become pregnant for the first time after age thirty-five and especially after age forty are more likely to develop this problem.

Careful monitoring of blood pressure and preventive care (such as good nutrition and increased rest) can minimize the potential risks. One experimental approach that has shown promise is a daily combination of a gram of calcium and a low dose (60 mg) of aspirin to prevent hypertension. Several studies have found that low doses of aspirin late in pregnancy greatly reduce the risk of high blood pressure and related problems.

Gestational diabetes. Pregnancy makes unusual demands on metabolism, including an increased need for insulin, the hormone that regulates the levels of glucose, our basic body fuel, in the blood. Women over thirty-five are less likely to produce as much insulin as their pregnant bodies demand, and they can develop a condition called gestational diabetes. If they do not recognize this problem and establish good blood-sugar control, they face a greatly increased risk of miscarriage.

Preterm labor. Women over age thirty-five are more likely to begin labor before the normal duration of pregnancy. The risk may be related not just to age alone but to other risk factors, such as previous abortions, miscarriages, and gynecologic surgeries. By learning to recognize and monitor early contractions, they can seek treatment early enough to halt labor and buy their babies more time in the womb.

Loss of the baby before or after birth. The overall miscarriage rate for women over thirty-five can be as much as two or three times higher than for younger women, depending on specific risks. According to a recent review of 1,579,854 births and 14,591 deaths by the Centers for Disease Control, infant mortality rates are only slightly higher among the babies of women thirty-five to thirty-nine years of age but rise sharply among babies of women forty to forty-nine. Only first-borns seem at risk; those with older siblings are not.

WHAT YOU CAN DO

You can't literally turn back the clock, but you can peel years off your chronologic age by enhancing your fitness and general health status. Here are some basic recommendations:

Get prepregnancy counseling. Your primary physician can evaluate your weight, overall health, nutrition, and habits to identify potential problems and areas for improvement.

Watch your weight. Many people find that as their age increases, so does their weight. If you've put on excessive pounds, especially if you are more than 10 to 20 percent over your ideal weight, you can prevent many problems if you slim down before you get pregnant. Even though you may be in a hurry to conceive, don't crash diet and cut your daily caloric intake to fewer than one thousand calories. If you try to lose too much too soon, your body will respond by slowing your metabolism. You'll lose muscle tissue so you'll feel tired and you may deplete your vitamin and mineral stores.

If you're already pregnant, don't diet. Eat carefully and nutritiously. Many overweight women gain less than the usual twenty-five to thirty pounds because their babies can draw on their stored-up nutritional reserves. However, your primary goal should be adequate nutrition for you and your baby.

Get in shape. If you've been exercising regularly, talk with your doctor about your typical workout schedule. While most women can remain active throughout pregnancy, you may want to modify your exercise program. When trying to get pregnant, you should be conscious of how high your temperature rises, because too-high temperatures can cause malformations. Older bodies tend to be less flexible than younger ones, and in designing your exercise regimen for pregnancy, remember that you may be more vulnerable to back and joint problems because of your age.

Break bad habits. Less-than-healthy habits, like smoking, may seem harder to break the longer you've had them. However, cigarettes are so dangerous to you and an unborn child that you may want to plan out a strategy to quit six months before you conceive. Other habits—such as skipping meals or working marathon hours

"I suppose all pregnant women get tired. But when you're forty-two you can't tell whether it's your age or your condition. I wake up dreaming about going back to sleep."

> "I'm smarter than I was in my twenties and thirties, and that's got to count for something. I like to think I'll have more to offer my baby as a 'mature' mother."

without rest—may not seem such obvious threats when you're not pregnant. But when you're eating and resting for two, regular meals and sleep become essential.

SPECIAL CONCERNS

If two women—one twenty-five and the other forty—become pregnant at the same time, most aspects of their pregnancies will be similar. At any age, morning sickness is just as unpleasant. The thrill of the first flutters of life is just as wondrous. The transformation of the body is just as amazing. The factors that make later pregnancies different often have more to do with the woman herself than with the pregnancy.

While age brings definite psychological, social, and financial advantages to a pregnancy, it also creates issues quite different from those facing younger couples. If every prenatal test is normal and every exam reassuring, these issues may never surface. If complications do develop, they may take on greater urgency. Here are some of the matters that *can* matter when women over thirty-five are high risk.

Career Issues

For many older women, pregnancy triggers a reevaluation of career goals and priorities. Some fear that they'll be nudged off the fast track and lose advantages they've worked hard to attain. Others, who've been achievement-oriented all their lives, may look at pregnancy as a project to be completed on deadline. If something should go wrong—for whatever reason—they blame themselves for "failing" at their assigned task.

Ideally, the best time to think through your feelings about pregnancy's possible impact on your career—and vice versa—is before conception. What would you do if you had to restrict travel or activity? What if weeks or months of bedrest seemed the only way to stave off preterm labor?

Some jobs and some employers are more flexible than others in helping women who find themselves in these situations. And women over thirty-five may have an advantage because they've proven their worth and may have considerable seniority and clout. Yet they may also feel that more is at stake because they've invested so much in their careers.

Child Care

Another concern is who'll care for the baby once it's born. Employers vary greatly in their policies on maternal leave and on special arrangements, such as part-time or flex-time schedules. Women over thirty-five, who may be in crucial management positions, may find it hard to plan for an absence of several months. The sooner that you start to think through your options and to discuss them with your spouse and employer, the more you can do to plan and prepare.

If you do return to work, you'll have to make arrangements for child care. If you want full-time, live-in help, you and your partner may have to reevaluate your living space and privacy needs. You may want to find out more about various nanny placement agencies or au pair arrangements. Perhaps your company offers daycare at your workplace. Or a neighborhood mother may care for other children along with her own. While it may be hard to imagine leaving a child you've waited so long to have, you'll feel better beforehand if you think through your needs, limitations, and priorities.

Financial Future Shock

Younger couples, who haven't had time to stash away savings, tend to worry more about the immediate expenses of having a child. But if a high-risk woman has to take leave or runs up high medical bills, older couples may also become budget conscious. The husband may feel burdened if he has to assume sole responsibility for supporting the household; the wife may feel guilty for not being able to contribute. If the baby should require intensive care after birth, a couple without adequate insurance coverage may find themselves facing unexpectedly high medical bills—some in the tens of thousands of dollars.

Another concern is the long-term economics of having a child. While they may never think twice about the cost of disposable diapers, partners around age forty may worry about putting their baby through college in twenty years—just when they're edging toward retirement. How will they be able to pay for tuition at a time when their own incomes may fall? What if their health fails unexpectedly or they're forced into early retirement? Couples may want to seek financial counseling to address their concerns, set up savings plans, and relieve the stress money worries can cause.

"Most of the time I'm glad we waited. I think of the things we've done, the places we've seen. But part of me wonders if it wouldn't be better for the baby to have younger parents. What if we run out of steam some time in the next eighteen years?"

THE AGING FATHER

Men can become biological fathers decades after a woman's reproductive years have ended. Yet even when their fathers are middle-aged or older, babies do not seem to be at increased genetic risk. Studies outside the United States, in Germany, Japan, and Denmark, have suggested that older fathers may be more likely to have children with Down syndrome. However, researchers in this country have never found any significant effect of paternal age, particularly in men under fifty-five.

Yet, in other ways, the father's age does matter—at least to him. In addition to their concern about their wives, older fathers may worry about having the stamina to care for a newborn. "How will I keep up?" is a frequent, if unspoken, question. Looking ahead, they may wonder whether they'll be able to play baseball with a ten-year-old or deal with the upheavals of adolescence as they enter their golden years.

As they look back on their childless pasts and ahead to their future as parents, older fathers may have to face their own mortality. Will they live to see their children graduate from college or get married? Will they ever see their grandchildren? While soul-searching confrontations with the reality of death are not uncommon at mid-life, they take on greater poignancy when a child's future is involved.

ADDING ONE TO TWO

If partners have been together a long time, they have a reservoir of shared memories, commitment, and love to draw on during a pregnancy. Yet they also have an accustomed way of relating to each other. That begins to change during pregnancy—ever so slightly in a low-risk pregnancy, dramatically if serious complications develop. If both had been fairly autonomous, the woman's increased dependence may disturb her and her spouse. Both partners may find themselves redefining their expectations and needs.

Older couples also may feel isolated. Even though the number of older parents is increasing, expectant partners in their late thirties or early to mid-forties may be the only ones at this life stage in their circle of friends. Their peers may have children in high school or college; some may be grandparents. Even though pregnancy may fill the couple with the exciting sense of beginning again, they may feel out of step. "You feel funny talking about morning sickness when your friends are complaining about hot flashes," comments a forty-two-year-old.

"At least when you're eight months pregnant, no one can mistake you for the kid's grandmother."

RECOVERY

One aspect of pregnancy that does seem harder for older mothers is getting back into shape after delivery. Women who've exercised all their lives, who remain active during pregnancy, and who resume working out soon after delivery may find that their weights—and waists—are back to normal within six to eight weeks.

For many older women, the road back takes longer. A great deal depends on weight gain and activity during pregnancy. If you gained a great deal of weight, were on bedrest for weeks or months or had more than one baby, you can anticipate a longer recovery period.

If you're frustrated in your struggle to get back the body you used to own, give yourself time. Older bodies are less forgiving. Your skin, which loses elasticity with time, will not be as tight as it was before pregnancy stretched your stomach. Stretch marks will lighten, but never entirely disappear. If you developed varicose veins, they may trouble you after delivery.

Sometimes the best you can do is try to keep these problems in perspective. "If I hadn't had my son, I still wouldn't have the body I did twenty years ago," one thirty-nine-year-old mother remarks. "And I wouldn't have a terrific little person in my life either."

CHAPTER 4

What to Expect

"When I've compared notes with other women, my pregnancy hasn't seemed so different. I see my doctor more. I've had more tests. But for the most part, it's business as usual."

In many ways, a high-risk pregnancy is just like any other, only more so. Every expectant parent worries about what could go wrong. Every pregnant woman finds herself, sooner or later, adjusting her habits and life-style for the sake of the baby she's never seen. And every pregnancy, like every child, provides plenty of surprises.

Many high-risk women require nothing more—and certainly nothing less—than intensive caring and close monitoring. Others need to alter their life-styles even before conception to reduce risks. Some have to work closely with a team of specialists throughout pregnancy to deal with complications as quickly and effectively as possible.

Because a high-risk pregnancy can make every aspect of pregnancy more intense, it's helpful to understand what you might be feeling and experiencing in a normal, low-risk pregnancy as well as what to expect because you are at risk.

KNOW WHAT'S NORMAL—AND ENJOY IT

Pregnancy is a time of constant change for every mother-to-be. As your child develops, your body adapts to its unspoken needs, transforming the way you look and feel. As a fertilized egg divides again and again, a microscopic cluster of cells forms itself into an embryo. In a high-risk pregnancy, the basic processes are the same.

YOUR CHANGING BODY

For the first few weeks, you experience few visible changes, although you may feel profoundly different: exhausted, nauseated, sick to your stomach. High levels of human chorionic gonadotropin (HCG), the compound produced by the placenta in early pregnancy, may trigger the nausea and vomiting known as morning sickness (which can occur at any time of day or night). Rising levels of the hormones progesterone and estrogen produce changes in the milk glands and ducts in the breasts, which increase in size and feel tender.

The midtrimester—the fourth through the sixth month of pregnancy—is usually a quiet time, although the transformation of your body becomes dramatic. Your waistline disappears; your breasts grow fuller; your belly becomes round and firm. Pregnancy hormones can cause changes in skin pigment, darkening the skin around the nipples, the areola, and the "linea alba," a white line that most people never notice that runs down the abdomen to the pubic bone. In pregnancy, it becomes a dark line or "linea nigra," but lightens again after delivery. Sometimes the pigment on a woman's face also darkens in a masklike pattern. Vaginal secretions, perspiration, and saliva increase.

By the end of twenty-four weeks, your uterus multiplies its weight by twenty times. The production of blood cells in the body accelerates; total blood volume increases by 30 to 50 percent. Your heart, working harder to pump the greater supply of blood, enlarges slightly and shifts position. By midpregnancy your breasts, functionally ready for nursing, secrete a thin amber or yellow substance called colostrum.

The most exciting experience of the midtrimester is feeling the baby moving inside the womb, which usually happens between the sixteenth and twenty-second week. At first the baby, swimming about with plenty of room to move, creates only gentle fishlike sensations. As it grows, its somersaults, kicks, and pokes become stronger.

During the final three months of pregnancy, the growing uterus pushes against the lungs, and many women feel breathless after any exertion, even though they are taking in more oxygen than before. When you sit or lie down for a prolonged period, the physical pressure of the growing uterus on the vessels that carry blood to and from the lower limbs makes it harder for them to empty.

In the final weeks, the baby "drops" or settles low in the pelvis, making breathing much easier. Some women feel tired, especially if the need to urinate frequently or the baby's kicks keep them awake at night. Many mothers-to-be look forward to delivery with both apprehension and eagerness, waiting restlessly for the day when they can hold their babies for the first time.

How a Mother's Body Changes

First Trimester
- Increased urination because of hormonal changes and the pressure of the enlarging uterus on the bladder
- Enlarging breasts as milk glands develop
- Darkening of the nipples and the area around them
- Nausea or vomiting, particularly in the morning
- Fatigue
- Increased vaginal secretions
- Pinching of the sciatic nerve, which runs from the buttocks down through the back of the legs, as the pelvic bones widen and begin to separate
- Irregular bowel movements

Second Trimester
- Thickening of the waist as the uterus grows
- Weight gain
- Increase in total blood volume
- Slight increase and change in position of the heart
- Darkening of the pigment around the nipple and from the navel to the pubic region
- Darkening of the face
- Increased salivation and perspiration
- Secretion of colostrum from breasts
- Indigestion, constipation, hemorrhoids

Third Trimester
- Increased urination because of pressure from the uterus
- Tightening of the uterine muscles (Braxton-Hicks contractions)
- Breathlessness because of increased pressure from uterus on lungs and diaphragm
- Heartburn, indigestion
- Trouble sleeping because of baby's movements or need to urinate often
- "Dropping" of baby's head into pelvis about two to four weeks before birth

Your Growing Baby

Sperm swirl around an egg in a silent dance. One penetrates its surface, and the long, intricate process of forming a new human being begins. In the next three to five days, as the fertilized egg travels down the fallopian tube, it divides to form a tiny clump of cells. The cells become tinier with each division, so the total cell unit stays about the same size as the original fertilized ovum—smaller than the head of a pin.

When it reaches the uterus, about a week after ovulation, the cell cluster burrows into the lining, a process called implantation. This may cause a small amount of bleeding at about the time you normally would have a menstrual period. Tiny fingerlike projections called villi burrow into the spongy uterine lining, and the embryo, as it is now called, takes on an elongated shape, rounded at one end. A sac (the amnion) envelops it. As water and other small molecules cross the amniotic membrane, the embryo floats freely in the absorbed fluid, cushioned from shocks and bumps.

A primitive placenta begins to supply the growing baby with food, water, and nutrients from your bloodstream and to carry waste back to your body for disposal. The placenta, which takes over the job of the villi, serves as a combination of lungs, kidneys, and digestive system for the baby. One of its key functions is the production of estrogen and progesterone, the hormones that regulate many of the physiological changes of pregnancy.

At the end of four weeks, an embryo is a little over a quarter of an inch long—ten thousand times its original size—and developing at amazing speed. Its cells differentiate into layers, tissues, and organs, grouping themselves according to the directions encoded in the genes, the parts of the cell that store inherited characteristics.

The neural tube, the beginning of the nervous system, remains open. There are gill-like arches that will develop into a mouth, lower jaw, and throat. Beneath them is a tiny U-shaped tube that will form a heart. The embryo begins to curl up so it will fit into its tiny home as it grows.

By the eighth week, the sculpting of the face has begun. Large dark circles appear where the eyes will be. Two tiny folds of tissue appear on either side of the head; they will develop into ears. There is a tiny depression where the nose will be and a thickening that will become the tongue. The head, larger than the rest of the body, seems to rest on the chest as if it were too heavy to hold up. The brain is developing rapidly, with the various sections, nerves, and membranes beginning to grow. Cartilage spreads upward to enclose it, although the skull will not knit firmly together for almost a decade, when the brain finally stops increasing in size. In medical terms, the embryo becomes a fetus.

By the end of the twelfth week, the body is completely formed.

How Your Baby Grows

First Month Embryo grows to about one-quarter inch in length and one-seventh ounce in weight

Foundations form for the nervous system, genital-urinary system, skin, bones, and lungs

Arm and leg "buds" begin to form

Rudiments of eyes, ears, and nose appear

Head is disproportionately large because of brain development

Second Month Length is 1.2 ins.; weight approximately one-sixth ounce

Distinct fingers and toes

Complete circulatory system

Third Month Length 2 ins; weight .5 oz.

Differentiated sex

Rudimentary kidneys excrete urine

Heart beats

Nose and palate take shape

Fourth Month Length 4 ins.; weight 2 oz.

Lanugo covers entire body

Fetal movements can be felt by mother

Heart sounds can be heard through special stethoscope

Fifth Month Length 8 ins.; weight 1.4 lbs.

Skin appears wrinkled

Eyebrows and fingernails develop

Sixth Month Length 11.5 ins.; weight 2.11 lbs.

Skin is red

If born, infant will cry and breathe, but rarely survives

Seventh Month Length 14–15 ins.; weight 3 lbs.

Fetus can survive outside the womb

Eyelids open

Fingerprints set

Vigorous movements

Eighth Month Length 15–17 ins.; weight 4–5 lbs.

Face and body have loose, wrinkled appearance

Lanugo disappears

Ninth Month Length 16–19 ins.; weight 6–7 lbs.

Smooth skin

Bones of skull harden

The heart beats rapidly. Eyes are visible behind closed lids. Nasal openings appear. Jaws become well defined, and teeth begin to grow within them. Primitive hair follicles have formed, as have the beginnings of vocal cords. The fetus can open its mouth, purse its lips, clench its fingers in a fist. The "buds" for its limbs have developed into arms and legs, and fingers and toes have been defined. The fetus begins to exercise its muscles and to move freely within its fluid-filled capsule, but its mother cannot yet detect any signs of activity. A boy has a penis; a girl, a clitoris. All major organs are in place.

The fetus grows rapidly, stretching to a length of more than six inches and a weight of five ounces by the sixteenth week. It begins to drink some of the amniotic fluid, which its kidneys process and pass back into the amniotic sac as urine. Its heart can be heard through a special stethoscope. A temporary covering of hair grows on its eyebrows, palms, soles, and upper lip. Its skeleton develops, with bone cells filling in and hardening the cartilage molds.

By the twentieth week, a fine down called lanugo, from the Latin for wool, covers its body. Most will rub off by birth. The eyes open and close. The ears are sensitive enough to detect sounds. Nails appear on the fingers and toes, and the ridges on the palms and soles are fully formed. The fetus begins testing its reflexes, grasping and sucking as well as kicking and moving. It still has plenty of room for somersaulting, but its mother can feel the twists and turns and detect a daily pattern of activity and rest.

By the end of the twenty-fourth week, the fetus is thirteen inches long. Although its vital organs are quite well developed, its lungs are not yet mature. If it were born at this time, it might not survive because it cannot breathe on its own. A protective coating, called vernix, forms over the lanugo, clinging to the hairy parts and creases of the body. The skin becomes more opaque, but remains very wrinkled.

In the last trimester, the fetus adds inches and pounds to its frame. Much of the weight is deposited under the skin as fat. This fat layer will provide necessary energy during birth and help maintain body temperature afterward. Gradually the fetus takes on a more "babylike" appearance, with pinkish skin and chubby limbs. In the last weeks in the womb, the lungs produce a crucial material that will line the small air sacs. This substance, called surfactant, will help the baby breathe on its own. In preparation for breathing, the fetus spends about half of the time making respiratorylike movements.

By the thirty-sixth week, the fetus usually settles into a head-down, or vertex, position in the mother's pear-shaped womb. In the ninth month, its head moves lower into the mother's pelvis, like an egg settling into an egg cup. Rather than moving its entire body, the fetus prods the mother with an arm or a leg.

By "term," or thirty-seven to forty weeks, the process of fetal development, growth, and maturation is complete. Two cells have grown to six thousand billion cells. A heart has been working for months. A brain, which will continue its development after birth, is responding to stimuli. Arms and legs have grown just so much and no more. A face has formed with a set of features that will distinguish this child from all others. In the darkness of the womb, a unique individual awaits its journey into the world.

Coping with Normal Discomforts

Pregnancy alters the workings of every major organ system in the body. It literally lifts your heart and takes your breath away. Your rate of circulation accelerates, and your pulse speeds up by about ten beats per minute. You produce more plasma and blood cells than usual, and your total blood volume increases by more than a third.

Often completely normal changes cause such unusual sensations and symptoms that you may fear something is wrong. However, problems such as backache, swelling of the ankles, indigestion, nausea, constipation, and hemorrhoids are common discomforts of pregnancy. In fact, they may even indicate that your body is acting and reacting as it should.

In a study of 9,098 pregnancies by the National Institute of Child Health and Human Development, women who vomited in their first trimester had a lower chance of miscarriages or stillbirths than women with steadier stomachs, possibly because of higher levels of crucial pregnancy hormones.

PREPARING FOR A HIGH-RISK PREGNANCY

As soon as you learn that you're at risk, you may have to alter the plans you've made for pregnancy, labor, and delivery. Like other pregnant women, you'll still have work to do, a family to care for, commitments to keep. The difference is that circumstances beyond your control demand that you invest at least some—and sometimes all—of your energy and time in the pregnancy itself. Your first and most important task is deciding who should take care of you and your unborn child.

Normal Discomforts of Pregnancy

Common Discomforts of Pregnancy and What to Do About Them

- *Nausea and indigestion; shortness of breath*

  Concentrate on good posture, pulling in your abdominal muscles and tilting your pelvis to give the stomach and lungs more room. Try sleeping on extra pillows to elevate your head and chest. Eat small meals every two to three hours rather than three larger meals. Avoid liquids with meals, acid- or gas-producing foods, and an empty stomach.

- *Pelvic pressure; thigh-hip pain; heaviness in legs; backache*

  Practice good posture while sitting, standing, and lifting. Using your abdominal muscles, try to lift the baby up off the big blood vessels in the pelvis and nerves that might be pinched. Relieve strain on your back with ample rest periods. Try pillow support under your top leg and arms and uterus to relieve the pull on your back.

- *Stretch marks*

  May be reduced by good posture to reduce pressure and stretching of the abdomen.

- *Swelling of the feet; varicose veins*

  Good posture and ample rest will help. You can improve circulation by raising your legs to drain fluid from them. Lie on the bed or floor with a pillow under your hips. Raise your legs up on the wall with knees bent and slowly make circles with your feet to the right and left. Point your heel rather than your toe. If you wear elastic support hose, drain your legs this way *before* putting on your stockings. Change body position often; wear sensible shoes and clothing that does not bind.

- *Swelling of the hands*

  Slight swelling of the fingers is common. Drink six to eight glasses of water daily and maintain a good diet, high in protein. Restrict salt only if instructed by doctor.

- *Leg cramps*

  These are common in the last three months because of the drain of calcium from your system for the baby's bone growth and decreased circulation as a result of the pressure of the growing baby. Adequate calcium in the diet—from dairy products, dark green vegetables, or calcium lactate (only if prescribed by your doctor)—is essential. Practice good posture. Straighten cramped muscles by standing up. Try warm baths, loose covers over your feet, pillows under your legs.

- *Constipation*

  Moderate exercise will help. Maintain intake of roughage in diet (fruits, whole grains, bran, raw vegetables). Increase fluids. Establish regular bowel habits; respond quickly to the urge to eliminate. Try relaxation and deep breathing during elimination to relax the anal sphincter. Use stool softeners only if prescribed.

(continued on next page)

- *Hemorrhoids (rectal varicosities)*
  Avoid constipation. Good posture will help to prevent pooling of blood in the rectal area. Try elevation of hips and extremities. Try soaking in a warm tub or applying witch hazel or Tucks to affected area.
- *Pelvic cramps during intercourse*
  Choose positions in which you can bend your knees. Ask your partner to massage your lower abdomen gently. Penetration should be shallow.
- *Fatigue/insomnia*
  Try deep breathing for relaxation and good pillow support for comfort. Sleep on your side with pillows under your top leg and arm and under your uterus. Or try a semisitting position, with pillows under your back, knees, and arms. Keep your feet up as much as possible during the day.
- *Dizziness*
  Get up slowly, moving your arms and legs to increase blood flow. Roll over onto your side and push yourself up with your hands to avoid back strain.
- *Feeling of warmth; heavy bodily secretions; oily hair*
  These are all caused by hormonal changes and increased metabolism. Wear cool, loose, comfortable clothing. You may feel more comfortable if you bathe and wash your hair more frequently.

Finding the Right People at the Right Place

Nurse-midwives and family practitioners provide quality care for many pregnant women, but if you're at risk, we recommend an obstetrician, who can offer the extra benefits of specialized training and experience in managing complicated pregnancies. "Perinatologists" specialize in high-risk pregnancies or "maternal-fetal" medicine. Most practice at major medical centers with sophisticated technology, specialized facilities, and a highly trained staff—all of which you or your baby may need.

If you go to a major medical center, you will usually work with a team of professionals. In the course of your pregnancy, you may see a genetics counselor, a nutritionist, a radiologist, a neonatologist, perhaps a neurologist or cardiologist. Usually you will have one primary caregiver, but each specialist can provide helpful and unique insights into your pregnancy. Perinatal centers are regionalized, so that one major institution may serve a fairly large geographic area. Women who live in the country or small towns may have to travel to the nearest big city to see a perinatologist.

Sometimes a qualified obstetrician closer to your home can safely and conveniently manage a high-risk pregnancy. However, women who require frequent evaluation or special treatments might fare better with a team of perinatal specialists at a medical center equipped to handle any and all complications.

If you have your own medical insurance, you generally can choose any private physician you prefer. If you belong to a prepaid practice plan or health maintenance organization, you may have to choose among certain individual physicians. If you don't know where to start, ask your family physician, gynecologist, or internist for some names. You also can call the obstetrical department at a local medical school.

Because you will be working closely with your obstetrical caregivers over a period of many months, we recommend taking the time to meet with each potential caregiver. In making your choice, keep these factors in mind:

• Look for an obstetrician with experience in managing high-risk pregnancies. Ask what percentage of patients in his or her practice have been high risk.

• If the doctor doesn't specialize in complicated pregnancies, ask how comfortable he or she feels with high-risk situations. Are high-risk consultants available? Who are they? Can you meet with them? Find out how specific needs, such as prenatal testing or hospitalizations, would be handled. What if unexpected problems further complicated your pregnancy? Would the high-risk consultant take over your case?

• Make sure the caregivers are "askable" professionals. Again and again, questions, fears, and concerns will require a medical opinion. You shouldn't feel so intimidated or so put off by your doctor's manner or reputation that you can't get the information you need. You should feel comfortable with your caregivers and with the way they answer your questions.

• Ask how often you'll schedule prenatal visits. Whom will you see—the physician, a nurse-midwife, other partners in the practice? Who is most likely to deliver your baby? Can you be assured of continuity in your care or of having a primary caregiver?

• Discuss your particular high-risk situation in detail. Ask what methods of diagnosis and treatment are most frequently used. How much emphasis does the physician put on prevention and self-care?

• Try to get a sense of how the doctor might react if you felt uncertain or disagreed with a recommendation. Would you be able to participate in the decision-making process? What if you wanted a second opinion?

"In my first pregnancy I was considered low-risk, so when things started going wrong, I felt betrayed. The second time around I was considered high-risk from the start, and I felt relieved. I knew it meant we would get special attention and stay one step ahead of the game."

"If I thought nature could do the job, I'd say, 'Great!' But I've struggled so hard to have this baby that I don't want to take any chances. When it comes to saving your baby, it doesn't matter that there are twelve doctors and a monitor in the room. You're just glad to know that they're there and they can help if you need them."

• If you have strong beliefs about prenatal testing or various interventions, voice them. Ask if the physician's philosophy about these subjects generally agrees with yours—or at least if he or she can accept and respect your desires.

• Try to meet the other people who may be involved in your care. You may want to find out if the high-risk team includes a certified nurse-midwife. While nurse-midwives mainly specialize in low-risk pregnancies, some acquire extensive experience in high-risk care. They always work closely with perinatologists, and they can offer an added dimension of caring as well as care.

• Check out the hospital your doctor is affiliated with. While most high-risk women do not require hospitalization during pregnancy, some do—to get premature contractions under control, to handle gestational diabetes, to bring blood pressure down, to minimize the risks of placental abruption or placenta previa. Can your local hospital handle such care? Would you have to travel to a larger institution?

• Where would your baby be born? Are there special facilities for high-risk deliveries? What if you went into labor early or developed a complication during labor? Also get information on care for high-risk newborns. While most high-risk pregnancies culminate in the birth of healthy babies, some infants do require intensive care. You may want to talk to a neonatologist (a specialist in caring for high-risk newborns) and tour the newborn intensive care units at different hospitals.

After meeting with possible caregivers, think about how comfortable you were asking questions and how willing they were to address your concerns. While you should hope for the best, try to think ahead and consider how you would feel turning to these people in a crisis. When you finally make your decision, choose caregivers you can trust—and who are worthy of your trust.

Prenatal Visits

Usually pregnant women see their health-care providers once a month until their twenty-eighth week, then every second week until their thirty-sixth week, then every week. A high-risk woman can expect to see more of her caregivers, primarily because frequent monitoring is necessary to detect problems early enough to prevent further complications.

During prenatal visits, you should expect routine screening in addition to specific evaluation of your high-risk condition. Among the standard measurements and tests are:

- weight
- blood-pressure reading
- fundal height (distance from the top of the uterus to the pubic bone), which can confirm normal growth or alert the caregiver to growth problems
- evaluation of the baby's heartbeat, which may be heard as early as the sixteenth week and almost always by the nineteenth or twentieth. An ultrasonic Doppler device can detect a heartbeat at about ten or twelve weeks of gestation.
- a "dipstick" test of urine for glucose, protein, or blood—all signs of potential danger
- urine cultures for the presence of bacteria (especially if you have a history or symptoms of infection, including vaginal discharge and painful urination)
- quantitative urine testing for protein and creatinine, which requires collection of all urine produced in twenty-four hours (most often used in women with high blood pressure or preeclampsia)
- a glucose screening test at twenty-six to twenty-eight weeks
- hematocrit (percentage of blood present as blood cells) and hemoglobin (concentration of the molecule that carries oxygen in the blood) to detect anemia
- cultures of fluid from herpes blisters to determine active infection. Women with known recurrent herpes may get a culture at thirty-six weeks of pregnancy, although many obstetricians test only if a woman develops symptoms.

Medications: Risks vs. Benefits

No pregnant woman should take any medication—prescription or nonprescription—without consulting her physician. Even aspirin, one of the most widely used drugs, can create problems if taken in standard doses in the last trimester, when it may prolong pregnancy and labor, increase fetal and maternal bleeding at delivery, and interfere with fetal blood circulation.

If you have a chronic illness, such as epilepsy or asthma, you may need medications to prevent or control your symptoms. Unfortunately, not all the medications that are safe for a mother are equally risk-free for her baby. Sometimes obstetricians, working closely with other specialists, may have to walk a thin line, carefully weighing the benefits to the mother and the possible risks to the baby.

To understand the relative risks of various medications, you can rely on the categories the Food and Drug Administration has developed for prescription medications in pregnancy:

• Category A drugs have been extensively tested in pregnant women and pose little, if any, threat to a fetus.

• Category B drugs have not been proven dangerous, but the available research is inconclusive. Animal studies may not have revealed any risk but the drugs may not have been tested in humans, or animal studies may have shown adverse effects while trials in humans have not.

• Category C drugs may be hazardous, but should be used if the benefits clearly outweigh the risks. There may not be adequate research data from animals or humans, or animal studies may have shown some dangers.

• Category D drugs definitely pose a hazard to the unborn baby, but they may be needed in pregnancy for the mother's well-being. They are used only when no better options are available.

• Category X drugs are so dangerous that they are never used in pregnancy.

Costs

Standard obstetrical fees include prenatal visits, labor, and delivery. In 1988 Metropolitan Life, an insurance company, estimated that the average costs of a normal pregnancy and baby are $2,900, although they ranged from a high of $4,210 in Washington, D.C., to a low of $1,790 in North Dakota. Doctors' fees account for about two-fifths of the average total. Hospital charges, which vary greatly across the country, usually make up the largest percentage of the final bill.

Care for high-risk newborns is extremely expensive. A March of Dimes cost evaluation at Babies Hospital, Columbia Presbyterian Medical Center in New York City, shows that newborns weighing less than three pounds three ounces (fifteen hundred grams) incurred an average cost of $25,275 in fifty-five days of intensive care. Nationally, 6 percent of all newborns require intensive care at an annual cost of $1.8 billion.

Because every high-risk pregnancy is different, it is hard to estimate exactly how much more special care will cost. However, diagnostic tests, additional visits, and longer hospital stays definitely can add to the total amount. Insurance policies vary considerably in their pregnancy benefits. Some cover most of the extra costs for testing, close treatment, and possible interventions. Others limit their coverage or do not provide any reimbursement.

As soon as you realize you're at risk, you and your partner should review your insurance coverage. You also might want to find out whether your insurance will cover the costs of special treatments for your baby if they become necessary.

Let your caregivers know about the coverage you have. If you do not have adequate insurance, you can work out a reasonable payment schedule. A social worker at the hospital where you'll have your baby can direct you to community programs and government sources that can provide assistance if you need it.

"Every day I thanked God I was still pregnant. Maybe that's the silver lining of being high-risk: you don't take a moment of your pregnancy for granted."

WHAT YOU CAN DO TO REDUCE RISKS

In a high-risk pregnancy, eliminating the risks that can be avoided or overcome is especially important. Good prenatal care can prevent problems that would add more complications to a pregnancy already in potential jeopardy.

Nutrition

The American College of Obstetricians and Gynecologists (ACOG) recommends a weight gain for most pregnant women of twenty-five to thirty pounds. If the woman gains substantially less, the risk to the infant is high. One of the biggest dangers is low birth weight. Since a well-balanced diet is critical for the baby's health before and at birth, ACOG has developed the following dietary guidelines for mothers-to-be:

• Expect to eat about 15 percent more calories than before and to gain about 20 percent over your ideal weight. For most women, that works out to about three hundred more calories a day than before pregnancy.

• Do not restrict salt unless instructed to do so. While doctors once feared that salt would lead to fluid retention and swelling of the hands or feet, they now feel that only excessive salt intake is potentially dangerous.

• Drink six to eight glasses of liquids each day, including water, fruit and vegetable juices, and milk.

• Concentrate on eating the right foods, not on watching your weight.

• Never diet during pregnancy. Dieting prevents adequate expansion of a pregnant woman's blood volume. And less blood flow to the placenta means less nourishment for the fetus. The result is a low birth weight and possibly a less healthy baby.

• Eat four or more servings each day from these food groups: fruits and vegetables; whole-grain or enriched bread and cereal; and milk and milk products. Eat at least three servings of meat, poultry, eggs, fish, nuts, or beans.

"EVERY PARENT'S NIGHTMARE"

Barbara and Bill felt like kids playing hooky from school. When she was twenty weeks pregnant, they both took the afternoon off from their jobs to go to the hospital for a routine ultrasound. "The doctor wanted to find out how pregnant I was," says Barbara. "I knew exactly when I'd conceived, and Bill and I were joking that the sonogram would show I was right."

In the examining room, Barbara and Bill eagerly watched the first, flickering images of their baby. Suddenly the technician froze. Then he pushed the scanning device hard against Barbara's belly, moving it back and forth over the same spot again and again, pressing harder and harder against her skin. Barbara looked at the grainy black-and-white image on the monitor and asked, "What is that?"

"The head," the technician said quietly.

"Oh my God," Barbara cried, suddenly realizing that fluid was sloshing around inside the skull. Every parent's nightmare, the unspoken, unspeakable fear that an unborn baby will have a hopeless defect, was coming true. Barbara and Bill stared at each other in horror.

Barbara called her sister, a physician, who immediately arranged for them to see the perinatologists at Johns Hopkins the following morning. "We'd come to the hospital in separate cars, and I was crying so hard I couldn't find the exit from the parking lot. The attendant asked me if I was too upset to drive. Upset? I was devastated."

The following morning a sonogram at Hopkins confirmed a very serious problem. "There was some brain, which made me feel better," she says. "But the baby had hydrocephalus." This build-up of excessive fluid within the skull is rare, and medical scientists know little about why it happens.

"We spent all day talking to doctors and reading the articles they gave us. We tried to find out everything we could. We wanted to know if the baby would survive, if it would be normal, what kind of life it could have."

The news was so grim that Barbara and Bill nicknamed one of the specialists "Doctor Doom." As he explained, more than 90 percent of babies with problems similar to their baby's die in utero or shortly after birth. If the baby were to survive, it would be severely retarded. "I had worked with retarded children, and I know how hard it can be as they grow older," says Barbara. "We decided that the best choice was an abortion."

But because Barbara was at the end of her second trimester and because of the size of the baby's head, obstetricians felt they could not safely perform an abortion. The pregnancy would have to continue. Knowing that the baby almost certainly would not, could not, survive, Barbara found herself grieving.

"I felt that the baby had already died," she says. "But Bill refused to give up hope. He had two teenage children by a previous marriage, and he said that all that mattered to him was that the child would be able to give and receive love. And he was so convinced that our baby was going to make it that I found myself believing—or at least wanting to believe."

Yet Barbara wouldn't let herself get anything ready for a new baby. "We didn't set up a nursery or have a shower. When strangers would see me and congratulate me on the baby, I never knew what to say." When she finally underwent a cesarean section (a vaginal birth was impossible because of previous uterine surgery), she wasn't sure how she'd respond to the first sight of her child. Filled with apprehension, she took a hesitant peek—and fell in love.

"William was eight pounds, fourteen ounces and a beautiful baby. His skull was larger than usual, but his face was normal. His features were perfect. The next day they operated and implanted a shunt to drain off the excess fluid from his head into his abdomen, so his head got much smaller. He was in an incubator and I couldn't pick him up for a week. That was the hardest part. Finally the doctors let us bring him down to stay with me."

Mother's Day was the first day that Barbara and William spent together. "He lay by my side. He slept a while, and then I fed him and held him. It was the sweetest, most beautiful day." Eleven days

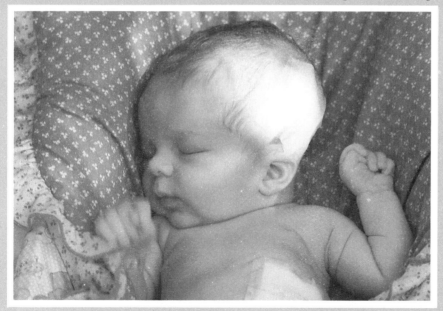

after the birth Barbara and Bill took their son home. "We learned how to take care of the shunt, but we were very tense. I was very protective. I never really relaxed."

The bond she felt with her son grew stronger every day. "William was normal in many respects. He was responsive and alert. He even smiled." Barbara remembers taking William back to the hospital for a CT-scan (a cross-sectional x ray) of his brain. "I was sitting there holding this baby, who I thought looked normal and acted normal, and seeing an x ray that showed half of his brain was missing. I couldn't deny how bad it was, but then I'd look at him again and not know what to believe."

When William was six weeks old, Barbara and Bill's friends gave them a baby shower. "Everyone was starting to think he was going to make it," she says. Two weeks later, William died quietly during his morning nap.

"We don't know if it was Sudden Infant Death Syndrome or if he had reached the point where his brain couldn't sustain life. We rushed him to the nearest hospital, but there was nothing anyone could do. We held him, had him christened, and said good-bye." An autopsy revealed multiple brain abnormalities.

Even though she had tried to prepare herself for losing William, his death tore Barbara apart. "I kept thinking: How could you do this? How could you wreck my body and then run off and leave me?" She tried desperately to find a reason, a cause.

"Part of the trauma was asking, 'Why did this happen?' I kept thinking about a threatened miscarriage in my second month, a vi-

rus that had made me very sick at the end of my first trimester. But no one could ever tell us what went wrong or why. I never dreamed that you could do everything right for a baby, and it still could die."

For a year Barbara couldn't even think about getting pregnant again. "I felt it would be disloyal. I knew that no other child could replace William, and I didn't want to try." But Bill was eager to try again. "One day, in front of his other children, he said, 'You know, some of us would still like to have another baby,' and I realized how deeply he felt. I decided to go ahead even though there wasn't a day that I didn't cry for William."

Once Barbara got pregnant, she knew that, because of William's anomaly, she would be categorized as high-risk. "I welcomed it. I knew I'd have regular sonograms, and if we could get past twenty-one or twenty-two weeks without anything showing up, we'd be okay. When we did, we relaxed." Because Barbara had no other complications, the high-risk specialists at Hopkins referred her to an obstetrician closer to her home for prenatal care.

"I let myself enjoy the fact that I was going to have a healthy, normal baby," she says. Yet the memories of William were with her always. "We bought a bassinet, and I was upset because it was the same as the borrowed one in which William had died. I wanted everything to be different."

On March 22, 1988, Barbara and Bill's second son, John Daniel, was born: big, healthy, and perfect from head to toe. The moment she held him, she once again fell in love. "It was so wonderful to have a baby in my arms again. I almost couldn't believe it."

Like many parents who have a baby after losing a child, Barbara and Bill checked on their new son constantly. "Fortunately he was a really noisy sleeper, but if he did get quiet for a few moments, we'd both rush in to see if he was okay," says Barbara. "The day after we made it past the point where William died, a friend called and said, 'Now you can really celebrate.' And she was right."

As their son has grown bigger and older, Barbara and Bill's anxious hovering has given way to the usual mix of feelings—and the inevitable fatigue—that all new parents feel. "When John got to be six months, I found myself taking him for granted at times," says Barbara. "If I was really tired and he started crying, I'd think, 'Oh why can't you be quiet and sleep!' Then I'd feel guilty because I'd remember how I yearned to hear a baby cry after William died."

But for the most part, memories of William no longer haunt Barbara the way they once did, although they remain with her always. "William will be part of me, part of our family, forever. He taught us so much about love. That was his gift to us."

• Keep an eye on your iron levels. A blood test called a hematocrit, performed routinely at your first prenatal visit to measure levels of iron, can determine if your iron supplies are low. Iron is a key element in red blood cells, and you need more than double your usual amount when you're pregnant because of the expanding demands on your blood supply. If you don't get enough, the fetus will get its iron directly from your bone marrow, which could make you severely anemic. If your doctor feels you need more, you can take 30 mg to 60 mg supplements. (Because iron can cause constipation or very hard stools, ask your caregiver about stool softeners. High-fiber foods may be sufficient, but safe prescription agents also are available.) This is especially important for women carrying more than one baby.

• Get plenty of calcium. Your needs for bone-building calcium soar during pregnancy. If you haven't stored enough, your metabolism may drain your bones of calcium to feed the fetus. You should work at getting 1,500 mg a day. If you drink a quart of milk a day or its equivalent, you probably don't need a supplement. If you aren't getting a good supply of dairy products, your doctor may advise calcium pills.

• Think zinc. This trace mineral plays a key role in very early fetal development because cells can't divide properly without it. Zinc supplements aren't usually necessary. You can get an adequate supply from red meat, leafy greens, and fish.

• Take your vitamins. Prenatal vitamin supplements can make up for some nutritional deficiencies, but they cannot replace or equal the benefits of a well-balanced diet. Most prenatal vitamin compounds include calcium, vitamin A, vitamin D, vitamin C, a B vitamin called folic acid (0.3 mg daily), and iron (30 to 60 mg daily).

• Don't take megadoses of any vitamins. Large doses of certain vitamins can be dangerous. Too much vitamin A, which can be obtained in adequate amounts from green and yellow vegetables, can cause severe birth defects. High doses of vitamin D, which can be obtained in adequate amounts from fortified whole or skim milk, have also been linked with malformations. (The bibliography at the end of the book contains our recommendations for books on nutrition in pregnancy.)

Exercise

While some pregnant women swim, ski, play tennis, even run marathons, high-risk women have to be realistic about the safety of vigorous exercise. You should not exercise if you develop placenta previa, placental abruption, preeclampsia, ruptured membranes, or premature labor. You also may be advised not to exercise if you have heart disease, a multiple pregnancy, or vaginal bleeding. Consult with your caregivers about exercise if you have any of the following conditions:

> hypertension
> anemia or other blood disorders
> thyroid disease
> diabetes
> heart palpitations or arrhythmias
> intrauterine growth retardation
> history of three or more miscarriages
> history of precipitous labor
> breech presentation in the final trimester
> you're extremely underweight or overweight

Often high-risk women who must avoid strenuous workouts can take walks, swim (sometimes only the sidestroke, which avoids strain on the lower back), or do basic stretching and toning exercises, such as side bends. Even those on bedrest can usually do head and shoulder circles or arm-strengthening exercises. Discuss with your caregivers the specific activities you can and can't do.

If you're given a green light for exercise, be sure to follow the guidelines developed by the American College of Obstetricians and Gynecologists:

- Don't exercise strenuously for more than fifteen minutes at a time.
- Check your heart rate. Stop if it reaches 140 beats a minute.
- Avoid vigorous exercise in hot, humid weather. Your core body temperature should never exceed 101.3 degrees.
- Don't bounce or jerk. For aerobics workouts, exercise on a wooden or carpeted floor to cushion shock and provide a firm footing.
- Stretch and flex carefully because the joints and connective tissue soften and loosen during pregnancy.
- Always warm up and cool down.
- After twenty weeks of pregnancy, don't do any exercises while lying flat on your back for extended periods.
- Drink plenty of fluids before and after exercising.
- Don't let your body temperature rise above one hundred degrees.
- Always stop exercising if you develop pain, bleeding, dizziness, shortness of breath, palpitations, faintness, a very rapid heartbeat, back pain, pubic pain, or difficulty in walking. (The bibli-

ography includes books and videos that can help you keep fit throughout your pregnancy.)

Rest and Work

Rest is as important as exercise, and if you're not used to taking time-outs during the day, you may have to schedule rest periods. If insomnia becomes a problem, pay attention to your sleep habits. Keep regular hours. Establish a soothing sleep routine that might consist of a warm bath, stretching, listening to soft music, or relaxation exercises. Cut down on fluids during the evening if frequent urination becomes a problem at night. Never take sleeping pills.

Many women continue working outside the home until the final weeks of pregnancy. The best guide to how long to continue is your own energy and comfort. Being on your feet for long periods of time may be uncomfortable. Women with other children at home may need extra help with their daily tasks during the final weeks of pregnancy.

Some high-risk patients have to restrict their activities. A diabetic may have to test her blood sugar eight times a day, yet have no restrictions on her activity. A woman at risk for preterm labor may have to cut back on standing or lifting. Ask your caregivers about your situation. They may not be able to anticipate every problem, but they can provide basic guidelines.

Avoiding Dangers

Tobacco. Cigarettes endanger two lives: the mother's and her unborn baby's. Smoking boosts the likelihood of miscarriage, fetal distress, stillbirth, low birth weight, heart defects, and premature birth, and also impairs growth. There is a direct correlation between the number of cigarettes smoked daily and the likelihood of having a short, underweight, or small-headed infant.

The sooner a mother stops smoking, the better are her baby's chances of growing to a normal weight for its gestational age. But it's never too late to quit. Even late in pregnancy, kicking the habit helps because babies gain a substantial part of their birth weight in the last trimester—when their brains are growing rapidly too.

Alcohol. One of every 750 babies in the United States is born with a cluster of physical and mental defects called fetal alcohol syndrome. An unknown number of babies whose mothers drink while pregnant suffer low birth weight, irritability as newborns, and various complications of pregnancy.

Alcohol is particularly dangerous during pregnancy because it crosses the placenta and reaches concentrations in the unborn baby's blood as high as in the mother's. The risk of fetal alcohol syndrome is greatest if a mother drinks three or more ounces of pure alcohol (the equivalent of six or seven cocktails) a day. Milder forms of this problem occur in about 10 percent of babies whose mothers consume one to two ounces of alcohol (two to four cocktails) a day. In addition to fetal alcohol syndrome, heavy drinking has been clearly linked to prematurity, smaller head circumference, smaller and shorter babies, and lower Apgar (newborn evaluation) scores. Even moderate drinking early in pregnancy can affect a child's intellectual ability and academic performance. The National Institute on Alcohol Abuse and Alcoholism and the U.S. Surgeon General advise pregnant women—and those trying to become pregnant—not to drink at all.

How Much Caffeine Is in Your Cup?	
Beverage	**Caffeine, mg**
Brewed coffee	75–150 mg
Instant coffee	30–80 mg
Tea	40–60 mg
Cola	30–60 mg
Cocoa	2–40 mg

Caffeine. Caffeine belongs to a chemical family called the xanthines, which include compounds found in chocolate, cocoa, coffee, and black tea. Whenever a pregnant woman drinks or eats a substance containing xanthines, her baby is exposed to the same amount. Studies have found no increases in birth defects in women using caffeine in pregnancy, but there is some evidence linking caffeine to pregnancy complications, including miscarriage, low birth weight, and prematurity. Moderate to heavy caffeine users (those ingesting more than 151 mg a day) are more likely to experience miscarriages than nonusers or light users (less than 150 mg. a day). The Food and Drug Administration's advice: "Prudence dictates that pregnant women and those who may become pregnant avoid caffeine-containing products or use them sparingly."

Illegal drugs. "Street" drugs have not been as extensively researched as medications, but they are a widespread threat. In a study of thirty-six U.S. hospitals, the National Association for Perinatal Addiction Research and Education found that at least one in ten newborns is exposed to illegal drugs in utero. The consequences include severe physical and neurological damage, including birth defects and disruption of normal development of the brain and nervous system. Physicians urge prospective mothers to stay drug-free for at least three months before they conceive and throughout their pregnancy.

Cocaine: In any form, cocaine can cause miscarriages, developmental disorders, and life-threatening complications during birth, including the bursting of blood vessels—the prenatal equivalent of a stroke—which can cause permanent physical and mental damage. Cocaine babies have higher-than-normal rates of respiratory and kidney troubles and may be at greater risk of sudden infant death syndrome. Visual problems, lack of coordination, and developmental retardation are common. They tend to feed poorly, sleep irregularly, suffer from diarrhea, and show marked irritability and increased respiratory and heart rates.

Sedatives. Barbiturates and other sedatives can cross through the placenta easily and cause birth defects and behavioral problems. Babies born to women who abused sedatives during pregnancy may be physically dependent on the drugs and develop breathing problems, feeding difficulties, disturbed sleep, sweating, irritability, and fever.

Marijuana. Women who smoke pot have smaller, sicker babies and a higher risk of stillbirths, according to available research data. A study of 1,690 mother-child pairs in Boston found that the use of marijuana in pregnancy can lower birth weight and cause abnormalities similar to those of fetal alcohol syndrome. The women who smoked pot while pregnant were five times more likely to have babies with small head size, irritability, and poor growth.

Radiation and other environmental risks. High levels of radiation of the type used for cancer therapy have been associated with defects. Diagnostic x rays are not a significant threat, particularly after the first trimester, because they involve low levels of radiation. The Committee on Radiology of the American Academy of Pediatrics says that because the possibility of birth defects resulting from x rays is extremely low, even abdominal x-ray examinations should be done if genuinely needed during pregnancy.

Dental x rays, which use extremely low radiation directed at the mouth, are not considered hazardous. As an added precaution, dentists routinely use lead shields that block any x rays from reaching a patient's major organs.

Few scientific data are available on fetal vulnerability to pollutants, toxic wastes, heavy metals, pesticides, gases, and synthetic compounds. There have been isolated reports—but no well-documented studies—that lead and cadmium are hazardous to a fetus and that exposures to certain chemicals may increase the risk of birth defects.

High temperatures. Researchers have long suspected that increased body temperature can harm very early fetal development. When University of Washington scientists looked back at various influences that may have contributed to otherwise unexplainable birth defects in human infants, they found one common factor: their mothers either had fevers or sat in hot tubs during the first three months of pregnancy. The best advice if you're pregnant or trying to get pregnant is to stay out of saunas or hot tubs. Keep bath water below one hundred degrees and limit soak time. And avoid intense exercise in hot, humid weather, which can boost internal temperatures to dangerous levels.

Travel

Babies are never as portable as when they're in the womb, and pregnant women generally can travel safely by car, boat, train, or pressurized aircraft. However, try not to go too far too fast. Limit traveling time to five or six hours or, if driving, three hundred miles a day. Sitting in a cramped seat increases the risk of blood clots. To boost circulation and minimize swelling, break up long trips with regular ankle rolls, leg massages, stops, or strolls. Spend about fifteen minutes each hour standing or walking. Emptying your bladder often reduces the risk of urinary tract infections. Drinking plenty of fluids helps ward off dehydration. Airlines may not allow pregnant women to travel after their thirty-sixth week and may require a note from a physician stating your estimated delivery date.

If you're at risk, the greatest danger may be being away from your perinatal team. Keep long-distance trips to a minimum. Check with your physician if you have complications, such as high blood pressure, abnormal bleeding, or a history of miscarriage or preterm labor, before planning a trip. At the very least, you may want to have names of specialists to turn to if problems should develop far from home. Many insurance carriers do not cover the costs of hospitalization for preterm labor or delivery in foreign settings.

The Tropical Medicine and International Travelers' Clinic at Yale University recently developed guidelines for pregnant women who travel. Among the recommendations:

• Try to undergo any required immunizations prior to pregnancy. Avoid vaccinations during the first trimester. Most live vaccines (such as those used in measles and rubella vaccinations) are best avoided entirely.

• To avoid the risks of tetanus, make sure you've had a booster shot within the last ten years. These can be given safely during pregnancy.

• Avoid foods that produce intestinal gas prior to a flight since gas expansion is particularly uncomfortable during pregnancy.

• Avoid high-altitude excursions, such as trekking in remote mountains. Some obstetricians advise against any vacation at an altitude higher than seven thousand feet.

Condoms During Pregnancy

The National Family Planning and Reproductive Health Association has recommended that condoms be used throughout pregnancy to prevent sexually transmitted diseases in women:

• whose partners have a history of genital herpes simplex virus infection, chlamydia, nongonococcal urethritis (NGU), venereal warts, trichomoniasis, gonorrhea, syphilis, hepatitis B, human immunodeficiency virus (HIV) or AIDS.

• who are diagnosed as having herpes simplex virus infection, chlamydia, pelvic inflammatory disease, inflammation of the cervix, venereal warts, trichomoniasis, gonorrhea, syphilis, hepatitis B, or HIV infection.

• whose partners are likely to have more than one sexual partner in the course of the pregnancy or who are bisexual or intravenous drug users.

• who have more than one sexual partner during pregnancy.

• Try to avoid any potentially contaminated food or drink. Check with your caregivers about safe treatments for traveler's diarrhea before leaving home.

• Pregnant women with diabetes or high blood pressure should carry urine dipsticks and home blood-pressure cuffs with them so they can monitor their conditions.

Sex

Most expectant parents can continue their usual sexual activities throughout pregnancy. In low-risk pregnancies, intercourse is not likely to trigger bleeding, miscarriage, or preterm labor. In certain high-risk pregnancies, such as those in which bleeding has occurred, the membranes have ruptured, or there is danger of preterm labor, intercourse may be hazardous and should be avoided. However, other forms of sexual activity, including kissing, cuddling, and holding, are not only safe, but soothing. Women at risk should check with their caregivers about whether orgasm should be avoided.

EXPECTING THE UNEXPECTED

"No one ever told me it would be like this." Almost all pregnant women say this sooner or later—although for very different reasons. While every woman brings certain expectations to a pregnancy, she always discovers something unexpected along the way. Even if you've been pregnant before, you'll find unique and surprising aspects in each pregnancy.

Being at risk adds more unknowns to a pregnancy. You may feel somewhat tentative, as if you're not sure what the next week, the next test, the next visit will bring. "After I found out I was high risk, I felt like I was always waiting for the other shoe to drop," says one woman. "I was never sure what might happen next."

Such uncertainty can be unnerving. Some women respond to it by holding back and not making a full commitment to the pregnancy. Others focus on the here-and-now, taking one day at a time and deliberately not looking ahead.

It wasn't until after her high-risk pregnancy, when she had a healthy child safely in her arms, that one woman could look back and see even the uncertainties in a positive light: "I didn't realize it at the time," she says, "but nothing prepared me for motherhood more than learning to expect the unexpected."

Prenatal Testing

In the last twenty years, major technological advances in prenatal diagnosis have opened up the long-hidden world within the womb to yield better information about fetal well-being than ever before. Today's tests can reveal more about an unborn child than once was thought possible. And largely because of the vastly improved precision and power of prenatal diagnostic techniques, more babies of high-risk mothers are surviving and thriving than ever before.

THINKING ABOUT TESTING

The perfect prenatal test would be save, painless, and precise. None meets all three criteria. That's why it's important for every woman to weigh the advantages and disadvantages, the possible benefits and the potential risks, before consenting to a test. Among the questions you may want to discuss with your caregivers are:

• *Is this test necessary?* What is the reason for it? Is there any other way of obtaining the information it might provide? Are any cheaper and safer tests available? How will the test findings affect the management of your pregnancy and the treatment of your baby?

• *Is the test safe?* Some tests, such as measurements of alpha fetoprotein (AFP) in the mother's blood, do not pose any direct danger to the growing fetus. Others, such as amniocentesis, carry a small but serious risk. It's important for you to consider the risks of testing versus the consequences of not getting the information testing can provide.

"I didn't look any different. I didn't feel any different. But, in my eighth week, I looked at an ultrasound screen and saw a tiny heart pulsing with life. From that moment she was as real to me as if I could have reached down and touched her. I think that's when I became a mother. I knew that I would do anything and everything to keep her safe."

● *Is the test accurate?* No test can rule out all possible problems. Unfortunately, some diagnostic tests produce a high percentage of false positives (results that indicate a problem when none exists) and false negatives (results that do not identify a problem that does exist). Talk with your doctor about what can be done to sort out any misleading findings.

● *Who will perform the test? Where?* Simple blood tests can be done at your caregiver's office. Most of the more complex prenatal tests are performed at large hospitals or major medical centers. However, some are so technically demanding or so new that only a few perinatal centers offer them.

● *How long does it take to get a result?* When you're waiting for test results, days can stretch into eternities. Some prenatal tests provide instantaneous information; others require weeks of analysis. Try to get a realistic estimate of how soon you can get the test findings. Find out if another laboratory or hospital can get faster results.

● *What do the results mean?* Make sure that someone will be available to explain the findings and their implications for you, your baby, and your pregnancy. You may want to talk about the possible need to repeat the test to rule out false positives or negatives and the chances of not being able to make a diagnosis on the basis of a single test.

● *What next?* Often one test requires another to clarify or confirm a finding. If a test detects an abnormality, find out if treatment is available during pregnancy or after birth. If no therapy is possible, you may want to discuss the baby's chance of survival and prospects for a normal life. If you would consider abortion, talk about the possible timing and dangers.

Ultrasound (Sonography)

What it is. High-frequency sound waves (outside the normal range of hearing) bounce off structures within the womb, producing echoes that are converted into images on a display screen. Ultrasound can create a two-dimensional still picture (a sonogram) or a series of pictures in rapid succession to show movement (real-time sonography). Standard ultrasound equipment can perform routine evaluations and screen for potential problems; more powerful and advanced equipment provides detailed, high-resolution images for specialized testing.

How it's done. A microphonelike device called a transducer sends sound waves produced by a small crystal into the body. A

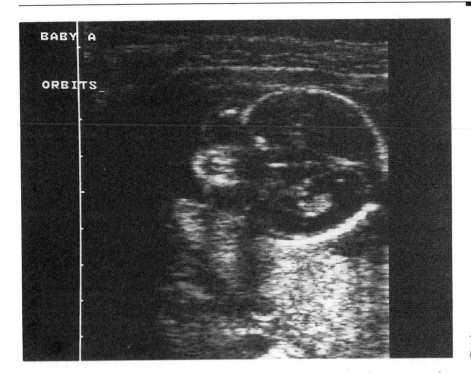

BABY A

ORBITS_

The face of a normal, healthy fetus, as shown on a sonogram.

technician or doctor moves the transducer painlessly across the skin, "scanning" a specific area. As the sound waves bounce off internal structures, they are converted into an image on a television-like screen.

What it can show. Ultrasound can establish gestational age (crucial information in timing other prenatal tests and delivery), reveal twins or triplets, identify possible causes of vaginal bleeding, pick up some serious birth defects, show whether the baby is growing as it should, and indicate if there is too little or too much amniotic fluid or whether the placenta has separated from the uterine wall or is blocking the birth canal.

What are the risks? Ultrasound has been used in pregnancies for twenty-five years with no reports of significant harmful effects. Like other tests, ultrasound can produce misleading results, sometimes triggering unwarranted concern over a problem that does not exist.

Why you may need this test. In many European countries, all pregnant women undergo ultrasound examinations routinely. In this country, the Consensus Development Conference sponsored by the National Institute of Child Health and Human Development has recommended scanning only when there is a specific reason.

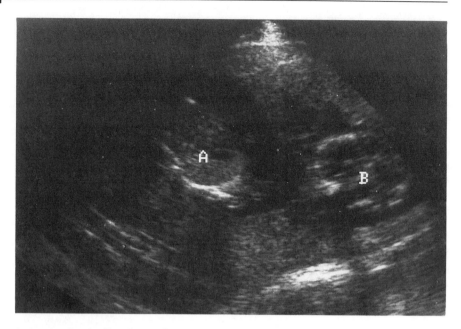

A sonogram showing two fetuses: Baby A and Baby B.

Among the indications for ultrasound testing are:
- establishing gestational age
- evaluating fetal growth
- finding the cause of vaginal bleeding
- determining the baby's position in the womb
- identifying multiples
- screening for fetal malformations
- determining the location and nature of a growth in the pelvis
- as an adjunct to other prenatal tests, such as chorionic villus sampling and amniocentesis
- evaluating a suspected ectopic (out-of-place) pregnancy
- diagnosing uterine abnormalities
- determining if a fetus is alive
- identifying presence and possible cause of excessive or insufficient amniotic fluid
- diagnosing separation of the placenta—complete or partial—from the uterine wall
- estimating fetal weight after premature rupture of the membranes
- evaluating possible neural tube defects if alpha fetoprotein levels are high
- identifying and monitoring fetal abnormalities

What to expect. Ultrasound does not involve x rays or injections of drugs or dyes. Since a full bladder helps create a clearer image of the uterus, you may be asked to drink several glasses of water about an hour before the exam and not to urinate before the test. A liquid gel rubbed on your abdomen assures adequate contact for the transducer. You will feel slight pressure as the transducer moves across your skin. Ultrasound itself is painless, but you may feel uncomfortable because of your full bladder. You may undergo several sonograms in the course of your pregnancy. But even if a woman is at high risk, sonograms usually are not performed more than once a month.

"After miscarrying in my first pregnancy, I was terrified when I became pregnant again. Being able to see the baby on ultrasound helped me so much. I knew then that our baby was alive and growing."

Alpha Fetoprotein (AFP) Screening

What it is. Performed between the sixteenth and eighteenth week of pregnancy, this test of the mother's blood measures a protein manufactured mainly in the liver of a fetus. AFP normally reaches peak levels between ten and thirteen weeks of pregnancy.

How it's done. AFP levels can be measured in a sample of the mother's blood or in amniotic fluid removed during amniocentesis. Most women simply undergo a standard blood test at sixteen to seventeen weeks.

What it shows. A high AFP in the mother's blood may indicate neural tube defects, in which the brain or part of the spinal cord does not form normally, or defects in the abdominal wall. Some of these problems are lethal; others can be corrected by surgery after birth. Further testing with ultrasound or measurement of AFP levels in the amniotic fluid is necessary to confirm a defect. Even if no defect is found, an elevated AFP can indicate increased risk of premature delivery, low birth weight, or other complications.

Low AFP levels can be an indicator of serious chromosomal disorders, such as Down syndrome (a form of mental retardation caused by an extra chromosome). Amniocentesis is recommended if a woman's risk of having a child with Down syndrome, based on her AFP and age, is greater than the risk of miscarriage as a result of the test. (Standardized charts are used to compute this risk.)

What are the risks? AFP screening is as safe and simple as any blood test for the mother and poses no risk for the fetus. Accurate gestational age is important since normal values vary according to the age of the fetus. More than 95 percent of abnormal readings are "false positives," often caused by an error in timing or by unsuspected twins. These misleading results can lead to unnecessary anxiety and to tests that may pose a risk to a fetus.

On the Horizon: New and Improved Prenatal Tests

Among the possible break-throughs in prenatal screening are experimental new tests that screen for Down syndrome, the leading cause of mental retardation, simply by testing the mother's blood. The tests measure the levels of two proteins, estriol and alpha fetoprotein (AFP), which are abnormally low in babies with Down syndrome, and another protein, human chorionic gonadotropin (HCG), which is abnormally high, at the sixteenth to eighteenth weeks. A computer program calculates the risk of Down syndrome based on the protein levels and the woman's age.

The major advantage of the new test, which is being used experimentally in Great Britain, is that it is so simple and safe that all pregnant women can be screened. A disadvantage is that, at this point, testing cannot be done accurately before the sixteenth week.

Even more experimental are screening tests that would separate fetal cells from a mother's red blood cells, grow them in a test tube, and analyze them for abnormalities. Scientists also are investigating the use of powerful magnetic fields in a technique called magnetic resonance spectroscopy to detect abnormalities in the amniotic fluid's chemical composition. This procedure might identify nongenetic defects, such as those caused by toxic chemicals and drugs.

Why you may need this test. Neural tube defects occur in one or two of every one thousand pregnancies in the United States. While screening is offered routinely to all pregnant women, genetic counselors strongly recommend it for women who have had a child with a neural tube defect, a strong family history of neural tube defects, or diabetes. Women may have to undergo two tests and a sonogram to get conclusive results. Screening detects 85 percent of neural tube defects. Its major drawback is the high rate of false positives.

What to expect. You will feel the momentary prick of the needle as a nurse or technician withdraws the blood sample from your arm. The results usually are available within a week. Check with your caregivers about the reputation and experience of the laboratory analyzing your blood sample and about the availability of counseling to interpret the results.

Figuring out what abnormal results mean can be difficult. In addition to neural tube defects, elevated AFP levels may indicate multiples, fetal death, too little amniotic fluid (oligohydramnios), or underestimated gestational age. An unusually low level may be a sign of a missed miscarriage, a "pregnancy" that consists of an abnormal growth or mole within the uterus, or chromosomal abnormalities.

In many cases, no explanation for high or low AFP levels can be found, even after sonography and amniocentesis. Yet women with unexplained elevated AFP levels have a significantly increased incidence of pregnancy loss, low birth weight, neonatal death, and congenital anomalies. Those with unexplained low AFP levels have a significantly greater risk of pregnancy loss but no increase in the incidence of low birth weight, neonatal death, or birth defects.

GENETIC TESTING

The two currently available methods for detecting genetic disorders before birth are chorionic villus sampling (CVS) and amniocentesis.

Chorionic Villus Sampling (CVS)

What it is. In this test for genetic defects, performed between the eighth and twelfth weeks of pregnancy, a physician removes a small sample of the chorionic villus, the tissue surrounding the early placenta, through a syringe or hollow tube.

How it's performed. Using ultrasound as a guide, the physician either places a catheter or hollow tube through the vaginal canal and into the uterine cavity or inserts a needle through the mother's abdomen into the uterus. Suction removes a sample of the fluffy wisps of chorionic villi, which develop from the fusion of the egg and sperm and have the same genetic makeup as the fetus.

What the test shows. Laboratory analysis of the chromosomes in the fetal cells can reveal serious genetic disorders, such as Down syndrome, as well as Tay-Sachs, beta thalessemia, and other hereditary problems. CVS cannot detect neural tube defects. Results are available within a week, early enough for a first-trimester abortion if the fetus has a major disorder and the parents choose to terminate the pregnancy. A woman who undergoes CVS must undergo a separate AFP blood test at sixteen weeks for neural tube defects.

What are the risks? The National Institute of Child Health and Human Development Chorionic Villus Sampling Collaborative Trial has concluded that CVS is about as safe for a mother and fetus as amniocentesis. The primary risk is miscarriage, which occurs in

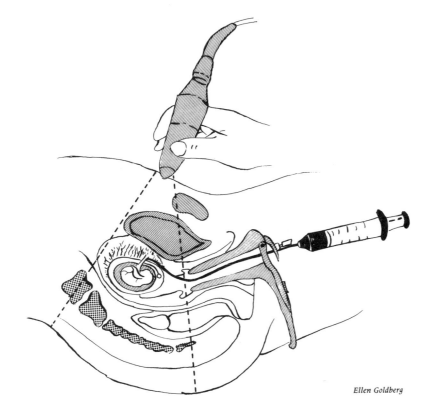

In chorionic villus sampling, a physician, guided by ultrasound, removes a sample of the tissue surrounding the fetus.

Ellen Goldberg

On the Horizon: Earlier Answers to Genetic Questions

The newest prenatal test for genetic defects can be performed as early as the sixth week of pregnancy. The fetus then is, as test developer Joseph Schulman, M.D., of the Genetics and IVF Institute of Fairfax, Virginia, puts it, "just a flicker of a heartbeat" on an ultrasound screen. The sac surrounding the fetus measures a mere six-tenths of an inch.

The new method involves insertion of a wandlike ultrasound probe into the vagina, where it bounces sound waves off the uterus. A needle on the end of the probe is guided through the cervix and into the uterus, where a sample of the chorionic villus—the tiny hairlike tissue that surrounds the developing placenta in the first trimester of pregnancy—is taken for analysis. The vaginal probe provides much clearer images than do standard sonograms used for regular CVS.

This experimental technique has been developed primarily for women at high risk of having a baby with a serious birth defect. Its developers feel it should be comparable in safety to CVS.

about .5 percent of women. CVS also can cause minor complications, including cramping, leakage of fluid for a few days, and spotting or bleeding.

In a recent Canadian analysis, the majority of women who participated in a comparative study of the two genetic tests stated that in future pregnancies, they would opt for CVS. One advantage, the researchers found, is that women who undergo genetic testing early in pregnancy are able to relax and become more "attached" in the second trimester, while women awaiting amniocentesis results may hesitate to invest too much emotional commitment in their pregnancies. Although genetic testing always evokes some anxiety, women undergoing CVS report feeling less anxiety for a briefer period of time.

Why you may need this test. Since the risk of Down syndrome and other chromosomal defects rises with age, counselors have recommended genetic testing for all women over thirty-five. Increasingly, that is changing to women over thirty-three. (However, not all insurers will pay for testing for women under thirty-five.)

Genetic testing also is recommended for women who have had a previous child with a genetic disorder, have a family history of hereditary illness or carry X-linked disorders (such as hemophilia) that they may pass on to their sons, and for couples who both carry a recessive trait for a hereditary disease (such as Tay-Sachs).

What to expect. To enhance the ultrasound images, you should have a full bladder for this test. You may feel momentary discomfort as the obstetrician inserts a needle through your abdominal wall into the uterus or maneuvers the catheter into the uterus. You may spot or bleed lightly after the test, and your doctor may advise you to stay off your feet or take it easy for a day or two. Report any leakage of fluid or heavy or persistent bleeding immediately.

Amniocentesis

What it is. Amniocentesis is a technique for sampling the amniotic fluid in which a fetus floats, either for genetic analysis of fetal cells in the fluid or to obtain information from the fluid itself about a baby's well-being.

How it's done. Guided by ultrasound, the physician inserts a slender needle through the abdomen into the amniotic sac and withdraws about an ounce of amniotic fluid. For genetic testing, amniocentesis is performed at about the fifteenth to seventeenth week. Some physicians are experimenting with earlier "amnios."

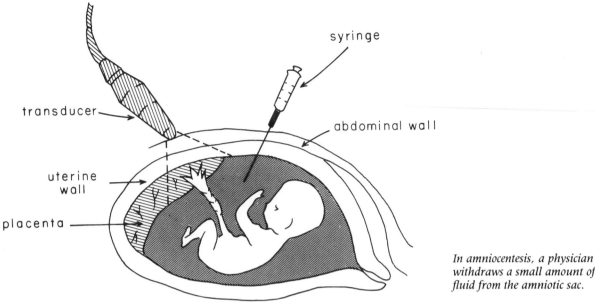

In amniocentesis, a physician withdraws a small amount of fluid from the amniotic sac.

Fetal cells in the fluid are cultured (permitted to multiply in a special fluid) and analyzed, a process that takes two or three weeks. The fluid itself is evaluated for alpha fetoprotein (AFP) levels. Later in pregnancy, amniotic fluid is tested for different components, such as chemical indicators of lung maturity, and results can be obtained within hours or days.

What the test shows. Laboratory analysis of the amniotic fluid and chromosomes from cells the fetus sheds into the fluid can reveal genetic disorders, other hereditary diseases, and neural tube defects.

In the final weeks of pregnancy, amniocentesis can determine if the baby's lungs have developed sufficiently for the baby to survive outside the womb. One indication of lung maturity is the ratio of two chemicals—lecithin and sphingomyelin. When there is at least twice as much lecithin as sphingomyelin in the amniotic fluid, the lungs generally are mature (for unknown reasons, this is not necessarily so in babies of diabetic mothers). Measurement of another substance, phosphatidylglycerol (PG), which increases as the lungs mature, also can help doctors determine the best time for delivery, especially when the mother is diabetic.

In Rh-sensitized pregnancies, analysis of the amniotic fluid can determine how severely a baby is affected and indicate the need for a blood transfusion in the womb or, after thirty-two or thirty-three weeks of gestation, for early delivery.

A sample of amniotic fluid late in pregnancy can identify a common signal of fetal distress: the release of meconium (fetal waste) into the fluid. Meconium can indicate lack of oxygen and a need for further assessment of the baby.

What are the risks? The major risk is miscarriage, which occurs in about one of every two hundred women tested. Usually the fetus seems to move out of the way, but in some instances, the needle pokes the fetus, causing a puncture wound, which is generally minor and heals itself.

Why you may need this test. Amniocentesis provides much of the same information that CVS does and is recommended for women over age thirty-three, women who've miscarried or whose husbands' ex-wives miscarried several times, those with family histories of chromosomal abnormalities, or anyone facing an unusually high risk of having a baby with a birth defect. Its major drawback is that results are not available for several weeks. This delay means that if a serious defect is found and a couple decides not to continue the pregnancy, the woman must undergo a riskier second-trimester abortion.

Later in pregnancy, your doctor may recommend amniocentesis if your baby has a blood-incompatibility problem (see chapter 10). If other tests indicate fetal distress, sampling of the amniotic fluid can detect meconium and help physicians determine whether a baby's lungs are mature enough for an early delivery.

What to expect. You may need a full bladder to enhance the ultrasound image. Some physicians apply a local anesthetic at the site where they insert the needle. Others use such a small, sharp needle that anesthesia isn't necessary. You may want to discuss the options with your physician.

You may feel discomfort when the needle enters your skin. Sometimes the needle must be repositioned and inserted more than once to obtain a sample. You may experience some cramping and spotting afterward. Your doctor may recommend that you rest for a day or two. Report continuing bleeding or cramping immediately.

For amniocentesis later in pregnancy, the woman empties her bladder before testing because there is a greater risk of inserting the needle into the bladder instead of the uterus. Ultrasound helps the physician pinpoint a "pocket" of amniotic fluid and remove a sample. Rh-negative women at risk always receive an injection of RhoGAM to prevent sensitization after amniocentesis.

Percutaneous Umbilical Blood Sampling (PUBS)

What it is. PUBS is a procedure for obtaining a sample of blood from the umbilical cord of an unborn baby. PUBS has generally replaced fetoscopy, a test in which obstetricians inserted a sort of minitelescope into the womb to guide them in removing blood cells or skin samples from a fetus.

How it's done. Using ultrasound to guide a needle through the abdominal wall, uterus, and amniotic sac, the physician removes a small amount of blood from the umbilical cord. The test can be performed as early as the eighteenth week. Results are usually available within hours or days.

What it shows. As a diagnostic test, PUBS enables scientists to analyze blood cells to detect genetic disorders, rare but devastating hereditary diseases, many blood disorders (such as hemophilia), and difficult-to-detect infections (such as toxoplasmosis). In high-risk pregnancies, PUBS can evaluate the baby of an Rh-sensitized mother to determine if it has developed anemia or other complications.

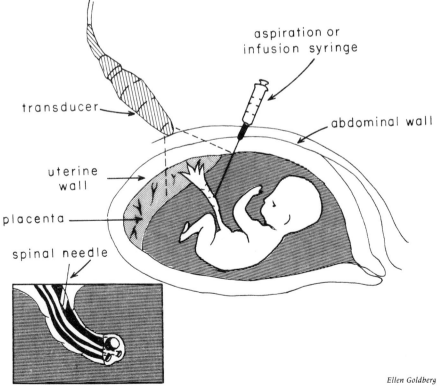

In percutaneous umbilical blood sampling, a physician inserts a syringe directly into the umbilical cord.

aspiration or infusion syringe

transducer

abdominal wall

uterine wall

placenta

spinal needle

Ellen Goldberg

"I think I was more nervous about prenatal testing because I'm a physician. Intellectually I knew the odds were in my favor, but I kept thinking about the one-in-a-hundred or one-in-a-thousand thing that just might go wrong."

What are the risks? PUBS is an experimental procedure, and the risks are not yet known. There does seem to be an increased risk of miscarriage. In the first six hundred procedures performed in the United States, 1.2 percent ended in miscarriage.

Why you may need this test. PUBS is performed if a woman has a family history of a serious blood disease or when one or both parents are known carriers. If amniocentesis fails to produce clear-cut genetic results, PUBS can provide a blood sample that can be analyzed for hereditary disorders. PUBS can detect possible fetal distress by helping to measure blood gases and platelets. It also can detect some serious infections, such as toxoplasmosis, and monitor the effectiveness of various treatments, such as bedrest, oxygen, or fluids. If the fetus develops life-threatening complications, an obstetrician can use PUBS as a therapeutic tool and perform an intrauterine blood transfusion. PUBS also can be used to administer medications directly to a fetus and monitor drug levels in the baby's blood.

What to expect. The abdomen is washed and coated with an antiseptic solution. While you'll receive a topical anesthetic, you may feel uncomfortable during the procedure because of your full bladder, the pressure of the ultrasound transducer, and the presence of the needle as it's being positioned. Depending on the position of the placenta, the test can require thirty to sixty minutes. Some women experience bleeding and cramping afterward.

Fetal Echocardiography

What it is. Fetal echocardiography is a means of detecting heart problems or defects before birth.

How it's done. A sonographer with special expertise in imaging, or viewing, the heart uses highly advanced ultrasound equipment to focus on the four chambers of the heart and the blood vessels leading to and from them. This test is best performed no earlier than the eighteenth week of pregnancy, when structures are large enough to be seen well.

What it shows. Fetal echocardiography can reveal various malformations in the chambers of the heart and abnormalities in the vessels that carry blood to and from the heart. It often can detect lethal heart defects early enough for parents to consider abortion. It also can alert perinatologists to problems or potential problems that require special care at birth or afterward.

Depending on the findings, obstetricians may recommend delivery at a high-risk center where a pediatric cardiologist (heart specialist) can be available for delivery and can perform any necessary corrective surgery as soon as possible after birth.

What are the risks. There are no known risks to the fetus or mother from ultrasonic exams like fetal echocardiography.

Why you may need this test. Obstetricians recommend this test whenever there is increased risk of a heart problem because of family history, maternal diseases, such as lupus and diabetes, or exposure to certain drugs, such as lithium (a treatment for manic-depression).

What to expect. The procedure is the same as for other ultrasound exams, but because of the need for highly specialized expertise, the test usually is performed only at high-risk centers.

Fetal Activity Monitoring (The Test Only a Mother Can Do)

What it is. In this do-it-yourself test, a woman counts how often her baby moves in a thirty- or sixty-minute period several times a day, beginning in the twenty-seventh week of pregnancy.

How it's done. Women at high risk can count movements three times a day for thirty minutes at a time or can keep track of movements throughout the day until they reach ten. Four strong movements in thirty minutes or at least ten movements every twelve hours are reassuring findings. Low-risk women can count movements two times a day for twenty to thirty minutes. You can record the movements on a daily record like the one on page 80.

What it shows. Vigorous activity provides reassurance that the baby is healthy. If the baby does not move at least three times an hour or does not move at all for twelve hours, further testing can determine if it is in jeopardy. If you note fewer than ten movements in a twelve-hour period, no movements in the morning, fewer than three movements in eight hours, or become concerned for any reason, contact your obstetrician.

What are the risks? Some caregivers have speculated that fetal movement counting might lead to unnecessary anxiety and unwarranted testing. But in a study of 394 pregnancies by University of Washington physicians, 85 percent of the women found counting their baby's movements reassuring; 91 percent wanted to do it again

How to Use This Chart

Each day you will mark on the chart the time you start counting. You will then keep track of how many times the baby "moves or kicks." When you reach ten movements or kicks, mark on the chart the amount of time it took for the baby to do this by darkening the block that matches this amount of time. For example, if you started counting Monday A.M. at 8:30, and the baby moved or kicked 10 times in 2 hours, mark the chart like this:

Start Time	Hours taken to feel 10 movements				
		1	2	3	4	5
M	8:30 A.M.		■			

Babies can vary greatly in the amount they normally move; women also vary in the extent they feel these movements, so it doesn't matter what you count as your baby's movements so long as you stick to it. If after 10 hours your total is less than 10 movements, just fill in the actual number in the A column.

<u>Important:</u> If your baby moves or kicks less than 10 times for two days in a row, or if your baby does not move or kick at all for 10 hours in one day, call your caregiver. This could be a sign that the baby is having some difficulty and needs more tests, or it may be fine. The only way to be sure will be to check your baby at the hospital.

Courtesy of Johns Hopkins Hospital

Fetal Movements Chart

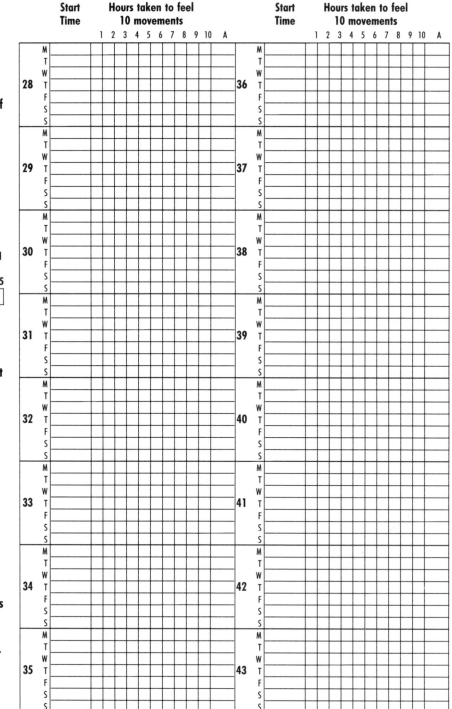

in subsequent pregnancies. There were twenty reports of decreased fetal activity; testing provided reassurance in nineteen of these cases. In one case, a nonreactive nonstress test and a suspicious contraction stress test led to the induced delivery of a healthy thirty-eight-week baby. There were no stillbirths. A Danish study also reported no stillbirths among women counting fetal movements.

Why you may need this test. All pregnant women are urged to notice the patterns of their baby's activity and to monitor movements at least once a day. In a high-risk pregnancy, the chances of fetal distress because of growth retardation, excessive or insufficient amniotic fluid, blood incompatibility, or maternal illnesses are greater—as are the benefits of conscientious monitoring.

What to expect. No one knows your baby's activity pattern better than you, but you should anticipate some normal changes as your pregnancy progresses. The average number of daily movements rises from about 200 at twenty weeks to as many as 575 at thirty-two weeks. As pregnancy continues and the growing baby has less room to move, the number of daily movements decreases.

Mothers don't notice every fetal movement, and some, because of their babies' size and position, feel fewer than others. Many factors can affect fetal movements, including time of day, sound, medications, blood-sugar levels, and smoking. What's most important is a dramatic change from whatever you know is normal.

Don't be afraid to call if fetal movements decrease. While it may be tempting to think, "It'll be better tomorrow," check it out. Let your caregivers decide whether your explanation of why the baby is moving less (you have a cold; you've spent most of the day in bed, etc.) merits further evaluation.

Electronic Fetal Monitoring (EFM)

What it is. Electronic fetal monitoring records the heartbeat of an unborn baby and measures contractions of the mother's uterus. Together, these two factors indicate how healthy and strong the fetus is.

How it's done. Measurements can be obtained in two ways: by external monitoring, which can be used during pregnancy and labor, and by internal monitoring, which can be used only after rupture of the membranes.

External monitoring usually requires two belts, placed around the mother's abdomen, to hold two small instruments in place. One uses ultrasound to detect the fetal heart rate. The other measures pressure changes caused by uterine contractions. A newer device combines both monitors on a single belt.

Internal monitoring uses a small device called an electrode, which is attached to the scalp of the fetus, to record the fetal heart rate and a tube, or catheter, to measure the pressure of uterine contractions. Both are inserted into the vagina after the cervix has opened or dilated during labor and the amniotic membranes have ruptured. (See chapter 13 for more on internal monitoring during delivery.)

What it shows. The external and internal monitors send information to a machine that records a "tracing" of the heart rate and uterine contractions on a long sheet of paper. The tracing shows the patterns of the fetal heartbeat, including:

Fetal Heart Rate Variability: A healthy baby's heart usually beats quite fast—about 120 to 160 beats a minute—with a fair amount of variability in the number of heartbeats per minute. This variability gives a normal tracing its characteristic jagged, sawtooth appearance. A flattened tracing may indicate oxygen deprivation.

In this tracing of a normal fetal heart rate during labor, the baby's heart speeds up with each contraction.

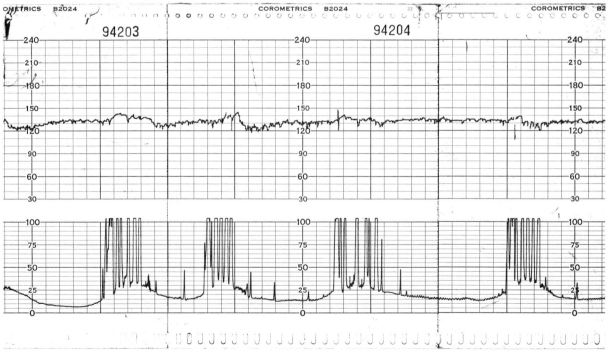

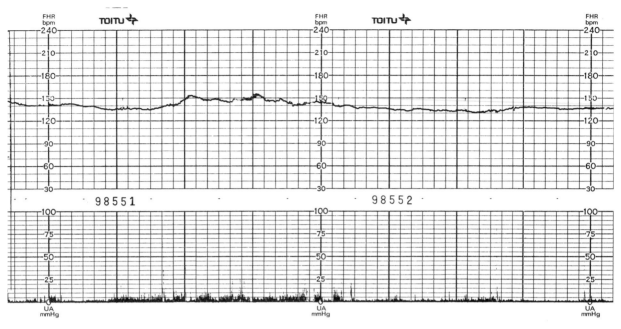

Above: This tracing shows decreased heart rate variability, which can be a sign of fetal distress.

Below: This tracing shows variable heart rate decelerations but good variability between decelerations and a rapid return to normal.

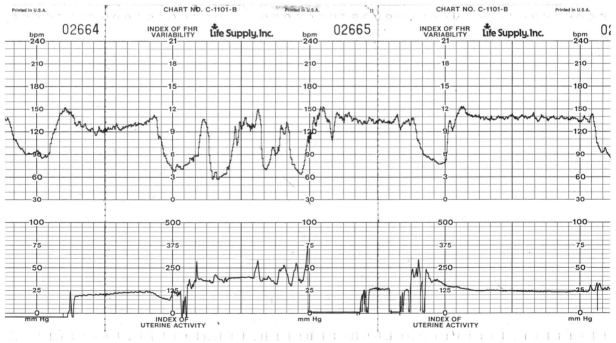

On the Horizon: A Test for Preterm Labor?

A simple monitoring technique may be able to detect the women with no recognized risk factors who are most likely to go into preterm labor. The test, which requires an hour in a doctor's office from the twenty-eighth to thirty-second weeks of pregnancy (the key danger period for preterm labor), uses a portable tocodynamometer, a small instrument worn around the waist that measures contractions of the uterus.

In two studies—one of 139 black inner-city women in Philadelphia and one of 520 non-black middle-class women in San Francisco—obstetricians from the University of California, San Francisco (UCSF), and the University of Pennsylvania had women wear a monitor either while waiting for doctors' appointments or at home. The women who carried their babies to term (thirty-seven to forty weeks) averaged three or four contractions during an hour of monitoring. The women who had six or seven or more contractions an hour were six times more likely to give birth prematurely. (See chapter 11 for more information on detecting early signs of preterm labor.)

Temporary Rise in Fetal Heart Rate (Acceleration): The heart rate normally goes up in response to fetal movement, a contraction, or an external stimulus, such as loud noise.

Early Slowing of the Fetal Heart Rate (Deceleration): This occurs about 15 percent of the time at the beginning of contractions during labor and does not indicate a problem.

Variable Slowing and Quickening of the Fetal Heartbeat: This change can indicate compression or squeezing of the umbilical cord, which is dangerous only if it is prolonged.

Delayed Slowing or Deceleration of the Fetal Heart Rate: This ominous change, which may take place during or after a contraction, may indicate that the fetus is not receiving enough oxygen, a potentially dangerous situation for the baby.

What Are the Risks? External fetal monitoring during pregnancy poses no known danger to a growing baby. Misleading or misinterpreted results may lead to tests that may not prove necessary and possibly to an unnecessary induction and an early delivery.

Why you may need this test. In a high-risk pregnancy, electronic fetal monitoring can provide assurances that the baby's heartbeat is normal and responding as it should to contractions and movements. This information can be critical in determining the timing of delivery and possible interventions.

What to expect. The following descriptions of nonstress and contraction stress testing provide information on how fetal monitoring is used during pregnancy:

Nonstress Testing (NST)

What it is. This test measures a baby's response to its own movement.

How it's done. An external fetal heart monitor, strapped around the mother's belly, measures the baby's heart rate when it moves.

What it shows. The results of NST can be:

Reactive: Normally the heart rate speeds up when the baby moves. A reactive or normal test shows two accelerations, each lasting fifteen seconds or more, as the baby moves in a twenty-minute period.

Nonreactive: There may be fewer than two accelerations or they may not last as long as fifteen seconds.

Unsatisfactory: The findings are insufficient or cannot be interpreted.

What are the risks? As with ultrasound, there are no known side effects.

Why you may need this test. Your doctor may suggest nonstress testing as part of a fetal biophysical profile or simply as a check on your baby's condition. NST is most often used for women with threatened preterm labor, placenta previa, postdate pregnancies, and other high-risk conditions.

What to expect. Nonstress testing is painless. However, sitting completely still for twenty or thirty minutes can be uncomfortable.

Contraction Stress Testing (CST)

What it is. This test measures how a fetus may respond to the stress of labor.

How it's done. A fetal heart monitor measures the baby's heart rate during contractions induced either by stimulation of the mother's nipples (with her hand or warm towels) or by intravenous administration of oxytocin (Pitocin), a hormone that triggers uterine contractions.

What it shows. The baby's response indicates how well it may cope with the physical stress of labor and alerts doctors to potential problems during delivery. The test can be:

Negative (normal). Three contractions lasting forty or more seconds occur, with good variability of fetal heart rate (see illustration on page 82). The heart speeds up when the fetus moves and doesn't slow down suddenly.

Positive (abnormal). In more than half of the contractions, the heart rate slows down and may not speed up at all when the fetus moves.

Suspicious. Occasionally the heart rate dips during or after a contraction. Your doctor may repeat the test in twenty-four hours.

Unsatisfactory. The findings cannot be interpreted because of movement by the fetus or mother, excessive amniotic fluid, fetal hiccups, bowel sounds, the mother's weight, or the absence of contractions.

What are the risks? Sometimes nipple stimulation or oxytocin triggers "hyperstimulation," contractions closer than every two minutes or lasting more than ninety seconds with late decelerations. Because this can be dangerous for the fetus, testing is stopped. If a baby with an abnormal heart rate shows continued signs of distress, treatment with labor-inhibiting drugs or an emergency delivery may be necessary.

A major drawback is the high rate of false positives. In more than half of the instances where the test indicates the baby is in distress, there is no problem. Generally, healthy babies show accelerated heart rates when they move, even when other patterns are troublesome. A positive CST, combined with no acceleration with fetal movement, is more ominous, and obstetricians usually will plan on an early delivery if the baby's lungs are mature.

Why you may need this test. In many high-risk pregnancies, nonstress testing is more widely used than CST. Fetal biophysical profiles also are becoming more common. However, CST may be a better indicator of risk in babies who are small, late, or at risk for stillbirth because of a previous miscarriage. It also can confirm or rule out problems after an abnormal or suspicious nonstress test.

What to expect. The test can last twenty minutes to two hours. You sit or lie on your side, usually in or near a labor and delivery unit at a hospital, with the monitors around your abdomen. During the first fifteen minutes, a nurse evaluates "baseline" movements, heart rate and contractions. If you experience three spontaneous contractions that last forty to sixty seconds within a ten-minute period, neither breast stimulation nor oxytocin will be necessary. Breast stimulation usually is tried first because this method takes less time, is less expensive, and causes less discomfort because no IV (intravenous line) is necessary.

To induce contractions by breast self-stimulation, brush your palm across one nipple through your shirt or gown. Stop when a contraction begins. Continue after a five-minute rest period. You'll continue the process for forty minutes or until three contractions at least forty seconds in length occur within ten minutes. If no contractions occur after fifteen or twenty minutes, stimulate the other nipple. While the contractions may be surprisingly strong, most women do not feel they're very painful.

If oxytocin is used, you will receive an IV infusion of the hormone until three contractions, lasting forty to sixty seconds, occur within ten minutes. The uterus may contract intensely. The breathing techniques taught in childbirth preparation class can help with painful contractions.

Fetal Biophysical Profile

What it is. This test, performed with an ultrasound scanner and an electronic fetal monitor, is the equivalent of a physical examination in the womb, including a check on the baby's breathing, movements, muscle tone, heart rate, and amniotic fluid.

How it's done. The biophysical profile relies on ultrasound and the nonstress test (see page 84) to provide information on a baby's well-being.

What it shows. The biophysical profile assesses fetal breathing, body movements, muscle tone, and amount of amniotic fluid, providing a score of two for each normal finding:

Biophysical Variable	Normal = 2 pts.	Abnormal = 0 pt.
Breathing	1 breathing movement at least 30 seconds in 30 minutes	None or none 30 seconds long in 30 minutes
Body movements	3 or more in 30 minutes	Less than 2
Muscle tone	1 or more active extensions of limbs or trunk	None or slow extensions
Amniotic Fluid	Standard volume	Less than usual
Heart rate	2 or more accelerations with fetal movement in 20 minutes	Less than 2 accelerations in 20 minutes

Total scores of eight to ten are considered normal. Lower scores indicate increased likelihood of oxygen deprivation and fetal distress.

What are the risks? Sonography and nonstress testing have no known risks.

Why it's done. The biophysical profile helps caregivers determine whether the baby is healthy despite high-risk conditions, such as a mother's hypertension or signs of growth retardation. As long as the baby's score is normal, the pregnancy can continue. If the baby's scores begin to drop, the obstetrician may perform other tests and monitor the baby more often. In cases of increasing danger (indicated by a persistent score of less than four), delivery may be essential to save the baby.

TESTING: FACING THE "WHAT IFS"

Of course, you want to know if your baby is all right. Every mother does. You want reassurance that he or she has the standard number of chromosomes and no more, that every organ system is developing as it should, that this child will be born healthy and strong. For most women, most of the time, prenatal tests are reassuring. A relatively small percentage of expectant parents get the news all couples dread: that somehow something has gone wrong, that the baby who has taken life in their imagination may not survive or may not be normal and healthy at birth.

Unlike low-risk women, who may undergo prenatal testing casually confident of hearing only good news, some high-risk women face each procedure with considerable anxiety. "What if . . ." is the question that haunts many such mothers-to-be as they pray for the best yet can't stop thinking about the worst. Admitting your concerns and fears won't make them go away, but talking about them—with your partner, with your friends, with your caregivers—can help you keep the real risks in perspective.

Coping

HANDLING THE STRESS OF A HIGH-RISK PREGNANCY

Sooner or later, you cry. You cry because you're worried about yourself and the child you've never seen. You cry because you don't know what the future might hold. You cry because you've lost your dream of having the perfect pregnancy. But through and after the tears, you do something else: you cope.

All pregnant women do. After all, every pregnancy is a life crisis that reflects and affects a family's deepest emotions and values. If you're pregnant and high risk, you'll experience the usual kaleidoscope of experiences and emotions, as well as some special concerns, all with an added measure of intensity. This chapter may help you anticipate some unexpected reactions and understand what's behind the emotions you're most likely to feel.

NORMAL PREGNANCY: HOW ALL PREGNANT WOMEN FEEL

Pregnancy is a special state of mind as well as body. Emotions push closer to the surface. Tears flow faster. Fears loom larger. A lifetime of feelings may be crammed into nine amazing months. Being at risk doesn't exempt you from any of these changes, and you may find it reassuring to realize that you're not the first or the only woman to be caught in an emotional whirlwind.

What may be most disconcerting is not just how varied your emotions may be but how quickly they change—from highs to lows and back again. Yet mood swings—or, in psychological terms, emotional "lability"—are characteristic of pregnancy.

You also may register each emotion much more intensely—as if, in one woman's words, you're "feeling for two." Some women, alarmed by the rage they feel when a driver swerves in front of them or the tears they shed when reading about a sick child, wonder whether they've become psychologically unglued. Yet true psychiatric disturbance in pregnancy is rare.

Typically pregnancy is a time of psychological development, and most women move through certain predictable stages from the time they first learn they're pregnant until delivery. In the first few months, when rising hormones bring on fatigue and morning sickness, many women feel weepy, irritable, or highly emotional. They're also likely to feel ambivalent about being pregnant.

Once "quickening" occurs in the second trimester and they feel the baby moving within them, women typically become more committed and positive. As their bodies adjust to higher hormone levels and begin to blossom, many feel tranquil, even sensual. This is a time of quiet excitement, when parents plan for and fantasize about their child.

The last, long stretch of the final trimester can be the hardest, physically and psychologically, and "prepartum blues" are not uncommon. In addition to the discomforts of being very pregnant, many women experience a certain letdown. They may feel that they've been pregnant forever, and the excitement and novelty have long worn off. Yet as they look toward labor and delivery, they may be anxious and apprehensive. First-time mothers in particular fear the unknowns: how painful birth might be, how they'll respond, how their mates will react.

By the end of pregnancy, most women have reached a point of psychological readiness. They've worked through their initial ambivalence. They've "connected" with their unborn baby. They've gained a sense of confidence in themselves and their bodies. They are ready—not just physically, but emotionally and psychologically—to mother the child they've yet to see.

THE STRESS OF BEING HIGH RISK

In a low-risk pregnancy, the mother-to-be continues her normal routines, with an occasional screening test or prenatal exam wedged into her schedule. She may cut back on some activities or modify her routine, but the changes are fairly small. During the quiet months of waiting, she and her family begin adjusting psychologically to the dramatic changes a new baby will bring.

In a high-risk pregnancy, the dramatic changes can start at a moment's notice. Suddenly it may seem that you're spending more time in doctors' offices and hospitals than you thought possible. And through it all, the other aspects of your life go on. None of your responsibilities, obligations, or problems disappears. Coping takes on entirely new and unexpected dimensions.

I'm Not Sick—Or Am I?

One fact that's easy to overlook when you're at risk is that pregnancy is a healthy, normal process. "When I first got pregnant, I thought of myself as being healthier than I'd ever been before," says one woman. "After I developed preeclampsia, pregnancy turned into something to treat rather than something to enjoy. I felt kind of cheated."

If you're at risk, your pregnancy does indeed become "medicalized." On the one hand, you may appreciate frequent, conscientious prenatal care, especially if you've lost a baby or run into unexpected problems in a previous pregnancy. But you may feel that the intensive care as well as caring has taken over your "old" life. You may undergo so many screening tests and diagnostic procedures that, as one woman put it, "pregnancy turns into one long medical exam."

If you have a chronic disease, such as diabetes or a seizure disorder, you may have had to make major adjustments in your lifestyle long before conception. Yet you may see your pregnancy as a triumph, as, in a psychiatrist's words, "a ray of hope against the ravages of chronic illness." The frequent checkups and tests required by your condition may be disturbing because they force you to confront, again and again, the precariousness of a deeply wanted pregnancy.

If you've been perfectly healthy, a sudden complication of pregnancy—such as placenta previa or preterm labor—may catch you psychologically off-guard. You may have to undergo tedious or uncomfortable tests or diagnostic procedures. If you must take medication, the drugs may make you uncomfortable, jittery, anxious, or depressed.

Most difficult of all is hospitalization for bleeding, preterm labor, or other serious complications. "You really feel out of control in a hospital," one woman says. "I didn't think of myself as the 'patient';

the baby was. Yet I was the one who had to put up with the inconvenience, the discomfort, and, worst of all, the complete lack of privacy."

In such circumstances, another source of stress—one you can do something about—is not knowing what's going on or what to expect. The best way to inform yourself and keep misconceptions, exaggerations, and unfounded fears in check is to make sure the lines of communication between you and your caregivers remain open.

Just as important as information about risk factors is information about what's normal about your pregnancy. Reading about stages of fetal development and keeping track of your baby's growth will remind you of the many ways in which your pregnancy is indeed just like any other.

THE PSYCHOLOGY OF BEING HIGH RISK

When you first find out you're at risk, you may not be able or willing to accept the fact. Denial is a common response. But as the signs and symptoms of a complication persist, denial breaks down. Very often women feel angry and bitter. "I did everything right," one woman tearfully recalls. "It didn't seem fair that this should be happening." Others take a highly intellectual, businesslike approach to pregnancy. They hold back emotionally, not totally involving themselves in their pregnancy, as if to protect themselves from possible disappointment.

Your reactions to being at risk may depend on your stage of pregnancy. If you begin to bleed in your first trimester, normal ambivalence about being pregnant may persist until the danger of miscarriage is past. If your baby isn't growing at the usual rate or shows signs of blood incompatibility, your confidence in yourself and your body may be shaken. Rather than worrying—as most women do—about what kind of mother you'll be, you may wonder whether you'll be a mother at all. If problems develop late in pregnancy, you may feel overwhelmed by the prospect of losing the baby or having a child with serious defects or problems.

Common Feelings

According to the standard myth, all pregnant women glow with happiness. The fact is that no mother-to-be goes through pregnancy in a state of unadulterated bliss. If you're at risk, you are sure to have happy times, but you'll also experience some darker feelings, including:

Resentment. Every pregnant woman—low risk or high risk—has some negative feelings about the experience of sharing her body with her baby. Many a would-be mother, woozy with nausea, has mumbled, "This kid had better be worth it," or has wondered why she ever got pregnant in the first place. If you're at risk, you may feel that such normal responses somehow caused the complications, that your resentment or ambivalence is to blame for the problems you or your baby are encountering. You're innocent on all counts. Feelings are just feelings, after all, and you're entitled to "bad" ones as well as good ones.

Anxiety. Every mother worries at some stage of pregnancy whether her baby will be normal and healthy. While you can't will yourself to stop worrying, you can try to be realistic and informed. Regular prenatal care, discussions of any concerns with your caregivers, and good health habits can provide reassurance that you are doing everything possible to ensure that your baby will get a good start in life. Above all, don't leave questions unanswered, because then the concerns that are making you anxious remain unaddressed.

Guilt. Many women automatically assume that they are to blame for the complications that put them and their babies at risk. You may obsessively look for the one thing that you must have done wrong. Initially finding a cause for your problem—however illogical—may make you feel as if you're in control of the situation. After all, you'll know not to do *that* again. While such detective work is a way of trying to make sense of a difficult situation, self-incrimination only feeds into totally undeserved feelings of inadequacy or failure.

Dependence. While most of us do appreciate tender loving care, almost everyone hates losing independence—a little of it or a lot. If you're at risk and have to restrict your usual activity and routine, you may not be able to go where you want to go, do what you have to do, or carry on with the business of daily living. You may not only need help from others; you may have to rely on it. And while friends and family may not mind giving assistance, you may dislike having to ask for it—again and again. But dependence, like pregnancy, is a temporary state. Remember that you're relying on others so you can concentrate on helping your baby.

"Every response a mother has to her high-risk pregnancy is a normal one, no matter how negative, unrealistically positive, or seemingly detached. When life hangs in the balance, particularly one's child's life, one does not necessarily react in an expected way. The typically strong may react weakly, and the hesitant, with strength. Remembering why the pregnancy was begun in the first place (whether or not it was known that it would be high-risk) may offer the parents the strength they need to hold on. But no matter what the goal, they can only get there one day at a time."

Lenette Moses, *Intensive Caring Unlimited*

Why me? You look around a supermarket or your child's pre-school, where every third woman seems to be pregnant—*and* radiant *and* energetic *and* healthy—and you think, "Why can't I be like them?" You're bound to feel sorry for yourself at times throughout your pregnancy, and you shouldn't put yourself down for being down. But self-pity—like guilt—is a useless emotion. No one is exempt from some unfairness in life, and you might ask an equally apt question: "Why *not* me?"

Fear. Of course, you're scared—for yourself and your baby. One of the greatest fears is that your baby may be disfigured or handicapped. While you can't get any absolute guarantees, you can find out what the risks really are and do everything you can to avoid any additional risks that may jeopardize your baby.

Inadequacy. A woman who's accomplished a great deal academically or professionally may be stunned when her body doesn't behave as expected. "Millions of women have perfectly normal pregnancies and babies every year," one woman reflected. "I couldn't, so I concluded something had to be wrong with me. For the first time in my life, I felt like a failure."

If a baby is not growing properly or has a blood-incompatibility problem, the mother is particularly likely to blame herself. Feeling increasingly inadequate, she may lost confidence and self-esteem. Yet pregnancy is not an Olympic event, where worthy opponents vie for medals. Remind yourself that your best is all you can and all you should try to do.

Loss. From the moment she learns she's at risk, a pregnant woman may feel a sense of loss, if only of her expectations of how pregnancy and birth should be. "I had this fantasy of walking through a mall when I was nine months pregnant and everyone stopping to look at me," says a woman who spent two pregnancies on bedrest, "I wanted to go out in the world as a pregnant woman, and I never was able to. It still makes me a little sad."

Other women experience a sense of loss because they can't work or exercise or travel. Some also lose a certain image of themselves. "I always saw myself as the type of woman who'd have tons of kids," says one woman. "When I couldn't seem to have just one, I felt I must have been kidding myself all those years."

Anticipatory grief. The most painful loss to contemplate is the loss of the baby. When a very serious complication develops during pregnancy, parents may start to prepare themselves for a possible loss by beginning to grieve. They may feel that by imagining the worst, they'll be better prepared if it happens.

"I still felt very committed to the baby, and I really wanted her to pull through," says one mother. "But another part of my brain was dealing with the fact that we might lose her. I was afraid that the more I let myself love her, the harder it would be to lose her."

If you find yourself in this sad and difficult situation, remember that the vast majority of high-risk babies do make it. Talk with your caregivers so you have up-to-the-minute information about your baby. And reach out to your loved ones for support and comfort.

> "After losing a baby, the next pregnancy is a white-knuckle pregnancy. You don't just have a feeling that things could go wrong: you feel that, in your case, things *do* go wrong."

If You've Had a High-Risk Pregnancy or Baby Before

Many woman are classified as high risk because something went wrong in a previous pregnancy. Becoming pregnant again after a difficult pregnancy, the birth of a handicapped infant, or the loss of a baby is invariably stressful.

"Filled with the conflicting emotions of hope for a normal child and fear that I would again fail in achieving this, I became pregnant," writes Phyllis DiFelice, executive vice president of Intensive Caring Unlimited, a Philadelphia support group for women with high-risk pregnancies. "I spent many sleepless nights saying to myself, 'What have I done? Why have I dared to conceive this child?' After all, my only other experience with pregnancy had resulted in a child with so many problems. Why should I think this time would be any different?"

This woman, like many others, made sure there would be a difference: She got the best possible high-risk care, ate well, abstained from caffeine, alcohol, and additives, underwent regular prenatal exams and tests. Still she felt anxious: "I could not allow myself to picture a healthy, normal baby at the end for fear of too much disappointment." And when she finally did have a perfect baby, she plunged from great joy into "overwhelming and uncontrollable depression," as if she were reexperiencing the intense sorrow and grief she'd felt after her first child's birth.

In addition to such emotional upheavals, couples often experience what counselors call the "black cloud" phenomenon: whatever happens, they sense disaster and expect the worst. They cannot dare to believe that this time, things will work out. "We couldn't allow ourselves to get excited," says one husband. "We decided that we weren't going to relax until we had the baby in our arms."

"The man is the same after his first love as he was before. The man spends a night by a woman and goes away. His life and body are always the same. The woman conceives. As a mother, she is another person than the woman without child. She carries the fruit of the night nine months long in her body. Something grows. Something grows into her life that never again departs from it. She is a mother. She is and remains a mother even though her child dies, though all her children die. For at one time she carried the child under her heart. And it does not go out of her heart ever again. Not even when it is dead. All this the man does not know; he knows nothing."

Leo Frobenius

As delivery day approaches, some parents feel curiously "disloyal" to the baby they lost, as if by letting themselves become attached to the child they're carrying they are denying that they had another child who died. "A couple of weeks before my due date, we brought out all the baby stuff we'd gotten the first time around," one mother recalls. "Suddenly I thought that these things really belonged to Jacob, even though he'd never had a chance to see them. I felt we had no right to them."

In this case, Jacob's baby clothes had become highly symbolic, and his mother didn't want to turn them all over to a new baby. She resolved her conflict by setting aside a few things that would always remain Jacob's and using the rest for the new baby.

What helps many couples going through a pregnancy in the shadow of a loss is contact with other parents who've had a similar experience. In many communities support groups for couples who become pregnant after a previous loss meet regularly, providing comfort for the members.

"I see a dramatic change in couples over the course of a pregnancy," says a counselor in Rockville, Maryland, who leads one such group, "Often the husband won't say anything the first few sessions, and the wife will be very emotional. But as the pregnancy progresses and the mother gets more invested in it, she often becomes stronger, and the husband starts talking about his feelings. In the group, couples can express their grief, work through it, and get ready to love another baby. And it's possible only because everybody in the room has been through the same thing."

THE PEOPLE IN YOUR PREGNANCY

The mother is always at center stage in pregnancy. Yet having a baby is a group effort, involving the father, grandparents, friends, relatives, and health professionals. Your relationships with these people can be a source of comfort—or conflict.

Your Baby's Father

Pregnancy is a life-changing event for men as well as women. When a couple has been planning or hoping for pregnancy, a daddy-to-be may feel great pride in siring a child. But soon his overriding feeling may become a deep sense of responsibility. He may reevaluate his job, salary, and plans for the future.

Many men's attitudes toward their partners also change. Some husbands are almost overly protective, yet they may feel confused or put off if their wives seem more tired or emotional than usual. Some think their wives have never been more attractive; others find it hard to think of a bulging belly as sexy.

Like their spouses, men may fear labor and delivery. They don't want to see the women they love in pain, and they worry about whether they'll be able to provide comfort and support. Yet they feel that expressing such fears may make them seem less supportive.

In a high-risk pregnancy, fathers may feel particularly protective of their wives, anxious about their role as providers, and fearful of the vulnerability of their partners and unseen children. A husband may feel that his job is to "take care" of his family, yet there's little he can do. This lack of control can undermine his sense of self-worth. He also may feel cut off from his mate as she becomes preoccupied with the baby and may worry that she will no longer have time for him and his needs.

The Invisible Man

Expectant fathers often feel left out as everyone focuses attention on the mother-to-be. They may feel unneeded, even though their emotional support is more crucial than ever before. In normal circumstances, most fathers weather the experience with little more than a bruised ego. In high-risk situations, the father can find his role extremely trying.

As a father-to-be confronts the same fears and doubts as a high-risk mother, he, too, feels pressure. In our society, men are conditioned to think of themselves as responsible for their families. When a pregnancy becomes seriously complicated or a baby is born with a defect or disorder, many men experience a sense of failure, a feeling that they let down the people they were supposed to protect. Yet most never talk about what they're going through.

"How could I talk about myself when I knew how bad my wife felt?" one man explains. "I wanted to be strong for her." Unfortunately, many women misinterpret their husbands' stoicism as indifference, concluding that they just don't care.

What Does She Want from Me?

Behind the helplessness men feel is a sense of not being able to do anything for their wives or not knowing what their spouses want. Yet women at risk know their husbands can't magically take away their problems. What they want are certain basics that any husband can provide, including:

Physical support. Women who once ran marathons or companies may find themselves too tired to get off the couch without some help. A husband who relieves his wife of some of the physical burdens of daily living—household chores, shopping, taking care of older children—is giving her a wonderful gift: more energy and time to give to their baby.

Reassurance. A woman at risk lives with doubts and fears. Even though she knows that her mate can't guarantee that everything will work out, she still likes to know that he believes in her. A hug, a compliment on how well she's doing, or a willingness to listen are all wonderful ways of assuring a woman that whatever she's feeling is okay.

Commitment. Coping with a high-risk pregnancy is a challenge for a couple. A woman with a partner, accustomed to and expecting his support, may feel that the one thing she couldn't handle is losing him. She needs to know that he'll be with her when she needs him most and that he's as committed as she is to having this baby.

Empathy and sympathy. A man can't know what it's like to be nauseated around the clock, to gasp for breath after the slightest exertion, to feel a uterus tighten rhythmically months before it should. But a husband can sympathize. When a psychiatrist surveyed the emotional needs of a group of high-risk mothers hospitalized during pregnancy, he found that very few needed professional counseling. What helped these women most was a genuine appreciation for what they were experiencing.

Your Marriage: For Better or Worse

A high-risk pregnancy cements some relationships and splinters others. Usually couples respond to this challenge the way they typically react in any crisis. But there are special pressures. Because of the emotional upheavals, the partners may not be "in sync" throughout a pregnancy. She may be fearful; he may be confident—and both may switch roles the very next day. Ideally, couples can talk through their mixed feelings so that they approach their child's birth sharing one common emotion: intense anticipation.

Ironically, many men and women on the verge of becoming parents feel a great need for parenting themselves. Often the nine months of waiting are, in a very different way, as crucial for the new parents as they are for their child. During the time the infant is preparing for life, they are preparing for the most demanding and rewarding roles of their lives—those of mother and father. If both care about each other's expectations and anxieties, they may find themselves closer than ever as they count down to the day of their child's birth.

Sex. Sex during pregnancy isn't necessarily better or worse than before, but it definitely is different. Many couples find themselves reevaluating their sexual needs and making changes in the way they usually relate to each other sexually. In a high-risk pregnancy, medical complications may limit or preclude certain types of sexual activity. Even without any restrictions, stress and fatigue can dampen both partners' interest in making love.

Together, the couple should talk to the woman's caregivers about what's safe and what's not. For women at very high risk, sexual intercourse may not be allowed. Couples should ask if that ban applies to other activities that might lead the woman to orgasm. (The man's orgasm is never a danger to the pregnancy.)

Just as important as what a couple can't do is what they can: kissing, hugging, cuddling, massaging. Some rediscover the surprisingly sexy pleasures of "making out." Others feel frustrated but console themselves with the thought that their situation is only temporary.

Yet women—pregnant or not, high risk or not—yearn to know that their partners are still attracted to them. And men want assurance that they, too, are desirable and desired. That's why it's important for couples to stay in touch, literally and figuratively, throughout pregnancy. Here are some suggestions:

• Remember that there is more to love than making love. Think of romantic alternatives: long walks, bedroom talks, candlelit dinners, evenings out, backrubs, massages, shared showers, or meeting for an intimate lunch.

• Bring up your hidden fears. If you're worried about your sex appeal, ask if your mate still finds you attractive. If your caregivers say intercourse is okay, but you're still hesitant, say so. If one or both of you is less interested in sex than usual, talk about what's on your mind.

• Recognize the strains you're under and talk about problems openly. If they seem too overwhelming to handle on your own, seek professional help.

• Be realistic in your expectations. Your goal should be staying as close as possible, physically and emotionally, not setting new records for sexual activity or creativity.

A FATHER'S STORY
"Guarding the Quarterback"
by Scott Penniman

Being a father during a high-risk pregnancy took me back to my very limited career as a left guard in junior-high-school football. During almost the whole game my job was to protect the quarterback. The quarterback's job was to handle the ball.

They never give the left guard the ball. Each play I had to run into and get hit by some threat to the quarterback. I'd get thrown to the ground every time and get up huffing. The quarterback is never supposed to get hit.

If we won the game the quarterback got most of the accolades, made all the speeches, and was widely admired. They would present the game ball to the quarterback, which eventually got thrown around and I would get to hold the ball for the first time. Of course, high-risk pregnancy is not exactly like football and the analogy falls short. For instance, when I got to hold the game ball it did not make a mess on my pants.

Before our most recent pregnancy, my wife, Connie, and I had been through two premature births: one six weeks premature (piece of cake), the other eleven weeks premature (totally changed my life). So on considering a third child (you must be crazy!) we sought out a high-risk doctor. Through him we discovered that Connie had been blessed with uterus didelphum, meaning she has two uteri. I could never be one-upped in locker-room discussion again.

"Apparently," the doctor said, looking at the x rays, "this can work. After all, you have two children. Therefore, I see no reason why you cannot have another." I knew then that we were safe in the hands of science.

It seemed like three days later we were back at the doctor's and Connie was two months pregnant. He congratulated us and proceeded to give us what I call the "Omnipresent Risk" speech. Our risk, of course, was premature labor due to two uteri. Connie could continue to work but not too hard because there was always a risk . . . Connie could still work around the house but moderately because there was always a risk . . . Connie should not have too much stress because there was always a risk . . . Connie could still engage in sexual activities but there was always a risk . . . In short, life became something of a risk for Connie.

After we got home from the doctor's (did I carry her out of the car myself or did someone help me?) we set aside a room downstairs for Connie. This room was outfitted the way one might outfit a radar station in the antarctic. We tried to have everything she needed there for the duration, including sources of entertainment during the polar winter. Connie sat on the sofabed. To her left was a glass of lemonade and two empty glasses I had yet to remove.

There was also a four-pound box of generic tissues (she is allergic to pregnancy hormones!). On her right was a reading lamp and a compendium of perhaps one hundred and twenty mindless magazines lent to her by family and friends. There was also a waste basket perpetually overflowing with spent tissues. In front of my quarterback was the TV and newly acquired VCR (no sacrifice too great!). The TV was tuned to channel 12 (PBS) except when Phil Donahue was on.

Basically, the doctor wanted Connie off her feet as much as possible because there was always a risk. Now that risk phrase rang constantly in my ears as if there was a Greek chorus following me about chanting, "There is always a risk." It drove me to do things like fetch lemonade, empty waste baskets full of tissues, and care for the two little urchins. Of course that doesn't mean I liked it or that it endeared me to my wife. Indeed, I got a whole new way of looking at my wife in bed. The doctor had told me sexual activity was fine if done gently, moderately, and infrequently because there was always a risk. After hearing that, it is easy to have a satisfying sex life if you are, say, an air traffic controller who enjoys diffusing live bombs as a hobby.

Connie and I explained her pregnancy to our two children, Catherine, age five, and Jacob, age three. Mommy was now restricted in what she could do and they were going to help us, right? Well, the three-year-old responded to every statement of fact with the question "Why?" The explanation got rather lengthy and ultimately embarrassing. But two hours later the kids understood and agreed to help. The five-year-old helped for about four hours, the three-year-old twenty minutes at best.

Time dragged by. Things got pretty tense at the ice station. I was the screaming guard. The quarterback was bored and irritable. The children (the ones we loved so much that we wanted another one) were openly canvassing strangers for a new living situation. There was only one way out of the ice station—going to see the midwife once a week!

Who would have thought that I would relish the idea of standing next to my stirruped wife idly chatting about cervices and such. But I did! Anything to escape the ice station. The only thing better than the midwife visits were the trips to the doctor, because they took even longer.

Fortunately, prematurity is a risk that diminishes with time. We had a good three months of worry spiced with about four false alarms. Three weeks before her due date we abandoned the ice station and waited for the inevitable to happen. The risk became a hope. The days dragged by. The guard no longer protected the quarterback. In fact, he stopped helping the quarterback altogether. As the due date passed the hope became a fervent demand. How dare this kid be late!

She was, in fact, a week late. Anna came into the world happy, healthy, and ready to join us at home. We had a victory celebration and the quarterback told stories of the game. The game ball was passed around. The guard took off his shoulder pads and vowed to take up tennis.

Staying close. If you've been through crises before, you might want to remind yourselves that this one, too, will pass. And you might draw on the strengths you've built in your years together.

- Say "I love you" as often as you can.
- Spend some time just holding each other, not saying anything, every day.
- Don't assume you can read your partner's mind or your partner can read yours. Ask what he or she is feeling, and try, as best you can, to express your feelings—even when you're not particularly proud of them.
- When you feel yourself holding back for fear of hurting or upsetting your partner, remind yourself that not talking never solves anything. Choose your words with care, but plunge ahead.
- Inform yourselves. Both of you may find it easier to cope with the stresses of a problem pregnancy if you understand what is going on and why.
- Make your pregnancy a partnership. Men can become active participants in a high-risk pregnancy, helping a diabetic woman monitor and record her blood-sugar levels. Learning to work together before a baby's birth is the best possible preparation for working together as parents afterward.

If You're Single

Going through pregnancy with a partner can be difficult; going through it without a partner is even more of a challenge. Being at risk adds to the stress. You'll manage, if you don't try to do it alone.

What you need is a support system—friends, colleagues, family. You'll want someone you trust with whom you can talk through the issues that arise during pregnancy as well as someone who can be with you during labor and delivery. You also might want to seek out other single mothers-to-be or mothers, who will truly understand what you're feeling.

Because your path—though no longer rare—remains untraditional, you may need more than the usual share of courage and confidence. If you know in your heart that what you want most is a baby, you'll find the strength you need.

Loved Ones

You may appreciate the support of family and friends more than ever during a high-risk pregnancy. But if you're overwhelmed with anxious relatives and overly solicitous acquaintances, you may feel you're getting too much of a good thing.

Some Advice on Advice

Often the only thing your loved ones feel they can offer is the one thing you want least: advice. Since you'll get so much of it while you're pregnant, you may want to learn to live with it. The key to accepting it without getting defensive—or offensive—is keeping your ears open and your mouth closed.

Here are other strategies that can make advice easier to take:

• The best response is "Thank you, I appreciate your concern."

• Look at every offer of advice as an opportunity. Ask yourself: What can I learn from this information and can I use it? If there's nothing there, you can discard it.

• Reflect back what you're hearing. Phrases like, "So what you're suggesting is . . . ," show you're listening and buy you time to consider what's being said.

• Let the person know when you've heard all you can handle. Rather than squirm through a lecture, say that you'd like to digest what's been said before considering anything else.

• Don't feel obliged to follow the advice. You can always explain that your situation was different, or that you came up with another strategy that worked.

The Grandparents-to-be. The people with the greatest emotional stake in your pregnancy—next to you and your partner—are your parents and your husband's parents. After all, you're carrying their grandchild. If it's their first, they may be as jittery as first-time parents. Even if they have a brood of grandbabies, they'll still care intensely—because they care about you and your mate and because, well, grandparents are like that.

If you're at risk, your parents' concern for you and your baby may be comforting. It can also be aggravating. "My mother would call after every prenatal visit," one woman recalls. "I know she was genuinely concerned, but I felt like a little girl handing over her report card." And because you'll also be hypersensitive to their judgments, a casual remark, like a reminder to get plenty of rest, may sound like a criticism.

Your Caregivers

Many pregnant women develop close relationships with their caregivers; the ties between a high-risk mother and the perinatal team can become particularly close. Yet these relationships also can run into difficulties. Some specialists may be superbly competent, yet lack warmth and compassion. So many people may be involved in "management" of a high-risk pregnancy that a woman may see a different professional at every visit and not establish a strong bond with one primary caregiver.

While you may not be able to put together an ideal arrangement, you usually can find a way to make things better. Many problems arise from mutual misunderstanding and can be easily corrected. Here are some recommendations for how to go about improving your relations with your caregivers:

• If you prefer one particular member of the team as your primary caregiver, say so. Staff schedules may require that you see other team members at different times, but you can work out ways to provide more continuity in your care.

• Whenever possible, both parents should meet with caregivers. You both get a chance to know them; they get a chance to know both of you. As you become more comfortable, you should feel free to bring up particular fears or concerns. Your goal should be to have a realistic view of what's happening and why.

• If you're not completely happy with your relationship, express your wishes and needs. You might say something like, "We feel a need for something more than medical supervision, yet you always seem so busy that we feel you don't have time to talk with us." In this situation, you may be able to schedule an additional appointment when you and your doctor can sit down and talk.

• Interrupt if your caregivers use initials, words, or phrases you don't know, and ask if they could explain what they're talking about in simpler terms.

• Write down questions as they occur to you and bring the list to each appointment.

• Don't be afraid of asking questions you fear may be dumb. Often they're not, and the answers can help your understanding of what's going on.

• Repeat questions if you have to. In the stress of the moment, it's hard to hear and remember the information you get. Sometimes taking notes or bringing a tape recorder helps.

• Ask your caregivers for written information or references you can look up and read on your own. Even if the only available pamphlets or articles are meant for medical professionals, ask for them to help you understand what's going on.

• If you don't feel confident in your caregivers or you have doubts about a particular therapy, seek a second opinion. At the very least, getting a different perspective may help you sort out why you feel a lack of trust.

WHAT YOU CAN DO

In a high-risk pregnancy, you may feel distressingly out of control. Because you have to rely so much on your caregivers, you may forget some simple facts: It's still your body, your pregnancy, and your baby. You are involved every step of the way, and you remain the most important member of the perinatal team.

You'll feel more confident and competent and more in control if you rely on some basic coping strategies, including:

Information gathering
• If your response to discovering you're at risk has been, "I don't want to know," stop and think. Until you know exactly what is wrong and why, you may assume that everything is wrong and nothing can be done. One woman in preterm labor overheard her doctors talking about their concern for the baby's lungs. They were discussing lung maturity, but she assumed that her baby had no lungs and was doomed to die. Usually imagined fears are worse than reality.

Defusing Stress: A Relaxation Exercise

Lenette Moses, a founder of Intensive Caring Unlimited, a Philadelphia support group for high-risk mothers, and an instructor in yoga and meditation, developed the following positive visualization exercise for use throughout a high-risk pregnancy:

• Get into a comfortable, relaxed position, with eyes closed.

• Start with progressive relaxation: My toes are relaxed. My arches are relaxed. My heels are relaxed. My ankles are relaxed, etc.

• Repeat the following affirmations.

I feel that my uterus is relaxed.

My cervix is firm and secure.

All the muscles surrounding the baby will gently hold him or her in.

I feel good about this pregnancy.

I am doing all I can to maintain this pregnancy.

I am a good parent.

• Take a long, slow inhalation and say to yourself: *With each inhale, I am bringing health-giving oxygen and energy to this baby and my body.*

• Take a long, slow exhalation and say to yourself: *With each exhale, I feel relaxation flowing into every cell in my body.*

• Assert your right to know. Ask. Ask. Ask. If your caregiver doesn't give answers, find one who does. In a high-risk pregnancy, caregivers should be prepared to spend quality time explaining and listening. And the more you know, the more in control you'll feel because you'll understand all your options.

• Don't be silent during medical exams or tests. If a piece of high-tech equipment seems intimidating, ask one of your caregivers to explain how it works. If your doctor prescribes a medication, find out about side effects for you and the baby.

• Go to prenatal classes. Even if you may not be able to participate in all the exercises, you can listen and learn.

• Read. Do as much research as you can into normal pregnancy and into the specifics of your condition.

• Let others do their jobs. Ask questions, voice objections, make your opinion clear, but give the professionals you've chosen as your caregivers the freedom to act on their knowledge and expertise.

• Level with yourself. Being at risk is as much a fact of life as being pregnant. Once you accept the reality, you may be able to accept the consequences of coping with it.

Communicating

• Express your feelings. You may fear that admitting that you're resentful or angry may make you sound like a bad mother (already!). Yet simply letting your emotions out reduces their intensity.

• Admit your fears. Of course, you're scared. It's an appropriate way to feel. But rather than submerging your fears and living with constant anxiety, talk about them—with your partner and with your caregivers. You may find that some of your fears are entirely unfounded.

• Talk about the unthinkable. If you are haunted by fears of losing your baby or having a child with severe birth defects, don't try to deal with such frightening scenarios on your own. Your caregivers can help you put the actual risks into perspective. Your partner can help you shift to a more positive way of looking toward the future.

Taking care of your needs

• Learn to say no. In a high-risk pregnancy, your number-one priority has to be taking care of yourself and your baby. You may have to say no to out-of-town relatives, to your boss, even to your other children. At first, you may experience twinges of guilt, but as you set limits, you'll find it easier to stick to them.

• Realign your priorities. The extra hours you'll need for prenatal visits or various tests have got to come from somewhere. If you try squeezing them into your already-crowded schedule, you'll end up feeling squeezed. You may want to organize your time by making lists: an A list of must-do items, a B list of hope-to-do items, a C list of can-wait items. (You'll be surprised at how many things gradually make their way from the A list to the B or C lists.)

• Baby yourself. As you eat what's best for the baby, sleep more because the baby needs rest, count kicks, and practice breathing, you may well reach the point where you wonder, "What about me?" Treat yourself to a favorite pleasure: A bubble bath. A new record. A frozen yogurt shake. A bouquet of wildflowers. A new perfume. After all, aren't you worth it?

• Learn how to ask for support. Some women have so much trouble putting their needs into words that they end up blaming others for not recognizing their unspoken needs. "You never help around the house," they say to a husband, rather than, "I need your help." The result: he feels unfairly attacked; she becomes self-righteous; everyone is miserable. Learn to ask—for attention, time, encouragement, or a helping hand—directly.

• Let others take care of you. One woman remembers that, at first, she began every request with "I'm sorry." "I was always apologizing for needing help or wanting a backrub," she says. "Finally, my husband asked, 'What are you apologizing for? Your job is taking care of the baby, and mine is taking care of you.'"

Taking a positive approach

• Accept yourself. If you keep comparing yourself to the pregnant dynamos you see at the office or around the neighborhood, you may hear yourself saying—as one woman did—"They're so active and productive, and all I can do is grow a baby." But growing a baby is the greatest achievement of all. If you accomplish nothing else for a few months, you'll still achieve an amazing feat.

• Commit yourself to your pregnancy. To some women, a high-risk pregnancy seems like the nine longest months, dragging on and on. To others, it's a rapid roller-coaster ride of ups and downs and hairpin turns. Whatever your pregnancy brings, you will get more out of it if you invest yourself in it. Rather than counting down days or crossing off weeks, pay attention to what's happening at this special time of your life. It won't last long, yet your memories will last forever.

• Analyze your emotions. If you find yourself on edge or overwrought, pull back and think through the reasons why. Of course, hormonal upheavals play a role, but if you find yourself bursting into tears over a dented fender or burnt roast, you may be crying

For Family and Friends: What You Can Do

• **Be there when you're needed.** What you say, what you do matters less than the comfort of your presence.

• **Listen.** Women at risk need to "process" or talk through their feelings. Your nonjudging, empathic listening can help enormously.

• **Provide practical assistance.** Prepare dinner. Pick up and drop off dry-cleaning. Volunteer to take older children on an outing.

• **Resist the temptation to second guess.**

• **Be positive, but not Pollyanna-ish.**

• **Let your loved one know you think she's doing a great job.**

because of a much deeper sense of fear or sadness. If you can acknowledge and express those feelings, you may be able to take some of the edge off them.

• Turn to your spiritual beliefs. Many people draw strength from religion or basic beliefs about life in times of crisis. Your beliefs may help you see the bigger picture and realize that everything that happens happens for a reason.

• Think positive thoughts about the pregnancy, the baby, your new family. "I deserve to enjoy being pregnant as much as any other woman," one high-risk mother would tell herself every day.

Relaxation/Imaging. Just when you think you're already worrying about everything that possibly could go wrong, you may discover something new: worrying about worrying. Medical scientists speculate that stress, including intense worry, increases risks in pregnancy because the body responds by producing more adrenaline (epinephrine). This hormone can increase blood pressure and impair the flow of blood and nutrients to the placenta and the developing baby.

While you can't make your concerns disappear with a flash of a magic wand, you can learn to ease the physical stress of anxiety. Relaxation and imaging techniques, such as those in the box on page 106, can help you help your baby now—and help you during labor and far into the future.

Reaching out. Whenever researchers have studied stress in pregnancy, they've found one factor that serves as a buffer: a support system. All people need people. Pregnant people need them more. Talk to your family and friends. Share your feelings and experiences with them. If possible, join a support group for high-risk pregnancy or ask your caregivers for names of mothers who've gone through similar experiences. You are not the only woman who's had to deal with the special stresses of being at risk, and sharing your feelings with others can be a great comfort and release.

Hope. E. B. White once commented that "No one should come to New York to live unless he is willing to be lucky." The same may be true of anyone who becomes pregnant. Despite the inevitable worries, you are in the middle of one of the most special times of your life. You may feel tuned in to the creative energies of your body. You may glow with the excitement of being full of life. And because that's what life is all about, you may also feel full of hope—for your pregnancy and for your unborn child. It's a wonderful way to feel. Enjoy it.

Bedrest: A Survival Guide

On a cold day in early February, Denise, thirty-six, an attorney in suburban Washington, D.C., took to her bed. Except for regular prenatal checkups, she remained horizontal while winter melted into spring and spring sizzled into summer. In mid-July, in her thirty-seventh week of pregnancy, she was allowed outside for a stroll for the first time in almost six months. After walking past four houses, she was so exhausted she had to head home. In early August, three days before her due date, Denise went into labor, and her second son was born: eight pounds, four ounces, and perfectly healthy.

"I figure I spent five and a half months on bedrest during each of my last two pregnancies," Denise says. "It was very, very difficult. But it was what I had to do to have a healthy, full-term baby." In fact, after two miscarriages, surgery to remove a septum (membrane) dividing her uterus, and the insertion of a cerclage, or stitch, to keep her cervix closed, bedrest was Denise's last, best hope. "Now I've got the payoff: two healthy boys," she says. "I never doubt that every minute was worth it."

Bedrest is one of the oldest "treatments" in obstetrics. Once women took to their beds for extended periods of confinement or "lying in." Today, despite space-age technology and therapies that have revolutionized the care of the unborn, bedrest remains the most common treatment prescribed for women at risk.

RX: BEDREST

Despite bedrest's long history, little scientific research has been done to prove its efficacy. That doesn't mean it doesn't work, just that there are no absolute answers about when it can help and when it can't. Studies have shown that bedrest improves birth weights for infants at risk and that it's effective in controlling blood pressure. Sometimes it's the least a mother and her caregivers can do for a baby at risk; sometimes it's the most.

Among the reasons caregivers prescribe bedrest are:

- history of miscarriage
- spotting or bleeding early in pregnancy
- DES-caused changes in the reproductive tract
- malformed uterus
- incompetent cervix
- multiple gestation
- history or high risk of preterm labor
- high blood pressure
- edema (fluid retention)
- mother's heart disease
- growth retardation
- placental separation (abruption) or placenta previa
- premature rupture of the membranes
- bleeding in the last trimester.

"Bedrest is safe, it makes sense, and time after time, we've seen it work," explains obstetrician Emily Haller, M.D., of Johns Hopkins. "The high-risk woman who goes on bedrest may be able to do more for her baby than we can with all our fancy equipment."

Caregivers list the following among the benefits of bedrest:

- Blood flow to the placenta and uterus increases, which means the fetus gets more oxygen and nutrients—exactly what's needed for pregnancies complicated by growth retardation, multiple gestation, or hypertensive disorders.

- By staying off her feet, a woman doesn't have to contend with the silent tug of gravity, which pulls the baby down on a weak cervix, increasing the risk of miscarriage or preterm labor.

- Because bedrest reduces physiological strain, a woman's blood pressure drops or stays stable. One study described bedrest as the "single most important part of management of the chronic hypertensive during pregnancy."

- If a woman is carrying more than one baby and is, therefore, at risk of an early delivery, bedrest helps assure that the babies will get as much time in the womb as possible.

• If the placenta has begun to separate from the uterine wall or is covering the cervix, bedrest minimizes the danger of hemorrhage.

• If preterm labor is a threat, bedrest lessens pressure on the uterus and eliminates virtually all physical activity that might trigger contractions. Women on bedrest also are more tuned in to their babies' movements and to early warnings of labor.

• If the membranes rupture prematurely, bedrest is crucial for delaying labor and preventing the umbilical cord from dropping through the cervix (prolapse).

• If a woman develops edema (fluid retention), bedrest, with legs elevated, helps reduce swelling.

• For women with heart problems—pregnant or not—bedrest is standard treatment. In women whose left ventricles of the heart weaken in the last month or first five months postpartum (a condition called peripartum cardiomyopathy that occurs for no known reason in women with no previous history of heart disease), the primary treatment is bedrest until the heart gradually returns to normal size.

Women at high risk of miscarriage may be put on bedrest in the first months of pregnancy and allowed up once they reach the twenty-fourth week. If blood pressure rises ominously in the middle of pregnancy, women may spend part of the second trimester in bed. If they go into preterm labor in the final trimester, mothers-to-be may wind up their pregnancies in bed. Women with multiple risk factors—like Denise, who had a malformed uterus, a stitch inserted around her cervix (cerclage), and a history of previous miscarriages—may begin bedrest in the first trimester and remain on it until their thirty-seventh week.

"I stayed in that bed for three months, absolutely immobile. I didn't even risk sitting up to eat my meals and taught myself a technique for eating flat on my back. I focused my mind on one thing and one thing alone: having the child . . . I thought about my insides constantly, about what was happening to me. I didn't even dare touch my stomach for fear I would disturb something . . . surely no prison confinement could be worse than these months in bed. I felt a constant uneasiness, an anxiety about my condition, despite my efforts to be tranquil."

Sophia Loren, in *Sophia: Living and Loving,* A. E. Hotchner, Morrow, N.Y.

The Basics of Bedrest

Bedrest is a specific treatment for pregnancy complications. While on bedrest you should lie on your left or right side, with your head elevated. Traditionally obstetricians have recommended the left side, but newer research indicates that the important factor is being on your side—either left or right. Avoid lying flat on your back for any extended period of time because the uterus presses against your major blood vessels, reducing the blood flow to the placenta.

Use the following checklist, developed by Lenette Moses of Intensive Caring Unlimited, a parents' support group in the Philadelphia area, to question your caregivers and find out exactly what you can or can't do.

What Is Bedrest?

The term "bedrest" is a familiar one to mothers experiencing high-risk pregnancies, but these women are often confused about the exact parameters of their limitations. Variabilities depend on each mother, the extent of her complications, and on the physician. This chart has been developed in an attempt to help mothers and their caregivers mutually define needs in specific situations. Because variables change during each individual pregnancy, you may wish to make several copies of this chart, to complete at various stages of your pregnancy.

What Can I Do Right Now?　　　　　　　　**Date**　　　　　　　　　　　　　　　　　　**Date**

1. Activity Level
Maintain a normal activity level　　　　＿＿＿
Slightly decrease activity level　　　　＿＿＿
Greatly decrease activity level　　　　＿＿＿

2. Working Outside the Home
Maintain my full-time job　　　　＿＿＿
Work part-time (how many hours?)　　　　＿＿＿
Work in my home (how many hours?)　　　　＿＿＿
Stop work completely　　　　＿＿＿
　　Why: _____

3. Working Inside the Home
Continue doing all housework　　　　＿＿＿
Decrease housework including:　　　　＿＿＿
　　Heavy lifting (laundry, moving furniture,
　　　etc.)　　　　＿＿＿
　　Preparing meals (standing on feet for a
　　　prolonged period of time)　　　　＿＿＿
　　Vigorous scrubbing　　　　＿＿＿
　　Other: _____
　　Why: _____

4. Child Care
Care for other children as usual　　　　＿＿＿
No lifting children　　　　＿＿＿
Have another caretaker watch an active
　　toddler　　　　＿＿＿
Have permanent caretaker for children　　　　＿＿＿
　　Why: _____

5. Mobility
Continue normal mobility　　　　＿＿＿
Limit mobility (sit down frequently)　　　　＿＿＿
Lie down each day (how many hours?)　　　　＿＿＿
Recline all day (propped up)　　　　＿＿＿
Lie down flat all day (on side?)　　　　＿＿＿
May walk stairs (how many times a day?)　　　　＿＿＿
Stairs forbidden　　　　＿＿＿
Take a shower/wash hair　　　　＿＿＿

Eat lying down? Sitting up? Sitting at table?　　＿＿＿
　　Why: _____

6. Driving
May drive a car　　　　＿＿＿
May be a passenger in a car (frequency?)　　　　＿＿＿
May not ride in a car, except to doctor　　　　＿＿＿
　　Why: _____

7. Bathroom Privileges
May use bathroom normally　　　　＿＿＿
Should actively avoid constipation　　　　＿＿＿
May not use bathroom (use bedpan)　　　　＿＿＿
　　Why: _____

8. Sexual Relations
May continue normal sexual relations　　　　＿＿＿
Should limit relations
　　(maximum times a month?)　　　　＿＿＿
Should avoid sexual intercourse　　　　＿＿＿
Should avoid all types of relations which
　　stimulate female orgasm　　　　＿＿＿
Should abstain from sexual relations　　　　＿＿＿
　　Why: _____

9. Maintenance of Pregnancy
Should monitor fetal activity ＿＿ hours
　　each day by hand, counting movements　　　　＿＿＿
Should drink wine each day
　　(When? How much?)　　　　＿＿＿
Should abstain from alcohol　　　　＿＿＿
Should limit cigarette smoking (no. per day?)　　　　＿＿＿
Should stop smoking cigarettes　　　　＿＿＿
Should monitor fetus by Termguard ＿＿
　　hours daily　　　　＿＿＿
Should take (drug) _____
　　＿＿ times daily, dosage: _____
　　Reason: _____
Should take (drug) _____
　　＿＿ times daily, dosage: _____
　　Reason: _____

Should follow these dietary rules:
Plenty of: Protein, vegetables, fruits, calcium, other:

_____

Avoid: Excess salt, excess fats, junk food, spicy foods, other:

_____

Approximate number of calories a day: _____

What Might I Expect in the Future?   Date

1. Decrease in Activity Level   _____
2. Limitations of Work
   Stop working completely   _____
3. Decrease Housework   _____
4. Need for child-care helper   _____
5. Need to recline in bed   _____
   Need to stay in bed (total bedrest)   _____
6. Limit driving   _____
   Stop driving   _____
7. Limit sexual relations   _____
   Abstain from sexual relations   _____
8. Need to self-monitor fetal activity   _____
9. Need to use a home monitor   _____
10. Need to take labor-inhibiting drugs   _____
11. Need to have a cervical stitch put in   _____
12. Need to stay in hospital for some
    period of time   _____
13. Need to have amniocentesis   _____
14. Need to have sonograms/ultrasounds   _____
15. Need to visit caregiver more frequently
    than normal   _____
16. Need to visit a high-risk specialist   _____
17. Need to have alpha fetoprotein levels
    done   _____
18. Need to have blood-sugar screening   _____
19. Need to have a nonstress test   _____
20. Need to have a stress test   _____

If Problems Arise and I go into Premature Labor . . .

1. When should I contact my caregiver?   _____
2. Where will I be hospitalized?   _____
3. Where might I be transferred?   _____
4. Name of physician at other hospital?   _____
5. Where would my baby be hospitalized?   _____
6. Could my husband be present at delivery?   _____
7. Is there a possibility of a cesarean?   _____

Hospital Bedrest

1. **What position do I have to be in?**   _____
   Trendelenberg (head lowered)   _____
   On side (left or right?)   _____
2. **Do I have to use a bedpan?**   _____
3. **Can I reach for things, or should I
   use a reacher?**   _____
4. **Personal hygiene**
   Can I take a shower?   _____
   Can I take a bath?   _____
   Do I have to take a bed sponge bath?   _____
   Can I get out of bed to wash my hair?   _____
5. **Mobility**   _____
   Can I walk the halls?   _____
   Can I walk in my room?   _____
   Can I sit in the chair in my room?   _____
   Can I take a wheelchair to the lobby?   _____
   Can I take a wheelchair to the nursery?   _____
   Can I take a wheelchair to hospital support-
   group meetings? (If applicable)   _____
6. **Visitors**
   When can my husband visit? _____
   (If you do not have a husband:) Can I have
   another friend or relative visit at the times
   husbands are normally permitted to visit?   _____
   Who can visit? When? _____
   Can my children visit? When? _____
   How many people can visit at a time?   _____
   If I am admitted to the labor room, who can
   visit? _____
   Who can be present in the delivery room? _____
7. **Consults**
   If appropriate, may I see:
   a physical therapist   _____
   an occupational therapist   _____
   a neonatologist (about fetal development
   and/or a typical preemie)   _____
   a social worker   _____
   an ophthalmologist   _____
   a dermatologist   _____
8. **Other directions:**

_____

_____

Reprinted from *Intensive Caring Unlimited*, May-June 1986, 4. (3) by Lenette Moses

Prenatal Care

While you're on bedrest your caregivers will want to keep close tabs on your condition—and your baby's. A few high-risk centers have set up house-call services in which a nurse goes to a bedresting woman's home to perform prenatal exams. However, most medical centers do not have staff available for home visits, and the diagnostic equipment or tests you need may be available only in your doctor's office or at the hospital. You'll need someone to drive you to your appointments (unless your caregivers have no objection to your driving), and if you're traveling a considerable distance, you should adjust the passenger seat so you're as horizontal as possible.

Home Monitoring

Beginning at the twenty-seventh week, all pregnant women should start counting fetal movements for a thirty-minute period twice a day (see page 80 for instructions). If you're on bedrest, careful monitoring of your baby's movements should be part of your daily routine.

If you are at risk for or have had an episode of preterm labor, you also should monitor for uterine contractions. You can either use your fingertips or a portable monitor (both methods are described in Chapter 11) that relays data on uterine activity to trained professionals via the telephone.

Hospitalization

Thanks to the development of portable monitors for preterm contractions, fewer women have to spend extended periods of time in the hospital. However, some need to enter the hospital for tests, an initial trial of a medication, or the round-the-clock surveillance that some conditions, like placental abruption, require.

If at all possible, ask for a room that is not in the labor and delivery unit. You'll rest easier away from the commotion and excitement that are common in birthing areas. You also may want to be sure the hospital has perinatologists skilled in pregnancy complications available around the clock and an intensive care nursery, just in case you deliver during your stay and your baby requires specialized treatment.

HORIZONTAL LIVING

Imagine that you're thirsty, but you can't get a drink. Your nose is running, but you don't have any tissues. You need to write down a phone number, but your only pen is out of ink. These are the sorts of scenarios that can and do happen to women on bedrest. You'll be much more comfortable and confident if you plan ahead for life in bed. The following sections, adapted from "Bed—and Bored" by Susan Schwartz (a pamphlet available from Birthways in Berkeley, California; see "Resources" in the appendix), may help:

> "My friends at work thought lying in bed, being waited on hand and foot, sounded heavenly. I couldn't make them understand that it gets old very, very fast."

- Choose the most appealing or convenient location in your home. You may want to have your bed moved near a window or bathroom or to set up alternative resting spots in the living room or outdoors.
- Establish a daily schedule for meals, activities, calls, etc., and stick to it as much as you can. "A daily list, as soon as you've washed up, made up, and put on a fresh nightgown, also will help you feel more in control," observes Marguerite Kelly, author of *The Mother's Almanac* and *The Mother's Almanac II.* "Set aside a special time for writing letters, paying bills, being with your child."
- Make up a list of the foods, quantities, and brands you usually buy and post it so someone can keep track of supplies and do the shopping for you.
- Call for take-out menus and deli price lists.
- Pack a suitcase with everything you'll need for a sudden trip to the hospital.
- Check your health insurance, so you know exactly which treatments for you or your baby will be covered.
- Keep careful records of your expenses, including child care and domestic help. They may be deductible.
- Make plans for handling money. While you can pay bills and make deposits by mail, getting cash can be more difficult. Never give anyone a blank check, your credit card, or your code for an automatic teller machine. You can write the purpose of the check—such as "for cash for (your name)"—on the back of a check made out to your account.
- Make a list of daily chores (meal preparation, shopping, cleaning, etc.). Divide responsibilities up among as many people as possible: relatives, neighbors, friends, church volunteers, hired employees. When friends ask what they can do, make a specific

request, such as preparing one dinner a week or driving a child to and from soccer games. If you can afford it, hire a weekly or biweekly housecleaner.

What You'll Need

Buy, borrow, or rearrange items you already own to create a "nest" for yourself. Among the most helpful items are
- a large bedside table.
- pillows—lots of them, for your head, back, legs, hips.
- a bedside storage unit, such as a low bookshelf or stacked crates.
- water pitcher, Thermos, ice bucket, cooler.
- a tray table for meals.
- an alarm clock, if you're taking medications on a regular schedule. (Some women set several alarms if they have to wake up more than once during the night.)
- a firm headboard and footboard for you to push against if you're allowed to do isometric exercises.
- mild indigestion remedies and laxatives, if needed, that are approved by your caregiver.
- a cordless phone or an extra-long cord for a bedside phone.
- a home intercom (the type you'll use later for the baby is the best buy).
- mood brighteners, such as plants, flowers, and attractive house-dresses or sweatsuits.
- sources of entertainment, such as a tape player, bedroom TV set, VCR, home computer, etc.

What You Can Do

Keeping busy helps the time pass faster and keeps you from worrying. Among suggested activities are

Reaching out. In many cities, hundreds of women are on bedrest at any given time. Some areas have telephone network systems that put bedresters in touch with each other. Check with parents' support groups to find out if such a program is operating in your area. If not, ask your caregivers or local Lamaze groups if they can refer you to other mothers who are or were on bedrest. Most will be more than glad to talk with you, and you'll find comfort in knowing you're not alone.

Volunteer calling. Your favorite museum, charity, or political group may need help in fund-raising. You also can make volunteer calls through community organizations to latchkey children, shut-ins, or elderly people who live alone.

Computer networking. Lap-top computers can sit next to you in bed and, with a modem, put you in touch with the world. This may be your chance to master new computer programs or to shop or visit electronically.

Puzzles. You can do some with your children, others with your friends, and crossword puzzles on your own.

Arts and crafts. Try sketching, knitting, crocheting, embroidery, or hand-sewing. If you've never had time to learn, you do now.

Collections. You might make a cookbook or file of your recipes, work on family albums, or organize souvenirs.

A journal. In addition to recording your thoughts, feelings, and fears, you may want to take a stab at a poem, short story or novel.

Adult education courses. Some are available by mail, and some are on television. You might learn a language from books, records, or tapes.

Financial analysis. In addition to keeping track of bills and preparing tax information, you can shop by telephone for the bank with the best services or highest interest rates, for savings plans, insurance, etc.

Bargain hunting. Clip ads from the newspapers; check the classified section; send for catalogues. Even if you buy very little, you may enjoy comparing prices and fantasizing about what you might purchase. But beware of the temptation: One woman ordered $2,000 worth of merchandise during her six weeks on bedrest.

> "Everyone had creative ideas about how I should spend my time. To me, they seemed like busy work. I preferred to think my thoughts and do just about nothing. Oddly enough, I didn't feel bored, and I wished everyone would just let me be."

Exercise

Don't even try to exercise without your doctor's approval. The purpose of bedrest is to reduce physical strain, and you don't want to risk any setbacks. When you talk with your caregivers, ask them to be very specific about what's safe (neck rolls, for instance) and what might not be (leg lifts, perhaps). A hospital physical therapist can tailor an exercise program to your condition. (Some insurance plans cover a "prescription" for a one-time consultation with a physical therapist.)

Establish a regular exercise time, not immediately after a meal but after using the bathroom. Like all pregnant women, you should start slowly and be sure to warm up. Breathe regularly, and avoid using your abdominal muscles or lying flat on your back.

Because of the risk of blood clots, massage your legs, calves, and feet every day to keep blood circulating. You also can flex your feet and push gently against a board at the foot of your bed. While such isometric exercises help maintain muscle tone and enhance circulation, they can cause contractions in some women, so pay attention to your body's signals. Rest if you feel weak, achy, or tired. Stop if you feel a contraction.

Sleep Problems

Paradoxical as it may sound, rest isn't good for sleep. The lack of activity and the tendency to doze off for a few minutes throughout the day undercut your usual sleep efficiency. In addition, you have to deal with the typical sleep problems of pregnancy (such as the difficulty in finding a comfortable position or turning over), the added anxiety of being at risk, digestive problems, and the side effects of medications. If you must take medicine around the clock, you'll have to get up every few hours and may have problems getting back to sleep.

Here are some suggestions from *How to Sleep Like a Baby* that may help:

- Keep a regular daily schedule, with consistent wake-up and sleep times.
- Develop a soothing presleep ritual—a nightly routine that might consist of a massage, warm milk, meditation, and listening to soft music—to help you unwind at day's end.
- Practice relaxation techniques, such as deep breathing and tensing and relaxing different muscles, to help yourself fall asleep. Take five deep breaths, counting as you breathe and telling yourself, "I am getting sleepier and sleepier."
- As you prepare to fall asleep, visualize a soothing scene, such as floating on a raft on a clear blue lake in the warm summer sun.
- If you have a problem falling back to sleep after waking in the night, light a candle in your imagination and focus on keeping

its flame upright. See how each distracting thought makes it flicker.

Eating Right

You need the same basic nutrients as other pregnant women, but fewer total calories each day (at least 2,000 calories, depending on your prepregnancy weight and overall condition).

While you may find it hard to eat as much as you should because you're anxious and inactive, remember that your baby needs regular meals. Many bedresting women get "meal privileges" so they can sit with their families at the table at least once a day. Others have to master the rather ungainly art of eating horizontally, with head propped up on an elbow.

The best bedrest foods are healthy finger foods such as raw vegetables and fruit. To prevent or overcome constipation, drink a lot of fluid and eat a lot of raw fruits and vegetables.

Work out a menu and a schedule with your spouse or a friend. One mother describes her family's routine: "My husband would fix breakfast for the three of us, bring me a tray, and then get our son ready for school. Before he'd leave, he'd pack a picnic basket with my lunch, snacks, and cold drinks. When he came home, he'd make and serve dinner. Usually it was very simple: a hamburger and applesauce, grilled fish and salad, spaghetti. On weekends, when he was with our son all day, we'd get take-out food for dinner."

Childbirth Preparation

While you probably won't be allowed to go to regular childbirth classes, you don't have to give up on your plans for natural childbirth. Local childbirth-education groups can recommend instructors to give private lessons to you and your partner or you can rent videotapes to watch at home.

Finances

If you're employed you can apply for an extended leave of absence because of temporary disability. This is the same sort of leave you'd need if you had an emergency appendectomy. You should receive your usual salary and benefits while using up your sick leave and annual leave. You also may qualify for state disability benefits or assistance through various government programs.

"I had a three-year-old and an eighteen-month-old when I went on bedrest with the twins. They couldn't begin to understand. They would cry because I couldn't or wouldn't do something they wanted. And I would cry because I felt bad for letting them down."

THE PERSONAL IMPACT

Bedrest changes all the rules you've played by and all the roles you've played. Others will have to readjust their expectations of you. And you'll have to adjust your expectations of yourself.

The Bedresting Mommy

Mothering, not an easy job for women who are fully mobile, becomes more complicated for women confined to bed. The very idea that Mommy can't walk or play is almost unimaginable to youngsters. After all, from their perspective, Mommy knows everything, can do anything, and is always there when they need her. Very small children may act out their fears and frustrations by throwing tantrums. School-age children may pull away, sulk, complain, or develop temporary behavior or school problems.

Whatever arrangements you work out, don't try to do it alone. One woman on bedrest realized how dangerous that could be when her preschooler turned on the gas on the stove to "make Mommy some tea": "I heard the click because I had a monitor in the kitchen, and I panicked. Should I run to the kitchen and make sure he was all right, or should I stay in bed and hope for the best? I ended up screaming for him until he came and then calling a neighbor to turn off the gas."

The best things a bedresting mother can give her children are her time and attention. Regular snuggle hours or story sessions give children something to look forward to every day. Young children will be delighted to eat breakfast on a tray sitting next to Mommy in bed or to cuddle up and watch "Sesame Street" with her in the afternoon. Older children can bring coloring books and crayons, games, or homework into the room and set up a work area next to their mother's bed.

Bedresting mothers may underestimate their children's ability to cope. "I kept worrying about these deep psychological scars my little boy would suffer because I was on bedrest for four months," says a mother. "But after the first two weeks, he took it in stride, as if it were the most normal thing in the world to have a Mommy who never left her bedroom."

Bedrest and the Working Woman

Pat had two weeks to get a major textbook through production. Nicole had a case to try. Helen had an advertising campaign to launch. Lisa had a new computer system to install. Then each of them had to go on bedrest.

"I tried to negotiate," Lisa recalls. "I said something like, 'If I can just have 'til next Tuesday, I'll be a good girl and go to bed for the rest of my pregnancy.' My doctor said, 'By next Tuesday there may not be a pregnancy,' and I realized how serious the problem was. I also realized, after some frantic phone calls, that not even I am indispensable."

For many mothers-to-be, bedrest comes as a complete surprise. Some are hospitalized immediately. Others are sent straight home without a chance to swing by their workplaces. "I had to give my principal fewer than twelve hours notice that I wouldn't be teaching my fourth-grade class and that I had no idea when I'd be back," one teacher says. "I felt terrible for leaving her out on a limb."

While such situations are always difficult, emergencies occur in everyone's life, upsetting schedules and commitments. Once women realize that indeed they are having an emergency, just like having an automobile accident, they feel less guilty about letting people down.

Many women don't have to quit working entirely. They can use the telephone to make calls, write memos or review manuscripts in bed. Those who work with computers can set up a work station on or next to their beds.

But sometimes the stress of meeting deadlines or attempting long-distance office management can jeopardize the well-being of a woman on bedrest. "I felt that I wasn't doing a good job professionally, and I wasn't doing a good job bedresting," says a stockbroker who decided to concentrate all her energy on her high-risk pregnancy. "I had to set priorities."

> "The nicest payoff has been that my husband and our son have gotten much closer. Before, he was always Mommy's little boy, but since I've been on bedrest, he's become Daddy's helper. Now he tells me that girls aren't allowed to do a lot of things we used to do together."

The Bedresting Wife

"We're pregnant," you may have happily announced as soon as you got the news, convinced that you'd be equal partners from beginning to end. Then something happens, and the mother-to-be is put on bedrest. Nothing is quite the same again. Almost every little routine woven into the fabric of your daily life is upset. Gone, for at least the near future, is any reassuring semblance of predictability.

The mother's world shrinks to the size of a mattress. Often she seesaws between resentment and guilt: "I saw him running from the moment he got out of bed until he collapsed at the end of the day," says one woman who spent two pregnancies on bedrest. "I

"At times I couldn't resist pushing the limits. I'd stay in the shower for ten minutes or carry my tray back to the kitchen. If nothing happened, I felt like a kid who got away with playing hooky. But if I felt even one contraction, I'd slink back to bed and promise never to be such a bad girl again."

once asked him if he was disappointed in me. I told him I really felt sorry for him. His response was that having a child is very important to him and that he felt sorry for *me* because of what I have to go through."

In most families the father-to-be becomes sole breadwinner, cook, housekeeper, personal maid, errand-runner, and, if there are other youngsters, child-care provider. Like his wife, he may be scared and confused, but too overwhelmed to say or do anything about his feelings.

One common danger for couples is second-guessing each other. A wife whose husband buys the wrong brand of toilet paper or puts the good silver in the dishwasher may think she's being helpful when she corrects him. All he hears is that he's doing something wrong. Similarly, husbands who give their wives "assignments" to do in bed (like filing receipts or darning socks) may make their spouses feel worthless if they can't or don't want to do them.

The section on relationships in chapter 6 may help—as can frequent reminders that this, too, will pass.

Psychological Survival

"I went nuts," one woman who spent months on bedrest recalls. "I felt like I was in solitary confinement. Each month I got more depressed. When my husband had to travel or work late, I resented his busyness. I tried social services agencies, I tried telephone sales, I tried making recordings for the blind. I even hired a graduate student to come over and speak French with me twice a week. I had no patience for writing. My ability to concentrate and my discipline went out the window. I gained thirty-eight pounds and developed gestational diabetes. It was not a good situation."

How did she survive—and willingly launch another high-risk pregnancy, knowing that once again she'd be on bedrest for months? "I thought of the babies I'd lost, and I told myself that I was doing something no one else could do for me and for the baby I was carrying."

During long periods of bedrest, there are few emotions you won't feel. Here are some that may affect you the most:

• Denial. Many women—particularly if they have a "silent" problem like high blood pressure and feel fine—think their caregivers are exaggerating the risks and treating pregnancy like a disease. "I don't really need to be doing this," they tell themselves, adding to their frustration. If you don't believe bedrest is necessary, ask your caregivers why they've recommended it. Listen to their explanations. Ask questions. Find out about the risks of not going to bed. You'll feel better about bedrest if you clearly understand the reasons for it.

• Guilt. Many women obsessively think about everything they did—or didn't do—that might have caused the complication that's forced them into bedrest. Maybe you and your baby would be fine if only you hadn't carried the laundry upstairs, gone for a long drive in the country, eaten the chili rellenos. Grant yourself an unconditional pardon. Tell yourself, firmly, that what's past is past and that you're going to devote your attention to what you can do for your baby now and in the future.

• Feelings of inadequacy. Your friends may have spent their pregnancies taking care of business or jogging three miles a day up to the minute they went into labor. Because you aren't even allowed to climb stairs or cross a street, you may feel that somehow you don't match up. If so, remind yourself (again) that pregnancy isn't a pass-or-fail test.

• Loss of stimulation. If you were accustomed to a fast-paced career, you may feel less informed and creative, as if you were cut off from stimulating people and ideas. Yet, in our plug-in society, you can get in touch with almost anyone, almost anywhere, without leaving your bed. Use your telephone. Watch the news. Read the newspaper. Listen to the radio. And remember that you are engaged in the most creative project imaginable every minute of every day: the making of a new life.

• Ambivalence. On the one hand, you want to do everything possible for your unborn child. On the other, you yearn to be back on your feet, getting on with your life. Such feelings do not mean you'll be a bad mother, just that you're human. You may feel better if you talk through your frustrations with your partner or a friend.

While a lot of emotions associated with bedrest are negative, there is good news: Usually bedrest gets easier as you go along. The days develop a rhythm, and while some stretch longer than others, they do pass. And as they do, you're sure to learn a thing or two about managing your time, setting priorities, achieving goals, and putting someone else's welfare before your own. That's quite a lot for a few months' effort.

"After two months in bed, my doctor said it would be okay to go on a 'nonstressful' outing. My husband made a sort of bed with a futon and cushions in the back of our pickup, and we went for a ride. I felt like a queen."

BEYOND BEDREST

If no complications develop and you don't deliver early, you'll reach a point where you can get up and move around again. Your blood pressure may be back to normal. You may no longer be in danger of miscarriage. You may simply have held out for thirty-seven weeks. While you may be tempted to leap out of bed and head out the door, remember that bedresting has taken a toll on your body.

A walk to the bathroom may make you dizzy; you may have to lean against a wall or pause to catch your breath. If you've been on complete bedrest, even standing at a sink to wash your face can tire you out. Some women have back problems when they get up in their ninth month because they're unaccustomed to their baby's weight.

Your caregivers can give you guidelines for how you can gradually build up your strength and stamina. Most women feel much stronger within a week and are thrilled to be up and about. "I usually hate shopping," one woman recalls, "but the biggest treat of my whole pregnancy was walking through a supermarket when I was thirty-eight weeks pregnant, after twelve weeks of bedrest. I felt like a little kid at the circus."

Looking back, some women feel that bedrest, by forcing them to confront the risks of carrying and having a child, helped prepare them psychologically for motherhood. They see themselves as more realistic about what to expect and more confident in their ability to cope, come what may.

"Months of bedrest may seem like forever," Marguerite Kelly observed in her syndicated column, "The Family Almanac." Her advice is to remind yourself often that bedrest is "the most important job you've ever had, and the most difficult. . . . [But it also leads to] the greatest reward in the world: a child."

Chronic Health Problems and Pregnancy

"When you've had a chronic disease for a long time, like I have, you take it for granted. It's part of who you are. Once I got pregnant, I had to deal with the reality of it every single day. That bothered me more than anything else."

A few generations ago, women with serious health problems often did not dare to become pregnant. Some feared for their own lives as well as for the well-being of their unborn children. Today millions of women with chronic illnesses are discovering that their chances of having a healthy baby have never been better.

The keys to overcoming the very real risks that chronic disease can pose during pregnancy are doing everything possible to achieve optimal health *before* conception, carefully monitoring yourself throughout pregnancy, and working closely with the perinatal team through labor, delivery, and the first days after birth.

DIABETES MELLITUS

Insulin, a hormone secreted by the pancreas, regulates the way our bodies store and use their basic fuel, glucose or sugar. Normally, every time you eat, the level of glucose in your blood rises, triggering the release of insulin. By converting glucose into energy or storing it for future use, insulin brings down the level of glucose in your blood, usually within two hours of eating.

In diabetes, the pancreas either stops producing insulin or does not produce a sufficient amount to meet your body's needs. Because a diabetic's body absorbs little, if any, of the available glucose, the level of sugar in the blood remains high—so high that the kidneys cannot process all of it and some sugar "spills" into urine. A condition similar to starvation develops, no matter how much the diabetic eats.

There are two main forms of diabetes mellitus:

• Type I (also called juvenile-onset or insulin-dependent diabetes), which usually occurs in young persons. The pancreas produces little or no insulin, so daily doses of insulin are required.

• Type II (also known as maturity-onset or insulin-independent diabetes), which usually develops in adulthood. Insulin-independent diabetics can control their disease by eating a well-balanced diet, exercising, and controlling their weight.

From 2 to 3 percent of pregnant women are diabetic. The keys to successful pregnancy and a healthy baby are prepregnancy evaluation, good control of blood-sugar levels, starting before conception, and frequent checkups.

Are you at risk? About half of all Americans with diabetes have not been diagnosed. You are most likely to be among them if you:

• have close relatives who are diabetics (your risk is then 2½ times that of others)
• are obese (85 percent of diabetics are or were overweight)
• have given birth to a large baby (over 10 pounds). This may be an indication of a predisposition to diabetes.

What happens during pregnancy. During a normal pregnancy, the level of sugar or glucose in the blood before a meal ranges from 60–90 mg/dl; after a meal, glucose rises to 120 mg/dl. The pregnant diabetic's goal is to keep her blood-sugar levels under 100 before a meal and under 120 afterward. This is difficult because of certain physiologic changes in pregnancy.

Early in pregnancy, insulin needs tend to decrease. But as pregnancy progresses, a hormone produced by the placenta—human placental lactogen—counters or resists insulin, so a much greater amount is needed. During the final ten to twelve weeks of pregnancy, diabetics may require two to three times more insulin than before pregnancy. After delivery, insulin requirements fall dramatically.

Possible effects on the mother. If you normally use insulin, you'll have to readjust your doses frequently during pregnancy, after delivery, and while nursing. If you have not required insulin prior to pregnancy, you may have to begin using insulin in order to keep your fasting blood sugar under 100. However, you should be able to return to dietary control after delivery.

Pregnancy generally has no long-term effect on diabetes, unless blood-sugar levels stay high, increasing the risk of damage to various organs. Women who develop gestational diabetes (page 163) are at increased risk for developing diabetes later in life.

If you've already developed early signs of eye or kidney damage as a result of diabetes, you may face greater risks for various complications of pregnancy. However, if you have proper care and good metabolic control, there's no increased risk of permanent damage to your vision as a result of pregnancy. Kidney function can worsen temporarily, but usually improves after delivery.

Diabetics face an increased risk of gestational hypertension (page 131) and preeclampsia (page 160), disorders related to high blood pressure. About 10 percent of diabetics develop hydramnios, or excess amniotic fluid, a condition that increases the risk of premature rupture of the membranes. Anemia and infection also are more likely to complicate a diabetic's pregnancy.

Ketoacidosis (the buildup of weak body acids called ketones), which can result from insufficient amounts of insulin and high blood sugar, may develop rapidly in pregnant women, and if not treated, can lead to coma and death.

Possible risks to the baby. Glucose freely crosses the placenta from mother to baby. If the mother's blood-sugar levels are high, so are her baby's. Because insulin does not cross the placenta, the baby's pancreas, responding to the high blood-sugar levels, produces large amounts of insulin. The combination of very high blood sugar and very high insulin creates serious risks, including a greater-than-usual chance of stillbirth.

Very high blood-sugar levels in the first seven weeks of gestation seem to be responsible for the increased incidence of birth defects among the babies of diabetics. Congenital anomalies are two to four times more common in diabetics. The most frequent ones involve the heart, central nervous system, and skeleton.

Since insulin stimulates fetal growth, diabetic women are more likely to have very big babies. This condition, called macrosomia, makes babies more vulnerable, particularly in late pregnancy and at delivery, because overly large babies often have excess fat and blood sugar and immature pancreases. Tight blood-sugar control before thirty-two weeks of gestation may prevent macrosomia. Because advanced diabetes may affect the mother's blood vessels, restricting the flow of blood to the placenta, some babies develop the opposite problem of growth retardation and are small for their gestational age.

After birth, many babies of diabetic mothers have very low blood-sugar levels and need oral glucose. Diabetics' babies also are prone to low calcium levels and high bilirubin levels, which can lead to jaundice, a not-uncommon problem treated by exposure to bright lights. The major long-term effect is a greater disposition to diabetes. If the mother alone is diabetic, the baby's risk of developing diabetes is 20 percent. The risk increases if both parents are diabetic.

Preventing problems. Because high blood-sugar levels have the greatest impact in the very first weeks of fetal development, women with diabetes should establish good metabolic control before conceiving. Every diabetic who's considering pregnancy should have a prepregnancy examination.

Your doctor can perform a blood test that measures hemoglobin A_{1c}, a component of red blood cells. This test will indicate how well you've controlled your blood sugar during the preceding month. High levels of this substance very early in pregnancy are associated with an increased likelihood of birth defects. By regulating your diet and insulin levels and checking blood-sugar levels several times a day, you can bring hemoglobin A_{1c} down to safe levels. The closer to normal that a diabetic woman's sugar metabolism remains during pregnancy, the better the outlook for her and her baby.

In general, the outcome of pregnancy depends on how long a woman has had diabetes and whether it has damaged her blood vessels, especially those in the eyes and kidneys. If you're a diabetic, you and your baby may require special care before, during, and after delivery, so your doctor may suggest that you plan to have your baby at a perinatal center with all the facilities you may need.

What to expect. A diabetic woman has to make a total commitment to her pregnancy and unborn child. You can expect frequent medical visits, strict dietary guidelines, monitoring of blood-sugar levels several times a day, and the full battery of fetal fitness tests. Simply sticking to this regimen may feel like—and become—a full-time job.

Ideally, both husband and wife work together for their baby's sake. Both should learn the principles of insulin therapy, the types of insulin to use, and the correct procedure for insulin administration. The more the husband understands about his wife's disease, the more support he can provide. Husbands should be particularly aware that symptoms can develop if blood sugar drops too low and should treat signs of hypoglycemia (low blood sugar) by giving their wives juice.

To keep blood-sugar levels at optimal levels, a pregnant diabetic has to check them several times a day and keep a detailed record of the readings at different times of day. Most women need two daily doses of insulin, one before breakfast and one before dinner. Occasionally a third injection at noon is necessary. Oral diabetes drugs are not considered safe for use in pregnancy.

Ultrasound early in pregnancy establishes the baby's gestational age and may identify multiple pregnancy or birth defects. Later in pregnancy repeated scans can monitor fetal growth for macrosomia or growth retardation. Close monitoring of the baby's well-being may begin with weekly nonstress tests at about twenty-eight weeks, and twice-weekly ones at thirty-four weeks.

After birth, insulin requirements fall dramatically. Often diabetics go through a "honeymoon" period in which they require little or no insulin for several days after delivery. Diabetics can breastfeed without risk to themselves or their babies, but nutritional requirements remain complex, and mothers must work closely with their health-care team.

What to watch for. Some of the normal changes and discomforts of pregnancy carry more of a threat for a diabetic. Among them:

Morning sickness. Vomiting at any time of the day may cause dehydration and upset sugar and insulin needs.

Low blood-sugar levels (hypoglycemia). Very low blood-sugar levels, perhaps because of an overdose of insulin, can cause drowsiness, weakness, irritability, and nervousness. (See the chart on page 129 for a list of the symptoms of hypoglycemia.) In severe cases, hypoglycemia can lead to a loss of consciousness, coma, or shock. To prevent such complications, always have with you a quick supply of sugar, such as fruit juice or a candy bar.

Ketoacidosis. High levels of sugar and ketones in urine and blood indicate a medical emergency. During pregnancy, ketoacidosis can become severe and lead to a coma much more rapidly than usual, sometimes in a matter of hours. The risk increases after the fifth month, and both the mother and unborn child are endangered. If untreated, ketoacidosis can lead to intrauterine death. The first symptoms are nausea and vomiting. Seek medical care immediately.

Infections. Even minor infections of the urinary or respiratory tract can upset insulin requirements by increasing the physiological stress. They also may trigger increased breakdown of fats for energy, resulting in higher levels of ketones—and a higher risk of ketoacidosis.

What you can do

Prepregnancy exam. As soon as you begin to think about getting pregnant, see your doctor, who will evaluate your blood-sugar levels, vision, kidneys, and heart. You may also want to talk to an

Recognizing Hypoglycemia

Your sugar levels can drop too low from too much insulin, too little food, or increased activity without increased food. Watch for the following symptoms, which can develop suddenly:

- nervousness
- shakiness
- weakness
- hunger
- perspiration
- cool, clammy skin
- pallor
- blurred or double vision
- headache
- disorientation
- shallow breathing
- irritability

Hyperglycemia

You may have excessive sugar in your blood if you take too little insulin, ingest too much food (especially carbohydrates), develop an infection, or are under stress. The symptoms develop slowly, often over the course of several days:

> dry mouth
> increased appetite
> increased thirst and urination
> tiredness
> nausea
> hot, flushed skin
> abdominal cramps
> rapid, deep breathing
> acetone-smelling breath
> paralysis
> headache
> drowsiness
> little or no urine output

obstetrician specializing in high-risk care, who can give you more information on what to expect and what the risks to you and your baby may be.

Blood-sugar monitoring. You will have to check blood-sugar levels several times a day with a reflectance meter so you can regulate your insulin dosage. Be sure to prick the sides of your fingertips instead of the more sensitive tips and clean the area to avoid infection. Follow directions for timing and washing or wiping the blood off the reagent strip exactly.

Good nutrition. Your diet will be critical. In early pregnancy your normal daily calorie intake should not increase. During the second and third trimesters, your caloric intake should average two thousand to two thousand five hundred calories a day. Approximately 45 percent of your calories should come from complex carbohydrates with adequate fiber to slow absorption, about 20 percent from protein, and 30 to 35 percent from fat. Ideally you should work with a nutritionist so you can vary and plan meals that suit your life-style and food preferences.

Careful timing of meals. Divide your total intake into three meals and three snacks. Usually you should have 25 percent of your total calories at breakfast, 30 percent at lunch, 30 percent at dinner, and 15 percent in snacks. Your prebedtime snack is the most important and should include protein and complex carbohydrates to prevent hypoglycemia during the night.

Insulin injections. Most pregnant diabetics administer insulin in multiple injections; some rely on continuous subcutaneous infusion pumps. Most take a mix of intermediate-acting (NPH) and short-acting (regular) insulin.

Exercise. You can keep up the exercise regimen you followed before pregnancy, if you've checked with your doctor. If you haven't been exercising, start gradually. Your blood glucose should be well controlled before you launch your workouts, and you should monitor your blood glucose to determine its variations with exercise.

Exercise after a meal, not when blood sugar may be low. Don't administer insulin into an extremity that will be immediately used in the exercise (such as your arm if you're going to lift weights). Carry Life Savers or some other hard candy with you when exercising, and wear diabetic identification. Have a snack immediately after your workout.

Travel. If you must travel, carry insulin (which can be kept at room temperature en route) and syringes. Keep them with you rather than in your suitcase. Wear an identification necklace or bracelet. Arrange meals with the airlines a few days before traveling.

Check with your doctor for any instructions, including prescriptions and advice before leaving.

Coping. Many communities have diabetes support groups. Learning how others coped with diabetes or pregnancy or both can be enormously helpful. At many medical centers, diabetes nurse-educators are available to provide information and support and to answer questions.

Medical treatment. In the past, obstetricians had to do a great deal of guesswork about the best time for delivery of a diabetic's baby. If pregnancy continued too long, the baby might grow too large and face increased risk of stillbirth. If the doctors attempted delivery too early, the baby's lungs might not be mature.

Technological advances have taken the guesswork out of the timing for delivery. Ultrasound can monitor fetal growth; various fetal fitness tests can warn of increasing dangers within the womb. And sampling of the amniotic fluid can determine if the baby's lungs are mature (see page 74).

Most doctors induce labor if the baby's lungs are developed and tests indicate that the baby may be safer outside the womb. During labor, a continuous infusion of insulin and glucose eliminates the risks of very high blood-sugar levels in the mother and very low blood-sugar levels in the baby.

About half of diabetics have cesarean deliveries, usually because of obstetrical complications or because their babies are too large to pass through the birth canal safely. Because of the increased likelihood of a cesarean, discuss this possibility with your doctor and seek out information or a class on cesarean birth preparation.

CHRONIC HYPERTENSION

High blood pressure, or hypertension, occurs when artery wells squeeze down excessively on the blood flowing through them. For most women of childbearing age, normal blood-pressure readings, measured in millimeters of mercury (mmHg), are lower than 120 mmHg systolic pressure (during heart contractions) and 80 diastolic pressure (between contractions). In obstetrics, the term *chronic hypertension* refers to high blood pressure (defined as 140/90 mmHg) present before conception or diagnosed before the twentieth week of pregnancy.

Are you at risk? You may have a predisposition to hypertension but not realize it until the unique physiological demands of carrying

"I never took my hypertension that seriously before I got pregnant. I wasn't all that good about watching what I ate or taking my diuretics. It just didn't seem like any big deal. But when I realized that my blood pressure could be a threat to my baby, I got religion. I became the most conscientious patient you ever saw."

a baby reveal a problem. This is more likely to happen if you:

- are over thirty-five
- smoke
- are overweight
- have kidney disease
- have a family history of hypertension

Your chances of developing complications in pregnancy because of high blood pressure are greater if you're over forty, have had high blood pressure for more than fifteen years, have insulin-dependent diabetes, cardiomyopathy (weakening of the heart muscle), kidney disease, or connective tissue disease.

What happens during pregnancy. Typically blood pressure drops about 10 to 15 mmHg in the first half of pregnancy and then begins to climb back to prepregnancy levels. Women with chronic hypertension generally do not experience any drop; their blood pressure remains constant and, if not carefully monitored and controlled, may climb higher.

Possible effects on the mother. Hypertension is a silent disease that may not cause noticeable symptoms for years. If undetected and untreated, it can trigger headaches, dizziness, and chest pain and lead to heart disease, brain hemorrhage, visual disturbances, and damage to the kidneys.

The greatest danger for a pregnant woman with chronic hypertension in pregnancy is "superimposed" preeclampsia and eclampsia, serious disorders that involve elevated blood pressure, swelling because of fluid retention, and deteriorating kidney function. These complications, described on page 160, greatly increase the risks to mother and child.

Possible risks for the baby. While pregnant women with hypertension may feel fine, their high blood pressure can diminish the blood supply to the placenta and fetus, jeopardizing normal growth and development. If no other complications develop, women with chronic hypertension are no more likely to lose a baby than any other group of pregnant women. Pregnancy losses can and do occur, however, especially in women who develop preeclampsia and have had previous pregnancies that ended in a miscarriage, stillbirth, or neonatal death.

Preventing problems. A prepregnancy physical is essential for any woman with diagnosed or suspected hypertension. The exam can establish a "baseline" blood pressure that will help your obstetrician in monitoring any changes that occur during pregnancy. Your doctor also can "work up" the causes of hypertension before pregnancy. If your blood pressure is high, a combination of exercise, weight loss, and not smoking can bring blood-pressure readings out of the danger zone before you get pregnant.

If you are taking antihypertensive medication, talk with your internist and an obstetrician who specializes in high-risk pregnancies about the relative benefits and risks. Often women need to continue medication only if they have other risk factors for cardiovascular disease, such as diabetes mellitus, elevated cholesterol, a family history of early heart disease, or a diastolic blood pressure higher than 105 mmHg. If medication is necessary, your obstetrician may prefer that you switch to a drug that has been extensively used and proven safe in pregnancy.

What to expect. Checkups usually are scheduled once every two to three weeks during the first half of pregnancy and then weekly until delivery. In addition to blood-pressure readings, expect regular laboratory tests of your blood and urine. Many women monitor their blood pressure at home, eliminating the danger of "white-coat hypertension," a surge in blood pressure because of the stress of a medical exam.

Repeated or serial ultrasound scans, usually beginning at thirty to thirty-four weeks, provide the best information on fetal development and can pick up any signs of growth retardation. If blood pressure has risen or other complications have developed, tests of fetal fitness may begin as early as twenty-six weeks. Most physicians rely on evaluation of fetal heart rates and ultrasound to determine the optimal time for delivery.

If your blood pressure rises, your doctor will tailor a treatment approach to your individual needs and condition. The goal is to avoid further increases in blood pressure, to reduce the risk of pre-eclampsia, and to prevent eclampsia.

What you can do

● Try to get at least eight hours of rest at night and to spend an extra hour or two resting on your side, especially after meals, to enhance blood flow to your baby.

● Work out a system for monitoring your blood pressure at home. Using a sphygmomanometer (blood-pressure cuff), you can take your own readings or ask your partner to help. Because you're more relaxed at home, these readings may be more accurate than those performed at a doctor's office and give a better reading of "average" blood pressure when you're home or on bedrest.

• Avoid prolonged vigorous exercise, including strenuous lifting or exertion on the job or at home.

• While you don't have to restrict your intake of sodium, avoid excessive salt.

• Eat balanced, nutritious meals.

• Avoid cigarettes and caffeine, since both can increase blood pressure.

• Stress can push blood pressure higher so try the various coping strategies in chapter 6 to ease the emotional strain.

• Beginning at the twenty-eighth week, you can begin daily fetal movement counts to check on your baby's well-being.

Medical Treatment. Mild to moderate hypertension usually does not require antihypertensive drugs; severe hypertension must be treated to safeguard both mother and child. Some physicians prescribe drugs if diastolic pressure reaches 90 mmHg in the first half of pregnancy; others wait to see if it rises to 110. At Johns Hopkins, the high-risk team generally begins treatment if diastolic pressure rises to 100 mmHg.

Many drugs are available for lowering blood pressure in pregnancy. Some have been studied extensively. Others are relatively new. Most obstetricians are very conservative about any drugs in pregnancy and prefer those with well-established safety records. However, in some situations, newer drugs may provide greater benefits.

In hypertensive patients who are not pregnant, diuretics (medications that accelerate the elimination of fluids from the body) are standard treatment, and many women with hypertension become pregnant while taking diuretics. Once a woman is pregnant, obstetricians generally prefer other agents because diuretics can cause a temporary drop in blood plasma and blood volume, which lasts for about ten days and can be risky for the fetus. They also may lower stores of potassium, a crucial trace mineral.

The most extensively used and studied antihypertensive drug is methyldopa (Aldomet), which is safe for a fetus and generally lowers the mother's blood pressure and her risk of early pregnancy loss. Its side effects include dry mouth, lethargy, and drowsiness. A newer group of agents used to treat chronic hypertension are the beta-blockers, particularly propranolol. Although it appears safe, it has not been tested as extensively in pregnancy as has methyldopa.

If blood pressure remains only mildly to moderately elevated, your obstetrician will simply continue close monitoring of your baby's condition. As long as the results are reassuring, you can expect a normal course of pregnancy and labor and, unless obstetrical complications develop, a vaginal delivery. Anesthesia can be risky for hypertensive women. If you have a cesarean delivery, your blood pressure will be closely monitored. If your blood pressure remains high after pregnancy, you will need follow-up for life.

HEART DISEASE

The healthy heart can withstand the extra demands of pregnancy with little difficulty. For the 1 to 1.5 percent of pregnant women with heart disease, the increased workload of pregnancy can create potentially serious problems. However, with precautions and appropriate care, most of these women can have healthy babies and remain healthy themselves. The heart conditions that most commonly affect pregnancy are:

Rheumatic fever (about half of all cases). This is the delayed result of an infection, usually of the throat, by group A streptococcus bacteria (strep throat), which strikes most often between the ages of five and fifteen. Infection can spread to the heart and lead to rheumatic heart disease, a chronic condition caused by scarring and deformity of the heart valves. Its incidence has declined dramatically because of the use of antibiotics that eradicate strep infections before they worsen and spread.

Rheumatic fever is most likely to complicate a pregnancy if the infection has caused stenosis (failure to open completely) of the mitral valve. This increases the likelihood of congestive heart failure. Even women with no symptoms before pregnancy are at risk if stenosis has occurred.

Congenital heart defects. In the past thirty years, advances in surgery and drug treatment have made it possible to repair many congenital defects so more women with these problems are surviving into adulthood and becoming pregnant. The specific problem is less important than whether it's been surgically corrected. The prognosis for pregnancy depends on how close to normal heart function is after corrective surgery. If there are no remaining indications of heart disease, the chances for a healthy pregnancy and baby are excellent.

Mitral valve prolapse. In this condition, a heart valve is pushed back too far (prolapsed) during a contraction so blood flows "backward" toward the lung when the heart is pumping blood to the body, causing a gurgling sound called a "murmur." Brief murmurs are not uncommon in young women, and if no other symptoms—such as chest pain or a heart rhythm abnormality—occur, mitral valve prolapse is not a threat before, during, or after pregnancy. In fact, most women with this problem are surprised that they can continue their normal activities. A few do develop palpitations, a problem that sometimes can be eased by limiting caffeine.

Artificial heart valves. Implanted to replace diseased or deformed valves, they present a risk because they often require ongoing use of drugs called anticoagulants, which prevent blood clots. One widely used agent, warfarin, may cause birth defects if taken early in pregnancy and may increase the risk of hemorrhage if used in the final weeks. Most obstetricians switch pregnant women to another anticoagulant, heparin, which is safe but can be taken only by injection.

Atherosclerosis. Although this is the most common heart problem in the United States, it is uncommon in pregnancy. Women over thirty-five and those with hypertension or diabetes are more likely to develop this age-related condition. Severe atherosclerosis can endanger the mother's life, and she may be advised not to conceive. In women with milder disease, the major risk to the baby is an inadequate supply of oxygen and blood, which can cause growth problems. Standard treatment is increased bedrest.

The various heart disorders usually are characterized by how well a person can function:

• *Class 1.* No limits on physical activity. Ordinary activities cause no discomfort or chest pain.

• *Class 2.* Slight limitation on exertion. Ordinary physical activity causes fatigue, breathlessness, palpitations, or chest pain.

• *Class 3.* Moderate to marked limitation on activity. During less than ordinary physical activity, the person experiences excessive fatigue, breathlessness, palpitations, and chest pain.

• *Class 4.* Inability to perform any physical activity without discomfort. Even at rest, the person experiences pain or other symptoms.

Women in classes 1 and 2 usually have relatively uncomplicated pregnancies without any unusual risks to them or their babies. Those in classes 3 and 4 are at risk for serious complications. For some women, the risk may be too high, and doctors will advise against pregnancy.

What happens during pregnancy. In the first thirty-two weeks of pregnancy, blood volume increases by 50 percent and the heart has to increase its output by 30 to 35 percent to assure adequate blood supply to the placenta and fetus. Even women with healthy hearts feel the extra strain. They tire more easily, become short of breath, and sense their hearts beating rapidly. If you have a heart disorder, your heart may have difficulty meeting these extra demands.

Possible risks for the baby. The greatest dangers are miscarriage, growth impairment, and preterm birth. Your baby's long-term prognosis depends on its size and maturity at birth. If you have certain congenital defects, your baby faces a 2 to 4 percent risk of also having a congenital heart problem (about twice the usual risk).

A woman who has had one child with a heart malformation faces a risk as high as 5 percent of bearing a subsequent child with a common defect, such as a hole in the wall between the chambers of the heart (ventricular septum), or 1 percent for rarer problems. There is no increased risk of a defect in a child if the mother has rheumatic heart disease.

What to expect. During the first half of pregnancy, exams may be scheduled every two weeks, increasing to every week in the second half. Expect a check of your pulse, respiration, and blood pressure as well as questions about your activity level and any changes since your last visit. Be sure to point out any factors that could increase strain on your heart, such as anemia, infection, anxiety, lack of a support system, or insufficient help at home. Report any symptoms, such as shortness of breath, cough, or lack of usual energy.

As further preventive care, you may be given antibiotics during any dental procedures, at the first hint of a respiratory or urinary tract infection, and during labor and delivery. Some doctors prescribe antibiotics throughout pregnancy for women with serious valve problems. Women with grave heart conditions may be hospitalized to assure continuous care. Surgery to replace valves in a pregnant woman is rare, but has been performed successfully without jeopardizing the baby.

Cardiologists advise a vaginal delivery, unless obstetrical complications require a cesarean. Throughout labor, continuous oxygen relieves breathlessness, chest pain, and a faster heart rate; most women also receive medications for pain and anxiety. Your obstetrician may use low forceps during delivery to reduce the strain of bearing down and pushing out the baby. The preferred position for delivery is sitting up or lying on one side rather than flat on the back. Close monitoring minimizes the risks of bleeding, infection, shock, or heart failure.

If you have moderate to severe heart disease, your doctor may want you to remain in the hospital after the delivery until your heart function returns to normal. Within a few weeks, your heart should be back to its prepregnancy size, position, and functioning. The time required for complete recovery depends on the severity of your heart problem. With proper care before, during, and after delivery, you shouldn't sustain any heart damage or long-term impairment.

If you have advanced disease, talk with your doctor about breast-feeding. Because of the extra fatigue and because you may be taking medications that pass into breast milk, you may be advised not to nurse your baby.

What to watch for. The symptoms of a heart's decreased ability to meet the demands of pregnancy are:
- frequent cough
- breathlessness upon exertion, getting worse over time
- edema (progressive swelling throughout the body, including the face, eyelids, hands, and feet)
- heart murmur detectable through a stethoscope
- palpitations
- rales (abnormal respiratory sounds)

Some of these symptoms can and do occur in normal pregnancies. However, if they worsen, they could indicate a greater risk of congestive heart failure.

What you can do. If you have severe heart disease or are taking medication, consult your cardiologist and a high-risk obstetrician before becoming pregnant. Even mild heart disease can impair your heart's ability to meet the demands of both pregnancy and physical exertion.

Rest reduces the heart's workload. Make sure you get eight to ten hours of sleep, with frequent rest periods during the day. More serious forms of heart disease may require you to spend most or all of your time on bedrest. You need a nutritious diet high in iron, protein, and other essential nutrients. Your doctor may advise you to restrict salt intake and to take iron supplements to prevent anemia.

ASTHMA

Asthma is a respiratory disease characterized by periodic attacks of wheezing, difficulty in breathing, shortness of breath, and mild to severe coughing. The three main triggers of asthma attacks are external irritants such as dust or pollen, respiratory infections, and stress. During an attack, the bronchioles, small tubes inside the lungs, contract as a result of a swelling of their lining, spasm, or constriction or mucus blockage of the tubes. At Johns Hopkins, about 1 percent of pregnant patients are asthmatics.

What happens during pregnancy. About half of pregnant patients have no change in the course of their asthma. A smaller percentage show improvement. The smallest group worsen. About a third of patients react differently in every pregnancy, regardless of the sex of the fetus.

Possible risks to the baby. Severe asthma attacks can drastically lower the amount of oxygen in the mother's blood, increasing the risk of growth retardation. There also is a greater risk of preterm birth and a slight increase in losses or complications during or after birth.

What to expect. Your doctor's goal will be to reduce the number of asthmatic attacks, prevent severe attacks, and assure adequate oxygen to the fetus. If you regularly undergo allergen desensitization, you can safely continue throughout pregnancy. If you require a flu immunization (which the Centers for Disease Control recommend for chronic bronchial asthma), you should schedule it for your second or third trimester. The risk of an insufficient oxygen supply to the fetus because of asthma attacks is greater than the risks of antiasthma medication.

What can you do. Because stress and heavy activity aggravate asthma, you may want to restrict what you do and incorporate relaxation exercises, breathing techniques, and other coping strategies into your daily schedule.

Medical treatments. The mainstay of asthma treatment are the theophyllines, including aminophylline. Aminophylline has shown no harmful effects for a fetus. Your doctor will monitor blood levels at least monthly and adjust dosages accordingly. Beta-mimetic drugs are safe and can be used. Terbutaline is the most commonly prescribed.

Aerosols are popular because they affect only the lungs and breathing passages and have few body-wide or systemic side effects. Corticosteroid aerosols, which help when other preparations fail to control symptoms, are safe in pregnancy. Oral corticosteroids are used if aerosols fail, and they carry a slightly increased risk of growth retardation. Check with your doctor before using any over-the-counter asthma remedies.

"RIGHT FROM THE START"

When she was twenty-one, Rae Jean started losing weight. "My legs were like toothpicks," she recalls, "and I was thirsty all the time." When she learned that she had diabetes, the first question she asked was, "Am I going to die?"

The answer was no, but as she discovered, a chronic condition—one that may get better or worse or recur through a lifetime—changes the rules of the game. Suddenly a disease that would never go away altered every aspect of her life.

"I had to learn everything—a new way of eating, how to give myself injections, how to calculate doses. Once I came close to going into a coma. I'd always wanted children, but I didn't even think of that at the time. I was overwhelmed."

Gradually Rae Jean adjusted to the demands of her illness and learned how to manage her condition. She kept working as a computer systems analyst, got married, and settled into a comfortable life. When she was thirty-four, Rae Jean and her husband, Wayne, started talking about having a child.

Their primary concern was that Wayne might be a carrier of a rare genetic disease. A genetic counselor provided reassurance that he wasn't but suggested that Rae Jean consult a perinatologist before becoming pregnant. "I had no idea how diabetes would affect pregnancy and how pregnancy would affect it," says Rae Jean. "The luckiest thing for me was that we got counseling before I got pregnant so I was in the best possible condition to have a baby."

Since her blood-sugar levels were high at the time of her prepregnancy exam, Rae Jean spent three months bringing them under control. "I'd check my blood sugar four times a day and write down everything I ate," she recalls. Once her blood-sugar readings reached optimal levels, she got pregnant. Throughout the next few months Rae Jean continued monitoring, kept a log book of her food intake and insulin doses, and saw her perinatologist every two weeks. "I'd eat six meals a day to keep my blood-sugar levels stable," she explains. "I'd also try to walk a few miles four or five times a week."

Like many diabetics, Rae Jean developed a blood-pressure problem. As her blood pressure rose to a worrisome 142/78 and her ankles began to swell, she was put on modified bedrest and could not return to work. "I was willing to do whatever it would take to have a healthy baby," she says. "I took it a day at a time."

Rae Jean's blood pressure stabilized, and all went well until her eighth month, when she developed an asymptomatic urinary tract infection. The silent infection, which never caused fever or burning on urination, led to premature rupture of her amniotic membranes.

"When my water broke, my doctor's office told me to go to the hospital as soon as possible," she says. "Wayne and I were very excited. We didn't panic or think that something awful might happen." In fact, something wonderful happened.

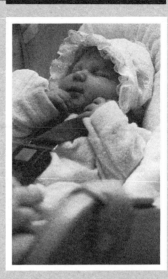

On June 15—six weeks before her due date—their daughter, Kelsey Whitney, arrived, weighing seven pounds nine ounces. Kelsey, whose lungs were not fully mature, developed several serious complications and spent twelve days in the intensive care nursery at Johns Hopkins, her mom recalls, "monitored twenty-four hours a day by the most wonderful, reliable people in the world." Because she required so many tests and treatments Kelsey "had so many bruises and holes in her body that Rae Jean thought she would never look normal. Of course, we were wrong."

Since her rocky start, Kelsey has been healthy and happy. "She's a real butter ball," says Rae Jean. "And her doctor says she is a healthy, thriving baby. I'm just so glad that I was able to give her the best possible start in life."

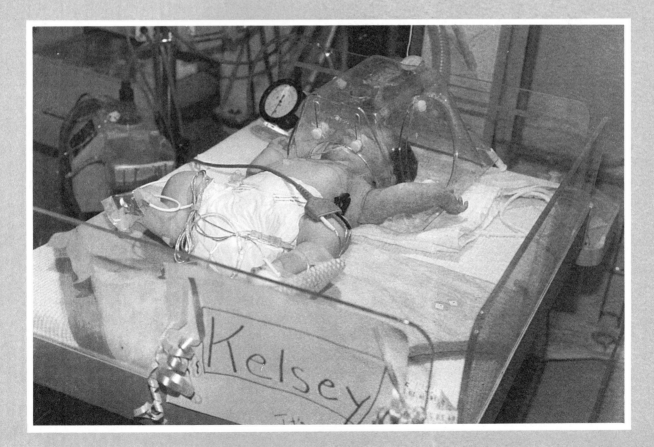

Neurologic Problems
Epilepsy and Seizure Disorders

Epilepsy and similar brain-function disorders are characterized by sudden, recurring attacks of violent muscle contractions (seizures) and unconsciousness. Some individuals with these problems have seizures involving the entire body while others experience only brief periods of unconsciousness, eye or muscle flutterings, and loss of muscle tone.

What happens during pregnancy. Pregnancy has different effects on the frequency of seizures. In one study of 155 women with epilepsy who became pregnant, the incidence of seizures increased in 45 percent, remained unchanged in 43 percent, and declined in 12 percent.

Possible risks to the baby. With carefully monitored control of seizures, epileptic women do not have a higher rate of complications, miscarriages, preterm labor, or perinatal loss. Seizures are the primary danger because they temporarily interfere with the oxygen supply to the uterus and fetus, jeopardizing the baby's well-being. Anticonvulsant drugs are remarkably effective in controlling seizures. However, not all are safe during pregnancy.

Both seizures and the medications that prevent them can pose a potential danger to an unborn baby. Several studies have found an increased rate of malformations in infants whose mothers had epilepsy, regardless of whether they were taking medications. The drugs and a genetic predisposition or vulnerability are probably both significant and codependent. Other risks include growth retardation and smaller head size.

Preventing problems. The vast majority of women with seizure disorders have successful pregnancies without endangering themselves or their babies. However, if you have epilepsy or a similar problem, you will have to work closely with your obstetrician and neurologist.

The best time to start is *before* you get pregnant. If you haven't had seizures in many years, your neurologist may gradually withdraw your medication before conception. Some pregnant women remain free of seizures without any medication; most require some treatment for seizure control. If seizures recur, your doctor will resume treatment because preventing seizures is essential for your health and your pregnancy. More than 90 percent of women on antiseizure medication have normal babies.

If you are taking anticonvulsants before conception, you should take vitamin supplements and an additional folic acid supplement each day. This will correct any potential Vitamin D deficiency caused by the drugs and prevent folate anemia in pregnancy. Folate supplementation requires weekly monitoring of anticonvulsant drug levels to keep them sufficiently high.

What to expect. In addition to regular monitoring of the level of medication in your blood, your obstetrician will schedule detailed ultrasounds of your baby, beginning at eighteen weeks, to pick up any possible malformations. Fetal echocardiography can rule out heart defects. Serial ultrasound scans monitor fetal growth. At twenty-eight weeks, prenatal fetal evaluation usually begins. If you are taking phenobarbital, primidione, or phenytoin, your doctor may recommend vitamin K supplements at about thirty-four weeks to prevent any coagulation (blood clotting) problems in your newborn.

As long as tests provide reassurance that your baby is doing well, you can expect to carry to term and to have a vaginal delivery unless obstetrical complications develop. After birth your baby may be given vitamin K to prevent blood clots. Your anticonvulsant medication levels will be monitored often after delivery, when rapid physiological changes occur.

What you can do. Beginning before pregnancy, if possible, or as soon as you discover you are pregnant, your primary goal should be adequate control of seizures. Take your medication regularly. Be sure you get enough sleep, since sleep deprivation can exacerbate seizures. If you suffer severe morning sickness, alert your doctor, who may recommend antinausea drugs so you can keep down your oral anticonvulsants.

Medical treatment. Choosing the best anticonvulsant and the optimal dose is a crucial decision. The most widely prescribed anticonvulsants in nonpregnant women are the hydantoins; the best-recognized trade name among this family of drugs is Dilantin. From 90 to 95 percent of pregnant women who use Dilantin have healthy, normal babies. Other hydantoins are more likely to cause fetal hydantoin syndrome, a cluster of birth defects that includes growth impairment, mental deficiency, and facial malformations, as well as occasional cleft lips and palates and heart defects.

Another anticonvulsant, trimethadione (Tridione), also can cause defects. As many as 80 percent of the babies of mothers taking Tridione have impaired physical and intellectual development, un-

> "The worst part of having a chronic illness is that you're always waiting for the other shoe to drop. You find out you have epilepsy or lupus or whatever. Then you keep wondering, 'What next?'"

usual facial features, cleft palates, and heart defects. Valproic acid and carbamazepine (Tegretol) also can cause birth defects and should not be used, if possible.

To avoid any danger, your neurologist may switch you to phenobarbital, a barbiturate that is considered the safest anticonvulsant in pregnancy. While there is some concern that this drug may interfere with growth, the risk seems to occur only with very high doses. If you take phenobarbital, you will undergo frequent blood tests to monitor the amount of the drug in your body, and doses will be carefully regulated.

Keep in mind that the most important factor is keeping the blood level of anticonvulsants high enough to prevent seizures. The dosages that worked before pregnancy may not be adequate during pregnancy.

Multiple Sclerosis

This neurologic disorder is characterized by the loss of the myelin sheath that surrounds and protects nerve fibers. Usually it strikes young adults, is marked by periods of remission, and progresses to marked physical disability in ten to twenty years. An estimated two hundred fifty thousand Americans have MS; an equal number may have a form so mild it hasn't been diagnosed.

Often MS goes into remission during pregnancy. Drugs usually are not necessary, but rest is important. Because sensation is diminished, labor may be almost painless. The disease itself does not endanger a baby, but there may be an increased genetic risk of passing MS on to a child. For years, physicians believed MS flared up after pregnancy, but recent studies have found no long-term harmful effects of pregnancy on the course of the disease.

THYROID DISORDERS

Hypothyroidism—production of too little thyroid hormone—rarely complicates pregnancy because women with this problem generally are infertile. Women taking replacement doses of thyroid hormone should check their dosages with their doctors before and during pregnancy. Hyperthyroidism, an excess of hormones produced by the thyroid glands, is a more common and dangerous risk—if it is not recognized and treated.

What happens during pregnancy. Pregnancy triggers major

changes in the thyroid gland and the hormones it produces. The gland itself enlarges, and basal metabolic rate speeds up. The most common symptoms of hyperthyroidism—excessive warmth, nervousness, rapid pulse, and fast heart rate—are similar to feelings many pregnant women experience. However, hyperthyroid women also often lose weight or fail to gain weight.

Possible effects on the mother. Most women with mild to moderate hyperthyroidism have uncomplicated pregnancies. Pregnancy does not make the disease worse or more difficult to treat. But control of thyroid production is essential for mother and baby. A "thyroid storm" or surge in the amount of thyroid hormone in the bloodstream intensifies the usual symptoms of hyperthyroidism to a dangerous extreme. The mother may develop tachycardia (rapid heart rate), dehydration, delirium, diarrhea, vomiting, a very high fever, and ultimately, heart failure.

Some standard medications for hyperthyroidism, such as iodide, are not used during pregnancy because they can cause goiter (enlargement of the thyroid gland) in the fetus. The most commonly used drugs are propylthiouracil (PTU) and methimazole (Tapazole), given at the minimum dose needed to maintain normal thyroid levels. They inhibit the synthesis of thyroid hormones. Propranolol can prevent complications, especially at delivery.

Possible risks to the baby. If treated, hyperthyroidism does not produce physical or intellectual abnormalities, and there is no increased rate of loss. However, if untreated, the risk of miscarriage, low birth weight, preterm birth, intrauterine death, and stillbirth increase. After delivery, all newborns of hyperthyroid women must be watched very carefully for neonatal hyperthyroidism. Fewer than 1 percent of these babies develop this problem, and most cases are temporary. However, they must be treated because of the danger of impaired central nervous system development.

What to expect. Once diagnosed, your condition will be monitored at regular checkups. Weight gain and a normal pulse are two excellent indicators that your thyroid levels are optimal. Thyroid activity will be assessed every two weeks, and your medications adjusted as necessary. About 5 percent of patients on antithyroid medications experience minor side effects, such as rash or itching. However, other symptoms, such as a sore throat or fever, also could be drug-related and must be reported immediately.

Medical treatments. "Antithyroid" drugs control the amount of thyroid hormone produced by an overactive thyroid gland. They do cross the placenta and could affect the baby's thyroid gland as well as the mother's. Your doctor may taper your drug dosages in the final weeks of pregnancy to lessen the risks of complications from abnormal thyroid function in the baby after birth.

Severe hyperthyroidism may require treatment with iodides to block the release of thyroid hormone. They carry a risk that the baby will develop a thyroid goiter and low thyroid hormone levels, so they are used only with caution and when essential.

In rare cases, medical treatment fails to control thyroid levels, and surgical removal of the thyroid is necessary. Sometimes a thyroid nodule needs to be removed. The optimum time for surgery is the midtrimester because of the danger of miscarriage in the first trimester and of preterm labor in the third. After removal of the thyroid, a woman must take oral doses of thyroid hormone to maintain normal levels.

Occasionally thyroid disease flares up after delivery. If you have thyroid problems, your thyroid levels will be checked before you leave the hospital and periodically for about a year. If you are taking antithyroid medication, you may be advised not to breastfeed because the drug is excreted in milk. If your drug doses are low, your doctor may allow breastfeeding, as long as your baby's thyroid levels are monitored.

GYNECOLOGIC PROBLEMS

Some women become aware of a problem with their reproductive organs long before they become pregnant because of symptoms, such as pain or bleeding. Other conditions are picked up during routine gynecologic exams. However, pregnancy is the ultimate test of reproductive health, and conditions that may never have caused the slightest problem before pregnancy—such as a bifurcated or split uterus—may become serious complications. A prepregnancy physical can detect many reproductive disorders. Sometimes corrective measures, such as surgery, can be taken before conception to improve the odds of a successful pregnancy and a healthy baby.

Myomas (Fibroids)

No one knows exactly why muscle tissue forms benign growths in the wombs of some women, but fibroids are common in women of childbearing age. Sometimes they produce no symptoms. Sometimes they lead to heavy bleeding and intense pain. Fibroids also can contribute to infertility by making it more difficult for a fertilized egg to implant in the uterus. In women no longer interested in having children, a hysterectomy or removal of the entire uterus might be performed. Myomectomy is a less drastic but more delicate procedure, in which the fibroids are removed while the uterus remains intact. The odds of becoming pregnant after this procedure are good to excellent.

Fibroids that remain during pregnancy can grow larger, causing severe pain as they outgrow the available blood supply. Very rarely a fibroid may block the birth canal, making a cesarean necessary. Usually obstetricians take an "expectant" approach, hoping for the best but constantly watching out for any hint that something might go wrong. Occasionally bedrest, hospitalization, and pain therapy are necessary.

Endometriosis

This relatively common condition is a major cause of infertility and may increase the risk of an ectopic pregnancy. Various treatments, including drugs and laser surgery to vaporize growths, can remove endometrial growths and increase the odds of conceiving. Once a woman is pregnant, endometriosis usually improves. After pregnancy, long-term remission may occur.

DES Exposure

In the 1940s and early 1950s, more than a million and a half American women took diethystilbestrol (DES) to prevent miscarriage. Their daughters are at greater risk of vaginal and cervical cancer and of reproductive problems, including infertility. When they do conceive, changes in the normal development of the cervix and uterus put them at greater risk of early miscarriage, preterm labor, and ectopic or tubal pregnancy.

Women who know they were exposed to DES in utero should have a thorough examination before becoming pregnant. Many doctors recommend a hysterosalpingogram, an x ray of the reproductive organs that can detect structural abnormalities that could increase the risk of preterm labor or miscarriage. Sometimes surgery can correct specific problems.

Even if they have no structural anomalies, DES daughters should expect close monitoring throughout pregnancy because of their heightened risk of miscarriage and preterm labor. Eventually more than 80 percent of these women have successful pregnancies and healthy infants.

Uterine Malformations

About one in every three hundred women has an unusually formed uterus. Sometimes the uterus is divided into two compartments (septate); sometimes it is forked (bicornuate). Some women have two complete or partial reproductive tracts. With a relatively minor defect, the prognosis is good. However, there is a higher risk of miscarriage, growth impairment, and preterm labor. Surgery can correct some problems.

Ovarian Cysts

A cyst or growth on an ovary can impair fertility, but usually does not have any impact on pregnancy. A "corpus luteum" cyst can be normal in the first twelve weeks of pregnancy. Large cysts that persist throughout pregnancy may make it difficult for doctors to check the size of the uterus and the baby's growth. If a cyst must be removed, surgery is scheduled between fourteen and twenty weeks. Cysts also may interfere with normal progress in labor and make a cesarean necessary.

CONNECTIVE TISSUE DISEASES

Women of childbearing age are the primary targets of diseases that affect connective tissue and blood vessels. In these disorders, the immune system fails to recognize body tissue as self and forms antibodies to attack parts of the body. The autoimmune diseases most likely to complicate pregnancy are systemic lupus erythematosus, scleroderma, and rheumatoid arthritis.

Systemic Lupus Erythematosus (Lupus)

Systemic lupus erythematosus, called SLE or lupus, afflicts about one of every seven hundred women between fifteen and sixty-four years of age. In black women, the prevalence is higher: one in every two hundred forty-five. About 80 percent develop skin rashes, including a classic "butterfly" rash across their faces, and sensitivity to the sun. About 90 percent develop muscle and joint soreness. About half develop neurologic or psychiatric symptoms. Many also experience kidney and blood abnormalities. Sometimes lupus first appears during a pregnancy. The key to overcoming risks is working closely with both a rheumatologist (a specialist in connective-tissue diseases) and an obstetrician or perinatologist.

What happens during pregnancy. According to Dr. Michelle Petri, an assistant professor of medicine at Johns Hopkins, the prospect for a successful pregnancy for women with lupus is brighter than ever. Until recently, many physicians felt that pregnancy was so dangerous that they recommended therapeutic abortions for the sake of the mother's health. Today, with optimal care and close supervision, most women with lupus can have healthy babies without endangering their own health. The prognosis is best when lupus has been in remission for six months or more prior to conception.

Pregnancy usually does not affect the long-term prognosis for lupus, but the disease is more likely to flare up during or after pregnancy. If you have lupus, you should be careful not to conceive during a flare-up to avoid added stress on yourself and exposure of your baby to high doses of medication. The disease also is more likely to flare up during pregnancy if it's active at the time of conception.

Possible effects on the mother. Lupus flares occur in about a third of pregnancies. However, most symptoms, such as skin rashes and joint swelling, do not affect critical organ systems, and usually minor changes in medication can control them. The major risk is exacerbation of kidney problems. But most women with kidney disease do well if their lupus is in remission at the time they get pregnant. Rarely, pregnancy can lead to permanent kidney damage or life-threatening complications.

Possible risks to the fetus. The risk of miscarriage in women with lupus is 25 percent or greater. Several factors contribute to this high risk: whether the disease is active, whether the kidneys are affected, and whether the woman has certain lupus antibodies in her blood—lupus anticoagulant and anticardiolipin—that may hurt the placenta. Miscarriage can occur in any trimester; late intrauterine death, or stillbirth, also is a danger.

Babies of mothers with lupus are at increased risk of heart abnormalities, including a condition called heart block, which is sometimes fatal. The danger of heart block is highest in women with two specific antibodies in their blood: anti-Ro and anti-La; they can be

"When you start a pregnancy with one strike against you, you need people who believe in you. My husband was my number-one cheerleader, and my doctor was just as enthusiastic. They made me believe I could do it— and I did."

measured early in pregnancy. If a woman with lupus has them, fetal echocardiograms can pick up any early evidence of heart block. This problem may be treated with corticosteroid drugs or plasmapheresis (removal of the antibodies from the mother's blood so they can't get to the baby). Most children born with heart block but no other heart abnormalities survive but require surgery to implant a pacemaker in their preteen years.

The babies of mothers with lupus may be born with neonatal lupus, brought about if the mother's autoantibodies cross the placenta. This temporary problem, which may cause a rash on the face or scalp, disappears in a few months.

Preventing problems. All women with lupus who are considering pregnancy should undergo a complete prepregnancy exam, including blood tests to determine the presence of lupus antibodies. Therapy with prednisone (a steroid) and low-dose aspirin can reduce risks before conception in some women. Blood tests early in pregnancy can also detect the lupus antibodies associated with congenital heart block; a fetal echocardiogram can confirm early signs. If a baby does have this problem, a neonatologist and pedriatic cardiologist should be at the birth.

What to expect. Usually obstetricians and rheumatologists see women once a month during their first two trimesters, then every two weeks during their third. Regular exams include assessments of weight, blood pressure, and kidney function. Women with lupus may be asked for twenty-four-hour urine collections every month to check creatinine and protein clearance (indicators of kidney function). Accurate gestational dating is crucial because of the risk of preterm labor and growth retardation.

Medical treatments. Standard treatment involves corticosteroids, which have not been associated with birth defects. Ideally a fetus should not be exposed to any drugs during the first trimester. If that's not possible for a lupus patient, prednisone and azathioprine (Imuran) have been used successfully. Some drugs occasionally used for lupus, such as hydroxychloroquine, are avoided in pregnancy because of potential danger to a fetus.

Scleroderma

Scleroderma, a collagen vascular disorder characterized by tight, bound-down skin, affects women four times more than men and usually begins between the ages of thirty and fifty. In some patients, the disease shows no change in pregnancy; in others, it worsens; in yet others, it improves. Preterm birth, preterm rupture of the membranes, and stillbirths are more common in patients with scleroderma. Women whose disease is so severe that it has affected their lungs, heart, or kidneys may be advised not to get pregnant or to terminate a pregnancy because of the risk of fatal complications.

Rheumatoid Arthritis

Rheumatoid arthritis, which usually strikes between the ages of twenty and sixty, singles out women two or three times more than men, but generally has no adverse effects on pregnancy. The majority of patients go into remission during pregnancy, although some experience a flare-up after delivery.

Classic symptoms include fatigue, low-grade fever, pain and swelling of joints, morning stiffness, and pain on movement. While extra rest relieves the burden on weight-bearing joints, women should continue their usual range-of-motion exercises.

If the disease goes into remission, no medication may be necessary. The usual therapeutic recommendations are rest, physical therapy, aspirin or other salicylates and, if necessary, corticosteroids. Heavy aspirin use late in pregnancy poses several risks: prolonged pregnancy, longer labor, greater blood loss at delivery, and anemia.

DIGESTIVE DISEASES

According to the National Digestive Diseases Advisory Board, almost half of the U.S. population will suffer a digestive problem at some time. Most disorders of the digestive tract affect only one section: the esophagus, the stomach and duodenum (the first part of the small intestine), the small intestine, the large intestine, the liver, the pancreas, the gallbladder, or the rectum. Many pregnant women develop reflux esophagitis, a regurgitation of stomach acids into the esophagus. The best means of avoiding this problem are staying away from spicy foods and eating small meals.

Among other digestive problems that can affect pregnancy are:

Ulcers

Ulcers (open sores in the lining of the stomach or duodenum) often improve in pregnancy. The primary treatments for patients with symptoms are antacids and dietary restrictions, including no caffeine, aspirinlike drugs, alcohol, or gastric stimulants. Most obstetricians advise against use of cimetidine, a widely used drug. It has not shown any teratogenic effect, but researchers believe its effects in pregnancy are not fully known.

Inflammatory Bowel Diseases

The inflammatory bowel diseases—ulcerative colitis and Crohn's disease, or regional enteritis—reach their peak incidence during the reproductive years. The symptoms of ulcerative colitis (development of raw, inflamed areas in the large intestine) include acute attacks of bloody stools, diarrhea, abdominal cramping and pain, weight loss, and dehydration. Crohn's disease (inflammation of part of the digestive tract) tends to be chronic, with symptoms including fever, diarrhea, and cramps.

Women with ulcerative colitis generally have successful pregnancies, especially if their disease was not active at the time of conception. Sometimes the disease goes into remission during pregnancy or improves; sometimes there is no change or worsening. Crohn's disease usually poses a minimal—if any—increased risk for a mother and her baby. However, there may be a greater chance of miscarriage in patients with active disease at the time of conception.

The medical treatment of inflammatory bowel disease does not change greatly in pregnancy. Since emotional tension can exacerbate ulcerative colitis and Crohn's, women should rely on the relaxation techniques to help with emotional strain.

Diet, always important, is even more critical in pregnancy. Women with mild ulcerative colitis often do well on a low-roughage diet or, if they're lactose intolerant, exclusion of milk products. Your doctor or nutritionist can offer dietary guidelines for pregnancy.

In addition to regular checkups to make sure you are gaining weight appropriately, your doctor will be concerned about diarrhea. Sulfasalazine and steroid therapy—both proven safe in pregnancy—are the usual treatment. Women who become profoundly dehydrated may require hospitalization so they can receive intravenous fluids. Very occasionally women whose acute episodes of inflammatory bowel diseases do not respond to medical treatment undergo surgery for a perforated or obstructed bowel. Most fare well after surgery, although the risk of preterm labor does increase significantly during and after the operation.

CHRONIC KIDNEY DISEASE

The kidney problems that complicate pregnancy can be temporary or chronic. Because chronic kidney disease often is "silent" and produces no symptoms until advanced stages, pregnancy or a routine medical examination may reveal the first signs of a developing problem. More than 85 percent of women with chronic renal diseaes can have successful pregnancies and healthy babies—if kidney function has not deteriorated.

Preventing problems. A prepregnancy evaluation is crucial because the potential problems of pregnancy are directly related to the severity of kidney disease and the damage it has caused. For some women, the dangers to their lives—and to any children they'd conceive—may be too great to risk pregnancy. Women with one normal kidney should also get prepregnancy counseling, because no backup kidney can provide reserves for them and their babies if any problems develop in pregnancy. However, keep in mind that one normal, healthy kidney is all a woman needs for pregnancy.

What to expect. Women with chronic pyelonephritis, a long-term kidney infection that damages the collecting system for urine, or chronic glomerulonephritis, which destroys the waste-filtering system within the kidneys, require conscientious prenatal care. Regular checks for infection and any signs of deteriorating kidney function are crucial. Some women may have to collect all urine produced in a twenty-four-hour period every two weeks until thirty-two weeks and then every week until delivery. Control of hypertension is critical, because blood-pressure problems can make kidney disease worse—and vice versa. If symptoms worsen, hospitalization may be necessary to reduce blood-pressure and assess fetal well-being.

Babies of women with kidney disease undergo regular prenatal testing, including serial sonograms for growth retardation and tests of their overall condition beginning at twenty-eight weeks. If the mother's blood pressure rises significantly, more frequent testing may begin.

Dialysis

Women undergoing kidney dialysis can have successful pregnancies, although they require longer and more frequent periods of dialysis, a controlled diet, and care to avoid anemia and hypertension.

Their babies are at greater risk of preterm birth. Ultrasounds follow fetal growth; prenatal testing begins at twenty-eight weeks. Vaginal delivery is possible and preferred; cesareans are performed only if obstetrical complications develop.

Transplants

More and more women with transplanted kidneys are becoming mothers of healthy babies. Most doctors recommend waiting for two to five years after receiving a transplant before becoming pregnant. This allows time for renal function to stabilize and drug doses to be well established. Women also should not have significant hypertension or problems with kidney function. The source of the transplant—whether the kidney came from a dead or living donor—does not seem to influence pregnancy.

The key to a successful outcome is *not* discontinuing the medications that prevent rejection of a kidney. Prednisone and prednisolone, the most commonly used steroids and immune suppressants, are safe because only minute amounts reach the fetus. No studies have noted any increase in birth defects.

The risk of rejection of a transplanted kidney is no greater in pregnant than in nonpregnant women. However, pregnant women may not show the classic signs of rejection (fever, no urine, tenderness, decreasing kidney function). Their symptoms may resemble pyelonephritis or preeclampsia (which occurs in about a third of transplant patients). Infection is a serious threat, and you can expect monthly urine cultures and prompt treatment at the earliest sign of infection.

Serial ultrasounds assess fetal growth. Prenatal heart-rate monitoring begins at the twenty-eighth week. About half of kidney transplant recipients deliver before thirty-seven weeks, and preterm labor, preterm rupture of the membranes, and growth impairment are common. Vaginal delivery is preferred. Kidney function worsens in a small percentage of women in late pregnancy, but improves after delivery.

Medical Problems That Can Develop in Pregnancy

When you're pregnant, medical problems seem especially dangerous and forbidding. You worry about your own health as well as the impact your illness or any medications you require may have on your baby. If a medical complication develops during pregnancy, you may feel responsible and guilty. Yet prompt diagnosis and treatment can prevent many medical problems from developing into a serious threat to your pregnancy or your baby.

ANEMIA

Anemia is a deficiency either of the protein hemoglobin, the main component of red blood cells, or of the total number of red blood cells in the body. The chief component of hemoglobin, which carries oxygen throughout the body, is iron. If you do not get enough iron, your body cannot make an adequate amount of hemoglobin. The result is iron-deficiency anemia, the most common medical complication of pregnancy.

A lack of folic acid (folate), a water-soluble vitamin needed for red blood cell division, can cause similar problems. Without adequate folic acid, red blood cells fail to divide and become enlarged and fewer in number, causing folic acid anemia. Because of the increased demand for red blood cells in pregnancy, mothers-to-be are at much greater risk of developing this problem than other women.

What happens during pregnancy. The need for iron increases as the body produces increasing amounts of red blood cells for mother and baby. The hematocrit, a measure of red blood cells, typically falls because plasma increases blood volume. In as many as half of pregnant women, hemoglobin decreases so drastically that they become anemic. The greatest need for iron is in the second half of pregnancy. If a woman begins pregnancy a bit anemic, she can rapidly develop severe anemia.

In pregnancy, the need for folic acid increases three to four times. Folic acid deficiency, which occurs in 1 to 4 percent of pregnancies, also can develop quickly and is most common in twin pregnancies.

Simple blood tests, usually performed routinely in all pregnancies, can show if a woman is anemic.

Possible effects on the mother. Without adequate iron and hemoglobin, pregnant women become more susceptible to infection, tire more easily, and are at greater risk of excess bleeding at delivery and of problems following delivery. Severe anemia, rare in women receiving regular prenatal care, can lead to heart failure.

Possible risks for the baby. Anemia jeopardizes the growing baby's supply of oxygen and essential nutrients. Generally the mother feels the effects before the baby. However, severe anemia does increase the possibility of growth problems, so a baby could be born small for its gestational age. In extreme cases, there is increased risk of stillbirth. During delivery, the baby of an anemic mother is at greater risk of hypoxia, or oxygen deprivation.

What you can do. You need approximately 1,000 mg more iron every day during pregnancy. Between 300 and 400 mg goes to the fetus; 500 mg goes for your increased red blood cell mass; another 100 goes to the placenta, and about 250 replaces iron lost in sweat, urine, and feces.

- To assure an adequate intake of iron, choose foods high in this mighty mineral, including red meats, legumes, fresh fruits, whole-grain cereals, and broccoli. Eating foods high in vitamin C at the same meal boosts iron absorption.
- To prevent folic acid deficiency, eat plenty of leafy green vegetables, red meats, fish, poultry, legumes, peanuts, and liver.
- Do not cook in large volumes of water, which can dilute 50 to 90 percent of folic acid.
- Limit microwave cooking, which destroys more folic acid than conventional cooking.

Medical treatment. If you become anemic, daily supplements of iron, folic acid, or both can boost your hemoglobin and red blood cells. Severely anemic women and mothers of multiples may need to take iron supplements two or three times a day. If you need iron tablets, be sure to take them with meals to decrease nausea and with orange juice since Vitamin C increases absorption. Your stool may turn black and hard. If you become constipated or have difficulty moving your bowels, inform your doctor. A stool softener can eliminate discomfort.

It can be hard to obtain adequate folic acid from diet alone. The standard therapeutic dose for supplements is 1 mg a day. This vitamin does not produce side effects for mother or baby.

BLOOD PRESSURE PROBLEMS

About 7 percent of pregnant women develop blood-pressure problems. Their impact ranges from minor to life-threatening for both a mother and her baby. In the past, the hypertensive disorders of pregnancy were labeled "toxemia," because physicians believed a poison, or toxin, was responsible. Now we think this isn't true. However, many people still use the term *toxemia* to refer to high-blood-pressure problems in pregnancy. Most caregivers use the following terms for different hypertensive disorders:
- Pregnancy-induced or gestational hypertension
- Preeclampsia
- Eclampsia
- Chronic hypertension, which can occur with "superimposed" preeclampsia and eclampsia. (This problem, along with other chronic illnesses, is described in chapter 8.)

What happens during pregnancy. Pregnancy brings about enormous changes in blood volume and pressure. During the first twenty weeks, blood pressure typically falls below prepregnancy levels. It then begins to rise steadily in the second half of pregnancy, usually back to prepregnancy levels.

Pregnancy-Induced Hypertension

Pregnancy-induced hypertension is the most common hypertensive disorder of pregnancy. Its cause is unknown. Most women of childbearing age have blood-pressure readings lower than 120 mmHg

"The idea of medication bothered me more than finding out that I had gestational hypertension. When my doctor agreed to try bedrest first, I was relieved. I hardly moved for a week. Fortunately, it worked."

(millimeters of mercury) diastolic (during contractions of the heart) and 80 mmHg systolic (between contractions). By definition a woman has pregnancy-induced hypertension if her blood pressure rises to 140/90 mmHg after the first twenty weeks of pregnancy or in the first twenty-four hours after delivery or if her systolic pressure rises by 30 mmHg and/or diastolic increases by 15 mmHg. These readings must be made on at least two different occasions, at least six hours apart.

Most women who develop pregnancy-induced hypertension had normal blood pressures before conception, although some may have had an unrecognized predisposition to hypertension. In most cases, blood pressure returns to normal after delivery.

Are you at risk? You are more likely to develop hypertension in pregnancy if you:
- are pregnant for the first time
- are over 35
- smoke
- are overweight
- have kidney disease
- have a family history of hypertension

While hypertension is always a serious consideration, the chance of complications during pregnancy increases considerably if you:
- are older than 40
- have a blood pressure higher than 160/110 mmHg early in pregnancy
- are an insulin-dependent diabetic
- have cardiomyopathy (weakening of the heart muscle)
- suffer from kidney disease
- have connective tissue disease, such as lupus
- have had previous blood clots
- have previously developed preeclampsia early in pregnancy
- have previously had a separation of the placenta from the uterine wall (placental abruption)

Possible effects on the mother. Usually blood pressure rises only slightly in pregnancy-induced hypertension, and the mother may feel fine. The primary medical concern is lowering the risk of preeclampsia.

Possible risks for the baby. Mild hypertension is not considered dangerous, but the hazards to your baby depend on how high your blood pressure rises and how long it remains elevated. Moderate to severe hypertension can cause fetal growth problems, and babies who do not grow well face a much greater risk of complications before, during, and after birth.

The biggest danger is that the baby, unable to get the oxygen and nourishment it needs, may die suddenly in the final months of pregnancy. There also is increased danger of placental abruption (separation of the placenta from the uterine wall before delivery). If preeclampsia does not develop, the prognosis for mother and baby is excellent.

Diagnosis. The first clue to a potential problem may be a high blood-pressure reading at the first prenatal visit. If your blood pressure does not drop 10–15 mmHg in the course of early pregnancy, your doctor will monitor it closely. If it reaches 140/90 or higher in the first twenty weeks of pregnancy, you will be diagnosed as having pregnancy-induced hypertension.

What to expect. Your doctor will schedule frequent checkups, usually once every two weeks during the first half of pregnancy and then weekly until delivery. You also may be asked to check your blood pressure at home. In addition to blood-pressure readings, you will undergo laboratory tests of your blood and urine for any indications of preeclampsia.

To monitor fetal growth, most physicians start regular sonograms at thirty-four weeks. Tests of the baby's well-being usually begin with weekly nonstress tests after twenty-eight weeks. As long as the results of fetal testing are reassuring, pregnancy continues without any intervention. If the tests indicate increasing danger to the baby, amniocentesis for lung maturity is performed, and labor may be induced as quickly as possible.

What you can do
- Bedrest usually is the first recommendation. Your doctor may advise you to get at least eight hours of rest at night and to spend an extra hour or two resting, especially after meals.
- Try lying on either side to enhance blood flow to your baby.
- Avoid all prolonged vigorous exercise, including strenuous work on the job or at home.
- While you don't have to restrict your intake of sodium, avoid excessive salt.
- Eat balanced, nutritious meals.
- Avoid cigarettes and caffeine, which increase blood pressure.

- Since stress also affects blood pressure, practice relaxation exercises, and try to cut down on commitments and chores.
- At the twenty-eighth week, begin daily fetal movement counts to monitor your baby's activity.

Medical treatment. Low doses of aspirin late in pregnancy can reduce the risk of high blood pressure. Mild to moderate hypertension usually can be controlled without antihypertensive drugs. Generally pregnancy-induced hypertension requires treatment with pressure-lowering drugs only if other complications, such as kidney disease, exist or problems like preeclampsia develop during pregnancy. Severe hypertension must be treated to safeguard both mother and child.

Preeclampsia

Preeclampsia refers to a spectrum of complications, ranging from mild to extremely serious. This disorder, which occurs only in pregnancy, is characterized by three key symptoms:

- An increase in blood pressure by at least 30 mmHg systolic or 15 mmHg diastolic or a reading of 140/90 mmHg after twenty weeks of gestation. In mild preeclampsia, diastolic blood pressure remains below 110 mmHg.
- Edema, or swelling caused by fluid retention. You may be developing edema if you gain more than 3.3 pounds a month in the second trimester or more than 1.1 pounds a week in the third trimester.
- Proteinuria. A concentration of .1 gram/liter of protein or more in two random urine specimens collected six hours or more apart or .3 grams in a twenty-four-hour collection. This indicates that the kidneys are not functioning as they should to prevent a loss of protein.

Women with severe preeclampsia may also develop serious blood and liver abnormalities.

Are you at risk? The chance of developing preeclampsia rises if:

- your mother or sisters had severe preeclampsia
- this is your first pregnancy
- you developed preeclampsia in a previous pregnancy

If severe preeclampsia occurred before thirty-four weeks, women are at greater risk of early development of preeclampsia, fetal growth impairment, and seizures in subsequent pregnancies.

What to watch for. If you are at risk, you should realize that the following symptoms can indicate increasing danger:

- headache
- blurred vision or spots before the eyes
- breathlessness
- pain in the right upper quadrant of the stomach
- nausea and vomiting
- irritability

What you can do. For mild preeclampsia, your doctor may recommend:

- bedrest
- a high-protein diet
- cutting back on salt

Medical treatments. Women with worsening preeclampsia generally must be hospitalized. They may receive replacement fluids and electrolytes intravenously and an antihypertensive to lower blood pressure. The drug of choice is a vasodilator (a drug that widens blood vessels) called hydralazine (Apresoline), which lowers blood pressure without affecting the fetus. Usually it is given when the diastolic pressure is higher than 110 mmHg. The greatest danger is seizures. While no one knows exactly why they occur, medical scientists theorize that decreased blood flow to the brain may cause this dangerous problem.

Traditionally an anticonvulsant, usually magnesium sulfate, has been used to slow down the central nervous system and prevent seizures. Occasionally, obstetricians also prescribe a sedative for anxiety. Some perinatal centers are using dilantin, a drug with potentially fewer side effects than magnesium sulfate.

Delivery is the definitive treatment. If the woman is near the end of pregnancy, labor usually is induced. If she is not near term, she'll receive medicine to lower her blood pressure. If her readings don't improve within twenty-four hours, delivery generally is necessary. Continuing the pregnancy jeopardizes the mother's well-being and her baby's life. During delivery, magnesium sulfate is given intravenously to prevent seizures.

Eclampsia

Eclampsia is the occurrence of convulsions or coma in women with preeclampsia. The ancient Egyptians and Chinese warned of its dangers, and throughout history, obstetricians have struggled against

"I always thought that the only people who got preeclampsia were malnourished teenagers. I had been so proud of myself for doing everything right. I couldn't believe it was happening to me."

this life-threatening problem. In recent years, we've become increasingly successful in preventing eclampsia, and cases of full-blown eclampsia are rare.

Are you at risk? The chances of developing eclampsia are greater:
- in first pregnancies
- in very young women and those over 35
- in poor women who do not receive prenatal care
- in women whose sisters or mothers had eclampsia
- in women who developed severe preeclampsia or eclampsia before 35 weeks in a previous pregnancy

Early eclampsia in one pregnancy also increases the likelihood of growth retardation in subsequent pregnancies

What to watch for. Prenatal care and treatment of preeclampsia can prevent many cases of eclampsia. Prompt treatment is critical. Eclampsia begins gradually, starting with rapid weight gain and ending with generalized seizures or coma. Its early warning signs are:
- weight gain of more than two pounds a week in the last trimester
- a rise in blood pressure higher than 30 mmHg systolic or 15 mmHg diastolic
- high amounts of protein in urine
- headache
- visual disturbances
- stomach pain

Medical treatments. Eclamptic convulsions are a life-threatening emergency and require immediate care. To control the seizures, obstetricians administer magnesium sulfate, an anticonvulsant, intravenously. Hydralazine, an antihypertensive, is used to lower blood pressure. Once the woman's condition is stabilized and if she is past thirty-two weeks, obstetricians generally induce labor or perform a cesarean section. Continuing the pregnancy increases the risks of fetal growth retardation, placental separation, and fetal distress during labor.

Growth retardation is the most common problem in babies whose mothers develop eclampsia. They also have a higher incidence of blood abnormalities. However, follow-up studies have shown that most infants born small for gestational age because their mothers had eclampsia caught up in growth within two years.

GESTATIONAL DIABETES

Because of the unusual metabolic demands of pregnancy, a woman's risk of developing diabetes is higher while she's pregnant. About 3 percent of pregnant women develop gestational diabetes.

What happens during pregnancy. Pregnancy normally produces various hormones, including human placental lactogen, a hormone produced by the placenta, cortisol, estrogens, progesterones, and prolactin. One not-fully-understood effect of these hormones is to modulate the action of insulin, the hormone that maintains normal blood-sugar levels. As pregnancy progresses, the pancreas has to work harder to manufacture a sufficient amount of insulin. If it cannot meet this challenge, the result is gestational diabetes.

Are you at risk? You are more likely to develop gestational diabetes if you:
- have a family history of diabetes
- have had glycosuria (sugar in your urine) or a positive glucose tolerance test in the past
- had a baby who was large for gestational age (over 4,500 grams or 10 pounds at birth) or an infant who died within a month of delivery
- had a previous stillborn or malformed baby
- are overweight (more than 120 percent of your ideal weight)
- are over age 35
- have an excessive amount of amniotic fluid (hydramnios)
- have recurrent urinary tract or kidney infections
- have a history of hypertensive disorders of pregnancy

About half of the women who develop gestational diabetes do not have any risk factors. That is why most doctors routinely screen all pregnant women for gestational diabetes between the twenty-fourth and twenty-eighth week of pregnancy. If your risk seems greater than usual, your physician may suggest earlier or more frequent testing.

Diagnosis. The standard screening test for gestational diabetes consists of drinking a glucose solution followed, one hour later, by a blood sample. Normally, blood-sugar levels fall lower than 140 milligrams/deciliter (mg/dl). If they don't, a woman undergoes a more precise glucose tolerance test.

In this test, fasting blood-sugar levels are measured every hour for three hours after ingestion of a glucose solution. About 15 to 25

"My grandmother had diabetes. I thought only old people were diabetic. When my doctor told me I might have gestational diabetes, I thought it was a joke. I learned pretty quickly that it wasn't."

percent of the pregnant women who undergo a glucose tolerance test have gestational diabetes. The test is performed at twenty-six to twenty-eight weeks or earlier, if the mother is at high risk of gestational diabetes because of previous disease, obesity, or glycosuria.

Possible effects on the mother. A woman who develops gestational diabetes is more likely to develop other complications of pregnancy, including:

- pregnancy-induced hypertension
- anemia, because of changes in the blood vessels and poor nutrition
- infection of the vagina and urinary tract because of high sugar levels in the urine
- hydramnios, or excess amniotic fluid, a condition that increases the risk of premature rupture of the membranes

Possible risks to the baby. The greatest danger for the unborn baby is that gestational diabetes is not recognized or treated. The risk of fetal losses is high in diabetic women who do not receive adequate prenatal care or have good blood-sugar control.

Women with diabetes and gestational diabetes are more likely to have very big babies because they produce excess amounts of sugar and glucose. This condition, called macrosomia, makes babies more vulnerable, particularly late in pregnancy and during delivery. Although many people think of big babies as healthy babies, macrosomia often indicates excessively high body fat and blood-sugar levels and an immature pancreas—which can mean greater difficulty after birth. Tight blood-sugar control before thirty-two weeks of gestation may prevent or control excess growth in diabetics' babies.

The babies of women with gestational diabetes may be susceptible to various temporary problems after birth. If delivered early, they may require intensive care. About 15 to 50 percent have very low blood-sugar levels and need glucose. If they can suck and are in fairly good condition, they receive an oral solution. If they are weak, floppy, or premature, they may require intravenous glucose. Some have high bilirubin levels and develop jaundice, a not-uncommon problem simply treated by exposure to bright lights.

What to watch for. Women with gestational diabetes should be on the alert for the symptoms of hypoglycemia (low blood-sugar levels) and hyperglycemia (high blood-sugar levels). Blood-sugar levels can drop from too much insulin, too little food, or increased activity without increased food. The signals of hypoglycemia, which can develop suddenly, are:

- nervousness
- shakiness
- weakness
- hunger
- perspiration
- cool, clammy skin
- pallor
- blurred or double vision
- headache
- disorientation
- shallow breathing
- irritability

If untreated, these could lead to convulsions and coma.

Hyperglycemia, or excessive sugar in your blood, occurs with too little insulin, too much food (especially carbohydrates), infection, or stress. This condition may develop over several days. Warning signals include:

- dry mouth
- increased appetite
- increased thirst and urination
- tiredness
- nausea
- hot, flushed skin
- abdominal cramps
- rapid, deep breathing
- acetone breath
- paralysis
- headache
- drowsiness

If untreated, hyperglycemia can progress to stupor and coma.

What to expect. As with chronic diabetes, the secret to a successful pregnancy and healthy baby is good control of your blood-sugar levels. Most women with gestational diabetes can accomplish this simply by regulating what and when they eat; about 15 percent require insulin therapy.

You usually will be examined at least once every two weeks during your first thirty-six weeks and weekly thereafter. Your doctor will evaluate your fasting blood-sugar levels at every visit. If they are normal, no medical therapy is necessary. If they are too high, you may need insulin.

Close monitoring of your baby's condition may begin at about twenty-eight weeks, possibly with a nonstress test every week and then twice a week starting at thirty-four weeks. If a nonstress test is nonreactive, you'll probably undergo a contraction stress test. At twenty-eight weeks, you can start monitoring fetal movements on your own. Repeated ultrasounds monitor fetal growth.

What you can do.

- Check blood-sugar levels several times a day with a reflectance meter. You prick your finger (use the sides, not the more sensitive tip) and smear a drop of blood on a specially prepared test tape. The color changes in the strip indicate the amount of sugar in your blood, and the reflectance meter translates the color reaction into a digital readout of your blood-sugar level. Your goal should be a pre-meal blood-sugar level of 60–100 mg/dl.

- Pay close attention to your diet. Ideally, you should work with a nutritionist so you can vary and plan meals that suit your life-style and food preferences. Your total intake should be about sixteen calories per pound of body weight each day.
- Rather than eating three big meals, have six small ones to prevent a sudden drop in blood-sugar levels. A bedtime snack is important to avoid low blood sugar during the night.
- Try to schedule your meals for approximately the same time every day.
- If you were exercising before developing gestational diabetes, you should be able to continue, but be sure to check with your doctor. Your blood-sugar levels should be well controlled before you launch a strenuous regimen.
- When exercising, schedule workouts for after a meal, not when blood sugar may be low. Carry Life Savers or another hard candy with you when exercising, and eat after prolonged exercise.

Medical treatments. Some physicians admit women with gestational diabetes to the hospital for several days so they can learn about managing their condition. Others do so only if blood-sugar levels are very high and insulin seems necessary.

In your last month, your doctor's primary concern will be deciding when it may be healthier for your baby to be in the world than in your womb. Amniocentesis can show whether a baby's lungs are mature. If they are, labor may be induced, particularly if fetal fitness tests indicate that the baby may be in jeopardy. During labor, you may be given a continuous infusion of insulin and glucose to avoid very high blood-sugar levels in your body and very low blood-sugar levels in your baby. Most obstetricians encourage breastfeeding for both the mother's and the baby's sake.

Women with gestational diabetes are more likely to become diabetic later in life and should undergo periodic screening tests.

KIDNEY INFECTIONS

With prompt diagnosis and treatment, most kidney infections do not present a grave threat to a mother or her baby. However, if they are not corrected, they can have serious consequences.

What happens during pregnancy. The kidney's basic function is to remove the waste products of metabolism from the bloodstream and maintain a proper balance of water, salts, acids, and bases. Within each kidney are about a million tubular structures called nephrons. In each of them is a ball of small blood vessels called a glomerulus, which filters blood. As the blood passes through the glomerulus, blood cells and large molecules, such as proteins, are retained, while smaller impurities become urine, which passes through the ureter into the urinary bladder. During pregnancy, the flow of fluids slows, and the levels of sugar in urine can increase.

Urinary Tract Infections

The most common problem is called asymptomatic bacteriuria, in which a culture shows bacteria but the woman does not have any symptoms. All pregnant women are routinely screened for asymptomatic bacteriuria at their first prenatal visit. Left untreated, this problem can and usually does develop into a symptomatic infection.

Approximately 15 percent of women with one asymptomatic infection will develop another. Because of the danger that the infection will spread later in pregnancy, prompt treatment with oral sulfonamides early in pregnancy or ampicillin and nitrofurantoin later in pregnancy is necessary.

Cystitis is a symptomatic infection of the lower urinary tract, characterized by increased frequency and urgency in urination, low-grade fever, and blood in the urine. Treatment is the same as for asymptomatic bacteriuria. If not treated, infection can spread to the kidneys and develop into pyelonephritis.

Pyelonephritis

Pyelonephritis, a serious bacterial infection that spreads from the bladder or through the blood vessels and lymphatic system to the kidneys, occurs in 1 to 2 percent of all pregnancies. It can increase the risk of growth retardation and preterm labor. Symptoms include fever, chills, aching pain in the back, loss of appetite, nausea, vomiting, and an abnormally high or low temperature.

An acute case will require hospitalization and intravenous antibiotics. Most women improve rapidly but must continue on antibiotics for ten days and on low-dose antibiotics throughout pregnancy. Prophylactic antibiotics throughout pregnancy are usually necessary to prevent recurrence.

"I FELT LIKE A FAILURE"

Roberta's job is saving babies. As a neonatologist, she spends her days—and many of her nights—fighting for the lives of the smallest, sickest babies. When she became pregnant, she was excited about having a baby of her own—and nervous about all that she knew could go wrong.

"I had amniocentesis because I was thirty-four," she recalls. "What amazed me most was how attached I was and how difficult it would have been to lose the baby." The results were reassuring: she was carrying a healthy, normal boy.

But within a few weeks Roberta had new reason to worry: A sonogram indicated that her baby wasn't growing normally. "Intellectually, I reacted like a neonatologist," she says. "I knew that usually there isn't a higher rate of mental retardation or cerebral palsy in growth-impaired babies, but emotionally I was a wreck."

Like a small percentage of first-time mothers, Roberta began to show the classic signs of a complex and potentially life-threatening problem called preeclampsia: rising blood pressure and traces of protein in her urine (a signal of declining kidney function). Sent home on bedrest in her thirty-fourth week, she discovered that just lying down can be terribly hard to do, but this doctor did everything her doctors ordered.

However, Roberta's blood pressure and the protein levels in her urine kept rising. She soon went back to the hospital—this time as a patient. "I remember that I wasn't feeling well. I went into the bathroom, and I started to bleed. My first reaction was to try to clean it up."

Roberta's obstetrician discovered that the placenta had separated from the wall of her uterus and that her preeclampsia was worsening. Her condition was critical. She was vomiting. Her blood platelets were falling. Her kidneys and liver were shutting down, and the pain in her abdomen was intense.

Administering a spinal anesthetic, the obstetrical team worked quickly to perform an emergency cesarean and deliver the baby. Born almost six weeks early, Joshua weighed a little over four pounds. Roberta, foggy from medications, her blood pressure still perilously high, got only a brief glimpse of him as he was whisked away. "I could see his little chest caving in with each breath. I wanted more than anything to go over and help him, but I couldn't move. Yet I felt this enormous relief because I had complete trust in my colleagues, who were doing everything they could for him."

At first Roberta and her baby fought separate battles. "I was too sick to go to him, and he was too sick to be brought to me. But someone had taken a Polaroid right after Joshua's birth. It was wonderful. I was only awake for five minutes of every hour, but I'd look at the Polaroid and feel this wonderful connection though I had never held him."

Even after she was out of danger, Roberta had such splitting headaches—a common complication of spinal anesthesia—that she couldn't sit up. "I needed to see my baby, so they wheeled me to the nursery on a stretcher with an IV pole attached. I lay next to his isolette and reached in and touched him."

Yet like many mothers whose babies develop problems after birth, Roberta felt profoundly guilty. "I felt like a failure. I wanted to have another baby right away just so I could do it right. I apologized to my son for having had to force him out on his own so early. And the first time I held him, when he was still on the respirator, he turned a little blue, which was scary—even for me."

After three days, Joshua was off the respirator, and Roberta was elated. "It was funny, but I felt all the things other mothers have told me about when I was taking care of their babies. I thought that the doctors and nurses knew him better than I did, and I was jealous. They would talk about how he moved around a lot, and I'd think, I should be the one noticing that. And I couldn't wait to undress him and see what he looked like."

Mother and son recovered rapidly, and ten days after the birth, both were ready to go home. "I felt a tremendous panic about taking him home and taking care of him myself," says Roberta. "And this is what I do for a living! He weighed four pounds, twelve ounces, and we dressed him in Cabbage Patch doll clothes. Once we got home, the more time I had with him, the more comfortable I felt."

Yet, like many parents of high-risk infants, Roberta kept worrying long after she brought her son home. "The more time passed and I could see how normal he was, the more reassured I felt. I think when you've had a high-risk baby, you never get over the feeling that, since something did go wrong once, it could happen again. Maybe that's what makes these children so precious."

INFECTIONS

An infection that you may scarcely have noticed before pregnancy can become a far more serious danger when you're expecting. Common microbes that may cause no more than a few days of misery for an adult can have devastating effects on an unborn child. They can interfere with fetal development and produce birth defects, increase the risk of miscarriage and preterm birth, and lead to complications after delivery.

The infections most likely to cause serious harm to a developing baby belong to the "TORCH" group: toxoplasmosis, rubella, cytomegalovirus, and herpes virus type 2. (Some say the *O* in TORCH stands for other infections). The babies of women who contract these infections in their first twelve weeks of pregnancy have a greater risk of developmental abnormalities.

Toxoplasmosis

The toxoplasmosis protozoa, primarily carried by cats, can harm an unborn baby if a pregnant woman unwittingly acquires the disease and passes it on to her fetus. About 20 to 30 percent of American women have been exposed to toxoplasmosis, which also can be found in soil and in raw or poorly cooked meat. Infection in pregnancy is fairly uncommon, and about .6 to 6 babies per 1,000 show signs of exposure. About a third of women infected during pregnancy pass on the virus to their unborn children.

Possible effects on the mother. Ninety percent of women experience no symptoms. Extreme cases produce flulike symptoms, such as achiness, sore throat, and malaise. Diagnosis can be made by blood testing. Treatment with sulfadizine or pyrimethamine can reduce the risk of fetal infection by approximately 50 percent.

Possible risks to the baby. The earlier in pregnancy that infection occurs, the more severe the damage to the fetus is. The high-risk period for serious birth defects is between gestational weeks ten and twenty-four. About one-fourth of women infected at this time will pass toxoplasmosis on to their offspring, and one-half of the infants will suffer severe effects. Infection in the third trimester is passed on in two-thirds of the cases, but most babies are normal at birth. However, some investigators have found neurologic or vision problems in eight-year-olds who had been infected with toxoplasmosis late in their mother's pregnancy.

Toxoplasmosis has been linked to increased danger of miscarriage, prematurity, stillbirths, neonatal deaths, and congenital anomalies as well as eye infections. Severe infection could lead to convulsions, coma, microcephaly (small brain), and hydrocephalus. Infants may die soon after birth; survivors may be blind, deaf, and severely retarded.

What you can do. To prevent toxoplasmosis infection:
- Eat only well-cooked meat (especially pork, beef, and lamb).
- Thoroughly scrub hands, utensils, and kitchen surfaces after contact with raw meat.
- Wash fruits and vegetables, especially if they come from a home garden.
- If you have a cat, don't change its litter box yourself. Have someone else change the litter often because it takes about forty-eight hours for cat feces to become infectious. The box can be disinfected by treatment with nearly boiling water for five minutes.
- Wear gloves when gardening, and avoid working in soil where cats frequently defecate.

Rubella (German measles)

Usually a mild illness in adults and children, rubella can have a devastating effect on a fetus. If you haven't had rubella, vaccination provides complete protection but it is not recommended during pregnancy. A prepregnancy exam is the ideal time to screen for rubella and, if necessary, schedule a vaccination. Couples are advised not to conceive for three months afterward. Women who have had rubella prior to conception are not at risk.

Risks to the baby. If infection occurs in the first four weeks of pregnancy, half of the embryos will die or suffer severe defects. In the second month, 25 percent are severely affected; in the third month, 15 percent. In the second trimester, the most common fetal effect is permanent hearing impairment. Other problems linked with rubella are congenital heart disease, growth retardation, cataracts, mental retardation, cerebral palsy, diabetes, sudden hearing loss, glaucoma, and encephalitis (inflammation of the brain).

Cytomegalovirus (CMV)

The most common perinatal virus, CMV has infected most people in the United States, and antibodies have been found in 40 to 100 percent of the adult population. CMV is spread by intimate contact

"You always hate finding out something is wrong with you, but when you're pregnant, you flip out. You don't know who to worry about more: you or the baby."

with infected bodily fluids, such as breast milk, cervical mucus, semen, saliva, and urine. In adults it rarely causes symptoms. The risk of getting an infection for the first time while pregnant is very low—about 1 percent—and the odds of the fetus becoming infected are 30 to 40 percent.

Possible risks to the baby. About 10 to 15 percent of infants born to women who first contract CMV in pregnancy suffer growth retardation, small head, deafness, blindness, mental retardation, jaundice, and other disorders. Blood, brain, and liver are most susceptible, but all major organs are at risk. About 20 percent of infected babies die. It isn't clear whether damage is greatest if infection occurs early in pregnancy.

A mother can transmit CMV to her infant in utero and after delivery. An estimated .2 to 2.2 percent of newborns are infected; one in every five thousand to twenty thousand suffers a severe complication.

What to expect. CMV is difficult to diagnose or treat. There is no test that predicts whether a mother will pass the virus to her baby. The CDC recommends routine screening for women in "high-exposure" areas, such as child-care providers in daycare centers, nurses, and physicians. However, the extent of their risk is unknown. Furthermore, testing is not readily available and risk is difficult to assess on the basis of a single test.

What you can do. To prevent CMV, the best advice is rigorous personal hygiene, especially frequent handwashing in any setting in which you may be in repeated close contact with infants and children. If possible, avoid working in high-risk settings.

Herpes Genitalis Type 2

About 1 percent of all women have herpes virus in the cervix, and one in every seventy-five hundred infants is infected during the birth. Unlike other infections, herpes is most dangerous at delivery—but only if the baby comes in contact with active lesions in the vagina.

Possible risks to the baby. In the first trimester, an infection carries a 20 to 50 percent risk of miscarriage or stillbirth. After twenty weeks, there is increased chance of preterm labor. Infections during delivery can have devastating consequences, including central nervous system disease and a mortality rate of 50 percent. The babies who survive often develop neurologic or vision problems.

About 54 percent of babies born vaginally when a women is ac-tively infected develop some form of infection. About 70 percent of babies infected at birth will die if untreated, while 83 percent of survivors will have permanent brain damage.

What to expect. In the past, obstetricians tested all women with herpes weekly from the thirty-sixth week to delivery. Now only women with lesions or symptoms are tested. If women are free of active infection, they can deliver vaginally. A cesarean is performed if there are lesions. Even in this case, breastfeeding is permitted, as long as the mother practices careful handwashing and keeps her baby away from any lesions on her body.

Recent studies have shown that the risk of infection for a baby whose mother first acquired herpes prior to pregnancy is low (less than 8 percent in one study of thirty-four women with active infec-tion at the time of delivery), possibly because the mother passes antibodies to the infant. By contrast, half of babies whose mothers acquire herpes during pregnancy show signs of infection, yet most do not develop any symptoms.

Increasingly, physicians are not routinely screening all women with a history of herpes and perform a cesarean only if the mother has vaginal lesions when she goes into labor. However, babies of all mother with herpes are observed carefully after birth. At first in-fected babies may show no symptoms, but after two to twelve days they may feed poorly and develop fever or loss of body temperature, jaundice, and seizures.

Varicella-Zoster Virus (Chicken pox)

The virus that causes chicken pox and shingles—the second most reported infectious agent in the United States after gonorrhea—also can cause birth defects. About 5 to 15 percent of American women of childbearing age are susceptible to infection. Varicella affects .7 in one thousand pregnancies and infects 30 to 40 percent of infants born to mothers with active disease. The risk of congenital malfor-mations is small, although no one knows an exact percentage.

If a mother develops chicken pox around the time of delivery, her infant may develop a rash one to two weeks after she first developed sores. Chicken pox is life-threatening for newborns, particularly if the mother becomes ill between the fourth day before birth and the second day after. If infection occurs at least a week before delivery, the fetus will share the mother's antibodies. If delivery occurs within five days of infection, the baby will not have the benefit of the moth-er's immune response.

If a woman becomes infected before her sixteenth week, her baby may suffer several malformations, including limb reduction, growth retardation, cataracts, chorioretinitis (eye infection), and small head size. Ultrasound can detect most of the major anomalies.

If a women who may be susceptible is exposed to chicken pox in her first or second trimester, she may be given a solution of immunoglobin and protective antibodies. However, there is no evidence that such injections will prevent fetal infection or its complications. In fact, some doctors feel that immunoglobin does more for the mother by preventing complications than it does for the fetus. It is given to newborns whose mothers developed chicken pox within five days before or forty-eight hours after delivery.

Chlamydia

This bacterial infection is the most widespread sexually transmitted disease in Western society. Of all pregnant women with inflamed cervices, 30 to 60 percent have chlamydia. The highest risk group are poor, nonwhite, unmarried, and between eighteen and twenty-four years of age.

Chlamydia has been implicated in a host of pregnancy problems, including preterm labor, premature rupture of the membranes, and postpartum endometritis (inflammation of the lining of the uterus). If infected at delivery, a baby can develop conjunctivitis (an eye disease) or pneumonia. Every year in the United States an estimated seventy-five thousand newborns develop conjunctivitis and thirty thousand develop pneumonia because of chlamydia. The risk to the infant of an infected mother is 60 to 70 percent of acquiring the disease, with a 10 to 20 percent risk of pneumonia and 25 to 55 percent of conjunctivitis.

Rapid, inexpensive tests for chlamydia have become available throughout the country, and many obstetricians routinely screen all pregnant women. The CDC's recommendation for treatment in pregnancy is erythromycin base or stearate. Tetracycline is not used in pregnancy because it can discolor fetal teeth.

Syphilis

Because of screening, the incidence of the devastating defects associated with congenital syphilis has fallen dramatically. The number of infant deaths from syphilis has fallen 99 percent since the 1940s. Poor women who have little if any prenatal care or immigrants from countries with widespread syphilis are at greatest risk. Treatment consists of penicillin for the mother, which eliminates the risk of second-trimester miscarriage, stillbirth, and a congenital infection in the baby. Babies with congenital syphilis suffer liver and spleen abnormalities, rhinitis (stuffy nose), or pemphigus (skin lesions).

Gonorrhea

Prepregnancy or prenatal screening picks up almost all cases. Nonpregnant women are treated with tetracycline, pregnant women with penicillin or spectinomycin. Routine preventive treatment for gonorrhea at delivery prevents eye problems in newborns.

Condlyoma (Genital warts)

A woman with condlyoma or genital warts can transmit the human papilloma virus to her baby at delivery, creating a risk of laryngeal papillomas, growths that develop when a baby reaches ten years of age. About 1.5 percent of women are infected with HPV, putting about forty-five thousand infants at risk each year.

Hepatitis B

Hepatitis B virus is carried by two hundred million men and women around the world. In the United States, two hundred thousand new cases occur each year. Worldwide, mother-to-child transmission is a major route of spread. The women at highest risk:

- are of Asian, Pacific Island, or Alaskan-Eskimo descent, whether immigrant or U.S.-born
- come from Haiti or subsaharan Africa
- have acute or chronic liver disease
- work or receive treatment in a dialysis unit
- work or reside in institutions for the retarded
- have been rejected as blood donors
- have received repeated blood transfusions
- have frequent occupational exposure to blood in medical or dental settings
- live in the same household as a carrier or a dialysis patient
- have had multiple episodes of venereal disease
- use drugs injected through the skin

If a pregnant woman tests positive for hepatitis B, her infant will be given immunoglobin within twelve hours of birth and the hepatitis B vaccine within seven days, with repeat immunizations at one and six months.

Hepatitis B usually does not affect the course of pregnancy. The babies of infected women do not have a higher rate of birth defects. However, infected newborns have an 80 to 90 percent risk of becoming carriers, which means a one-in-four risk of dying of liver-related disease. An infant born to a mother with hepatitis can be treated with hepatitis B immunoglobin within twelve hours of birth, followed by vaccinations during its first six months.

FIFTH DISEASE

First described 100 years ago, fifth disease (or *erythema infectiosum*) is a common viral infection caused by the human parvovirus B19. This highly contagious illness usually strikes between the ages of 5 and 14. About half of all adults in the United States have been infected.

Spread by respiratory secretions from coughing and sneezing, fifth disease causes no symptoms in about a quarter of infected children and adults. Others develop mild flulike symptoms, including fever, headache, sore throat, achiness, runny nose, cough, congestion, nausea, and diarrhea, generally beginning from 4 to 20 days after exposure. The last symptom to appear is a red "slapped cheek" rash on the face, which may be followed by a lacelike red rash on other parts of the body. Adults often develop temporary joint pains or arthritis.

About half of all pregnant women have lifelong immunity to fifth disease and are at no risk during pregnancy. If a pregnant woman with no prior infection works in a setting such as a school or daycare center where the disease is widespread, she has a 30 percent chance of infection. If a child in her own home has fifth disease—with the diagnosis confirmed by a physician—she has a 50 percent chance of becoming infected.

Ninety percent of women infected during pregnancy develop no problems. Ten percent may miscarry. Overall, the risk of miscarriage for a pregnant woman who does not know whether she's had fifth disease and who is exposed in a school setting is 1.5 percent. If she's exposed to a child with the disease at home, the upper limit of risk is 2.5 percent.

Obstetricians can perform blood tests, available from state and federal health agencies, to confirm possible fifth disease infection and use ultrasound to "follow" the development of a fetus in an infected mother. No specific treatment or vaccine is available. A woman who feels she may be at risk because of her work setting should consult her caregivers.

HIV INFECTION

HIV (human immunodeficiency virus), which causes AIDS, can be passed from a mother to her child in utero or at delivery. In at least one case involving a woman who received AIDS-contaminated blood in a transfusion after delivery, the virus was transmitted via breast milk. The risk of passing the infection on to an infant is about 40 percent. Less than half of babies born to women with AIDS have acquired the disease. Some states require testing of all pregnant women for AIDS exposure. Sometimes pregnancy exacerbates the disease in the mother, and her health status deteriorates.

If infected, babies may develop neonatal AIDS. Its symptoms include failure to thrive, blood and spleen problems, pneumonia, recurrent infections, and neurologic abnormalities. Infection can occur early in development and create specific facial characteristics. Active AIDS usually kills its smallest victims within a year or two. Some children who test positive for the AIDS virus have lived for eight years or longer without developing the disease.

ACCIDENTS

Accidents and injuries complicate about 6 to 7 percent of pregnancies. In early pregnancy, physiological changes may increase the risk of fatigue and fainting spells, which can make injuries more likely. Later, balance and coordination may become more difficult, increasing the chance of a fall. Usually the fetus is well protected by the abdominal and uterine muscles and the amniotic fluid. The greatest danger comes from trauma: a car accident, knife and gunshot wounds, or bleeding so severe as to lead to shock.

In addition to treating the mother, obstetricians work to assure that the fetus receives a continuous supply of oxygen. Prompt treatment is critical. Depending on the nature and severity of the injuries, surgery may be necessary. In addition to the direct risks, surgery can increase the danger of preterm labor or separation of the placenta.

The best approach to accidents at any time is prevention. Always wear your seat belt when driving or riding in a car. As your center of gravity changes, take extra care as you sit, stand, or climb.

CHAPTER 10

Complications of Pregnancy

"I saw myself having my baby on a beach, surrounded by people I love. I thought I was an earth mother. I was twenty-five, young, healthy. I didn't think anything could go wrong–until it did."

Even though it is a natural phenomenon, pregnancy is such a complex biological, physiological, and psychological experience that complications can and often do occur. Many require nothing more than increased monitoring. However, some are emergencies that endanger a mother and her unborn child. One of the major missions of high-risk pregnancy care is recognizing the potential for such problems and acting fast to prevent harm to a woman and her unborn baby.

MULTIPLES

After the surprise of discovering that you'll be seeing double–or more–at delivery, you may balk at the label "high risk." However overjoyed or overwhelmed you may be, chances are you feel perfectly fine. After all, you may argue, a multiple-baby pregnancy should be just like a single-baby one–only more so. However, the "more so" also applies to risks.

The risks are lower now than they were in the past, in part because mothers and doctors have advance warning. Once, more than half of multiples were surprise arrivals. Today almost all are identified early in pregnancy–by routine ultrasound, by high levels of alpha fetoprotein, or by detection of more than one heartbeat.

In fact, ultrasound has become so advanced that obstetricians have observed an unexpected phenomenon: a much higher incidence of twins very early in pregnancy (before ten to fourteen weeks) than anyone had suspected. For unknown reasons, a "vanishing twin" disappears in early pregnancy, probably reabsorbed into the mother's body. Usually the remaining fetus develops normally.

Twins can be either identical or fraternal. The differences start at conception. Identical or "monozygotic" twins, genetic carbon copies of each other, develop when a single egg, fertilized by a single sperm, divides in two. Fraternal or "dizygotic" twins form when a woman releases two separate eggs, which are fertilized by two different sperm. These twins are no more genetically similar than any other siblings.

Identical twins are an accident of nature. They occur in about four of every one thousand births among women in every country, regardless of heredity, age, or race. In contrast, a host of factors influences the incidence of fraternal twins, which ranges from four to fifty per one thousand births in different countries.

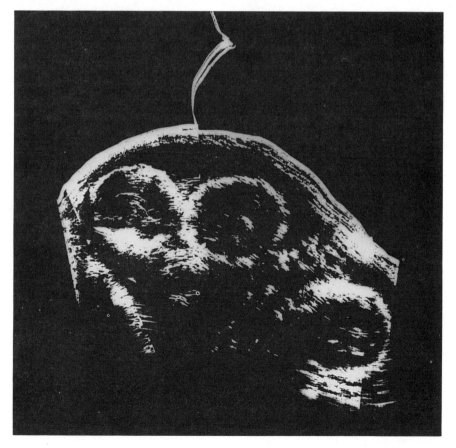

Triplets, like these shown on a sonogram, occur in one of every 6,400 pregnancies.

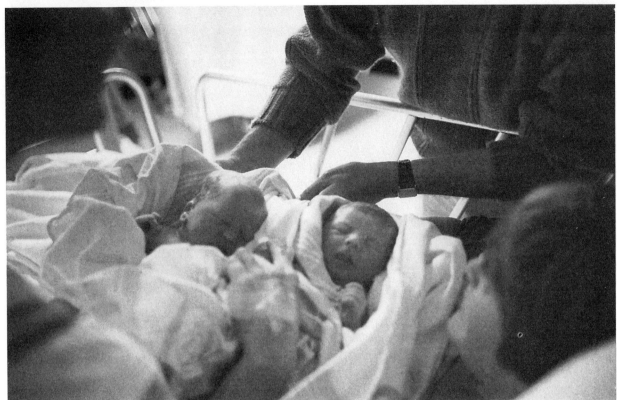

George Fry

Twins develop in one of every 80 pregnancies

The Baby-Baby Boom

Throughout the last decade, the number of babies arriving in pairs, trios, and larger groups has soared. Twins, who develop in one of every eighty pregnancies, account for 97.8 percent of multiple births. Triplets occur in one of every six thousand four hundred pregnancies; quadruplets, in one of every five hundred twelve thousand. Although they make the most headlines, quintuplets and sextuplets are the rarest multiples.

The recent rise in plural births in this country is no accident. If American women really wanted to increase their odds of having more than one baby at a time, they couldn't be doing a better job. Among the reasons more parents are finding themselves doubly—or triply—blessed are:

Delayed pregnancy. The prime age for women to conceive fraternal twins is the thirties, with twin rates peaking in thirty-five- to thirty-nine-year-olds. No one knows exactly why, although some speculate that, as women near the end of their reproductive years, they ovulate erratically and sometimes release more than one egg per menstrual cycle. Once past age forty, a woman's fertility declines dramatically, and she's much less likely to conceive multiples.

The pill. Women who've used oral contraceptives for at least six months seem more likely to conceive multiples after they stop. Some women experience a hormonal surge after going off the pill that stimulates the release of more than one egg. In large-scale studies in the 1970s, women who conceived in the first cycle after going off the pill were almost twice as likely to have twins as non-pill users.

Fertility drugs. Among the most common treatments for women who do not ovulate regularly are Clomid (clomiphene), which uses the body's own hormones to stimulate the pituitary gland to direct the ovaries to produce eggs, and Pergonal, which stimulates the ovaries themselves. Since more than one egg usually is released after treatment, more than one may be fertilized. About 7 or 8 percent of women taking Clomid conceive twins. With Pergonal, a much stronger stimulant, the multiple-birth rate can be as high as 20 percent. In the past, a small but significant minority of women taking Pergonal conceived four, five, or even more babies. Now fertility specialists carefully monitor doses and the number of eggs released to reduce the likelihood of mega-multiples.

In-vitro fertilization (IVF) and gamete intra-fallopian transfer (GIFT). Women undergoing either of these treatments generally take a fertility drug first. In IVF, several eggs are then removed from a woman's ovaries, fertilized in a laboratory, and, after a few days of development, inserted into her uterus. In GIFT, several eggs, removed from the ovaries, are placed in the fallopian tubes along with sperm so fertilization can occur within the woman's own body.

Both procedures use several eggs to increase the odds that one will "take" and result in a normal pregnancy. Sometimes these treatments are more successful than anyone had hoped. The result: a multiple-birth rate of 20 to 25 percent.

Race. Black women are most likely to have twins; Oriental women, least likely. Nigeria, where twins occur in one of every forty-five pregnancies, reports more double births than any other nation. China and Japan have the lowest incidence of twins: about four in every one thousand births. In the United States, a white woman's odds of conceiving twins are one in one hundred five; a black woman's, one in seventy-three.

Family history. Of all multiples, only fraternal twins run in families and only on the mother's side. In a study of Mormon family

"We were so happy to be having twins. It bothered me to think about them as a complication."

records, women who were twins gave birth to twins in 17.1 of every thousand pregnancies, compared to 11.6 per thousand for "singleton" mothers. Women with brothers or sisters who are twins also have more twins.

Previous pregnancies. The more often a woman has conceived, the greater her odds of having multiples. While mothers of identical twins are not more likely to have a second set, mothers of fraternal twins are.

For some multiples, the only explanation is just plain luck. But as long as women delay pregnancy, rely on oral contraceptives until they're ready to conceive, take fertility drugs, or undergo fertility procedures, more babies are sure to arrive in groups.

What happens during pregnancy. Multiples grow at the same rate as singletons for the first half of pregnancy; then their growth slows down. In a twin pregnancy, both babies gain as much as a single fetus in the last months of pregnancy. The average birth weight for 40 to 60 percent of twins is less than 5 1/2 pounds. In identical twins sharing a single amniotic sac, there is greater competition for nutrients, and one or both may have impaired growth.

Possible effects on the mother. The mothers of multiples literally have a heavier load to carry, and the normal discomforts of pregnancy can double—or triple. Typical complaints include severe morning sickness, shortness of breath or difficulty breathing, backaches, and itchy abdomens.

Miscarriages are twice as frequent among multiples, possibly because of genetic defects or poor placental implantation or development. There also is a greater risk of pregnancy-induced hypertension because of the oversize uterus and increased amounts of placental hormones and of third-trimester placental bleeding problems. Some obstetricians have reported that 20 to 30 percent of mothers carrying multiples develop blood-pressure problems in pregnancy.

Anemia is four times more likely when the maternal system is nurturing more than one fetus. The risk of gestational diabetes increases. An unusually large amount of amniotic fluid may fill the womb, leading to a condition called hydramnios. And a mother with multiples is much more likely to begin labor early.

Possible risks for the babies. From conception to birth, multiples lead more dangerous lives than "singletons," who have no competition for space or nutrition in their mothers' wombs. Although twins account for only .8 percent of babies, they represent

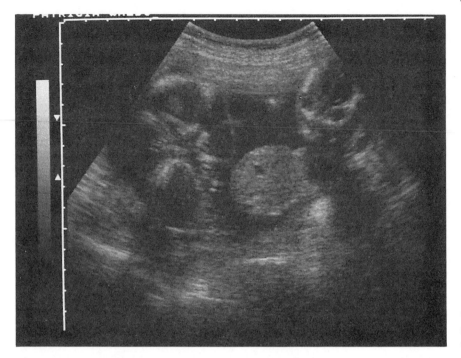

Triplets, like these shown on a sonogram, occur in one of every 6,400 pregnancies.

11 percent of neonatal deaths. Babies sharing a womb have a higher incidence of placenta previa, placental abruption, preeclampsia, cord accidents, and unusual presentations.

In about one of every one thousand cases of identical twins sharing a placenta and amniotic sac, one twin receives a much greater share of nutrients and develops much greater blood volume. This is called twin-twin transfusion. While the larger infant looks healthier, it is at greater risk because of its excess blood, low blood pressure, and tiny heart. This baby is at risk of heart failure and circulation disorders, which can prove fatal. The smaller, anemic twin must struggle with the difficulties of being small for its gestational age.

While birth defects are uncommon in all pregnancies, they are more likely in multiples. The incidence of major malformations is 2.12 percent in twins; minor malformations have an incidence of 4.13 percent. Some defects occur somewhat more often in identical twins: club foot, extra fingers or toes, heart abnormalities, and neural tube defects. The reason may be a delay in the splitting that takes place when identical twins form.

The greatest threats for all multiples are preterm birth and growth retardation. About 21.5 percent of multiples are born before thirty-five weeks of pregnancy; half of twins weigh less than twenty-five hundred grams (five pounds, eight ounces) at birth.

What you can do. A mother's health status—critical to every baby—becomes doubly or triply important if her body is serving as the lifeline to several growing babies. The better your overall health before pregnancy, the better you'll be able to cope with the greater demands of a multiple pregnancy.

• Good nutrition. You need to take in about three hundred more calories a day. Most caregivers recommend daily iron and folic acid supplements. Be sure to eat well and adequately. Most twin mothers put on about ten to twelve pounds more than singleton mothers.

• Morning sickness. Because you're getting a larger dose of pregnancy hormones, nausea and vomiting may persist past the first trimester. Try a diet of dry, nongreasy food. Rather than a few big meals, try frequent small snacks.

• If your blood pressure rises—a not-uncommon occurrence in multiple pregnancies—take frequent rest periods during the day.

• For back discomfort, try pelvic rocking (rock back and forth while on your hands and knees on the floor).

What to expect. Checkups are generally scheduled every other week through the first half of pregnancy and weekly thereafter. Expect close monitoring of your blood pressure and blood-sugar levels because you are at increased risk for gestational high blood pressure and diabetes. Prompt treatment can prevent further complications.

Because of the increased risk of preterm labor, you may have to restrict your activity and spend time "bedresting." Some researchers have documented beneficial effects from bedrest; others have questioned its value. Studies of twin mothers hospitalized on bedrest beginning as early as twenty-three to twenty-four weeks have shown a dramatic reduction in perinatal deaths. Many caregivers routinely advise a program of bedrest beginning in the twenty-sixth week.

Prevention is always the best approach to preterm labor. Be sure you know how to recognize early contractions. Chapter 11 provides detailed information on preventing preterm birth. The treatments are the same for multiple as well as single-baby pregnancies, but the risks and potential complications may be greater.

Regular ultrasound scans can improve the outcome of a multiple pregnancy by following the growth of each baby. Testing of fetal health usually begins at thirty to thirty-four weeks and may include a nonstress test (NST), fetal biophysical profile, and sometimes a contraction stress test. NSTs are done every three to seven days until delivery.

Delivery isn't necessarily more dangerous, and vaginal births are possible. However, if the babies are in unusual positions, if they are very premature or growth-retarded, or if there is a long delay after the emergence of the first baby, a cesarean will be performed. Approximately half of twins are delivered by cesarean, and mothers of multiples should learn more about C-sections before the end of their pregnancies.

A vaginal delivery is more likely when:
- pregnancy has lasted for more than 32 weeks
- each fetus weighs more than 2,000 grams
- the larger twin is closer to the cervix
- the closer twin is head-down or vertex
- the second twin is vertex and smaller
- there is no sign of fetal distress
- the first twin's head can pass through the birth canal

Usually one obstetrician and one neonatologist are available for every baby. If the babies are premature or small, they may require intensive care.

RH AND OTHER BLOOD INCOMPATIBILITIES

"Rh" refers to a group of substances in the blood first identified in rhesus monkeys. About 85 percent of whites, 95 percent of blacks, and 99 percent of Orientals carry one particular factor, Rh_D, and are called Rh positive. Those without this factor are Rh negative. If an Rh-negative woman carries an Rh-positive child and becomes "sensitized," her body produces protective antibodies. In a subsequent pregnancy, her antibodies will cross the placenta to attack and destroy her baby's red blood cells.

Twenty years ago thousands of babies died as a result of Rh incompatibility. Since then obstetricians have rewritten the book on Rh disease. Today they can prevent its occurrence in the vast majority of pregnancies. If it should develop, treatment is available—and highly successful.

Are you at risk? Rh disease is a risk only if:
- you are Rh negative.

and

- your partner is Rh positive. If the father of your child is also Rh negative, your baby will not have Rh factor in its blood and is not in danger.

and

- your unborn baby is Rh positive. If the father has both an Rh-negative and an Rh-positive gene, the odds of conceiving an Rh-

"In a sense, being high risk makes pregnancy more precious. It was much more stressful the first time I was pregnant, when I hadn't defined myself as high risk. But the second time I knew what I was getting into, and it was easier to make a commitment to the pregnancy."

negative baby are 50 percent. If both his genes are positive, the baby will be Rh positive.

What happens during pregnancy. In your first pregnancy with an Rh positive fetus, there is almost no danger because the blood of a mother and her baby rarely mix until pregnancy ends. Fewer than 2 percent of Rh-negative women become sensitized and produce antibodies against their baby's blood before delivery. However, there is a 10 to 15 percent chance that fetal blood cells will enter the mother's bloodstream and trigger production of Rh antibodies during abortion, miscarriage, or delivery. Because of individual variability, some women are not sensitized even if their blood mingles with a fairly large amount of the baby's, while others respond to even tiny amounts.

In a subsequent pregnancy with an Rh-positive baby, the mother's antibodies destroy the baby's red blood cells in a process called hemolysis. Producing more and more replacement cells, the baby becomes anemic because it can not maintain an adequate supply of blood. Lacking healthy blood cells, the baby's body may become swollen before or after birth; this condition is called hydrops. Pockets of fluid, called ascites, may form within its abdomen. Its heart, struggling to pump blood through its body, may be unable to function properly. The baby may die or suffer severe brain damage because of this combination of problems, called erythroblastosis fetalis.

Preventing problems. In 1968 medical scientists discovered that they could prevent Rh disease by injecting a substance called RhoGAM (or Gamulin or HypRho-D) that contains anti-Rh antibodies. The borrowed antibodies coat and destroy any foreign fetal cells in the mother's blood. Since the mother's body never manufactures any Rh antibodies, there is no threat of damage to any future children.

The key to success is timing: The mother must receive the injections at any time when fetal blood cells might enter her bloodstream. That means during amniocentesis or PUBS as well as after delivery. Because the mother's blood vessels and the placenta are so close to each other, separated only by a membrane, they can mingle through small breaks between the placenta and the uterus. RhoGAM is 98 to 99 percent effective in preventing production of Rh antibodies.

Most obstetricians advocate a two-stage approach: one injection of RhoGAM at twenty-eight weeks to prevent the 1 to 2 percent risk to all Rh-negative women and one after delivery in all Rh-negative women with Rh-positive babies, regardless of whether they show any signs of sensitization. This double protection reduces the number of women who become sensitized before delivery from 2 percent to fewer than .5 percent.

What to expect. A blood test at your prepregnancy or first prenatal visit can determine if you're Rh negative and, if so, whether you've been sensitized. If you have no antibodies to Rh, your blood will be checked periodically throughout pregnancy and you will be given RhoGAM if you undergo amniocentesis and later in pregnancy.

If you are sensitized, you will be monitored closely. In the first pregnancy after sensitization, your level of Rh antibodies may rise steadily, indicating greater danger. Once they reach a certain level, your doctor will perform an amniocentesis to sample the amniotic fluid for evidence of bilirubin, the yellowish pigment released in the destruction of red blood cells. The color and density of the fluid indicates the severity of Rh disease and the extent of red-blood-cell deficiency in your body. Another alternative is percutaneous umbilical blood sampling (PUBS), which allows doctors to obtain a blood sample for direct testing for anemia.

Medical treatments. If a baby appears to be in jeopardy, a transfusion of fresh blood cells into the womb can prevent complications and save its life. First performed in the mid-1960s, this once-revolutionary procedure has become more sophisticated and more effective. In the past there was a 5 to 10 percent risk of miscarriage during each transfusion, as well as risk of premature rupture of the membranes, preterm labor, infection, or puncture of a blood vessel.

Two major innovations have made intrauterine transfusions much easier: ultrasound's enhanced precision in guiding the obstetrician and the development of PUBS to infuse blood into the umbilical cord. About 80 to 90 percent of babies who require transfusions survive.

Transfusions must be repeated every few weeks to replace red blood cells destroyed by the mother's antibodies. As the pregnancy continues, regular testing assesses the baby's well-being and maturity. The obstetrician must carefully weigh the risks of continuing the pregnancy with those of an early delivery. Labor may be induced if the cervix has begun thinning and widening in preparation for delivery and the baby's lungs are mature. A vaginal delivery may be possible, unless labor becomes long and difficult. A cesarean may then be necessary because a baby with Rh disease cannot tolerate much stress.

If bilirubin has built up in the baby, immediate treatment is crucial. The baby may need a supply of fresh blood cells. If necessary, its blood, with its dangerous amounts of bilirubin, destructive Rh antibodies, and immature red cells, is drawn out and replaced with Rh-negative blood. A baby may require several such exchange transfusions in its first week.

ABO Incompatibility

This problem can develop if the mother has Type O blood and the father Type A or B. In 20 to 25 percent of pregnancies, the mother's blood contains antibodies to either A or B antigens in her baby's blood. Because this problem is so common, it accounts for 60 percent of the blood disorders in newborns. Fortunately its effects are usually not serious. Most often the baby experiences a mild to moderate elevation in bilirubin in the first twenty-four hours, which is treated with exposure to bright lights. Only about 1 percent of affected babies require an exchange transfusion.

Other Blood Incompatibilities

From 2 to 5 percent of blood disorders in newborns are the result of irregular maternal antibodies directed against unusual blood-group antigens. These "irregular antibodies" are found in about .5 percent of the general population. An antibody screen of the mother is performed before pregnancy or at the first prenatal visit. If the test is positive, the father is tested for the antigen.

If there is a potential problem, the obstetrician follows the pregnancy carefully. Depending on which antigen is involved, amniotic-fluid bilirubin studies may be performed. Only a few antigens are associated with moderate to severe blood disease in newborns. However, they have become as common and as serious a threat to affected mothers and babies as Rh incompatibility was before the invention of RhoGAM. The mothers and babies are monitored and tested just as they would be for Rh disease.

GROWTH RETARDATION

The smallest newborns face the biggest risks. Some babies are tiny at birth because of prematurity. Others fail to grow as they should within the womb. Growth retardation occurs in 3 to 7 percent of pregnancies, and these babies are eight times more likely to die before, during, or after birth. They also are more vulnerable to a host of serious problems after birth.

Infants born below the tenth percentile in weight for their gestational age are considered growth retarded. Some physicians base their diagnosis of growth retardation on the ratio of soft-tissue mass to the skeletal frame (birth weight times crown-heel length). Short, slim infants may share the same risks as those dubbed growth retarded because of their gestational age.

Why Some Babies Don't Grow

Chromosomal abnormalities and congenital malformations. These problems have been associated with 10 to 30 percent of growth retardation. The growth impairment shows up early and affects all parts of the body equally.

Infection. Herpes, cytomegalovirus, rubella, toxoplasmosis, and other viruses are suspected in about 10 percent of cases. The infectious process disrupts cell growth. If it occurs early, it may impede normal development.

Placental problems. Any disorder of the placenta—the organ that supplies the fetus with nutrients—can jeopardize fetal growth.

Multiple gestation. The greater the number of babies competing for nutrients, the greater the likelihood of growth retardation.

Maternal disease. Any condition that affects the supply of oxygen-carrying blood to the placenta and fetus can impair normal growth. This includes hypertension (chronic or pregnancy-induced), diabetes (if blood vessels are affected), respiratory problems, and heart disease. Women living at high altitudes are also at higher risk.

Poor weight gain. A woman's failure to gain weight may mirror the poor nutrition and weight gain of her baby. Some obstetricians feel that a nutritious diet can make a difference; many feel that other factors, such as illness or infection, have a greater impact.

Smoking. Because it interferes with blood flow and oxygenation, smoking can be a culprit in growth retardation.

Alcohol. Consumption of one or two alcoholic drinks a day increases the risk of growth retardation.

Prior growth-retarded infant. Women who've had one too-small baby are at high risk of having another, particularly if the previous child died as a result of its growth problems.

What happens during pregnancy. Growth problems tend to follow two different patterns:

• asymmetrical or brain-sparing growth retardation (approximately two-thirds of all cases), in which the baby's head diameter increases normally until late pregnancy but body growth lags behind. This pattern is most often associated with maternal disease, particularly hypertension.

• symmetrical growth retardation, in which both head and body are small. This pattern tends to occur much earlier, often because of infection or fetal malformation.

Possible risks to the baby. Very small babies can develop very big problems in their first days in the world. They're more likely to suffer meconium aspiration, which can lead to lung problems. They may have low blood sugar as well as low calcium and phosphate levels. Their blood may be extremely dense or viscous, interfering with circulation. They may have impaired liver function and problems regulating their temperature.

Because of tremendous advances in neonatal care, too-tiny babies are facing brighter futures. Their ultimate growth potential is good, and most do some "catch-up" growing so they score above the tenth percentile for their height by age eight. Infants who are small because of prematurity alone often catch up to normal levels by two years.

In general, the babies who suffered growth retardation near the time of delivery catch up in size while those with earlier and more long-standing growth retardation lag behind. Some develop learning disabilities when they reach school age, but major neurologic problems are rare.

Diagnosis. Ultrasound is the most reliable and useful means of monitoring fetal growth. Some obstetricians also use a three-hour glucose tolerance test to predict fetal growth retardation. It picks up low blood-sugar levels in the mother, which may reflect metabolic abnormalities.

What to expect. Therapy has to be tailored to the cause of the problem. If the mother is anemic, for example, treatment consists of iron supplements. If the supply of blood to part of the placenta has been cut off—a problem called placental infarction—heparin (an anti-clotting drug that increases blood flow) can help.

Repeated ultrasound scans follow the baby's growth. Biophysical profiles can determine its well-being. Twice-weekly nonstress tests may begin as soon as growth retardation is detected. As long as a growth-retarded baby has a reactive test, it is not in immediate danger. Abnormal tests need to be carefully interpreted and confirmed. If the test is positive, a complete fetal profile is necessary. A mother's monitoring of fetal movements also provides useful information on her baby's health.

Delivery may be induced early because the majority of fetal deaths occur between the thirty-sixth week and delivery. Timing is based on gestational age, the baby's growth, and test results. Amniocentesis can determine lung maturity. A cesarean may be necessary if the baby can not withstand the stress of vaginal delivery.

What you can do. At the very least, stop smoking and drinking. Your obstetrician or nutritionist may recommend dietary changes, including supplements with vitamins, iron, and folate. Another cornerstone of treatment is bedrest to increase the flow of blood to the placenta.

"I'd gone through thirty-three years of life thinking I was perfectly healthy, head to toe and inside and out. Then I discovered my cervix isn't competent. I felt as if I were being blamed."

INCOMPETENT CERVIX

About 15 to 20 percent of second-trimester miscarriages stem from an incompetent cervix. The cervix dilates (opens) and effaces (thins) gradually some time after the twentieth week of pregnancy. This problem usually is diagnosed only after a woman loses a baby. Often each subsequent pregnancy becomes shorter.

Are you at risk? No one knows exactly why a cervix opens, suddenly and painlessly, in the middle of a pregnancy. The risk factors include:

- a possible congenital predisposition
- cervical trauma, particularly from obstetric or gynecological procedures, such as a cone biopsy or lacerations from a previous delivery
- a previous abortion in which tapered cervical dilators or laminaria (natural chemicals that soften the cervix) were not used
- DES exposure, primarily when there are significant uterine, cervical, or vaginal changes

Treatment. Treatment consists of a pursestringlike suture called a cerclage (the McDonald procedure) or a tightening of a band around the cervix (the Shirodkar technique). Both can be put in place through the vagina.

The procedure may be uncomfortable because of the bulky instruments that are used to lift the uterus off the cervix. Most obstetricians use regional or general anesthesia. Occasionally a woman with a very short cervix requires a stitch that must be inserted by abdominal surgery, a much more extensive operation requiring general anesthesia and a hospital stay.

Cerclages are most effective when inserted before eighteen weeks of pregnancy (the ideal time is between twelve and sixteen weeks) and before the cervix has begun to dilate. After twenty-six weeks, a cerclage is usually too dangerous because of the risks of inducing premature rupture of the membranes or preterm labor.

After cerclage, women must decrease their physical activity and spend at least part of their day on bedrest. Some must remain on total bedrest throughout pregnancy. Intercourse is usually prohibited. Most caregivers examine the cervix every week or every other week and remove the cerclage at thirty-seven weeks.

Some physicians use a pessary, an instrument placed in the vagina to support the uterus, as an alternative to cerclage. This device is simpler to insert and less risky but has not been proven as effective as cerclage.

PLACENTA PROBLEMS

The placenta transfers oxygen and nutrients from a mother's blood to her baby's; waste products pass the other way for disposal by the mother's lungs and kidneys. Any disorder that impairs the placenta's development or blood supply may increase the risk to the baby.

If blood does not reach a part of the placenta, an area of tissue may die; this is a placental infarction and it may jeopardize your baby. It is most likely to occur if your pregnancy continues long past your due date. If the placenta cannot provide proper nourishment—a problem called placental insufficiency—the baby cannot grow as it should. The usual "treatment" is inducing labor.

Placental Abruption (abruptio placenta)

The premature separation of a normally implanted placenta from the uterine wall occurs about once in every 120 births. Some small abruptions (about 40 percent of all) cause slight bleeding and do not affect the mother's blood pressure or the baby's heart rate. More serious abruptions (45 percent) involve mild to moderate bleeding, some contractions, rapid pulse rate, and some signs of fetal distress. The most serious (15 percent) cause moderate to severe bleeding, uterine pain, a drop in maternal blood pressure, and death of the fetus.

Why abruptions occur. No one knows exactly why a placenta sometimes tears away from the uterus. For many years, obstetricians suspected the number of a woman's pregnancies, her age, or poor nutrition, but studies have failed to show any correlation. More likely factors include:

• Hypertension of more than 140/90 mmHg. High blood pressure increases the risk of any type of abruption and is strongly associated with the most severe types.

• Trauma. From 1 to 2 percent of the most severe abruptions are caused by trauma, such as injury in a car accident.

• Previous abruptions. Reoccurrences occur in 5 to 17 percent of women who've had one abruption. If a woman has had two abruptions, the chance for another is 25 percent.

What to expect. Vaginal bleeding in the third trimester occurs in 80 percent of women with this problem. Ultrasound can detect only 2 percent of abruptions but it can rule out another common and dangerous cause of bleeding: placenta previa.

Because an abruption threatens your baby and you, you will require very close attention. With a partial abruption, you'll be put on complete bedrest in the hospital, with constant monitoring of your baby's heart rate and your blood pressure. One of the risks is preterm labor. If contractions begin, you may be given magnesium sulfate to forestall labor. The chance of losing the baby is about 15 percent—but much greater if the separation is extensive.

If the abruption is severe and the baby is not terribly premature, delivery may be the best option, with continuous fetal monitoring and checks of the mother's blood volume and pressure. Women who lose a great deal of blood may require a transfusion of whole blood.

A placental abruption can be life-threatening and requires close medical attention to prevent massive blood loss and shock. Often a cesarean is the safest option for birth, although if the separation is mild, labor usually is induced. With a complete separation, an obstetrician may perform a complete hysterectomy to save both the woman and her child.

Placenta Previa

If the placenta blocks the opening to the birth canal–either in whole or in part–this condition is called placenta previa. The more extensive the blockage, the greater the blood loss and risk to the mother. It occurs in one of every 250 births and is more common after several pregnancies.

A placenta previa can be:

• *incomplete:* the placenta may lie low down along the side of the uterus; the edge of the placenta may be at the mouth of the cervix; or the placenta may partially cover the cervix.

• *complete:* the placenta lies totally over the cervix.

Placenta previa often occurs near the end of the sixth month of pregnancy, many times without warning in a woman whose pregnancy had seemed entirely normal. The first sign is bleeding, which may be scant or heavy. The source of this blood is not the baby, but the mother, whose blood is escaping from the lower portion of the uterus. Ultrasound confirms the diagnosis.

Are you at risk? The reasons for placenta previa are not clear. In many instances, it seems a chance occurrence that happens when the fertilized egg implants itself in the lower segment of the uterus. This complication is more likely to occur in older mothers who've had many previous pregnancies, in women who smoke, or in those carrying more than one fetus. Scarring of the uterus during previous cesarean deliveries, fibroids, or poor circulation to the uterus may increase the risk.

What to expect. Treatment for placenta previa depends on whether the infant is premature (less than thirty-six weeks), whether the woman is between her thirty-seventh and fortieth week of pregnancy, whether she is in labor, and whether she is bleeding so heavily that her life is in danger.

If the pregnancy is between twenty-four and thirty-six weeks, the goal is to maintain it without jeopardizing the mother's well-being. This may mean complete bedrest, with bathroom privileges only, preferably in a hospital; a transfusion to replace the blood she's lost; RhoGAM if the mother is Rh negative; and, if contractions develop, drugs to prevent preterm labor. Every day that the fetus stays in the uterus before the thirty-third week cuts its stay in an intensive care nursery by two days. And sometimes the placenta moves away from the cervix, lessening the danger.

Hospitalization is recommended because half of women who deliver early develop heavy bleeding but have no contractions to alert them to the beginning of labor. About 25 to 30 percent make it through thirty-six weeks without bleeding or preterm labor forcing early delivery. The type of delivery depends on circumstances and bleeding.

If placenta previa occurs with persistent bleeding or contractions in a woman past thirty-seven weeks of pregnancy, delivery is the usual recommendation. Amniocentesis may be performed to check if the baby's lungs are mature.

Risks to the baby. If placenta previa leads to an early emergency cesarean to save the lives of the mother and baby, the infant may face the dangers of prematurity. If the mother has lost a great deal of blood, her baby may not get sufficient oxygen, which may affect its growth and development.

Risks to the mother. The risk to the mother depends on the amount of blood lost. Even after delivery, a woman may continue to bleed because the lower portion of the uterus may not contract to stop bleeding. Blood loss also increases her risk of infection.

AMNIOTIC-FLUID PROBLEMS

An unborn baby swims in about two quarts of fluid—some of it water from the mother's body, some of it urine from the baby's kidneys. Too much fluid creates a condition called hydramnios. Too little leads to oligohydramnios.

Hydramnios

About one of every sixty pregnant women produces more than the usual two quarts of amniotic fluid, but usually only to a minor extent. Multiple gestation, diabetes, and Rh incompatibility all lead to greater amniotic fluid volume. Severe hydramnios of more than about three quarts of fluid occurs only once in every one thousand pregnancies. The cause could be a fetal defect that interferes with swallowing, such as constriction of the esophagus, or a neural tube defect that spills cerebrospinal fluid into the amniotic sac.

In most cases, hydramnios develops slowly. The first symptom may be difficulty breathing, caused by the enlarged uterus pressing against the lungs. Because the bulging uterus can interfere with normal circulation and drainage, the woman's legs and abdominal wall may become swollen. Ultrasound and a physical exam confirm the

"I WASN'T GOING TO LOSE ANOTHER BABY"

"My mother had six children," says Rebecca. "I never expected that I'd have any problem at all." Throughout her first pregnancy, when she was twenty-nine, she felt great. In her second trimester, she and her husband, Bruce, went hiking in the Cascade Mountains of the Pacific Northwest. All seemed right with her world.

Then, at twenty-eight and a half weeks, Rebecca started spotting. She spent an anxious weekend on bedrest. The spotting continued, and she began to feel more discomfort in her lower abdomen. When she rushed to the hospital, a fetal monitor showed that the baby was in fetal distress. Performing an emergency cesarean, the doctors delivered a two-and-a-half-pound boy. After delivery, they discovered that Rebecca's placenta had separated from the uterine wall—a potentially catastrophic complication called a placental abruption.

"Robert had the typical problems of a premature, low-birth-weight baby," says Rebecca. "He had very severe respiratory distress syndrome. His fingers were like matchsticks. His head was smaller than my fist. I was in the hospital for about a week and then I had to go home without him. I was very depressed."

Despite numerous scares and setbacks, Robert made it through and came home, weighing four pounds, ten weeks after his birth. "He wasn't a Gerber baby, but he was alive," his mother says.

Encouraged to conceive soon to lower the risk of complications in subsequent pregnancies, Rebecca soon was expecting again. In

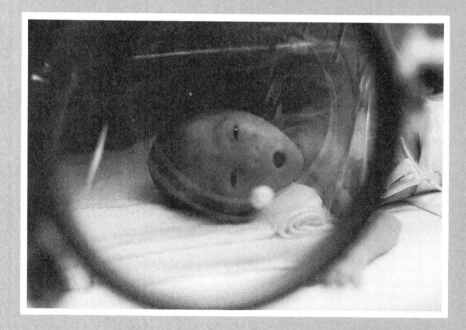

her sixth month, she began to feel funny. She wasn't quite sure whether anything was wrong. Her doctor wasn't sure either. The ultimate diagnosis: another placental abruption.

Rebecca underwent another emergency cesarean. The baby, a girl, died after little more than a day in the world. "That was so hard because I felt that maybe if we had another doctor, maybe if I went to a different hospital, they could have saved her. You never let go of what you should have done."

A few months after this loss, Bruce and Rebecca sought prepregnancy counseling at Johns Hopkins. "We wanted to know the score from someone with the best information possible. The perinatologists weren't overwhelmed by our questions, and they felt there were things they could try if we got pregnant again."

Rebecca suffered three miscarriages over the next few years. Both she and the perinatal team at Johns Hopkins were determined to keep trying. When she became pregnant again early in 1983, she took daily progesterone supplements. At twenty weeks, she began receiving weekly injections of medication to control contractions. At twenty-two weeks, she began bedrest at home. At twenty-four weeks, she entered the hospital.

"Because I was at high risk for another abruption, the doctors and nurses wanted me right in front of the nurse's station," she recalls. "I was determined to do whatever I had to do. I wasn't going to lose another baby. And they weren't going to let me." In all, Rebecca spent forty-two days in a hospital bed, knitting, reading, and taking care of bills and paperwork. Relatives and friends looked after four-year-old Robert, who visited every day. At twenty-seven weeks, she went into preterm labor, but a labor-inhibiting drug stopped the contractions.

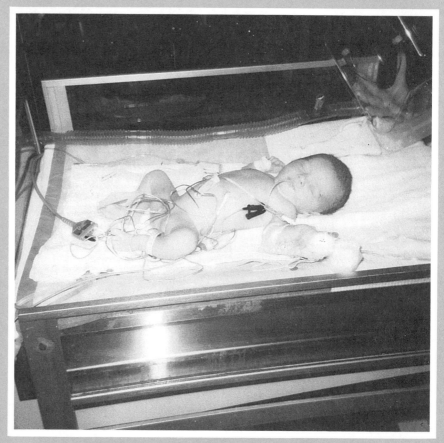

"The doctors told me that the most important thing I could do was to be aware of the baby's movements and keep track of them several times a day for an hour at a time. That became my job, my mission."

When Rebecca made it through her thirty-second week, her doctors let her go back home. "I had been dreaming about going home, but when they said that, I didn't want to go. I was scared that something would happen."

After three weeks at home on bedrest, in her thirty-fifth week, Rebecca went into labor. Back at Johns Hopkins, Rebecca's doctor performed a cesarean. Elizabeth—all five pounds, three ounces of her—entered the world with a lusty cry. She spent eleven days in the neonatal intensive care unit, struggling with respiratory distress, and she required a home breathing monitor for her first six months at home. But she has thrived ever since.

Now a fourth-grader, Robert is thin and athletic, swimming on local teams. His little sister, Elizabeth, is starting grade school. "We are blessed with bright, healthy children," their mother says. "They add a dimension to our life that isn't measurable."

diagnosis. Whenever there is excess amniotic fluid, obstetricians suspect a blockage in the baby's digestive tract, such as duodenal atresia. Ultrasound can detect any abnormalities.

Minor degrees of hydramnios, often associated with diabetes and Rh sensitization, require no treatment. Because of the risk of preterm labor, placental abruption, and bleeding after delivery in severe cases, the doctor may withdraw some excess fluid by repeated amnioconteses. Hospitalization may be recommended for close monitoring of mother and baby.

Oligohydramnios

Oligohydramnios, a much less common problem, is dangerous because it removes the protective fluid around a baby and increases the risk of abnormal organ development. Unable to float, the baby could sit on its umbilical cord, cutting off its basic supply line.

Medical scientists do not know why oligohydramnios occurs. Often the cause is a malformation, such as an obstruction of the baby's urinary tract, lack of kidneys, or a leak in the membranes. If it occurs late in pregnancy, early delivery may be performed to avoid potential risks.

Sometimes a saline solution is infused into the amniotic sac during delivery to relieve pressure on the umbilical cord. Such infusions also are being tried experimentally prior to labor. Babies who do not have an adequate supply of amniotic fluid are at high risk of lung problems after delivery.

BIRTH DEFECTS

Birth defects occur in 2 to 4 percent of babies, affecting about two hundred thousand newborns each year. About 20 percent are hereditary. The other 80 percent are caused by a variety of factors. Some can be anticipated before conception, and some can be detected early in pregnancy. However, most occur as a result of unexpected events during pregnancy or labor and delivery.

Familial Abnormalities

In addition to purely genetic diseases or defects, some common abnormalities occur more often in some families than others. However, they are not caused by an identifiable chromosome defect, and they're not inherited like a classic single-gene disorder. Such "multifactorial" defects probably result from a combination of genetic and environmental factors. They include:

Congenital hip dislocation, problems in which the hip and its socket do not fit together properly.

Cleft lip with or without cleft palate (14.8 per ten thousand births), incomplete fusion of two sides of the roof of the mouth or upper lip, correctable by surgery and speech therapy.

Clubfoot (28.4 per ten thousand births), an abnormally positioned foot that can be corrected by a cast or surgery.

"Limb reduction" defects (10.2 per ten thousand births), shortened or missing arms, legs, fingers, or toes.

Neural tube defects, such as spina bifida or open spine, which often can be corrected or improved by surgery, and anencephaly, the lack of a normal brain, which is always fatal (12.5 per ten thousand births).

Pyloric stenosis, overdevelopment of part of the muscle at the outlet of the stomach that causes vomiting in young infants.

Heart malformations, including defects in the heart valves, blood vessels, and chambers (48.3 per ten thousand births).

Couples who have one child with any of these problems have a 3 to 5 percent chance of having a second affected child. After two children with the same problem, the risk rises to 10 percent.

Pressure Problems

Some malformations are the result of crowding or pressure on the uterus—a common occurrence after the thirty-fifth week. Since the bones are soft and pliable, normal babies may be born with bowed legs, turned-in feet, and long, pointed heads. Pressures that occur early in development can create more serious problems, such as clubfoot and congenital hip dislocation, which happens most often when babies are in the breech (foot-first) position.

The risk of such problems increases in the following circumstances:

- first pregnancies (the uterus has not been stretched)
- small mother
- very small pelvis
- malformations of the uterus
- large uterine fibroids (which take up space in the uterus)

On the Horizon: Fetal Surgery

While fetal surgery is experimental and risky, occasionally it offers one last hope for babies who otherwise might never have a chance at life. According to the International Fetal Surgery Register, more than seventy operations have been performed around the world for hydronephrosis, obstruction of the urinary tract and subsequent backup of urine, and hydrocephalus, the buildup of fluid within the brain.

Fetal surgery is performed only when the mother's life and reproductive system are not jeopardized and the baby has no other serious problems. Only a few obstetricians in the world have attempted any interventions before birth. Their greatest success has come in treating hydronephrosis and diaphragmatic hernia, a hole in the diaphragm separating the chest and the abdomen so the intestines push into the chest cavity, interfering with lung growth.

The complications and risks of prenatal operations have limited their usefulness. With greater experience and continuing advances in technology and technique, fetal surgery may someday help more unborn babies, possibly allowing correction of common defects, including facial deformities, before birth, when the operations might not leave scars. But for now, the field remains in its infancy.

- multiples
- too little amniotic fluid (oligohydramnios)
- unusual position
- engagement of fetal head too early in pregnancy

While some deformities caused by crowding require special treatment, they are almost always correctable, and the child can have a full, active, productive life.

Blood Supply Interruptions

Another cause of birth defects is interruption of the fetal blood supply—either in a single, devastating accident or as a chronic problem. Both the severity and the timing of a lack of blood flow—and therefore of oxygen and nutrients—influence the impact on the fetus.

Sometimes the result is growth retardation. Sometimes, if the lack of oxygen to the fetal brain and other organs is severe, long-term damage can result.

Some blood-supply interruptions may be related to very early rupture of the fetal membranes, which produces scars called amniotic bands. These fibrous bands may stretch across part of a fetus's body or encircle a leg, cutting off blood and impairing normal development. This may be how a clubfoot occurs.

Hydrocephalus

Prenatal hydrocephalus, excessive fluid within the skull, occurs in one of every five thousand deliveries, affecting about two thousand five hundred babies a year. Half to two-thirds are stillborn; only about 25 percent of newborns with hydrocephalus survive infancy. Often hydrocephalus develops in babies with spina bifida and can cause cerebral palsy and mental retardation.

Traditional treatment includes surgical implantation of a shunt, a tube to drain the brain's fluid into another part of the body where it can be absorbed, soon after birth. While shunts have greatly improved the outlook for hydrocephalic babies in the past thirty years, the devices frequently become blocked or infected, which can lead to further brain damage or repeated surgery.

Specialists have attempted to insert shunts before birth to drain the excess fluid, but the results have been discouraging. About 10 percent of unborn babies have died as a consequence of prenatal surgery; more than half of the survivors have suffered serious neurologic handicaps.

Hydronephrosis

This buildup of urine within the kidneys occurs because of an obstruction in the urinary tract. Severe hydronephrosis can interfere with normal kidney development and limit production of amniotic fluid, which can impair the growth of the lungs. In a few cases, surgeons have operated before birth to allow urine to drain into the amniotic fluid.

Complications of Labor and Delivery

Unexpected complications late in pregnancy or during labor and delivery account for other permanent defects. Often these result in damage to the nervous system—either temporary or permanent. One danger is asphyxia, the lack of oxygen and buildup of carbon dioxide. The effects of too little oxygen can range from temporary difficulty in breathing to mild to severe brain damage, seizures, cerebral palsy, and developmental problems.

Sometimes certain nerves are damaged during difficult deliveries. Pressure or pulling on an arm or hand may cause brachial palsy, paralysis that may be partial or complete. Pressure on the facial nerve, located close to the skin just in front of the ear, may lead to facial palsy, a weakness or paralysis of the muscles on one side of the face. This can disappear within several weeks or months.

One of the most agonizing dilemmas for parents is early recognition of a serious birth defect. Routine sonography may reveal an unusual problem, such as hydrocephalus, along with other defects, such as spina bifida. Should the parents abort the pregnancy? Should they agree to highly experimental treatment, such as insertion of a shunt in utero? No one may be able to tell them precisely what impact the abnormality will have on their baby's intellectual and physical development. Each case is unique, and there is no single right answer for every parent and child.

PROLONGED PREGNANCY (POSTDATES)

About 8 to 11 percent of pregnancies continue past the mother's "due date." Often the baby isn't really overdue; rather, the estimated date of conception is wrong.

A pregnancy that continues for more than forty-two completed weeks since the first day of the last menstrual period is considered prolonged or "postdates." Being overdue is not a complication in itself, but a reason for increased surveillance of mother and baby. Babies who remain in the womb are at risk because they could develop a combination of complications called postmaturity syndrome, which develops in as many as 40 percent of postdates pregnancies.

Prolonged pregnancies create a great deal of anxiety. In one survey, women had more difficulty coping with this particular complication than with many others. Certainly, after carrying a child for nine months, every pregnant women is eager to hold her baby. Each extra week she has to wait can seem endless.

Are you at risk? The likelihood of a prolonged pregnancy increases in women:
- who've had a threatened miscarriage
- who are in their first pregnancy
- who are very young or over 35
- who are poor
- who've had a previous prolonged pregnancy (the odds of another are about 50 percent)

Diagnosis. One of the greatest diagnostic challenges is figuring out whether a pregnancy is indeed prolonged. If you had regular menstrual cycles, know for certain the first day of your last menstrual period, or charted your shift in basal body temperature in the cycle in which you became pregnant, your obstetrical team can be sure of how long you've been pregnant.

Other key indicators are:
- Positive pregnancy test at six weeks from your last menstrual period
- Fetal heart rate detected at 18–20 weeks
- Fundal height at the navel at 20 weeks
- Early exam and recording of dates before 13 weeks
- Early ultrasound "dating" of your pregnancy

If a woman has gotten pregnant immediately after discontinuing oral contraceptives, there usually is a two-week delay in ovulation, so the gestation should be forty-two weeks, not forty, from the last menstrual period.

Possible risks to the baby. Prolonged pregnancy is associated with many risk factors: placental tears, lack of oxygen supply for the fetus, growth retardation, an overly large baby, meconium staining and aspiration, and death. One-third of prolonged pregnancies are complicated by fetal distress during labor, and cesarean section for failed progress, large size, or distress is more likely.

The postmaturity syndrome produces a constellation of problems, including the following:
- failure to grow normally
- dehydration
- dry, cracked, wrinkled, parchmentlike skin
- reduced fat deposits
- long, thin arms and legs
- advanced hardness of the skull
- no vernix or lanugo (which normally cover an unborn baby's skin)
- breakdown of skin surface
- brownish-green or yellow discolored skin, umbilical cord, and membrane
- alert, "little-old-man" appearance

Postmature babies experience more complications, including fetal distress, failure to progress in labor, more cesarean deliveries, and lower developmental scores at birth and four months of age. There is a sevenfold increase in the incidence of perinatal death. Some postmature babies experience more illnesses and more sleeping and eating disturbances in their first year.

In general the longer the pregnancy extends past term, the greater the dangers. The risk to a baby's life at forty-three weeks is two to five times higher than at term; the risks at forty-four weeks can be as much as seven times higher.

What to expect. In addition to the passage of forty-two weeks, the classic signs and symptoms of a postdates pregnancy are maternal weight loss, lack of uterine growth, too little amniotic fluid, and an absence of any pockets of fluid visible on a sonogram.

Your doctor will rely on your daily fetal movement counts, sampling of the amniotic fluid (for meconium, a distress signal), sonography, biophysical profiles, twice-weekly nonstress tests, contraction stress tests, and others to determine if there is any danger. Among the conditions indicating a need for immediate delivery are: serious maternal illness affecting the fetus (such as hypertension, preeclampsia, or eclampsia), growth retardation, birth defects, and tests suggesting fetal problems and/or postmaturity syndrome.

For years obstetricians have debated the wisdom of inducing labor in all women after they reach forty-two weeks. A study of two hundred Johns Hopkins patients whose pregnancies continued beyond forty-one weeks compared outcomes when caregivers simply waited for labor and when labor was induced after forty-two weeks—a practice that has been common in Great Britain for many years. Both approaches proved safe for the mother and fetus. Induction did not increase the cesarean section rate nor the number of large-for-gestational-age babies.

COPING WITH COMPLICATIONS

For women who start their pregnancies with eager anticipation, complications can be emotionally wrenching. Without warning, they're dealing with problems they thought would never affect them. "I remember my doctor saying, 'We're in a whole different ball game now,'" recalls one woman who suddenly became high risk. "All I could think was, What did I do wrong?"

The fact is that she—like other mothers whose pregnancies become complicated—did nothing to cause the problem. The conditions described in this chapter often occur without any clear reason. If they happen in your pregnancy, understanding what is involved and what can be done for you and your baby will help you adjust your expectations and work with your caregivers to overcome any additional risks.

CHAPTER 11

Preterm Labor

HELPING YOUR BABY TO WAIT NINE MONTHS

"When you've had one very premature baby who almost didn't make it, there isn't anything you won't do to buy more time for your baby the next time around."

"It's nothing," Cindy told herself as she felt her abdomen tighten ever so slightly. A nurse in a high-risk pregnancy clinic, she had just entered the fifteenth week of a perfectly normal, perfectly wonderful pregnancy. But when she pressed her fingertips gently against her stomach, just as she had taught so many high-risk women to do, her uterus was tightening and relaxing rhythmically.

Fortunately the contractions stopped, but Cindy knew that the risk of preterm labor wouldn't go away. As the weeks passed, regular exams revealed that the baby's head was moving down into her pelvis far too early. At thirty-one weeks, with her cervix beginning to open, Cindy began total bedrest. "I was too scared to move," she recalls. "I knew that just a few more weeks could make an enormous difference in how the baby would do."

Bedrest bought Cindy's child almost four crucial weeks in her womb. At thirty-four weeks, five days, her daughter, Whitney, refused to wait any longer and weighed in at five pounds, eleven ounces. Like many preemies, she had trouble breathing, and Cindy only had time for a quick kiss before the neonatologists whisked Whitney to the newborn intensive care unit. After several scary days when she needed a respirator to breathe, Whitney—like most premature babies born today—overcame her shaky start and began growing bigger and stronger.

From 6 to 10 percent of babies are born too soon. Preterm births

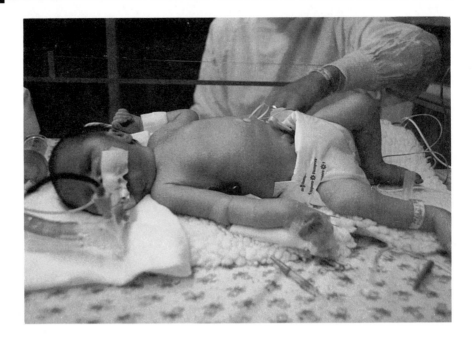

are associated with 75 percent of neonatal deaths of babies with major birth defects and 50 percent of long-range neurologic handicaps. Neonatologists have made tremendous progress in saving even those who weigh less than five hundred grams (a little more than a pound) at birth, yet they cannot give them what they need most: more time in their mothers' bodies.

Prevention is the key to conquering the problems of premature birth. If perinatologists could identify all women at risk and if every pregnant woman learned how to recognize the warning signals of too-early labor, as many as half of preterm births might be prevented. The savings, in human and financial terms, would be great: According to recent estimates, it costs as much to care for five premature babies as it does to provide prenatal care to 150 expectant mothers.

WHAT IS PRETERM LABOR?

The usual "term" or length of pregnancy is thirty-seven to forty weeks after the last menstrual period. In "preterm" labor, regular uterine contractions begin and the cervix starts to dilate (open) and efface (become thinner) between twenty and thirty-six weeks of pregnancy. If not stopped, preterm labor leads to the early delivery of a baby who may not be capable of surviving outside the womb. (Technically, labor and birth that occur before thirty-seven weeks of pregnancy are preterm; babies born too soon are premature. But the words "preterm" and "premature" are often used interchangeably.)

While most pregnant women experience some contractions before term, the contractions that characterize preterm labor are regular and persistent. However, they may be "silent," causing little if any discomfort, so they're difficult to detect unless women know what to watch for.

ARE YOU AT RISK?

Risk-assessment evaluations, like the one on page 211, can identify about half of the women who will go into labor too soon. Not all women with a high-risk rating will experience preterm labor. And not all women remain at risk throughout pregnancy. In some cases, a problem, such as a urinary tract infection, can be detected and treated early, eliminating the potential danger.

The risk factors for preterm labor include:

Previous preterm labor or delivery. After one preterm delivery, a woman is much more likely to have another. The risk increases if she has more than one premature baby and decreases after she has one or more full-term babies.

Uterine abnormality. The risk varies with the type of anomaly and is greatest if a septum, or membrane, divides the uterus in two.

DES exposure. An estimated one-fourth to one-half of DES daughters have reproductive tract anomalies (such as a T-shaped uterus, incompetent cervix, ridges, or other structural changes in the vagina and cervix) that can triple their risk of preterm labor. The higher the dose of DES that a woman was exposed to in her mother's womb and the longer her mother took the drug, the greater her risk of having her child too soon.

Abdominal surgery. Women who've undergone abdominal surgery are at greater risk because of the scarring and adhesions that surgery—especially gynecologic operations like myomectomies (removal of fibroids) or ovarian surgery—can leave behind.

More than two second-trimester miscarriages or elective abortions. It's unclear whether first-trimester losses or abortions increase the risk of preterm labor; second-trimester miscarriages or abortions definitely can and do.

Cone biopsy. Women who've undergone this diagnostic procedure, in which tissue from the cervix is removed for testing for precancerous changes or malignancy, are at greater risk of preterm labor.

Multiple pregnancy. Women carrying more than one baby face a greatly increased risk of delivering before term. The greater the number of babies sharing a womb, the less time pregnancy usually lasts.

Cervical changes and/or excessive uterine contractions before thirty-three weeks of pregnancy. An incompetent cervix can lead to painless dilation and early delivery.

Serious infection. Various microorganisms, including group B streptococci, chlamydia, and trichomonas, increase the risk of preterm labor. Recurring urinary tract infections, especially pyelonephritis (page 167), and infections of the amniotic fluid are especially threatening. Chronic vaginal and cervical infections also may lead to preterm labor.

Pregnancy complications. Placenta previa, placental abruption, excessive or insufficient amniotic fluid, and first-trimester bleeding all increase the risk of preterm delivery.

Vaginal bleeding. Women who develop bleeding for no known cause after twenty weeks of pregnancy are at risk.

Fibroids. Depending on their location and size, fibroids increase the danger of bleeding and of preterm rupture of the membranes.

Smoking. The risk of preterm labor increases with the number of cigarettes the woman smokes. Women who smoke more than ten cigarettes a day are at greatest risk.

Physical stress. Extreme exertion, such as heavy lifting, and environmental discomfort, such as working in wet, cold, or noisy surroundings, have been implicated in cases of preterm labor. In one review of 3,437 deliveries, occupational fatigue (determined by posture, work involving an industrial machine, physical exertion, mental stress, and environmental discomfort) was the strongest predictor of premature birth.

Psychological stress. Emotional upheavals, such as the loss of a loved one, can increase the likelihood of a too-early birth. Various studies have come to contradictory conclusions about whether the number of "life events"—moves, changes, triumphs, and traumas—in pregnancy also add to the risk. Chronic or ongoing stress seems most dangerous, possibly because it may increase uterine contractions in some women.

Who Is at Risk?

According to most risk-scoring systems for preterm labor, approximately 15 percent of all pregnant women face a high likelihood of going into labor after the 20th and before the 37th week of pregnancy. Below, some of the factors considered, and their relative importance.

What puts a woman at high risk?
- A previous premature delivery
- Repeated second-trimester abortions or miscarriages
- Twins or triplets
- Abdominal surgery during pregnancy

Moderate risk?
- Uterine malformation
- Exposure to DES (diethylstilbestrol) before birth
- One second-trimester abortion or miscarriage
- Placenta previa (placenta covering the opening to the birth canal)
- Excessive amniotic fluid
- Kidney infection
- Thinning or opening of the cervix
- Bleeding after the 12th week
- Age less than 18 years

Mild risk?
- Two or three first-trimester abortions or an abortion less than a year since last delivery
- Weight less than 100 pounds before pregnancy
- A weight gain of less than 12 pounds by 32 weeks or a weight loss of more than 5 pounds
- Heavy work
- Long tiring commute
- Fever
- Fibroid tumors
- Baby in breech (feet down) position at 32 weeks
- Age over 40 years
- Single parent
- Smoking
- Unusual fatigue during pregnancy
- High blood pressure during pregnancy
- Bacteria in urine during pregnancy

It is important to keep in mind that falling into one of these categories—even the high-risk group—does not mean you are destined to have a problem pregnancy or deliver prematurely. Rather, it's simply a signal to your doctor that you may need extra attention and care to ensure a successful pregnancy. Talk to your obstetrician if one or more risk factors apply to you and together you can put it in perspective for your individual pregnancy.

"I felt great all along. I couldn't understand all the fuss because I was carrying twins. Then I went into preterm labor at twenty-eight weeks. From that moment on, I realized I was going to have to fight for those babies."

Low socioeconomic status. Poor women, who often are unable to get prenatal care, are more likely to go into preterm labor than are middle- and upper-class women.

IF YOU'RE AT RISK

Some women at risk for preterm labor go through pregnancy with few, if any, modifications in their usual routine, except for more frequent prenatal visits. Others have to reorganize every aspect of their lives, including their professional responsibilities, household management, and favorite forms of exercise and entertainment.

What to expect

Prenatal Care. Women who do not get regular prenatal care are more likely to deliver early, regardless of their socioeconomic class or any other risk factors. In a study of 31,871 babies at Stanford University, regular prenatal care reduced the rate of premature births by 65 percent.

If you're at risk, expect frequent checkups. And while most women do not undergo pelvic exams during most of their pregnancy, you probably will, because your caregivers may need to check for cervical changes.

Work. Working women do not deliver more preterm babies than those who are not employed. However, strenuous jobs that involve standing, lifting, carrying, or long hours may present problems. Women in medical residencies and in the military have been shown to be at greater risk because of their jobs. You may want to speak with your employer about shifting to a different position or making other adjustments so you can continue working as long as you'd like.

Exercise. Like other pregnant women, you would be wise *not* to start any new types of exercise during pregnancy. Vigorous exercise, including running, riding, or skiing, also may be too demanding. Describe your usual exercise regimen to your caregivers to find out if any changes would be wise. When you do exercise, monitor for contractions during and after your workout.

Childbirth preparation. Women who know they're at risk for preterm labor sometimes arrange to attend classes prior to their twenty-sixth week and to come back for a couple of review sessions after their thirty-seventh week, avoiding the prime danger period.

If you attend childbirth classes during your last trimester, play it safe and monitor for contractions during the group practice sessions. Talk to your instructor, too. You and she may decide that you should sit out those exercises in which the mothers-to-be put pressure on their abdomens or bear down to simulate labor. Some couples prefer videotaped classes or one-on-one counseling in their homes. (See the listings on page 311 for information on national childbirth education organizations.)

Sex. In some studies, intercourse and orgasm increased the risk of preterm labor. In others, they have shown no effect. While orgasm can trigger contractions, it usually doesn't lead to labor. Talk with your caregivers about what's safe and what's not. You may be advised to avoid stimulation of your nipples, which can produce contractions. You and your partner should discuss the relative risks and try to find forms of intimacy that can satisfy your needs without jeopardizing the pregnancy.

Nutrition. The quality and quantity of what you eat can affect a baby's growth and birth weight. Adequate weight gain helps reduce the likelihood that your baby, whenever it's born, will be small for its gestational age.

What You Can Do to Lower the Risks

Despite years of research, medical science knows so little about what causes preterm labor that we can not offer a step-by-step, surefire guide to preventing it. However, a common-sense, conservative approach can help lower your risk:

• Take it easy. Two or three times a day, put your feet up and lie on your left side.

• Get plenty of rest. In addition to daytime breaks or naps, add an extra hour or two to your nightly sleep.

• Drink plenty of fluids. Aim for two or three quarts of water or fruit juice a day. Don't drink caffeinated beverages. Dehydration can trigger contractions, so increase your fluid intake if you develop a fever, vomiting, or diarrhea.

• Urinate often to avoid the pressure of a full bladder. Make sure you empty your bladder at least every two hours.

• Try to prevent urinary tract infections by drinking plenty of fluids, always wiping from front to back after going to the bathroom, wearing cotton underwear, not douching, and promptly reporting any signs of vaginitis (itching, burning, foul-smelling discharge) to your caregivers.

• To eliminate the need to strain during bowel movements, get plenty of fiber in your daily diet.

• Avoid lifting anything heavy, including small children.

• Pace yourself, avoiding unnecessary exertions.

• Monitor for uterine contractions at different times of the day and during different types of activity.

• Try to avoid the circumstances most often associated with preterm labor or contractions: stress, fatigue, long and tiring trips, poor nutrition, and climbing stairs.

• Do not do any breast preparations for nursing, such as rubbing your nipples with a towel. The stimulation can increase uterine activity.

• Find out about disability coverage from your employer and/or the government for any time you cannot work before delivery.

The Danger Signals

Preterm labor can develop silently, with few clues to alert the mother. You may feel nothing more than a sense of something different, something not quite right. Among the subtle changes that may occur are:

Contractions. When most women think of labor, they assume it must be painful. Yet in preterm labor, the contractions are usually painless. You may see your uterus tighten and rise up or, with your fingertips, you may feel the muscles of the uterus tighten and relax. Such contractions aren't unusual in normal pregnancy, but if they occur more frequently or at regular intervals, you may be in labor. Notify your doctor if you have four or more contractions within an hour or if contractions occur less than fifteen minutes apart.

Backache. While a sore back is one of the most common complaints of pregnancy, pain in the lower back that comes in waves and travels to the front of your abdomen may indicate that you're in preterm labor. Most backaches get better or worse if you move around. If you're in labor, the pain will persist regardless of your activity or position. Even if it eases and then returns, it may seem different from other backaches you've had in pregnancy.

Cramps. You may feel menstruallike pains in your lower abdomen. Often they are dull and aching, causing continuous discomfort, or they may come and go in a rhythmic pattern. Sometimes stomach cramps, with or without diarrhea, herald preterm labor. Persistent diarrhea, often accompanying a case of the flu, may irritate the uterus, leading to excessive uterine contractions.

Pelvic pressure. A feeling that the baby is balling up inside you or about to "fall out," as some women put it, can also be a warning signal. You may feel that you have to move your bowels when you really don't. This sense of pressure may come and go or remain constant.

Vaginal discharge. While many women have increased vaginal discharge during pregnancy, you should suspect preterm labor if there is a change in the type, amount, consistency, or color, especially if the discharge becomes brown or pinkish.

Monitoring for Preterm Contractions

Women who have one or more risk factors for preterm labor usually are taught how to monitor for contractions with their fingertips. Women who've had an episode of preterm labor, are at very high risk (if they're carrying triplets, for example), or are on bedrest to prevent early labor may use a portable monitoring device called a tocodynamometer, which records any contractions and transmits the information, via telephone, to trained professionals.

Self-monitoring. Recognizing preterm labor requires some practice and an idea of what to look for. Your caregivers can help you recognize what's normal for you and what's not. You should monitor your uterus at least once a day, *every* day. This way, you'll develop a sense of your regular pattern of contractions so you can detect any potentially dangerous variations. Here's how:

• Lie down on your left side. A pillow under your hip may help support your back.

• With your fingertips, gently feel the uterus for tightening. Think of it as divided into four sections, and move your fingers over each of the sections. When your uterus is relaxed, you should be able to indent it with your fingers. During a contraction, it will feel firm to the touch.

• If your uterus becomes firm on one side while the other remains soft, you are probably feeling your baby move. During contractions, your entire uterus becomes firm.

• If your uterus is tightening, try to determine how often and how long the contractions are. Start counting minutes from the time the uterus first begins to tighten. The time from the beginning of a contraction until the uterus becomes soft again is the length or duration of a single contraction. The number of contractions in an hour represents the frequency.

• You may be in preterm labor if you have four or more contrac-

"I'd never understood how a woman could be in labor and not realize it. But the last thing I expected at thirty-two weeks of pregnancy was labor. I thought it was indigestion, or the flu. If my husband hadn't insisted on taking me to the hospital, I probably would have had the baby then and there."

tions in an hour or the time between the beginning of one contraction and the beginning of the next is less than fifteen minutes.

You should monitor for contractions twice a day for half an hour at a time, ideally at about the same time each day. Some women feel more uterine activity in the afternoon or night, while others experience more contractions in the morning. You also may want to monitor your uterus after exercise, intercourse, or doing household chores. If you notice any other sign of preterm labor, stop and focus on monitoring alone. Whenever you suspect that something may be happening, stop and monitor.

Whenever you detect contractions, write down the time each contraction starts and its length. If you have other symptoms, but no contractions, make a note. You may notice that contractions tend to increase after a certain activity or when you're upset or hassled. This may be useful in modifying your daily routine. With your doctor, review your record so you can determine your usual pattern—two contractions an hour in the morning, for instance, and three in the evening. Once you know your pattern, pay special attention to any changes.

Your partner can help monitor your contractions. You can show him how to monitor by placing his hands on your abdomen and gently pressing each of the four sections. Let him feel your abdomen when your uterus is relaxed and when you're having a contraction.

Home Monitors. Self-monitoring is not foolproof and may not be adequate in many cases. If you are carrying twins or triplets, for instance, your uterine wall may normally be quite firm. Also, stomach cramps, a full bladder, or fetal movements can feel like contractions. An increasingly popular alternative for women at high risk is home monitoring with tocodynamometers that measure contractions and transmit the information via telephone.

A typical home monitor consists of a belt with a small pressure-sensitive recorder that detects contractions that often are not felt by the woman herself. The data are stored and then transmitted over the telephone for immediate evaluation by specially trained nurses, who also are available around the clock to answer questions from mothers at risk.

Most women put on the belt and monitor for about an hour twice a day. While they cannot move around, they feel no discomfort. Early studies indicate that monitoring, which costs about seventy-five to eighty dollars a day, can help identify excessive contractions and alert everyone to the need for prompt treatment to delay delivery. The only alternative for women at very high risk of preterm labor is hospitalization, which costs at least twice as much. Most insurance companies cover home monitoring costs.

Home monitors, which have been used by more than thirty-five thousand women in the last five years, do reduce the incidence of preterm births. However, the key to their success may be the mothers' close daily contact with trained, concerned professionals. Rather than feeling they are "bothering" their caregivers, women using home monitors feel that they *should* be reporting any small changes early and regularly. This attitude may be the most important factor in preventing preterm birth.

If You're Having Contractions or Any Worrisome Symptoms

- Call your caregivers.
- Report how often contractions are coming and how many you've had in the last hour.
- Report how active you've been during the day and what you were doing prior to noticing the contractions.
- Describe any other signs of labor you may have noticed.
- If you have a vague feeling that something's not quite right, play it safe. Go to the labor and delivery unit in your hospital for electronic fetal monitoring. A pelvic exam can determine if your cervix has begun to thin out and open.

Never hesitate to go to a hospital and get thoroughly evaluated. The worst that can happen is that you'll learn you are not in preterm labor. If you do not go, the worst that can happen is the unthinkable: the too-early birth of a baby who may be too small to survive.

TREATING PRETERM LABOR

Treatment for preterm labor depends on how advanced contractions and cervical changes are. If your cervix has dilated more than five centimeters, little can be done to postpone delivery.

To Treat or Not to Treat

A leading obstetrical textbook quotes Kenny Rogers's "The Gambler" in its chapter on management of preterm labor: "You've got to know when to hold 'em, know when to fold 'em." The decision to "hold" or "fold" can be difficult for the perinatal team and the parents.

A crucial factor is the baby's gestational age. Treatment helps

"Once you've had an episode of preterm labor, you feel like a walking time bomb—that at any moment it could happen again. When my doctor finally put me on complete bedrest, I was relieved."

most when labor begins relatively early in pregnancy—say, between twenty-four and thirty-two weeks. If born so early, babies can survive but face many life-threatening complications and require extended intensive care. Every week the risks to a baby diminish. After thirty-three weeks, premature babies still require extra care but usually suffer no long-term damage.

The mother's medical condition also influences what can be done. Women with many serious illnesses or pregnancy complications cannot safely take the most effective labor-inhibiting drugs because of their side effects. These medications also trigger anxiety and restlessness, particularly during the first four days of treatment. For some women, the additional psychological stress may be unacceptable.

Ultimately the decision to go ahead with treatment depends on both the individual circumstances and the relative risks and benefits. Parents, confused and anxious, shouldn't hesitate to seek a second opinion or to take time to talk through the situation with each other and their primary caregivers.

Bedrest

Bedrest is the classic approach to preventing preterm birth. In theory, bedrest takes weight and pressure off the uterus and, if the mother lies on her side, increases the flow of blood to the placenta and growing baby.

Some high-risk women, such as mothers carrying twins or triplets or women who've developed preterm contractions in previous pregnancies, begin bedrest at home, usually in the seventh month. No further treatment may be necessary if they do not go into labor. Depending on specific risk factors, perinatologists may advise bedrest earlier or later in the pregnancy. (See chapter 7.)

Hospitalization

Women in very active preterm labor are generally hospitalized for evaluation and treatment. While most women return home in a few days, about 10 to 15 percent require prolonged hospitalization, usually on complete bedrest and with continuous medication and monitoring.

If a woman is on bedrest in the hospital, she usually receives intravenous fluids (hydration therapy) because dehydration may increase uterine activity. She also may get a sedative, such as a barbiturate or morphine, to relieve anxiety.

Medications to Stop Uterine Contractions

Labor-inhibiting drugs, or tocolytics, have proven remarkably effective in buying more time in the womb for babies whose mothers go into preterm labor. More than 80 percent of women given labor-inhibiting drugs do not deliver for at least a day or two; 40 to 60 percent carry their babies until their thirty-seventh week or later. The disadvantage of labor-inhibiting drugs is that they have potentially serious side effects for the mother and, since they cross the placenta, for the fetus as well. The most commonly used medications are:

Beta-adrenergics. These drugs, similar in chemical structure to adrenaline, include: ritodrine (Yutopar); terbutaline (Brethine or Bricanyl); isoxsuprine (Vasodilan); solbutamol; and fenoterol.

Women in very active preterm labor initially need high doses of these drugs. That usually means intravenous (IV) administration, an increased risk of side effects, and a clear need for close monitoring in a hospital with perinatologists and neonatologists available to handle complications.

Once labor is under control for twelve to twenty-four hours, women can switch to pills or an infusion pump that boosts blood levels of the drugs whenever necessary. Most women can go home, but usually must remain on total bedrest and test, often with a home monitor, for contractions several times a day. Since beta-adrenergics stay in the blood for only a short time, mothers-to-be must take a pill every two to four hours around the clock—and often must continue on these drugs until the thirty-seventh week.

One recent innovation has been the development of infusion pumps that provide regular low doses of labor-inhibiting drugs, usually terbutaline, around the clock. This is a particularly appealing alternative when oral medications cannot control preterm labor and a woman faces the prospect of prolonged hospitalization. In a study of nine women in preterm labor, San Francisco researchers found that infusion pumps helped prolong pregnancy an average of 9.2 weeks, with the women delivering at a mean gestational age of 38.9 weeks (therapy was discontinued at thirty-seven weeks). The women reported fewer side effects with the pumps than with oral medication.

Side effects for the mother. Most side effects occur during initial high-dose IV treatment. After twelve to twenty-four hours, they become milder. Side effects are fewer when women use pills or an infusion pump.

The single most serious complication for mothers is pulmonary edema, the buildup of fluid within the lungs. Restricting fluid and salt intake may prevent this problem. Other potential side effects include: a very fast or very slow heart rate, skipped heartbeats, chest pain, significant shortness of breath, persistent headache, nausea, vomiting, and constipation. Some women feel warm, jittery, tired, nervous, moody or short-tempered, or can't sleep. These side effects lessen with time and disappear as soon as women stop taking the drug.

Mothers-to-be with heart disease, diabetes, or hyperthyroidism cannot take beta-adrenergics because of the side effects. These drugs are also not generally used for women with preeclampsia, eclampsia, heavy bleeding, infection of the amniotic sac, a baby with a serious abnormality or growth retardation, multiple gestation, preterm rupture of membranes, fever, chronic hypertension, or a history of severe migraines.

Regular exams and testing help detect side effects so doctors can adjust the dosages. One simple but effective way to monitor doses is by pulse rate. A pulse below 90 beats per minute with continuing uterine activity indicates too little medication. A pulse higher than 110 to 120 beats per minute for several hours may indicate too high a dose. Women on beta-adrenergics should check their pulse twenty to forty minutes after taking medication and again just before taking the next pill.

Effects on the baby. Beta-adrenergics speed up the baby's heart rate, cause a temporary drop in blood pressure, and may decrease blood-sugar and calcium levels after birth. If delivery occurs more than twelve to twenty-four hours after the drugs are stopped, the level in the baby's body at birth is very low, and no harmful effects have been reported.

Newborns whose mothers received beta-adrenergics are routinely watched for potential complications, such as very low blood-sugar levels and low blood pressure. These problems have no known long-term consequences but do require medical attention. Babies who have been followed for several years show normal development.

Magnesium sulfate. Used for decades to treat certain high-blood-pressure disorders in pregnancy (see chapter 9), "mag-sulfate" also has proven effective in stopping preterm labor. Its major advantages are that it has relatively few side effects and can be monitored in the bloodstream. However, side effects, including potentially serious ones such as pulmonary edema, develop in a small percentage of women.

Some obstetricians prefer to use magnesium sulfate first in active preterm labor because it is less expensive, easier, and safer. However, it can be given only by injection. Once contractions are under control, the woman switches to beta-adrenergic pills.

Side effects for the mother. Initial doses of magnesium sulfate can cause flushing, warmth, headache, nausea, and dizziness. Other complications include lethargy, sluggishness, and a 2 percent risk of pulmonary edema in women who are carrying more than one baby or have excess amniotic fluid.

Effects on the baby. Babies born within twelve to fourteen hours of magnesium sulfate therapy sometimes have lower calcium levels, decreased muscle tone, and diminished alertness. However, these effects are rare and temporary.

Other Medications. Other substances used to prevent preterm delivery include:

Prostaglandin-inhibitors. Drugs that block the effects of a hormone called prostaglandin have been successful in treating preterm labor if other drugs fail. Given primarily as pills or rectal suppositories, they seem effective but have not been thoroughly evaluated for safety for the baby. One concern is that they may cause premature closure of the opening in the heart that prevents the flow of blood into the lungs of a fetus.

Progesterone. Recent research indicates that large doses of natural progesterone, administered by injection, can prevent preterm delivery. However, the number of women in the studies has been small, and little is known about effectiveness and long-term safety. In some centers, progesterone is given prophylactically to women with cervical cerclages. It has no effect once preterm labor has started.

Calcium entry blockers. Drugs that block the action of calcium on the uterine muscle have been tried on a very limited basis to treat preterm labor. These agents, widely used in treating heart disease, have not been tested for safety during pregnancy. European physicians, who have tried them, report mixed success rates. Effects on the fetus are not known, but a few fetal and neonatal deaths have made American obstetricians wary.

If Preterm Labor Cannot Be Stopped

One of the greatest dangers a premature baby faces is respiratory distress syndrome (RDS) because its lungs are too immature to produce a substance called surfactant that keeps open the tiny air sacs within the lungs. Powerful hormones called corticosteroids, such as betamethasone or dexamethasone, can speed up lung maturation and enhance production of surfactant. They are most effective if given at least twenty-four to forty-eight hours prior to birth and before thirty-two to thirty-four weeks of pregnancy.

Administered by injections deep into the gluteal muscle of the mother's buttocks once a day for two days, they cannot be given to women with vaginal bleeding, hypertension, diabetes, or an infection because of the danger of side effects.

The benefits of corticosteroids seem greatest between twenty-eight and thirty-three weeks of pregnancy. For unknown reasons, white boy babies benefit less than others. Amniocentesis can determine if babies about to be born after thirty-three weeks have mature lungs and do not need steroids.

Long-term follow-up (to age six) has shown no impairment in cognitive or psychological development of babies treated with steroids before birth. The major short-term risk for mother and baby is infection and, in women with insulin-dependent diabetes, impaired glucose tolerance in the mother.

PREMATURE REPTURE OF THE MEMBRANES (PROM)

Premature rupture of the membranes refers to leakage of amniotic fluid through the cervix before thirty-seven weeks of gestation. Often the woman experiences a gush of fluid from the vagina, followed by persistent leaking. Careful examination and testing of the fluid can indicate whether the membranes have indeed ruptured.

No one knows why some membranes rupture early. They may have tiny defects or may have been weakened as the fetus grew or the uterus contracted. Infectious agents also may cause damage. Smokers are three times more likely than nonsmokers to experience a rupture before their thirty-fourth week. Women who've had premature rupture of the membranes in one pregnancy are at greater risk of another.

One serious danger is infection, which can jeopardize the lives of the mother and child. The fetus also is at greater risk of cord prolapse, fetal distress, umbilical cord compression, and lung disorders.

Medical therapy depends on the gestational age of the fetus and the presence of infection. Many physicians simply wait to see what will happen. If membranes rupture before twenty-six weeks, 30 to

40 percent of the pregnancies will continue for at least one week; 20 percent will continue for four weeks. If their membranes rupture between twenty-eight and thirty-four weeks, 70 to 80 percent of women will deliver within a week—more than half within four days.

The management of premature rupture of the membranes is highly controversial. Some obstetricians believe in letting nature take its course; others in immediate delivery or aggressive therapy to delay delivery. One point of agreement is that delivery is essential if infection occurs. If there is no infection, the perinatal team must weigh the relative risks of waiting against the possibility of serious problems developing because of the rupture.

Women whose membranes rupture between the thirtieth and thirty-fourth week usually undergo amniocentesis to detect infection and assess lung maturity—if there is enough fluid for the obstetrician to insert the needle safely. If bacteria are present or the lungs are mature, labor is induced.

If infection has not developed and the lungs are not mature, some obstetricians use drugs to prevent labor or to enhance fetal lung maturity. A still-experimental approach is infusion of a saline solution into the amniotic cavity if the baby's heartbeat is erratic to prevent occlusion, or blockage, of the cord.

Many obstetricians take an "expectant" approach, hospitalizing and carefully monitoring the mother. After initial evaluation, some women can return home on complete bedrest (with bathroom privileges). They must monitor their temperature four times a day and avoid intercourse, douches, and tampons. Warning signs of serious danger include fever, uterine tenderness, contractions, increased leakage of fluid, or a foul-smelling vaginal discharge.

PRETERM DELIVERY

Sometimes the most conscientious care can delay preterm birth only briefly. No one knows why some contractions are impossible to stop, but delivery becomes inevitable in about half of cases of preterm labor.

Some early deliveries do not just happen. The perinatal team may deliberately induce early labor or perform a cesarean section if various tests indicate that the mother and/or the baby are in great danger. Such "indicated" early deliveries account for as many as 40 percent of all preterm births. They're most likely to occur in pregnancies complicated by:

- severe hypertension
- severe premature separation of the placenta from the uterine wall, which cuts off the supply of nutrients and oxygen to the fetus
- extreme maternal bleeding
- signs of infection inside the uterus
- growth retardation
- a fetal death or an abnormality that eliminates any chances that the baby will survive after birth

The best place for any premature baby to enter the world is a hospital with the most sophisticated technology and a highly trained staff to care for high-risk babies. The best form of transportation for these babies is in their mothers' bodies, and regional networks, including airplanes, helicopters, and ambulances, have been set up to rush women in preterm labor to the hospitals with the best facilities for their babies.

Preterm labor is essentially the same as term labor. However, the premature baby may not be able to handle the stresses of labor so obstetricians try to deliver the baby in the gentlest, least traumatic way possible. That means minimal medication and manipulation and careful monitoring. In every major study, conscientious surveillance of premature fetuses has dramatically improved their outcome. For example, electronic fetal monitoring can detect ominous changes in heart rate, alerting doctors to act quickly to avoid such dangers as a lack of oxygen.

Vaginal delivery is possible if the baby is head-first and shows no signs of fetal distress and labor is not unusually long or difficult. Some obstetricians feel that a cesarean delivery is safer and more gentle, particularly for a very small, very premature baby in the breech position. You may want to talk over this issue with your caregivers.

Preterm babies seem more sensitive to pain medications given to mothers during labor and take longer to metabolize and eliminate these drugs because their liver and kidneys are not mature. The safest pain relievers are those, such as morphine and Demerol, that act quickly and clear the mother's and baby's bloodstreams by the time of birth. Another option is a regional anesthetic, such as an epidural, which is injected outside the spinal column and allows the mother to be alert while feeling no pain. Very little of this type of medication enters the mother's or the baby's bloodstream.

Some obstetricians use forceps to cradle and protect the especially fragile head of a premature infant from the pressures of the pelvic muscles during the final stage of delivery. Some favor use of vacuum extraction (see page 255), a technique in which a cuplike device is placed on the baby's head and attached to a vacuum, which gently pulls the baby from the body. While some obstetricians will delay an episiotomy to see if it's necessary in a vaginal birth, many perform one routinely in a premature delivery to reduce any pressures on the baby's head.

THE PROGNOSIS FOR PREEMIES

"What if . . ." The question that shadows so many high-risk pregnancies is inevitable if you're at risk for preterm labor. What if you do go into labor? What if contractions can't be controlled? What if your baby is born weeks or months ahead of schedule?

Your perinatal team will work hard to keep your questions purely theoretical. But because you can't help worrying about having a preterm baby, you may want to learn more about what can be done to help babies who are born too soon. (See chapter 14 on high-risk newborns.)

Today some infants born as early as twenty-two or twenty-three weeks and weighing less than a pound at birth survive, but they remain a fortunate few. At Johns Hopkins, 40 percent of babies born at twenty-four weeks survive. By thirty weeks, more than 90 percent survive, and more than 80 percent suffer no long-term handicaps.

The more premature a baby is, the more vulnerable he or she is to the most serious neonatal complications. After twenty-eight weeks, the risks decline dramatically. Yet even among the smallest, youngest babies, the hopes for a healthy future are bright. More than 85 percent of the very tiniest survivors suffer no long-term neurologic impairments.

CHAPTER 12

Pregnancy Losses

MISCARRIAGES, ECTOPIC PREGNANCIES, GENETIC ABORTIONS, AND STILLBIRTHS

Few medical events are more common, more mysterious, or more emotionally devastating than a pregnancy loss. The end of one brief life before it even begins leaves an indelible mark on parents who find themselves with empty arms and broken dreams.

One question in particular haunts every woman who has felt a tiny life slip from her body: Why? Only recently have medical scientists begun to find some answers—and to offer new hope of eventually having a healthy child. Today more than 90 percent of women who've lost a baby before its birth go on to have healthy pregnancies and normal children.

MISCARRIAGE

In medical terms, a miscarriage refers to the loss of a fetus before the twentieth week of pregnancy. Some three hundred thousand women miscarry every year. By very rough approximations, one of every four women has had a miscarriage; one of every three hundred has had three or more. The risk rises with age, so as more women delay pregnancy, the overall incidence of miscarriage will continue to rise.

In general, 10 to 15 percent of women with confirmed pregnancies miscarry. But this estimate refers only to miscarriages that occur after eight weeks of gestation. Many more pregnancies may end much sooner, often before a woman suspects she's pregnant. The single predominant cause of these early losses is genetic, most often a chromosomal abnormality.

In a large-scale investigation carried out at five medical centers, researchers, using highly sensitive tests to detect hormone changes within seven days of conception, found that 31 percent of "implanting" embryos miscarry. Medical scientists now believe that many miscarriages that *seem* to occur between eight to fifteen weeks of pregnancy actually occur much earlier. Although the pregnancy is doomed, the embryo remains in the uterus for several weeks before expulsion.

The fact that so many pregnancies end so soon may offer some comfort to a woman who's miscarried. While she may assume that something she did precipitated the miscarriage, the pregnancy, in all likelihood, ended weeks earlier for reasons totally beyond her control.

Why Miscarriages Occur

Among the most likely reasons for miscarriage to occur are:

Genetic defects. A single miscarriage seems to be nature's way of destroying a random genetic error—a system of "quality control" for the species. In at least 50 to 60 percent of first-trimester miscarriages, the embryo itself has a missing or extra chromosome. Because of this devastating defect, it cannot develop normally. Second-trimester miscarriages are more likely to stem from other causes, although more than a third also may be the result of genetic aberrations.

Major physical abnormality. About 20 percent of embryos have physical malformations that interfere with normal development.

A degenerating egg. An egg begins to disintegrate several days after its release. If fertilization occurs at this point, the embryo may never develop or it may be absorbed by surrounding tissue early in pregnancy. In the eventual miscarriage, the gestational sac that normally contains the embryo is empty.

Gynecologic abnormality. Women with unusually formed, double, or divided wombs are more likely to miscarry. Exposure to DES before birth also can alter the reproductive tract in ways that make miscarriage more likely.

"Incompetent" cervix. One of the most frequent causes of second-trimester losses is a cervix that opens without pain or warning as the baby and its amniotic sac grow larger and heavier. The result is the birth of a fetus far too immature to survive. Women who have neither borne children nor undergone cervical surgery are not at risk. (See chapter 10 for more on this problem and its treatment.)

Fibroids. Benign growths of muscle tissue within the uterus, called myomas or fibroid tumors, may increase the risk of miscarriage by interfering with normal implantation. The location of the growths is more significant than their size.

Uterine adhesions and scarring. Adhesions can develop after myomectomy, inflammation of the uterine lining, or curettage (scraping) of the uterus after a previous delivery. Scarring also may be the result of pelvic inflammatory disease (PID). Using hysteroscopes to look inside the uterus and microsurgical instruments and lasers, gynecologists can remove some adhesions and scars, reducing the risk of subsequent miscarriage.

Previous abortions. A first-trimester elective abortion does not seem to increase the risk of miscarriage, although several may. Two or more second-trimester abortions pose a somewhat greater risk.

Progesterone deficiency. Since progesterone prepares the uterine lining for pregnancy, scientists speculate that too little of this hormone might jeopardize a pregnancy. A sampling, or biopsy, of cells from the lining of the uterus (the endometrium) eleven to twelve days after ovulation can reveal a "luteal phase defect" caused by too little progesterone. Another way to spot this problem is monitoring your temperature throughout your menstrual cycle. If your temperature does not remain elevated by at least .6 degrees for ten or more days after ovulation, you may have a progesterone deficiency that could interfere with normal pregnancy.

Age. About 15 percent of thirty- to thirty-four-year-olds miscarry. Among women between the ages of thirty-five and thirty-nine, 17 to 18 percent lose babies. In women over forty, the miscarriage rate rises to 25 percent. The reason may be an increase in chromosomal defects, as well as more years of exposure to toxins, more chronic infections, diminished hormones, and poor blood supply to the uterus.

Smoking. Miscarriage rates in smokers, regardless of their age or alcohol consumption, are clearly higher than in nonsmokers.

Smoking should stop as soon as a woman tries to get pregnant, if not sooner.

Alcohol. Two major studies have found an association between alcohol and miscarriage. In one, 17 percent of the women who drank at least twice a week miscarried, compared to 8.1 percent of nondrinkers. Another study found a slightly increased risk of miscarriage in the first trimester. Recent data suggest that an occasional drink does not increase the risk of miscarriage, but does pose other threats to a fetus.

Thyroid abnormalities. Either too much or too little thyroid hormone interferes with normal fertility, and some physicians routinely evaluate thyroid function if a woman miscarries. If her thyroid levels are low, treatment consists of thyroid supplements. However, there is no solid evidence that extra thyroid hormone can prevent miscarriage.

Infections. Many bacteria and viruses can cross the placenta and possibly trigger a miscarriage. The one most frequently implicated in repeated miscarriages is *Ureaplasma urealyticum*. While this organism normally resides in the vagina and cervix, studies have detected unusually large colonies of these microbes in the fetus and placenta after miscarriage.

Chronic diseases. Women with kidney or thyroid disorders, uncontrolled diabetes, or flare-ups of lupus have a higher incidence of miscarriage. Establishing good control of a disease prior to pregnancy or conceiving during a time of remission lowers the risk.

Surgery during pregnancy. Physicians generally operate on pregnant women only when absolutely necessary. The risk of miscarriage is greatest after abdominal or pelvic surgery.

Immunologic mechanisms. According to a still unproven theory, a mother may not reject a fetus as she might a transplanted organ because blocking antibodies protect the baby. However, if a fetus is too genetically similar to its mother, these antibodies may not develop.

Prenatal diagnostic tests. The two methods of genetic testing in pregnancy—chronic villus sampling (CVS) and amniocentesis—carry a .5 percent risk of miscarriage, a risk parents must balance against the benefits of prenatal diagnosis.

Environmental factors. Irradiation and cancer drugs are proven agents of miscarriage, but they're rarely a danger in pregnancy. Among the more common chemicals associated with miscarriage are: anesthetic gases, aniline, arsenic, benzene, ethylene oxide, formaldehyde, and lead. Microwaves and video display terminals have been accused of playing a role in miscarriage, but we do not know how great a risk they may be.

What Doesn't Cause Miscarriages

Sex. The enlarging uterus moves out of the woman's pelvis into the abdomen during pregnancy. Neither vaginal intercourse nor a woman's orgasm pose a threat in a normal pregnancy.

Falls. While old-time movie heroines lost their babies after tumbling down stairs or off horses, real-life injuries rarely trigger miscarriage. The developing fetus, cushioned by amniotic fluid, is protected from all but the most severe trauma.

Forbidden treats. Often women torment themselves with the memory of a glass of wine, a quick cigarette, a cup of coffee that they had shortly before miscarriage. Keep in mind that the signs of a miscarriage often don't occur for days or weeks after a fetus dies.

Types of Miscarriages

Miscarriages occur in different ways and pose different implications for future pregnancies.

Threatened miscarriage. About 15 to 20 percent of pregnant women experience some bleeding in their first trimester. Early bleeding, particularly on the days you might have been menstruating, does not mean that you will miscarry. In more than half of such cases, miscarriage does *not* occur, and the pregnancy continues normally.

If the bleeding persists, your doctor may not know whether or not you've miscarried. Ultrasound is the best method for determining whether the fetus is still alive. If the sonogram shows a living fetus, your chances of continuing the pregnancy are good, despite the bleeding.

Restricted activity and bedrest are the primary recommendations. If the bleeding stops, you'll probably be able to get up in a day or two. If it persists, another sonogram can check for possible reasons, such as a blighted ovum (an egg cell that does not develop normally).

Imminent or inevitable miscarriage. Once the cervix or the membranes of the amniotic sac open, nothing can be done to save the pregnancy. Women usually feel strong uterine cramps and discharge heavy amounts of bright red blood, plus clots and occasional pink tissue fragments. Rarely is the embryo itself visible in an early loss.

Complete and incomplete miscarriages. A complete miscarriage lasts anywhere from a few minutes to several hours. Once all the tissue has passed through the cervix, uterine cramping stops. Bleeding greatly diminishes, and the woman feels much better. After an examination, she requires no further treatment.

In an incomplete miscarriage (which is more common), tissue remains in the uterus, causing continued bleeding and cramping for several days. If not treated, bleeding can persist for several months. Doctors usually perform a D & C (dilation and currettage, or scraping of the uterine lining), using a vacuum or suction device.

Missed miscarriage. If an embryo fails to develop properly or stops growing and dies, the mother may not realize what has happened because nothing has been expelled from her body. However, her uterus stops growing, her breasts become smaller, and she may lose several pounds. Eventually the embryo and products of pregnancy are expelled or reabsorbed into the body. If the woman is Rh negative, she receives RhoGAM to prevent sensitization.

The myth of the "habitual aborter." For decades, obstetricians believed that women who'd had three or more miscarriages faced an 80 to 90 percent of miscarrying again. The unfortunate term for a woman whose pregnancies repeatedly ended in spontaneous abortions was "habitual aborter." A conclusive study in 1964 showed that women who had at least one liveborn infant had only a 25 to 30 percent risk of miscarrying, regardless of how many times they had miscarried in the past. The risk is higher (about 40 percent) in women who've never had a successful pregnancy.

What to Expect

If you have a complete miscarriage, you need no further treatment other than bedrest for the next forty-eight hours. Notify your doctor immediately if you develop a fever. If you require a D & C, you'll be given a medication to relax your uterus and prevent additional cramping as a result of contact with the instruments. The procedure itself lasts several minutes and can be performed in a doctor's office

"I know you could say I never really had a baby, except during those few hours when it was already over and done with, but I guess these things aren't entirely logical. I loved my baby . . . absorbed in pain and self-pity, still I was flooded with adoration for this tiny, not-yet-shaped baby who had lived in me."

Penny Armstrong and Sheryl Feldman, *A Midwife's Story*

On the Horizon: Immune Therapy

One new approach to miscarriage stems from an old question: Why doesn't a pregnant woman's body "reject" a fetus just as it might an organ transplant? One theory is that tissues surrounding the fetus produce blocking antibodies that shield the tiny foreigner from the mother's usual immune defenses. However, if a woman and a husband are too genetically similar, the child they conceive may be so like the mother that her immune system doesn't respond as it should to protect the fetus.

A novel therapy has been developed by researchers in England and the United States to trick the mother's system into setting up the proper blocking reaction: injections of the husband's white blood cells or insertion of vaginal suppositories containing his seminal plasma (plasma made from spinning semen) *before* pregnancy. Several thousand women in England and the U.S. have undergone immune therapy, and 60 to 80 percent have become pregnant. But many scientists remain dubious for a simple reason: Even after several miscarriages and with no treatment at all, 60 to 80 percent of women become pregnant.

or an outpatient facility. You will have to remain on bedrest for several days. Your doctor will test to see if you have Rh-negative blood and, if necessary, administer RhoGAM.

If you miscarry in your second trimester, you may be given oxytocin, a drug that induces contractions, or prostaglandins to complete the expulsion of the amniotic sac. The process is longer, more stressful, and more uncomfortable; recovery also takes longer.

To prevent infection, don't have intercourse for two weeks or until bleeding stops. Even if you're eager to conceive again, obstetricians generally recommend birth control for at least two cycles. After a miscarriage, the uterine lining is rough and uneven, which may interfere with implantation of a normal fertilized egg. Some physicians advise waiting as long as six months before trying to get pregnant. The risk of another loss is highest in the first two months after a miscarriage.

Medical Options

A woman who has miscarried more than once may be the hapless victim of circumstance or she may have an undetected medical or gynecologic problem. In the past, obstetricians did not launch a thorough investigation unless three miscarriages had occurred; increasingly, they are beginning their detective work after two losses, depending on the woman's age and desire for children.

A miscarriage workup usually includes a physical examination, chromosomal studies, assessment of the uterine lining in the second half of the menstrual cycle, cultures for pathogens, x rays of the uterus and fallopian tubes (hysteroscopy and hysterosalpingography), and possibly immunologic evaluation. Based on the findings, couples have a variety of options.

Genetic counseling. A genetic counselor can help a couple find out more about their genetic makeup. To get the most information, geneticists examine the aborted fetus to detect any possible abnormalities. Extensive testing turns up a problem in 5 percent of cases.

Sometimes one parent is a carrier of a genetic defect that makes it impossible to have a normal child. If the father is the carrier, artificial insemination with another man's sperm is an option for the couple to consider. If the mother is the carrier, embryo transfer—in which her husband's sperm would fertilize another woman's ovum in the laboratory and then be implanted in the uterus—is a possibility. If both parents carry a recessive gene for the same problem, the chances of having another affected baby are one in four, and a counselor can advise the couple about prenatal testing and diagnosis.

Antibiotics. Your doctor may test for a range of pathogens. Some routinely recommend treatment with the antibiotic doxycycline (a form of tetracycline) for husband and wife for ten days, even though a specific organism has not been identified.

Progesterone. If either blood tests or an endometrial biopsy indicate a luteal phase defect, a progesterone deficiency in the second half of the menstrual cycle, the usual treatment is progesterone. Most women use vaginal suppositories, beginning when their temperatures rise at ovulation and continuing for six to eight weeks. Boosting progesterone levels before conception also may help, but there's no strong scientific evidence that it will.

Cerclage. After more than one midtrimester loss, an obstetrician may place a pursestringlike suture, called a cerclage, around the cervix, pulling it tight to prevent its opening. Usually a cerclage is put in early in pregnancy and removed at the thirty-seventh week. This method works—if the problem truly is an incompetent cervix. (See chapter 10 for more information.)

Uterine surgery. If the problem is a malformed uterus, reconstructive surgery is advised. If fibroids seem to be interfering with pregnancy, a myomectomy can remove the growths without removing the uterus. Laser surgery often can remove scars or adhesions. About 50 percent of women who undergo such surgery become pregnant again, but their miscarriage rate remains high.

Treatments for placental blood clots. Some women may have specific antibodies in their blood that increase the risk of blood clots in the placenta, which might make miscarriage more likely. Experimental treatments include prednisone, a steroid drug, and aspirin. Also under investigation is the anti-blood-clotting drug, heparin.

TLC. Everyone assumes, although no one knows for sure, that stress can provoke miscarriage. Emotional support can alleviate stress—and possibly help prevent miscarriage. In one study, a group of women who'd had repeated losses received increased attention but no specific medical therapy. They were more likely to have successful pregnancies than women who did not get such special consideration.

"WE WERE BORN TO BE PARENTS"

On an awful night in Baltimore several years ago, Janet lay in agony in a hospital emergency room. She was bleeding from her vagina. Her abdomen was rigid. The pain was relentless.

"As a nurse, I knew something was very wrong, although I didn't know what," she recalls. "At first the doctors in the emergency room thought an ovarian cyst had burst. But a blood test for pregnancy turned out positive, and a gynecologist guessed that an ectopic pregnancy had ruptured in one of my fallopian tubes. He performed emergency surgery to remove the tube and saved my life." By the time of the operation, Janet had hemorrhaged so heavily that she'd lost half of her blood volume and needed a transfusion of two units of blood.

Janet, a new bride of twenty-three, wondered about future pregnancies, but consoled herself with the thought that one fallopian tube was all that was necessary for a fertilized egg to travel to the uterus. She and her husband decided not to wait to have a child. "We both wanted kids, and we didn't want to take any chances," Janet explains.

For a year they tried to get pregnant. "I took my temperature, kept charts of when I was ovulating, went through a battery of infertility tests," she says. Finally Janet tried Clomid, a fertility drug, and got pregnant that month.

Seven weeks later she started spotting and cramping. An ultrasound showed only the remnants of an egg sac in her uterus. "We thought it was a very early miscarriage," she recalls. When cramping persisted, she underwent a D & C. But for the next month she continued spotting and cramping off and on.

When she went to Johns Hopkins for an exam, a pregnancy test turned out positive. The gynecologist discovered that a calcified egg had been sitting in her remaining fallopian tube for three and a half months. "I was devastated, because I knew that if I lost the tube, I'd lose my last chance for a normal pregnancy," Janet says. Using highly precise microsurgical techniques, her gynecologist was able to remove the egg and save the tube.

"Afterwards, he told me to try again," says Janet. "The risk of another ectopic was 50–50, but at least there was reason for hope." This time a fertilized egg managed to make its way through the repaired tube to her uterus. In January 1987, she gave birth to a healthy, normal little girl, named Natalie. "She made us realize that we were born to be parents," says Janet. "Being with her was what we loved most."

Janet was thrilled when she suspected she was pregnant again. But her levels of human chorionic gonadotropin (HCG), the telltale hormone of pregnancy, kept fluctuating. "I walked around like a human time bomb until a sonogram showed that there was nothing in my uterus." A fertilized egg had ruptured at the very tip of her sole fallopian tube. "It was a hard call, and we didn't know if the tube could be saved," she remembers. But once again her gynecologist was able to remove the egg without damaging the tube.

However, this time Janet's HCG levels didn't go down as they should have after the surgery. Tests indicated that microscopic cells were growing within her fallopian tube. Hoping to avoid more surgery and to preserve the tube, her gynecologist suggested a new therapy: methotrexate, a drug usually used to treat cancer.

Like other anticancer agents, methotrexate—even at doses much lower than those needed for cancer chemotherapy—kills fast-growing cells throughout the body. During the course of her therapy, Janet suffered mild forms of the symptoms that plague cancer patients, including nausea and bleeding gums. But the methotrexate did its primary job and destroyed the remaining cells in her fallopian tube.

The experience was emotionally as well as physically harrowing. "I felt guilty that my reproductive system kept failing me," she explains. "It's like having a chronic illness. You feel you can't trust your body. The psychological impact is worse than the physical recovery. It messes up your career; it messes up your marriage. And you feel grief because of what you lose every time you think you're pregnant and you're really not."

For Janet, deciding whether to try again was enormously difficult. "The odds were still 50–50, and I didn't know what to do next," she says. "On the one hand, I was just so grateful to have Natalie. On the other, we yearned for another child. I didn't know if I was being selfish by not wanting to go through another ectopic."

Finally, Janet and her husband's wish came true. As this book was going to press, she learned that, once again, a fertilized egg had made its way to her uterus and she was going to have another baby.

ECTOPIC PREGNANCY

An ectopic pregnancy refers to the implantation and development of a fertilized egg outside the uterus—in the fallopian tubes, the uterine muscles, the cervix, abdomen, or ovaries. The vast majority—98 percent—occur within the fallopian tubes. The gestational sac cannot grow, and if it isn't removed, it ruptures. Because of the risks of bleeding and infection, a ruptured ectopic pregnancy is a life-threatening medical emergency.

The incidence of this serious complication has almost quadrupled in recent years, rising from seventeen thousand eight hundred cases in 1970 to seventy-eight thousand four hundred cases in 1985. In 1970, ectopics occurred in 4.5 of every one thousand pregnancies. In 1985 the incidence was 20.9 for every one thousand. More younger women, including adolescents, are developing ectopic pregnancies, possibly because of earlier sexual activity or more widespread sexually transmitted diseases. However, the highest incidence is in women over the age of thirty.

While the skyrocketing incidence is bad news for would-be mothers, there also is good news for women at risk: The mortality rates have fallen dramatically because of advances in diagnosis and treatment. And because of new surgical techniques, women who've had an ectopic have better chances of having a normal pregnancy in the future.

Why Ectopic Pregnancies Occur

Normally tiny hairs called cilia within the fallopian tubes transport an egg from the ovary to the uterus—a journey that takes about eighty hours. Any obstruction, narrowing, scarring, or damage to the cilia can block the egg's passage, increasing the likelihood that it will implant itself in the tube. Among the causes of such damage:

Pelvic inflammatory disease, or PID, an infection that spreads from the uterus to the fallopian tubes, ovaries, and surrounding tissues, is responsible for about 50 percent of ectopic pregnancies. A woman with one documented episode of PID has a 1 in 24 chance of having an ectopic pregnancy, compared to 1 in 147 for other women. PID can be the result of use of an IUD or of sexually transmitted disease.

Previous surgery on the fallopian tubes. Any operation—including sterilization by blocking or cutting the tubes and corrective surgery to restore fertility—increases the risk of ectopics. About 16 to 20 percent of women undergoing tubal sterilization subsequently have ectopic pregnancies. After reconstructive surgery to restore fertility, women are twice as likely to have an ectopic.

Intrauterine devices (IUDs). While no one has proven that IUDs cause ectopics, there is a 1.2-fold increase in the ectopic rate among IUD wearers. The major risk factor is length of use, and the infections associated with IUD use may be responsible. Another theory for the link is that IUDs prevent intrauterine, not ectopic pregnancies. About 13 percent of the pregnancies that occur with an IUD in place are ectopic.

Previous sterilization procedures. Ectopic pregnancies seem to occur more frequently after sterilization, whether by blocking, cutting, or burning the tubes by electrocautery. Ten percent of pregnancies after such surgery are ectopic because the tubes, though reconnected and open, may be damaged.

Several abortions. Researchers have found an increase in the relative risk of ectopic pregnancy from 1.3 after one abortion to 2.6 after two or more first-trimester elective abortions.

Previous ectopic pregnancy. About half of women who've had one ectopic will go on to have a viable normal pregnancy. However, 12 to 20 percent will have another ectopic, possibly because of microscopic abnormalities in both tubes.

DES exposure. Daughters whose mothers took DES while pregnant may have abnormalities in their reproductive systems that increase the risk of ectopic implantation.

Endometriosis. The growth of endometrial tissue within the tubes is rare. However, the disease might impair the gentle motions by which an egg is transported to the uterus, making it more likely that the egg is trapped in a fallopian tube.

Previous abdominal surgery. Any operation within the abdominal or pelvic cavity increases the change of damage, adhesions, or scars.

What to Watch For

Early diagnosis is critical in saving a pregnant woman's life *and* her ability to have children. In the past, 80 percent of ectopic pregnancies went undetected until they ruptured. Today only about 20 percent reach that point of extreme danger, mainly because of early detection of the warning signals, which include:
  • a missed menstrual period

- abdominal pain, which may be mild at first and become severe
- vaginal bleeding
- fainting
- a mass within the abdomen

What to Expect

If you are at risk for an ectopic pregnancy or you develop any of the telltale symptoms, your doctor will try to determine whether you are indeed pregnant and whether the embryo is developing within the uterus or outside it. Various diagnostic techniques have greatly enhanced the chances of detecting an ectopic, including:

Measurement of pregnancy hormones. Blood tests can determine if you're pregnant within seven to ten days of conception. If you are not pregnant, your levels of human chorionic gonadotropin (HCG), the characteristic hormone of early pregnancy, will be very low. In a normal pregnancy, your HCG levels will double every 2.4 days. Almost all pregnancies that do not follow this progression are ectopic. If the readings are unclear, your doctor will repeat the test until the fifth or sixth week of pregnancy, when ultrasound can help with a diagnosis.

Ultrasound. After five or six weeks of pregnancy, a sonogram can reveal the typical signs of an ectopic pregnancy: an empty uterus and a suspicious mass or evidence of blood elsewhere.

Laparoscopy. In this test, a physician inserts a long, thin flexible instrument called a laparoscope through a small incision in the abdomen and examines the abdominal and pelvic area to check for an ectopic pregnancy.

Culdocentesis. This test, used less often than in the past because ultrasound has become more precise, detects the presence of blood in the cul-de-sac, a cavity in the pelvis that fills with blood if an ectopic pregnancy has begun to bleed.

A combination of these tests permits diagnosis between six and eight weeks in most cases—before rupture, which generally occurs after ten weeks. Early diagnosis allows for conservative therapy and a greater chance of saving a fallopian tube.

Medical Options

In determining what approach to take, physicians have to consider various factors: whether the gestational sac has ruptured, the extent of bleeding, the damage to the tube, the site of the pregnancy, the state of the opposite tube, and the woman's desire for future pregnancies.

Medical treatment. While a ruptured ectopic pregnancy always requires surgery, early diagnosis sometimes allows a more conservative approach. Some women, whose ectopic pregnancy is reabsorbed into their bodies, may require no treatment. In others, methotrexate, an anticancer drug, destroys rapidly growing new tissue. It produces milder forms of some of the same side effects as cancer chemotherapy, including nausea, vomiting, and bleeding gums.

Tubal "expression." Depending on the size and location of the ectopic pregnancy, the surgeon may be able to manipulate or press the tiny gestational sac out of the fallopian tube. Fine sutures or electrocauterization may be used to control bleeding at the implantation site.

"Conservative" surgery. Various microsurgical techniques can help preserve the fallopian tube for women who want to have future pregnancies. After such an operation, the chance of a normal pregnancy ranges from 25 to 55 percent.

Removal of the fallopian tube. This procedure, a salpingectomy, may be necessary if a tube has ruptured or been extensively damaged. If the other tube also has been damaged or scarred, the chances for a normal pregnancy range from 30 to 70 percent.

In-vitro fertilization. If there is no way of preserving the fallopian tube, this technique, in which a woman's eggs are removed, fertilized in a laboratory, and then reimplanted in her uterus, offers an alternative route to conception. Success rates average about 20 percent at most fertility centers.

GENETIC ABORTIONS

For 98 percent of the women who undergo genetic testing each year, the results are reassuring: The baby is normal. There's no reason for concern. They can relax and enjoy the pregnancy. But for 2 percent of couples, genetic testing reveals that their worst fears have come true. Their unborn children may never have a chance to survive or to live a normal life. Some parents, acting on the basis of deep religious or personal beliefs, continue the pregnancy. Others

"We agreed about the abortion. We knew the baby could never have any chance of a normal life. But still I felt guilty and sad about ending the life of a baby we had wanted so much. It's like losing a loved one, but people don't think you've suffered a loss because, after all, it was something you chose to do."

make the heartbreaking decision to undergo an elective abortion. Even women who oppose abortion on religious or ethical grounds often choose an abortion if the child has no chance of survival.

If a woman underwent chorionic villus sampling, she can arrange for a relatively simple first-trimester abortion. During the first twelve weeks of pregnancy, suction curettage is the most common method of abortion. After progressive dilation or widening of the cervix, a suction device draws out the contents of the uterus. A curette, a surgical instrument shaped like a spoon, is used to check for complete removal. Major complications occur in fewer than one in one hundred cases.

Between the thirteenth and fifteenth week, doctors generally use a technique called dilation and evacuation (D & E), in which they open the cervix and use medical instruments to remove the fetus from the uterus.

From the sixteenth to twentieth week, prostaglandins, natural substances found in most body tissues, are administered as vaginal suppositories or injected into the amniotic sac by inserting a needle through the abdominal wall. They induce uterine contractions, and the fetus and placenta are expelled within twenty-four hours. A variety of other methods also are used for second-trimester abortions, including injections of saline or urea solutions into the amniotic sac to kill the fetus and drugs that make the uterus contract.

While second-trimester abortions are more medically complex and risky, the timing makes little difference psychologically. Whether early in pregnancy or later, the loss remains devastating. "Women often say they want CVS so they won't have to have a second-trimester abortion," says Karin Blakemore, an obstetrician and geneticist at Johns Hopkins. "But they're just as attached at nine weeks as at sixteen, and emotionally the abortion is just as difficult."

In a study of twenty women who underwent elective abortions because of genetic defects discovered by amniocentesis, about half were ambivalent or had difficulty accepting the abortion. Yet all but one said they would recommend prenatal testing to friends, and all but one who became pregnant had amniocentesis again.

At any stage, abortion can be as profoundly painful as any other form of pregnancy loss—for both partners. "We lost this child, the chance to hold her, love her, and raise her; we lost the joy of anticipation about her future," a father wrote after the midtrimester abortion of a baby with Tay-Sachs, a fatal enzyme storage disease. "The worst part of our loss was the awareness that we would never know this child."

STILLBIRTHS

The death of a baby after the twentieth week of pregnancy is called an intrauterine fetal death or, more commonly, a stillbirth. About twenty thousand occur each year, and in more than half the cause is never discovered.

Among the conditions associated with an increased risk of still-birth are:

Genetic defects. From 5 to 10 percent of such losses are triggered by genetic anomalies, particularly an extra eighteenth chromosome (Trisomy 18). Despite this devastating defect, which is always eventually fatal, the babies may appear normal at birth.

Maternal disease, including high blood pressure, diabetes, heart disease, kidney disorders, and lupus. While the diseases themselves do not trigger the loss, they increase the danger if another risk factor—such as infection—develops.

Umbilical cord accidents, in which the cord becomes twisted or squeezed, cutting off the baby's oxygen and blood supply.

Placental abnormalities, such as abruptions, tumors, or growths.

Serious infection of the mother or fetus.

Often doctors can find no explanation, and parents have to come to terms with their loss and make plans for their future without a clear understanding of what happened and why.

Once doctors confirm the absence of a fetal heartbeat, the parents have to make the difficult decision of choosing between immediate induction of labor or waiting until labor begins on its own (usually within two weeks). The use of prostaglandins makes induction of labor safe for the mother and delivery easier without the need to wait weeks. However, waiting a few days may allow the parents to begin working through their grief.

If the parents choose to wait, physicians recommend weekly blood testing for infection or clotting. The trend is to induce labor once past the twenty-fourth week of pregnancy, although obstetricians will allow parents time for emotional adjustment before facing the trauma of delivery.

After delivery of the baby, parents can see and hold their child. Many arrange for a baptism or funeral service. Obstetricians generally request permission to perform an autopsy, since the results can provide clues as to what happened and why.

GRIEVING FOR BABIES WHO DIE BEFORE BIRTH

Each year hundreds of thousands of couples mourn for a baby who never laughed or cried or lived outside its mother's womb. What friends and relatives often don't understand is that this child, who may have slipped away unseen and unheld by anyone, was just as real, just as loved, as a youngster who spent years romping in the world. Psychologists have found that the length of time a fetus or infant survives has no correlation with maternal grieving. Mothers whose babies die before birth may mourn as intensely as those whose infants live for several months.

Even before conception, the parents may have begun planning and fantasizing. They've talked about names. They've teased each other about whether the baby would inherit his carrot-colored hair or her turned-up nose. The unborn child becomes the embodiment of their most cherished dreams. If the baby dies, the dreams die too.

An Invisible Loss

Some psychotherapists believe that losing a baby who never lived may, in its own way, be harder than mourning for a specific individual. "You grieve for the baby you never knew and for the child—the beautiful, perfect, wondrous child—who might have been," says one mother. Parents also grieve alone. Since there is no casket and no funeral, the loss is, to most of the world, invisible, and friends may not understand why the couple is so upset.

Women often feel the loss in an extremely intense, almost physical way. Many who miscarry have not yet reached the point in pregnancy where the fetus seems separate from them. "His flesh was my flesh; his blood was my blood," one woman recalls. "Losing him was like losing part of me."

Typically, women feel both vulnerable and responsible, as if they did something to cause the loss or should have done something to prevent it. They also tend to blame themselves, trying to identify the one thing that they did wrong: exercising or not exercising, working or not working, eating too much or too little.

Guilt, that ugly little intruder, preys at grieving mothers. If they—like many women—felt any ambivalence about being pregnant, they may feel that somehow their negative feelings led to the miscarriage or stillbirth. Some women interpret a loss as a punishment for past wrongs, imagined or real. As such self-inflicted guilt gnaws at them, their self-esteem shrinks and they may tumble into a depression.

Fathers also grieve, but in different ways and at different times. At first, their greatest pain is their helplessness. They see the women they love in distress, and they can do nothing. They, too, feel guilty—about traveling, working too hard, not helping around the house. And their wives seem so profoundly miserable that they cannot find the words to comfort them. "I have never felt so inadequate," one man recalls.

Some men, feeling that they're doing no good, pull away, burying themselves in work or drowning their pain in alcohol. Some strive to put the loss behind them and get on with their lives. To their heart-broken wives, such actions may seem hurtful. "He seemed almost indifferent," one woman says. "I felt that he mustn't have loved the baby very much to start with." The incidence of separation and divorce rises after pregnancy loss.

When couples can overcome their hesitations and talk, they often discover that the father is masking his own grief to appear strong for his wife. Sometimes, months later, once a woman has picked up the pieces of her life, a father will suddenly feel the heavy weight of sorrow that he'd put on hold for so long.

Often parents find great comfort in talking through their feelings. Some hospitals have perinatal mortality programs that include meetings with a genetic counselor and specialists so parents can get answers to their questions about what happened. In many communities support groups meet regularly to help parents deal with the emotional impact of a pregnancy loss.

Participating in these groups can be invaluable in working through grief. Both spouses feel freer to express painful feelings. And many individuals are relieved to discover that others share their "craziest" thoughts.

> "I was in the bathroom when I passed the fetus. I began to sob uncontrollably. My husband came in and held me. I felt as if my heart had just slipped out of my body."

What You Can Do

Counselors who provide support to parents who lose babies before or shortly after birth offer some basic advice:

- Name the baby.
- If the loss occurs after the fetus is formed and has features, hold it. Take pictures (the hospital usually will do this for you). Ask for a lock of its hair.
- Hold a memorial service that suits your religious beliefs and values.
- Be prepared to commemorate the most poignant day of all, your baby's due date.

- Talk to other children in the family about the loss, reassuring them that nothing they said, did, or wished caused the death of the baby. A pregnancy loss, confusing and frightening for parents, can deeply trouble young children, who do not understand why their parents are so upset. They need reassurance that they are loved and that, eventually, life will return to normal.
- Give yourself time—more than you might ever guess—to recover.
- Even if you desperately want to get pregnant right away, take time to work through your grief.
- Schedule an appointment with your caregiver a few months after the loss to discuss the possible causes and the implications for future pregnancies. A "genetic autopsy"—detailed analysis of your baby's genetic makeup—can provide clues as to whether any subsequent children will be at risk.
- Don't be shocked if you feel pangs of jealousy or resentment when you see women with healthy babies, especially if the infants are about the age your baby would have been.
- Join a support group for parents who've suffered pregnancy losses. Your hospital social worker or the national organizations listed in the appendix can refer you to a group in your area.

Are You Ready to Try Again?

Some women want nothing more than to have another baby immediately. "I lay on the table in the emergency room, bleeding and doubled over with pain, and all I could think of was getting pregnant again and doing it right the next time," says a woman who had an ectopic pregnancy. Yet most physicians advise waiting at least several months for physical and psychological healing to take place.

If a woman becomes pregnant too soon, the unresolved grief and anxieties may interfere with her ability to relax and relate to another child. Psychotherapists have described a "replacement child syndrome," in which mothers become pregnant again to "replace" the lost child. The mother never works out her original grief and may be overprotective and have unrealistic expectations. The child may live forever in the shadow of its older sibling.

While the ache never goes away completely, most couples who lose a child eventually reach a point of acceptance. "Finally you let go of the baby you lost," says a mother. "Some kind of compass inside you somehow points toward the future, and you know it's time."

The High-Risk Birth

Every pregnant woman has a fantasy of how she'd like her baby's birth to be. You may see yourself in a cozy room, surrounded by people you love, eagerly waiting to welcome your child into the world. Or you may think of the exhilaration of clasping your husband's hand and pushing the baby from your body. Or you may anticipate the sweet moment when your newborn, still wet from the womb, nuzzles against your breast.

Even in normal pregnancies, such fantasies don't always come true. Unexpected events can suddenly transform a simple delivery into a complicated and potentially hazardous one. About 20 percent of normal pregnant women become high risk during the process of giving birth.

While you may assume that all high-risk pregnancies culminate in high-risk deliveries, that isn't necessarily so. Many, even most, women who've had complicated pregnancies can have uneventful deliveries. Some risk factors, such as an incompetent cervix or preterm labor, which no longer are a threat after the thirty-seventh week, have little or no impact on delivery.

Even when complications persist, you can participate in the decisions concerning your baby's arrival. Like all parents, you'll find that the more you learn about the stages and phases involved in giving birth, the better prepared you'll be for the happy moment when your child enters the world.

"In our medicated society, we have eradicated some of the pain and anxiety, but I'm afraid we have eradicated more of the excitement and joy. Pregnancy, labor, and delivery are thought of as essentially a disease in the United States. As a result, the anxiety and fear and pain are medically treated as if they were evil and destructive symptoms of the 'condition' rather than positive forces that mobilize a woman for an awesome, prodigious, and usually enormously rewarding experience— the birth of a child."

—T. Berry Brazelton, M.D., *Be a Healthy Mother, Have a Healthy Baby*

COUNTING DOWN TO DELIVERY

At times you probably can't wait for the big day to arrive. At others you may almost hope it never will. Every pregnant women's emotions seesaw from excitement to apprehension, curiosity to concern, as she thinks about labor and delivery. If your pregnancy was tense because of risk factors or complications, you may look forward to the end of your anxious anticipation. But if you have reason to be concerned about your baby's well-being, you may worry about how your child will fare during and after birth.

Where to Have Your Baby

For a child who has weathered a high-risk pregnancy, the best place to be born is generally one of the four-hundred-plus hospitals fully equipped to handle problems before, during, and after birth. (The appendix contains a list of perinatal centers.) Like many other hospitals, these centers often have birthing or combined labor/delivery/ recovery rooms. Talk to your caregivers about whether you might be able to use one. If so, you'll have the combined advantages of a homey, comfortable environment and immediate access to medical care in case of an emergency.

Childbirth Preparation

Childbirth classes let parents know what to expect during labor and delivery. If you cannot attend regular classes because of restrictions on your activity, you can arrange for inexpensive private lessons. Another alternative is a videotape, available through many childbirth education programs.

While years of research have found that childbirth education does not decrease the pain of giving birth, it does increase the mother's satisfaction. Simply becoming aware—physically and psychologically—of what's happening can give you a greater sense of control, a feeling that relieves some of the stress of a high-risk situation. At the least, you'll have a better sense of the questions to ask and the options available to you.

Psychological Preparation

While some high-risk women may not be able to practice the more strenuous childbirth-preparation exercises, one method requires no physical strain: visualization. Fantasizing about labor often enhances understanding and helps women prepare for what will happen. By visualizing your baby's birth and the excitement you and your partner will share, you can see yourself as an active participant, prepare for the work and pain, and boost your confidence in your ability to cope.

Relaxation techniques (see page 106) also can help before and during labor. As your delivery date approaches, you might combine them with breathing exercises. For instance, you might visualize yourself gently rocking your baby as you inhale and exhale.

Pain Relief

All pregnant women worry about the pain of childbirth, especially the first time around. You may fear not just the pain itself, but the loss of control over your body and emotions. The type of controlled breathing taught in childbirth preparation classes can help, but there is no one way for all women to breathe in labor. What's important is finding a comfortable pattern of breathing that will enable you to relax as much as possible.

Your "coach" can be a tremendous help in many ways: assisting you into comfortable positions, breathing with you so you can relax, offering you clear fluids, ice chips, or a Popsicle, rubbing your back, holding a cool damp cloth against your forehead, providing reassurance, applying pressure to the small of your back to relieve the pain of back labor.

You also should discuss your options for pain-relieving drugs with your caregivers. The availability of certain types of anesthesia may influence where you deliver. Occasionally, a health problem, such as heart disease, may limit the choices, but even in a high-risk pregnancy, a variety of painkillers and anesthetics can provide much-needed relief during long or difficult labors.

Pain-relieving medications can produce unwanted side effects, such as making it harder for a woman to push during the second stage or making the baby somewhat lethargic after delivery. But, as always, you and your caregivers have to weigh the advantages and disadvantages, the risks and benefits. Using pain medications for childbirth isn't a matter of making a right or wrong decision, but of doing what seems best in the unique circumstances of your baby's birth. (See chart on page 247).

Pain Medications for Labor and Delivery

- Tranquilizers and barbiturates are pills given mainly early in labor to help the mother relax.
- Analgesics (painkillers), such as Demerol, a narcotic, are injected into the blood or a muscle to relieve pain.
- Anesthetics numb the body or part of the body completely. An *epidural block* involves insertion of an anesthetic into the membrane surrounding the spinal cord at the lower back to block sensation from the waist down. A *spinal block*, delivered by injection into the spinal canal, also numbs the lower body. A *pudendal block*, injected through the vagina, numbs the perineum for an episiotomy.
- General anesthesia, an inhaled or injected drug that puts the mother to sleep, is used only for emergency cesarean deliveries when there's no time to administer regional anesthetics.

GIVING BIRTH: WHAT TO EXPECT

As your body prepares for birth, you'll notice some subtle and not-so-subtle changes. Some women lose a few pounds; others experience a burst of energy or a strong nesting instinct. Among the biological signals to watch for:

• Engagement. In the last weeks of pregnancy, the baby's head settles into your pelvis, so you can breathe more easily and deeply. In first pregnancies, the baby's head usually engages two weeks before delivery. In subsequent pregnancies, the head may move down into the pelvis many weeks before birth or during labor. Women often speak of this as "lightening."

• Brief, irregular contractions, called Braxton-Hicks contractions, that feel like a tightening of your abdomen. If they persist, you may wonder if your baby is about to be born. In "false" labor, contractions stop if you walk around and they do not become stronger or longer.

• A "show" of pink-tinged secretions from your vagina that indicates passage of the mucus plug that sealed your uterus to protect your baby from infection. Labor usually begins within twenty-four to forty-eight hours.

• A trickle or gush of warm clear fluid, indicating that the amniotic sac enclosing your baby has burst. Notify your caregivers immediately. When the amniotic membranes break beforehand, labor generally begins within twenty-four to forty-eight hours; if not, the risk of infection increases.

• A sudden burst of energy. A day or two before labor, many women become restless or concentrate on "nesting," rearranging furniture and preparing their house for the baby.

True and False Labor

False labor contractions are irregular and do not increase in frequency, duration, and intensity. They may feel like a painless hardening or balling up of the abdomen or produce discomfort only in the lower abdomen or groin. Walking may stop the contractions and relieve any pain.

Real labor contractions often start at the back and radiate to the lower abdomen, becoming more frequent and more intense regardless of your position or activity. If your baby's head is pressed against the back of your pelvis, all of the pain may be concentrated in your lower back.

Don't hesitate to call your doctor if you think you may be in labor. Only a vaginal examination can determine if your cervix has begun the crucial prerequisites for delivery: effacement (thinning) and dilation (opening). In first-time mothers, effacement may occur gradually over several days; in women who've had children, it may take only a few hours.

Normal Labor

Labor consists of three stages: In the first and longest, the cervix opens to a width of ten centimeters (four to five inches). The second begins with complete dilation and ends with the birth of the baby. The third consists of the delivery of the placenta.

First-time mothers spend an average of twelve to fourteen hours in the first stage; women who've had previous deliveries, six to eight. In the earliest part, called the latent phase, contractions typically last from thirty to sixty seconds and occur every five to twenty minutes. Using a stopwatch or a watch with a second hand, you or your coach should note the time from the beginning of one contraction to the beginning of the next.

Once you enter the birth center or hospital, expect regular examinations to check on your cervix's dilation. In the active phase of labor, your cervix dilates from three or four to ten centimeters. Contractions are stronger, longer, and more intense, lasting for sixty seconds and occurring as often as every three minutes. If you remain relaxed, your uterus will work more efficiently. Change position often. If your back hurts, try getting up on your hands and knees and rocking back and forth. Keep the muscles of your face and throat as relaxed as possible.

For many women, the hardest part of labor is "transition," the period of very strong contractions—lasting for sixty to ninety seconds and occurring every two or three minutes—during which the cervix dilates from eight to ten centimeters. You may experience vomiting, nausea, leg cramps or shaking, irritability, problems concentrating, chills, severe low backache, deep pelvic pain, or pressure on your rectum.

The second stage of labor begins when the cervix is fully dilated and ends with the birth of the baby. Contractions become more intense, and you may feel an overwhelming desire to push. Once you can give in to it, you may feel tremendous satisfaction and lose awareness of everyone and everything else.

When the baby's head "crowns" (becomes visible), you may feel

Apgars

Designed in 1952 by Dr. Virginia Apgar, an anesthesiologist, this test measures a baby's ability to adapt to the stress of labor and delivery. The test consists of five observations, made at one minute, five minutes, and occasionally fifteen minutes. Each score represents different responses of the newborn's bodily systems, measured on a three-point scale (0 to 2):

Heart Rate: under 100/min. = 1; over 100/min. = 2.
Color: blue = 0; pink but with blue extremities = 1; pink all over = 2.
Respiratory Effort: weak cry = 1; strong cry = 2.
Muscle Tone: limp = 0; some flexion tone = 1; good flexion = 2.
Reflex Irritability (from foot stimulation): no response = 0; response and some motion = 1; withdrawal and cry = 2.

Scores of 8 and 9 are excellent; 4 and 6 show a baby born under stress who is gradually adjusting. A worrisome Apgar is below 6 at one minute and remains below 6 at fifteen minutes. A high Apgar score indicates that a newborn's nervous and cardiovascular systems are adequate. But babies who improve within fifteen minutes also have responsive systems.

a full, bulging, tingling sensation or pressure on the lower bowel, rectum, or vagina. The area around the vagina becomes numb as the baby moves from your body into the world. If necessary, your doctor will make an incision to widen the vaginal opening to prevent tearing or hasten delivery. Sometimes you can avoid an episiotomy by good nutrition throughout pregnancy, exercise, trying different birth positions, or having an attendant massage the perineal tissue. However, your skin's elasticity and the baby's size also will determine whether that's possible.

Most babies emerge gradually—first the head, then one shoulder, then the other, then the rest of the body. The obstetrician clamps the umbilical cord and suctions the baby's nose and mouth to remove amniotic fluid. Your child may be lifted onto your stomach for a first snuggle. Then it will undergo several routine procedures, including weight and height measurements and administration of eye drops to prevent infection caused by gonorrhea. Often blood is drawn from the cord to measure gases—another indicator of a baby's well-being.

A nurse observes a newborn's heart rate, breathing, muscle tone, reflexes, and color at one and five minutes after delivery and gives it an Apgar score—a rating on a scale that indicates how the baby has fared during its stressful passage—from zero to ten; most babies score seven or higher. The Apgars do not predict how a baby will develop, but indicate to the pediatricians which babies may need special support or resuscitation in the delivery room. Many very premature babies score low, not because they are sick but because movement and breathing are not yet fully developed.

Engrossed in the sight and feel of your new baby, you may not even be aware of the mild contractions accompanying the third stage of labor: delivery of the placenta. If your baby begins to nurse, its sucking will stimulate the production of a hormone that compresses the blood vessels in the uterus and reduces blood loss. The third stage usually lasts less then thirty minutes.

WHAT MAKES A BIRTH HIGH-RISK

Just as in pregnancy, "risk" doesn't mean a problem definitely will develop. But because of a greater potential for complications, your caregivers will be especially vigilant in watching for early indications of danger.

Pregnancy Complications

Some conditions can have an impact on labor and delivery as well as pregnancy, including:

Hypertension. The higher a woman's blood pressure climbs and the more related problems she develops in pregnancy, the more likely she is to have a high-risk labor and delivery. In addition to being at risk for preterm birth, women with hypertension may not be able to provide an adequate supply of blood and oxygen to the placenta and fetus, and the baby may develop fetal distress. Fetal monitoring (page 81) can pick up signs that the baby isn't getting enough oxygen. While women with mild hypertension can receive most forms of pain relief or anesthesia, there is increased risk of hypotension (low blood pressure) with women with more serious problems, and expert care is crucial.

Diabetes mellitus. Because of the greater likelihood of an extremely big baby or a growth-retarded infant, a diabetic is always at increased risk during labor and delivery. Fetal monitoring can detect problems with oxygen supply or distress. During labor, a continuous infusion of insulin and glucose prevents very high blood-sugar levels in the mother and very low blood-sugar levels in her baby. About half of diabetics have cesarean deliveries, usually because of obstetrical complications or because their babies are too large to pass through the birth canal safely.

Heart disease. The strain of labor may place a serious burden on the heart of a woman with advanced heart disease. Throughout labor, continuous oxygen relieves breathlessness, chest pain, and palpitations; most women also receive medications for pain and anxiety. Caregivers watch the mother carefully for any indication of bleeding, infection, shock, or heart failure. Anesthesia may have a beneficial effect.

Cardiologists encourage a vaginal delivery, unless obstetrical complications require a cesarean. The preferred position is sitting up rather than lying flat. The obstetrician may use low forceps during delivery to reduce the strain of bearing down and pushing out the baby. Women with moderate to severe heart disease may have to remain in the hospital after the delivery until their heart function returns to normal. Invasive monitoring of the mother's heart by inserting a catheter through her blood vessels into the heart may be needed.

Epilepsy. As long as tests provide reassurance that the baby is doing well, women with seizure disorders can expect to carry to term and to have a vaginal delivery, unless obstetrical complications develop. Labor is a high-risk time for seizures.

Complications of Labor and Delivery

Some circumstances develop, often without warning, during the process of labor and delivery and immediately place the birth at risk. These include:

Abnormal presentation. About 95 percent of babies enter the world head-first. About 3.5 percent are "breech," with their heads in the upper part of the uterus and either their feet or buttocks down. A small number lie horizontally in what is called a transverse position.

Abnormal presentations increase the risk of prolonged labor and cesarean delivery. An unusual position sometimes indicates that the baby is premature, growth-retarded, has a congenital abnormality, or will experience physical trauma during delivery. Some caregivers attempt external version, or turning by means of slow, gentle pressure, of a baby in the breech position so its head enters the birth canal first. If the baby does not move into the vertex position, a cesarean delivery may be necessary.

Dysfunctional labor (failure to progress). Dysfunctional labor is the obstetrical term for any problem that results in a delay in the process of giving birth. If labor is prolonged for more than twenty-four hours, the risks to both mother and baby increase.

Dysfunctional labor may be the result of ineffective or weak contractions or a halt in contractions. Bedrest and sedation may help establish a more effective labor pattern. The obstetrician may rupture the amniotic membranes or administer oxytocin to stimulate stronger contractions. If signs of fetal distress appear, a cesarean may be necessary.

Precipitous labor. Extremely rapid labor that lasts for less than three hours can be hazardous to both the mother and her baby. Women who've had many children, who've had previous precipitous labor, who have a large pelvis or a small baby—and who develop very strong contractions—are most likely to have fast labors. Close monitoring can detect early signs of a problem.

The greatest danger is that a baby, born before the mother can get medical assistance, may not get needed care in its first few minutes of life. If the woman is in a hospital, she may receive sedatives or drugs such as magnesium sulfate to slow contractions (see page 220). Panting or blowing with each contraction can help "pace" the delivery.

Prolonged labor. In about 1 to 7 percent of women—mostly first-time mothers—labor lasts more than twenty-four hours. The principal causes are cephalo-pelvic disproportion or CPD (the baby's head is too large to pass through the mother's pelvis), unusual presentation, dysfunctional labor, excessive use of sedatives and painkillers very early in labor, premature rupture of the membranes, and extreme anxiety. The exhausted mother is at risk for infection, bleeding, rupture of the uterus, or lacerations of the birth canal. The baby may develop fetal distress and also face increased risk of infection, prolapsed cord, and bruising or trauma to its head.

Treatment may consist of intravenous (IV) fluids to prevent dehydration, rupture of the membranes, or oxytocin administration to stimulate stronger contractions. If the baby shows signs of oxygen deprivation, either a forceps or cesarean delivery may be necessary.

Fetal distress. Fetal distress means that the baby is not getting an adequate supply of oxygen. The most common causes are compression of the umbilical cord, placental abnormalities, and maternal disease, such as hypertension. If hypoxia, or insufficient oxygen, persists, it can damage the baby's brain and increase the risk of cerebral palsy.

The most common signals of fetal distress are meconium-stained amniotic fluid and changes in the fetal heart rate, particularly late or severe variable decelerations (see page 215). A sampling of blood from the baby's scalp can help obstetricians evaluate how serious the problem is. Treatment includes changing the mother's position to her side, administering oxygen by a mask to the mother and, if distress persists, forceps or cesarean delivery.

Meconium aspiration. Meconium is the fetal waste that forms the first bowel movement, typically tarry and greenish, that a baby produces—usually after birth. Sometimes, possibly because of stress, the baby releases meconium into the amniotic fluid. Babies can suck meconium into their mouth and nose; caregivers remove it by suctioning at birth.

Much rarer and more serious is aspiration of meconium into the lungs, where it can interfere with the baby's breathing and jeopardize its survival. Babies with severe meconium aspiration may require immediate intubation (insertion of a tube into the windpipe) to provide oxygen after birth and continued treatment in an intensive care nursery.

Shoulder dystocia. Occasionally the shoulders of a large or oddly positioned baby become wedged in the birth canal. This problem is most common with the large infants of diabetic mothers. The obstetrician usually performs a series of maneuvers to manipulate the baby's body so it can move through the cervix and vagina.

HIGH-RISK BIRTH: WHAT MIGHT HAPPEN

If risks develop during labor and delivery, you can anticipate extremely close monitoring of you and your baby and quick action if either of you faces increasing danger.

Electronic Fetal Monitoring

Your caregiver can check your baby's heartbeat—a signal of how it's handling the stress of labor—with a special handheld Doppler stethoscope. In low-risk births, this method is as helpful as electronic fetal monitoring. If you're at risk, your doctors probably will use an external fetal monitor, a small ultrasonic instrument, strapped around your abdomen, that records both the fetal heartbeat and the pressure of the uterus during contractions. You can move around with the monitor, although it may have to be adjusted.

High-risk births often require more sensitive internal electronic monitoring via an electrode, attached to the scalp of the fetus, that records the fetal heart rate and a tube, or catheter, that measures the pressure of uterine contractions. Both devices are inserted into the vagina after the cervix has opened during labor and the amniotic membranes have ruptured. The fetus probably feels a prick, but the electrode is very shallow and does not have to be pushed deeply into the scalp.

External and internal monitors send information to a machine that records a "tracing" of the heart rate and uterine contractions on a long sheet of paper. In evaluating the fetal heartbeat, your doctor will look for poor variability, or little change in the number of heartbeats per minute, which can indicate oxygen deprivation. Another ominous sign is delayed slowing or deceleration of the heart rate, which may take place during or after a contraction.

Induction

If you or your baby are in increased jeopardy, you may not be able to wait for labor to begin on its own. Among the most common reasons for inducing labor are:

- fetal distress
- rupture of the membranes (if labor doesn't begin spontaneously within 24 hours)
- postmaturity
- diabetes, if the baby is very large and shows signs of inadequate oxygen and blood supply
- severe blood-incompatibility problems
- hypertensive disorders of pregnancy
- severe kidney disease
- growth retardation

Sometimes labor can be induced by rupturing or breaking the amniotic membranes (amniotomy), which releases the fluid and leads to stronger contractions. Nipple stimulation also may trigger contractions. However, the most reliable, effective, and widely used form of induction is IV administration of oxytocin (Pitocin), a hormone that stimulates contractions.

Carefully monitoring both mother and baby, the obstetrical team drips small amounts of oxytocin into the mother's veins, gradually increasing the dose until effective contractions begin. Some women find the sudden onset of strong contractions difficult to handle. Once contractions are regular, oxytocin may no longer be necessary, and labor progresses on its own.

Forceps

If your baby shows signs of distress or does not move through the birth canal quickly enough, your doctor may use forceps, metal devices that encircle the baby's head and dovetail into each other, to accelerate delivery. They are needed most often to protect the heads of preterm or small-for-gestational-age babies. The primary risks are temporary molding, or shaping, of the baby's head and cuts within the mother's birth canal.

Vacuum Extraction

This alternative to forceps is a small cap attached to the baby's head while it's making its way through the birth canal and hooked to a

"Even though it was a high-tech delivery, there were wonderful moments of intimacy. It was so exciting just to see Owen as soon as he was born and to hold him. And I was able to breastfeed him right away. Ultimately, it's the touching, not the technology, that you remember."

suction pump that exerts just enough force to speed up the baby's progress. Obstetricians use this technique primarily to accelerate delivery of a baby in distress. The baby must be head-first. Risks include cuts or tears of the baby's scalp and the mother's birth canal.

Cesarean Birth

In a cesarean delivery, a doctor lifts the baby out of the mother's body through an incision in the uterus and lower abdomen. The rate of cesarean births has more than doubled in the last ten years; 24 percent of babies were delivered by cesarean "section" in 1987. Among high-risk women, the cesarean rate tends to be higher.

Under certain circumstances, a cesarean is the safest way for a baby to enter the world. These include:

- a baby too big to pass through the mother's pelvis
- problems with labor, such as failure to progress (prolonged labor with very slow cervical dilation) or signs of distress in the unborn baby
- a breech baby
- a placenta or umbilical cord blocking the birth canal
- maternal medical problems, such as diabetes, active herpes lesions, or high blood pressure, which can interfere with the baby's oxygen supply and increase the mother's risk of a life-threatening condition called eclampsia
- a baby who has not grown normally in the womb or has developed problems such as Rh incompatibility, a disorder in which the mother's blood cells attack and destroy the red blood cells of her unborn baby

In most cesareans, the mother, given a regional anesthetic, is awake and aware of what's happening, and the father can remain at her side.

What to expect. A cesarean is an operation and is performed in an operating or delivery room. General anesthesia is usually used only for emergencies or very unusual circumstances; most mothers receive epidural or spinal anesthesia, which produces numbness in the lower half of the body. An IV line is hooked up to a vein in one arm; a catheter is inserted into the bladder to drain off urine. A blood pressure cuff is loosely draped around one arm; disks for an EKG, which monitors heart rate, may be placed on the chest or shoulders.

After being washed and swabbed with an antiseptic solution, the lower abdomen is covered with surgical "drapes" or cloths. Only the small area where the incision will be made is left uncovered.

Two kinds of skin incisions can be used for cesarean deliveries: a transverse or bikini incision very low on the abdomen, usually in the fold just below the pubic hairline, or a vertical incision from below the umbilicus to the pubic hair. It may be in the middle of the abdomen or to one side. Most obstetricians use a bikini incision. Ask your obstetrician what type he or she favors. If you have a preference, state it. If your doctor objects, find out why. After cutting through the skin, the obstetrician cuts through the fatty tissue just below and the fascia, the tough membranes that cover the abdominal organs, moving aside the muscles and bladder (which normally covers the uterus).

The incision on the uterus can be horizontal or vertical. Most common is the low transverse or horizontal uterine incision, which cuts into the lower segment of the uterus and which is easier to repair. It allows about four to six inches for delivery. A "classical" incision runs up and down and is made higher on the uterus. It can be lengthened quickly if delivery must be extremely fast or if the baby is very large. A low vertical incision runs up and down but is done in the lower segment of the uterus.

As the doctor cuts into the uterus, the amniotic fluid may gush out, or the obstetrician may rupture the amniotic sac. As the baby is gently lifted from the womb, the mother may feel some pressure or tugging. Often the doctor will begin suctioning as soon as the head is delivered, then clamp and cut the cord. The doctor manually removes the placenta and examines the uterus for remaining tissue.

It may take only three to ten minutes from the start of surgery to the emergence of your baby. Suturing, on the other hand, may require forty-five minutes, as each layer is carefully stitched. In all, a woman has six or seven separate layers of stitches. Only the top one, which may consist of special surgical staples, clamps, or adhesive materials, is visible.

One recent innovation has been the use of patient-controlled analgesia (PCA) for women who undergo cesarean deliveries. Rather than receiving pain-relieving drugs on a preset schedule, new mothers can use a special pump to increase pain medication when and if needed, for instance, prior to getting up and walking. Women are taught how to use the pump before undergoing a cesarean; most rely on it only for the first twenty-four hours after delivery.

If you've had one cesarean. Vaginal birth after a cesarean (VBAC) is not only possible, but highly encouraged. According to the American College of Obstetricians and Gynecologists, 50 to 80 percent of women who've had cesareans can safely have vaginal deliveries in future pregnancies.

For most women, the risk factors that made one C-section necessary never recur. If your first baby was a breech (foot-first), your second very likely will be head-first, and you can have a normal labor and a vaginal delivery. There are only a few problems, such as a malformed pelvis or large vertical scar on your uterus, that mean a woman will have to have another cesarean.

Special concerns. The more you learn about cesarean birth, particularly before delivery, the more easily you'll understand and accept it if it becomes necessary. While some mothers report feelings of helplessness, guilt, or failure afterward, most focus on the end result: a healthy baby. (See chapter 15 for more on recovery following a cesarean and the appendix for support groups for cesarean birth.)

Emergency Care for Your Baby

If your caregivers anticipate problems in labor and delivery—because of prematurity, pregnancy complications, or indications of fetal distress—a pediatrician and an intensive care nurse will be called to the delivery room. As soon as the baby is born, they will take the baby to a special table at the side of the room, carefully evaluate its condition, and, if necessary, start emergency treatment. That may mean oxygen through a mask or, if the baby doesn't breathe, a tube inserted into its airway. Depending on its condition, the baby may require immediate transfer to a newborn intensive care unit.

THE END OF THE BEGINNING

Expectant parents spend so much time and energy thinking, planning, discussing, and preparing for their child's birth that they may not realize that birth merely represents the end of the beginning. The real work of parenting, with its inevitable mix of joy, wonder, and anguish, lies ahead.

While babies are born in one unforgettable moment, a man and a woman aren't instantly transformed into parents. After your baby's birth, you and your partner will need time to adjust and to make room in your lives for the newest member of your family. Be patient with yourselves. After all, you've only just begun. And, like the newest member of your family, you have a very long way to go.

The High-Risk Baby

"The twins were so scrawny, not at all like the babies you see in ads. I think most parents look at their babies and feel proud. I looked at mine and felt ashamed—mainly of myself for not being able to have done a better job."

It's always too hot, too bright, too noisy. Especially on your first visit, a newborn intensive care nursery can seem the most alien of environments. Alarms go off constantly. Monitors blink. Ventilators hum and hiss. You find yourself listening for the one sound curiously missing: a baby's cry. Everywhere you look you see infants, but most are too small, too sick, or too weak to cry.

Encased in plastic incubators called isolettes, with oxygen, temperature, and moisture carefully regulated to mimic conditions within the womb, the smallest of hospital patients lie silently. Most are unbelievably tiny, so tiny that you want to scoop them up in one hand and gently tuck them back inside their mother's bodies. By comparison, the bigger, term babies look huge, yet their hold on life is often just as tenuous.

According to the National Center for Health Statistics, more than 1.3 million newborns each year require special care after birth because of prematurity, low birth weight, birth defects, jaundice, respiratory difficulties, or other problems. About 6 percent of newborns—more than two hundred thousand babies each year—require immediate intensive care for potentially life-threatening problems that developed before, during, or after birth.

Parents who learn that their newborns are at risk face one of the most wrenching experiences of their life. For months, they've pictured the way their baby might look and fantasized about the first moments they would spend with their child. They've also feared—even if they never said so—that the baby might be in some way damaged or unhealthy. When a high-risk baby is born, parents feel robbed of their wonderful dreams at the same time that they realize that their worst fears may indeed come true.

HIGH-RISK CARE

More than four hundred hospitals in the United States have Level III or tertiary-care newborn nurseries. Each of these units is somewhat different, but, like the babies who fight for life within them, they have a great deal in common.

Most large nurseries are divided into different areas. The sickest babies, often just hours out of their mother's wombs, lie out in the open under special warmers so staff members have easy access to them. Sometimes half a dozen people crowd around a table, each one inserting a different probe or checking a different monitor.

Babies who are not quite as critical but still require special attention are in an intermediate care area. At Johns Hopkins, this part of the nursery, where preemies gain weight and strength, has been dubbed "the pasture."

The ratio of staff to patients is high. Among the professionals who may make up the neonatal team are:

- *Neonatologists,* pediatricians who specialize in the care of newborn infants.
- *Neonatology fellows,* fully trained pediatricians who are completing extra years of training to become neonatologists.
- *Interns and residents,* medical doctors training to become pediatricians.
- *Nurses,* including neonatal nurse practitioners or clinical nurse specialists with extra training in newborn care, registered nurses who perform most of your baby's routine care, and licensed vocational nurses.
- *Technicians* who perform specific tests, such as drawing blood, taking x rays, administering extra oxygen, etc.
- *Specialists.* Depending on your baby's condition, your neonatologist may work closely with cardiologists, neurologists, or physicians in other fields of medicine.

Common Problems

Many babies spend brief periods of time in an intensive care nursery. They may have had breathing problems right after delivery and require oxygen so they can "pink up." Babies of high-risk mothers, such as diabetics, may be kept for observation to make sure they're not experiencing any aftereffects. The most common problems include:

Jaundice. The baby's liver faces an important task after birth: the breakdown of bilirubin, an orange or yellowish pigment that increases as the baby's body breaks down its normal surplus of red blood cells, sometimes making a baby look yellowish, or jaundiced. This condition occurs in about half of full-term babies and 80 percent of preemies. If the bilirubin climbs too high, phototherapy—exposure to bright light to accelerate bilirubin breakdown—is necessary for a few days because newborns, especially sick ones, are vulnerable to the toxic effects of too much bilirubin.

If the baby's bilirubin is exceptionally high—a problem called hyperbilirubinemia—and phototherapy does not help, the baby may require an exchange blood transfusion. Small quantities of the infant's blood are removed and replaced with an equal amount of donor blood.

Patent ductus arteriosus. Because the lungs do not function before birth, a special circulatory system diverts most of the blood from the lungs to the heart and brain. Small amounts of blood enter the vessels of the lung, but the fluid in the lung creates resistance, which pushes the blood back through the ductus arteriosus, a small opening into the heart.

The very first breath, along with other complex changes in the blood oxygen supply, decreases the resistance within the lungs so blood can enter. The ductus arteriosus thickens; within about three weeks it closes completely. If it remains open, a condition called patent ductus arteriosus, the baby will not receive an adequate oxygen supply and will appear blue.

Sometimes simply limiting the baby's fluid intake reduces the load on the heart and allows the ductus to close. In babies younger than thirty weeks at birth, this usually is not sufficient. A medication called indomethacin can stimulate closing of the ductus, but it is not always effective. If it fails, surgery is necessary to close the ductus. Although surgery is always a risk in infants, babies, who are given general anesthesia, usually tolerate this operation well.

Sometimes a baby's circulatory system fails to develop as needed to supply enough blood to the lungs. This complication, called persistent fetal circulation, is most likely to occur in preterm, postmature, or diabetics' babies. Drugs often can solve the problem. If they fail, a new experimental approach—extracorporeal membrane oxygenation (ECMO)—offers hope. (See box on page 261.)

Breathing for Babies Who Can't

Extracorporeal membrane oxygenation (ECMO) acts like an artificial heart and lungs for term or near-term babies with meconium aspiration, pneumonia, other lung infections, or persistent fetal circulation, in which the circulatory system fails to develop as needed to supply enough blood to the lungs. ECMO involves threading a tube into the right side of the heart to carry the blood outside the baby's body and through an artificial lung machine, where it is oxygenated and carried back through another tube into a major artery in the infant. This allows the lungs to rest and heal.

More than a thousand babies have been successfully treated with ECMO in the last decade. Most would have had less than a 20 percent chance of surviving without this new technology. More than forty centers around the country now offer ECMO.

While the costs are high—an estimated four thousand dollars a day, compared to two thousand five hundred for intensive care, x rays, and lab work—ECMO can drastically reduce the length of a baby's nursery stay. The machines have not been as successful in helping babies born before thirty-four weeks because they require use of a blood thinner that can cause brain hemorrhages in preemies.

Blood chemistry abnormalities. Some babies have either too many red blood cells (a condition called polycythemia) or too few (anemia). Those who are premature or small-for-gestational-age or whose mothers have diabetes are more likely to have polycythemia, which causes sluggish circulation. In a sick baby, this problem, if untreated, can lead to tissue damage. Usually removing some blood and diluting the remaining blood corrects this problem.

Anemia can be the result of bleeding during delivery, intrauterine infection, blood-incompatibility problems, a detached placenta, and other complications of pregnancy. Often high-risk babies are so sick for so long that they become anemic because of routine blood tests. Treatment consists of transfusions of whole blood or a solution of concentrated or "packed" red blood cells. Many nurseries have arrangements so family members can donate the small amounts of blood needed.

Pneumonia. This infection of the lungs is the most common serious infection in newborns. Caused by viruses or bacteria, pneumonia can develop before birth, and congenital pneumonia usually is a graver problem than pneumonia that develops after delivery. Chest x rays, blood counts, and cultures of lung secretions can confirm the diagnosis. Antibiotics and oxygen, if needed, treat bacterial pneumonia. Babies with viral pneumonia receive supplemental oxygen and are put on respirators if necessary.

PREEMIES

Usually about two-thirds to three-quarters of the babies in a special-care nursery have been born prematurely. Their appearance, overall condition, and prognosis depends on how much time they were able to spend in the womb. The chart on page 281 lists the percentage of babies of different gestational ages who survive at Johns Hopkins. The smallest and youngest survivors weigh a little more than a pound and are born after just twenty-three weeks of pregnancy.

Generally, babies born before the twenty-fifty week and weighing five hundred grams or less (about a pound) face the grimmest odds. Fewer than half survive, and those who do may suffer severe, lifelong complications.

Babies born between the twenty-sixth and thirtieth week usually survive but require extended care; their risk of potentially fatal or lifelong complications is high. If born between thirty-one and thirty-three weeks, infants are stronger and healthier, although they still can develop life-threatening problems. From thirty-four to thirty-seven weeks, many babies are so healthy that they may not need any special care.

Very premature babies look not quite finished. At twenty-four weeks, weighing just over a pound, they are dark red because skin pigmentation hasn't begun. Their eyes may be fused shut; their ears are mere flaps. At twenty-nine weeks, averaging two and a half pounds, their fat layer has begun to develop, creating a more rounded, plump appearance. Their eyes are partly open, and they're alert for longer periods. Some begin to suck. At thirty-five weeks, most babies weigh more than five pounds and see almost as well as term infants, showing a preference for human faces. They can suck, swallow, and breathe. Their skin is smooth; their muscles have tone.

The major threat to the preemie is the immaturity of its organ systems, which makes the baby more vulnerable to serious medical complications, including:

Respiratory Distress Syndrome (RDS). This breathing disorder, also called hyaline membrane disease, develops if a baby cannot produce enough of a soapy substance called surfactant that keeps the tiny air sacs or alveoli within the lungs inflated. By thirty-seven weeks, most babies have produced enough surfactant to breathe efficiently. Some have lungs that mature earlier; some, later. But almost all babies who are born before thirty weeks and weigh less than one thousand grams (two pounds two ounces) develop some type of respiratory distress. The younger they are, the more serious RDS usually is. For unknown reasons, boys are more susceptible to RDS than girls. The babies of diabetic mothers and of white women also are more vulnerable.

Treatment depends on the severity of RDS. Babies born before thirty weeks may require intubation, insertion of a plastic tube through the nose and mouth and into the windpipe to deliver needed oxygen. A ventilator hooked up to the tube provides mechanical breaths that are more efficient than the baby's own weak and irregular ones. Other babies get additional oxygen through a mask placed over the mouth and nose or a flexible nosepiece that provides "continuous positive airway pressure" (CPAP) and makes it easier for the baby to breathe on its own. In babies with milder RDS, extra oxygen can be pumped into a hood over their heads or into their isolettes. One problem is that too much oxygen in the baby's blood can lead to retinopathy of prematurity, which can cause blindness. That is why the baby's blood is carefully monitored.

A still-experimental therapy is injection of surfactant directly into the newborn's lungs. Researchers are trying different forms of surfactant (human, cow, pig, and synthetic), administered through a tube inserted into the upper airway immediately after delivery, to protect the fragile lungs of premature infants and reduce the severity of RDS.

None of these approaches are cures. They simply help babies breathe until they can do so on their own—but in itself this is an enormous accomplishment. A generation ago forty thousand infants died of RDS every year. Now more than 85 percent of the babies who develop RDS each year survive.

Intracranial hemorrhage. Any severe physical stress—insufficient oxygen, low blood flow to the brain, rapid changes in blood pressure—can damage the fragile blood vessels in a premature baby's brain, causing bleeding or hemorrhage. Ultrasound or a special, cross-sectional x ray called computerized tomography (a CT scan) can detect bleeding. There is no treatment, so the bleeding must stop on its own. Sometimes the baby receives medication to prevent seizures or a transfusion to maintain its blood supply. The long-term impact depends on the severity of the hemorrhage, but up to 85 percent of those who had milder hemorrhages do fine.

Infections. A premature baby is highly susceptible to infection for several reasons, including the immaturity of its immune system and its lack of protective antibodies, which mothers usually transmit to a fetus in the last trimester. Infections tend to spread rapidly and affect several body systems. Prompt antibiotic treatment is critical. Some babies receive routine antibiotics to prevent infection.

Feeding problems. Babies born before thirty-four weeks of gestation often are too weak to suck or swallow and require feeding through a gavage tube passed through the nose or mouth into the stomach. Some cannot digest formula or breast milk and require a special mix of nutrients and fluids administered through an intravenous (IV) line. Mothers who pump their breasts can store their milk for future use. Often breastmilk can be given by injection or gavage. Nursing can begin as soon as the baby can coordinate sucking and swallowing and can control its body temperature outside of the isolette.

Necrotizing enterocolitis. The most common serious intestinal disorder that premature babies encounter may begin because of an inadequate supply of oxygen and blood to the intestine. Usually harmless bacteria invade the tissue layers of the intestines, which can break open and spread infection through the abdominal cavity. Antibiotics treat the infection; occasionally surgery is necessary to remove dead intestinal tissue.

Apnea. Apnea is a disruption in normal breathing that can last for twenty seconds or more. Many premature babies pause for five to ten seconds and then take several rapid breaths. If they do not breathe within twenty seconds, their blood oxygen levels fall, their skin color changes, and their hearts beat at an abnormally slow rate. A monitor alerts the nursery staff by sounding an alarm.

Babies with apnea often need mild stimulation, such as rubbing their soles, ankles, or back, or medications, like theophylline or caffeine, to resume breathing. If that doesn't work, a nurse will squeeze oxygen from a soft, inflatable bag positioned over the baby's nose and mouth. Some babies with frequent or persistent apnea may require intubation and use of a respirator to establish regular breathing. If apnea persists after the baby is big and well enough to go home, a monitor can alert parents to breathing disruptions.

Hypothermia. Preterm babies have very little fat to insulate their bodies and keep them warm. If chilled, their metabolism accelerates, using up all available fuel. To prevent a dangerous drop in temperature, premature babies stay in heated isolettes.

Vision impairment. Premature babies are susceptible to changes in the retina, the light-sensitive tissue that lines the eyeball. This condition, called retinopathy of prematurity, is the result of excessive growth of blood vessels in an infant's developing retina. The proliferation, which occurs for unknown reasons, stimulates growth of abnormal tissue that may distort or pull the retina away from the eyeball, leading to retinal detachment.

Seven percent of babies weighing one thousand to one thousand five hundred grams at birth develop retinal problems. The incidence soars as high as 42 percent in babies who weigh less then one thousand grams at birth. More than twenty-six hundred infants suffer some eye damage each year from retinopathy of prematurity, and more than six hundred fifty become blind, according to the National Eye Institute. To prevent retinal problems, the neonatal team tries to keep preemies as stable as possible. If impairment does develop, new treatments can help.

One is cryotherapy, a surgical procedure that briefly freezes portions of the retina, cutting the risk of blindness in half. In a multihospital study of almost four thousand premature infants completed in 1988, cryotherapy, performed at about eleven weeks, stopped the abnormal growth of blood vessels, perhaps by killing the retinal cells that stimulate such growth.

OTHER HIGH-RISK BABIES

Being born at term prevents many of the problems preemies encounter—but not all. Among the reasons why term babies may require intensive care are:

Low birth weight. About 7 percent of babies born in the U.S. weigh twenty-five hundred grams (five and a half pounds) or less. Some are premature, but many are simply small for their gestational age. According to the March of Dimes, full-term babies with low birth weights are forty times more likely to die in their first month and twenty times more likely to die in their first year than other full-term infants. They also are much more likely to suffer long-term developmental disorders.

Very small babies may be chronically deprived of oxygen in the womb and unable to tolerate the extra stress of labor and delivery. If they gasp before birth, they may aspirate amniotic fluid and meconium into their airways, adding to their respiratory difficulties.

Small, skinny babies lack the protection of insulating fat layers and cannot regulate their body temperatures. They may have to stay in temperature-controlled isolettes until they grow and are capable of staying warm on their own. Some have low levels of blood sugar, a condition that can cause brain damage and mental retardation if not corrected by administering extra glucose.

While low-birthweight babies can "catch up" in weight, they tend to be shorter than normal-weight babies their age. Some, who suffered poor brain development before birth, may develop learning disabilities and problems such as hyperactivity, short attention span, and poor fine-motor coordination, which may make writing and drawing difficult for them.

Postterm birth. As many as 10 percent of babies arrive after forty-two weeks of gestation. Most are healthy at birth. However, about 5 percent show signs of postmaturity syndrome, a complex of problems that increases the mortality rate by two to three times compared with term infants. Most of these problems are the result of inadequate supply of nutrients from the placenta, decreased oxygen and glucose, and the stress of labor.

The most common complications postterm babies face are:
- hypoglycemia or low blood sugar
- aspiration of meconium (fetal waste)
- abnormal blood chemistry
- congenital anomalies of no known cause
- seizures
- temperature-regulation problems because of loss of subcutaneous fat.

Treatment consists of a warm environment, frequent monitoring, and IV administration of glucose for low blood-sugar levels.

Diabetic mothers. These infants tend to be very large, often over ten pounds, if their mothers' blood-sugar levels were high during pregnancy. While they are big, some major organ systems are immature, making them prone to problems similar to those of premature babies. The most common complications they encounter are:

- *Hypoglycemia.* After months of high blood-sugar levels, the baby's pancreas continues to produce extra insulin, which can drastically lower its blood sugar. This is less likely to occur in women who keep their blood-sugar levels low during pregnancy. Intravenous administration of glucose can help stabilize the baby's blood-sugar levels.

- *Jaundice.* Diabetics' babies may have more difficulty breaking down bilirubin and require phototherapy to speed up the process of clearing extra blood cells from their bodies.

- *Respiratory distress.* Even though testing before birth may indicate that the baby of a diabetic has adequate amounts of the lipids that make up surfactant, the baby may have difficulty breathing and require careful monitoring and oxygen after delivery.

- *Birth defects.* Babies exposed to high blood sugar and high insulin levels before birth have a greater incidence (as high as 8 to 10 percent) of malformations. See chapter 8 for information on reducing these risks prior to conception and birth.

Blood incompatibility problems. The major complication for babies with Rh disease or other blood incompatibilities (such as ABO) is hyperbilirubinemia. A baby with severe Rh disease may require immediate transfusion with fresh blood cells. If necessary, the baby's blood, with its immature red cells, bilirubin, and destructive Rh antibodies, is replaced with equal amounts of Rh-negative blood in an exchange transfusion. Babies with other blood-incompatibility problems usually require only phototherapy to break down excess bilirubin.

"A LOVE SONG FOR KATIE"

The first sight of her newborn daughter, Katie, almost broke Mary Ann's heart. "She was fourteen weeks premature, and she was so tiny. I wanted her back inside me. I wasn't ready to give her up. All I could think of was how I'd let everyone down—especially little Katie and my husband, Tom."

Tom and Mary Ann had waited to have children. He was forty, and she was thirty-four when they conceived Katie on a vacation in Italy. They were ecstatic. Mary Ann, a certified nurse-midwife who was completing her doctoral work, decided to undergo amniocentesis because of her age. For a week after the test, she felt menstrual-like cramps. Instead of going away, the cramps grew more frequent. Soon her uterus would tighten after almost any activity. "I'd get out of bed and have a contraction. By twenty-one weeks I was having contractions almost every time I moved."

Mary Ann went on bedrest and began taking medication to inhibit early contractions. "I felt panicky, but I knew I was doing everything I could," she says. In her twenty-sixth week, she started having more contractions and began spotting. One afternoon her membranes ruptured, and the contractions intensified. She was admitted to the hospital that day.

The obstetrical team tried everything to buy more time in the womb for Mary Ann's baby, including continuous high doses of intravenous medication to halt labor and tipping her bed so her feet were higher than her head. "I could feel my pulse," she recalls. "That's how fast my heart was beating because of the drugs."

On her fourth night in the hospital, she woke up with gas pains. When the obstetrician checked her cervix, it had completely dilated—without a single contraction. Delivery was quick and tense. The baby's cord prolapsed, or slipped through the cervix, and the doctor used forceps to lift the baby out. "I couldn't believe it. I felt so guilty. I'm a certified nurse-midwife, but I hadn't realized what was going on," Mary Ann says, blinking away tears.

Katie weighed just two pounds, five ounces. "Right after she was born, I didn't ask any questions because I didn't want to hear she was dead. At the same time, I found myself praying that she wouldn't be one of those babies they just keep alive. I hadn't even looked that pregnant, and I didn't feel like I'd had a baby. More than anything else, I had to see her." Two hours after the birth she did.

"The moment we saw her, we felt love for her. We didn't care about anything else except that she was alive." In her first forty-eight hours, Katie's biggest problem was superficial bleeding under

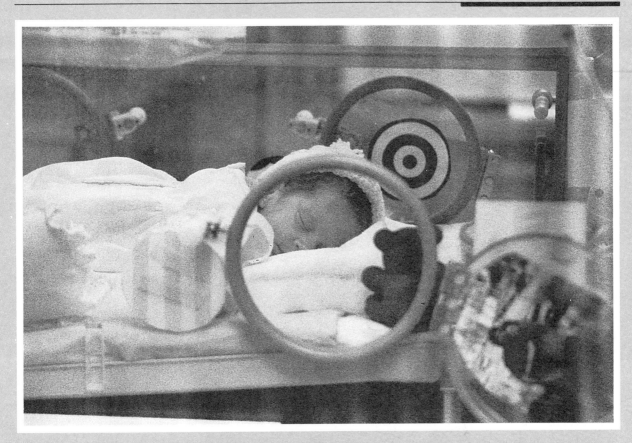

her scalp. "Her head felt like a sponge," Mary Ann recalls. Katie's bilirubin (a potentially harmful substance produced by the breakdown of red blood cells after birth) was dangerously high and she required several risky transfusions of her entire blood volume.

"I'd always thought that when our baby was born, the only ones handling her in the hospital would be me and Tom and our midwife. Instead every shift change brought new doctors and nurses. Worst of all, Katie looked like she was in pain. She was bruised from the forceps, and her eyes were swollen shut. She was writhing around. I felt so frustrated because I knew that if she were in my uterus, she'd be fine. I kept imagining her inside me and then I'd open my eyes and see her in front of me, suffering. I had this constant sense of dread, and I couldn't even get the relief of sleeping through the night because I was waking up every few hours to pump my breasts."

For the next few weeks, Katie and her parents rode a terrifying roller-coaster. Fortunately she never developed severe respiratory

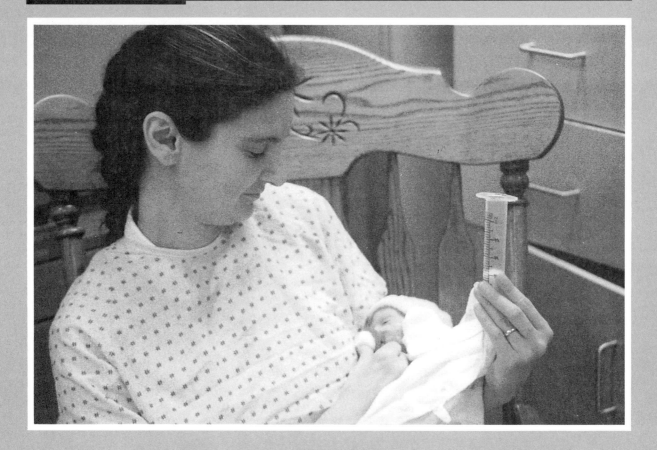

distress, although she went on and off a ventilator twice. "I was always afraid, especially when I had to leave her," says Mary Ann. "When I was at the hospital, I loved holding her, but I had to be careful not to overstimulate her. I wanted to go with my instinctive feelings, but I couldn't. If things were natural, she would still have been inside me."

Mary Ann struggled with the same doubts and fears of other mothers of preemies: "It's hard to feel positive at the beginning because the babies aren't real cute. They're so frail and sickly. And you feel so helpless. But I found that parents have more options than you think. You can make decisions. You can get involved in caring for the baby. And the more you do, the better you feel."

Because of the incessant noise and constant activity in the NICU, Mary Ann created her own world around Katie's isolette. "I wouldn't even look at the other babies. I would put up screens and pull up a rocker and just focus on Katie. I'd talk to her and stroke her hand. And I'd sing. My husband lost all his inhibitions when he was with her. He'd sing and talk and do anything to make her eyes light up. We made a special place for ourselves within the nursery. In time the NICU staff came to seem like members of the family too."

Mary Ann also made a real commitment to breastfeeding, even though for weeks Katie was too small and weak to suck. "I rented an electric pump for four months. It really took a lot of effort, but it was the one thing only I could do for Katie. And I believe she really thrived on my milk."

After a rocky few weeks, Katie turned into what one doctor called "a rose." She blossomed visibly, becoming stronger every day. On June 7, after eleven weeks in the nursery, Katie went home. She weighed a whopping four pounds, six ounces.

"She was hooked up to a monitor to make sure she didn't stop breathing. A couple of times, the monitor went off and gave us a real scare," Mary Ann recalls. Because she was so little, Katie woke up every hour or two to nurse. "It was exhausting, but we were so happy just to have her with us."

At her first birthday, Katie showed few signs of her struggle for life. "None of the follow-up tests have shown any serious impairments," says Mary Ann. "There may be some developmental delays, but we'll take whatever comes. Katie had to fight so hard just to get this far, and we're so proud of her. I don't think that will ever change."

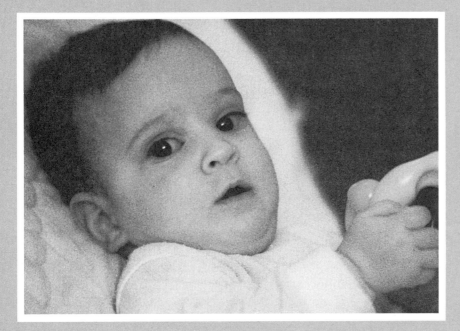

Birth defects. Birth defects occur in two to four of every one hundred births. About one hundred thousand babies each year have birth defects so serious they face lifelong handicaps.

Birth defects may be caused by environmental or genetic factors, and most are unanticipated. Some are life-threatening and require treatment within hours. All can cause deep anguish for a family. Among the most common birth defects are: cleft lip and/or palate (correctable by surgery), hydrocephalus (which is treated by insertion of a shunt immediately after delivery to drain excess fluid), neural tube defects (some of which can be surgically treated), and heart defects (surgery can correct some, but not all). Fetal echocardiography (page 78) can diagnose some problems before birth.

Most parents respond to the shock of learning that their baby has a malformation with initial denial. "It can't be," they might say again and again. The next stage usually is one of sadness and anger—at themselves, their doctors, whatever powers might be responsible.

Often it helps to focus on what's normal about the baby: its huge blue eyes, its silky skin, its curly hair. If surgical treatment is necessary, such as repair of a cleft lip or palate, pictures of how other babies look before and after can be tremendously encouraging. Gradually most parents come to accept the reality and to feel increased satisfaction with the baby and greater confidence in their ability to cope.

LOVING A HIGH-RISK BABY

"I was too sick to go see my son for four days, and I knew he was having plenty of problems himself," recalls a woman who required an emergency cesarean delivery. "When my husband finally was wheeling me to the nursery, I started crying. I was terrified that I wouldn't be able to love my baby."

This woman learned the same lesson many parents of high-risk infants do: that love is not an on-off switch that can be pushed only during one critical time period. The process of "bonding" or attachment begins long before birth, when you plan, prepare for, and begin a pregnancy. Through each successive month, your commitment to the baby grows.

For most parents, birth is the joyous culmination of the months of eager anticipation. Ideally parents and child can spend the following hours and days getting to know their baby. Families who cannot cement the bonds between them in the earliest stages of their lives together do miss out on something special—but that doesn't mean they can't make up for lost time.

According to pediatrician T. Berry Brazelton, the noted infant specialist, parents of high-risk babies initially relate to them by gathering medical information. They talk in numbers more than words: blood gas mixes, oxygen percentages, heart rates. They're almost afraid to touch or hold their fragile newborns. Gradually they begin to see their child as a baby, not a medical problem. Yet they may not feel that the infant is truly theirs until they can hold and rock and care for their child.

If the prognosis is bleak or guarded, parents may think they'll "be better off" if they don't get too close to their sick newborns. "I found myself staying away from the hospital," a father confesses. "My attitude was, 'What's the use? There's nothing I can do for him anyway.'"

While such feelings are understandable, parents who've gone through similar experiences—and professionals who've counseled and observed them—report that detachment doesn't blunt the pain. And often parents who, despite a poor prognosis, spend time with their child and become as close as possible feel a certain comfort, even if the baby dies, because they did as much as any parents could. "All we have are memories," says one mother whose son died two days after birth. "But they are wonderfully sweet ones."

From the very beginning, parents can look for the qualities that make their child unique—how tightly he holds on to the blanket or how she seems to respond to a teddy bear that makes a sound like a heartbeat. The bond between parents and child grows stronger faster when mothers and fathers feel they "know" their infant.

Even if parents do nothing more than look at or stroke the child, that can be enough to establish a connection. Most nurseries encourage parents to take over aspects of the baby's care, such as feedings, as infants grow stronger. Some centers have set up care-by-parents units where mothers and fathers provide all the care for babies who are stable, under the supervision of the nursery staff.

What to Expect

If you are apprehensive about your first visit to the high-risk nursery, ask what the baby will look like, what sort of equipment may be in use, if there's anything you should be aware of in advance. Most parents are initially put off by the barriers an intensive care

"When they showed me his isolette, I peeked in and almost hoped he wasn't mine. He was so small and red, like a little monkey. I was relieved when they told me I couldn't hold him in my arms. I thought that if I picked him up he might break."

> "At first I resented all the strangers taking care of my baby, but after a while, they came to seem like family. We spent so much time talking about the littlest things the baby did, and they seemed to care so much."

nursery creates between them and their babies: gowns, masks, isolettes with gloved openings for their hands, alarms that beep unpredictably. If you have any reason to think your baby may need intensive care after birth, arrange a tour of the nursery before delivery.

When you visit your baby, try to disregard everything else, focusing total attention on your child. Allow yourself several visits to become familiar and, eventually, comfortable with the nursery. Ask about the equipment: what each device does, why it's necessary, what the various lights and buzzers mean. The less alien and intimidating it seems, the easier it will be for you to take the equipment for granted. Many parents bring family photographs and tiny stuffed animals or brightly colored toys to place in the isolettes.

If your baby was very premature, his or her appearance may shock you at first. You may find it hard not to focus on what looks abnormal to you: red skin, large genitals, limbs that seem impossibly small. Ask how babies of this gestational age usually look and if the nursery has any photographs of how they change. At Johns Hopkins, a large bulletin board with week-by-week pictures of preemies at different ages often becomes a magnet for parents whose babies are in the nursery. "I used to stand there whenever I felt discouraged and say to myself, 'Someday my baby's going to be just as big,'" one mother recalls.

The Emotional Impact

The confusing barrage of emotions you may feel if your baby's at risk—sadness, guilt, disappointment, inadequacy, denial, anxiety—are normal. You are grieving for the perfect child you'd hoped to have and preparing yourself emotionally to care for the sick child you do have. At first, you may feel exactly the way most first-time mothers do: incompetent.

Many women feel at least some jealousy of the nursery staff, who are so expert and relaxed. "They knew my baby better than I did," one mother recalls. "I was grateful for all they were doing, but I resented their closeness to him." As mothers take over more of a baby's care—changing diapers, helping turn the baby, caring for breaks in the skin—this feeling eases.

The emotion that many parents find hardest to acknowledge and handle is anger, which may be surprisingly intense. Yet anger is a normal response to any loss, and the best way to deal with it is by expressing it. If you can talk through your anger with your partner, a friend, or a counselor, you may realize that you are angry with the fates or God or whatever caused your baby's problems. If you don't take time to "process" your anger, you might direct it at the staff, the doctors, your partner, the hospital regulations.

Mothers in particular feel the heavy burden of guilt. One mother recalls feeling guilty "when I watched the fat, rosy-cheeked, full-term infants being wheeled through the halls by their mothers." Others, preoccupied with their own recovery, may feel guilty about what they see as "selfishness." Yet mothers of high-risk babies are just as tired and achy and sore as other new mothers, and they have every right to concern themselves with hemorrhoids or itchy episiotomy stitches. You need to take care of yourself so you'll be able to take care of your baby, and this requires some self-absorption.

Perhaps nothing stirs more guilt than a negative response to your baby. One mother, looking at her child's severe cleft lip and palate, said, "God help me. I can't stand looking at her. I wish she wasn't mine." Her husband and caregivers listened without judging, helping her talk out her feelings. Gradually she learned how to hold and feed her daughter and became very attached to the infant long before surgery corrected the malformation.

If your baby was premature, you may need a longer period of time to work through your feelings. A preterm birth shatters nature's timetable for development for both children and parents. Just as the infant needs time to grow and prepare for life outside the womb, the parents need time to work through the complex feelings that every pregnancy brings.

What You Can Do

There is no formula for how to cope when your baby is in intensive care. But parents who've been through the experience suggest strategies that may help:

• Spend as much time as you can with your baby right from the start. Talk to your infant. Sing a lullaby. Comfort your child with the familiar sound of your voice.

• Name your baby. It'll make him or her more of a person—to you and the nursery staff. "I remember wondering whether we should 'waste' our favorite name on a baby that might die," says a mother. "Then I realized that name would live in our hearts forever."

• Touch your baby. After a normal birth, mothers begin their tactile explorations of their infants within hours. You may need to wait for several visits before you're comfortable enough to touch and cuddle your baby. Eventually both parents can take over the baby's skin care, rubbing moisturizer gently into its delicate skin and getting to know more about their baby in the process.

• Take pictures of brothers or sisters, drawings from them, small toys to the isolette. Make it *your* baby's home with your family's things.

• If at all possible, both parents should talk to the neonatal team at the same time. It's best to air your unspoken fantasies and fears so your baby's caregivers can dispel or confirm them.

• While neonatologists can provide a great deal of helpful information, they can not predict the future. Ask how other babies with the same problem have fared; the answers may help you get a realistic view of what your child may face.

• Interrupt if your caregivers use initials, words, or phrases you don't know, and ask if they could explain what they're talking about in simpler terms.

• Don't be afraid of asking questions you fear may sound dumb. Often they're not, and the answers can help your understanding of what's going on.

• Repeat questions if you have to. In the stress of the moment, it's hard to hear and remember all the information you get. Taking notes or taping conversations with caregivers may help.

• Keep a record of your baby's progress. Because recovery can be so slow and one step back may follow every two steps forward, you may find it reassuring to review the improvements your baby has made every week or so.

• Take photographs regularly. You may not be able to appreciate the progress your baby is making unless you look at the shots you took just a few weeks before. Years from now, you may not believe your child was ever so small or so sick.

• Accept your feelings—anger, depression, resentment, despair—without blaming yourself. You have a right to feel however you do.

• Fight against guilt. One woman told herself a hundred times a day, "Guilt does no one any good."

• Talk to each other, to your friends, to the nurses, to anyone who's willing to listen.

• Don't hold back the tears. Crying releases emotions too powerful to restrain.

• Get in touch with parents who've been through the same experience. (Many hospitals have support groups and networks to arrange this.) They'll understand the way friends cannot.

• Accept counseling if it's offered—even if you don't think you need it. You may be surprised at what it can do.

• If people offer to help, let them. Be specific about your needs: babysitting, house cleaning, cooking, transportation.

• Rest. You may feel guilty about lying down during the day for a nap, but the more rested you are, the better you'll be able to cope.

• Keep informed of your baby's condition. If the busy nursery staff doesn't volunteer information, ask.

• Be with your baby, if at all possible, if he or she seems to be losing the struggle for life. This time may be the saddest of your life, but many parents report that, despite the pain, being with their baby at its death helped them resolve their grief.

> "Nursing was the only 'natural' thing I could do. At home I'd prop up a Polaroid of the baby and look at it as I pumped. It wasn't the same as nursing a baby, but it was better than nothing."

Going Home Alone

One of the saddest moments the mother of a high-risk baby faces is the day she leaves the hospital—and leaves her baby behind. Going home with empty arms to an empty nursery can be traumatic. The mother feels the normal postdelivery discomforts, such as engorged breasts, exhaustion, and a sore perineum, yet has no "reward" to show for her pains.

Some women cope by spending as much time as possible at the hospital with their babies. Others, who may have children at home who need their attention, visit daily and keep in touch by phone. Sometimes women find that pumping their breasts and freezing the milk, if the baby is too small or sick to nurse, helps them feel useful.

Many women feel a sadness or depression far more intense than any they've ever known. The feeling is grief, no stranger for the parents of high-risk babies, and it enters the lives not just of those whose babies die in the first month of life, but those whose babies are perilously ill or severely malformed. Even a temporary separation from a premature or extremely sick child can precipitate profound sorrow and loss.

IF THE BABY DIES

The very thought of death can seem morbidly out of place amid the happy voices of new parents basking in the pleasures of their baby's first moments. Yet each year more than six thousand families lose a child at or shortly after birth.

Unanticipated losses usually produce a much more severe and overwhelming grief response. Parents who knew in advance that their baby might not survive have months to prepare themselves

"We never regretted having her. She was so sweet, and we have happy memories. I just wish we could have had more of them."

psychologically. The shock of a sudden loss can intensify feelings of denial so parents may not be able to accept the reality of their baby's death for several weeks. Many feel overwhelmed, unable to make decisions, and isolated for a prolonged period.

The Parents' Pain

The death of a baby is a tragedy that leaves scars that never completely fade. Often the first reaction is one of shock and numbness, as if the mind is trying to protect itself from the anguish of acknowledging the loss. Many parents, even while holding each other or hugging loved ones, feel profoundly alone.

Going home from the hospital after a child's death is especially wrenching. Family and friends, while hoping to help, may make remarks that hurt. The mourning parents should put their own needs first, letting people know as clearly as possible how they are feeling.

Postpartum depression can be especially severe after a loss. The mother's bond is just as strong as the connection with a healthy infant, but instead of feeling full of love, she may feel empty. Some mothers report that their arms ache for weeks after a baby's death, as if in longing for a child to hold. In a study of sixty-two women who suffered perinatal losses, about a third had psychological problems, primarily anxiety attacks, a year or two after the death of their infants.

When a baby dies, fathers tend to grieve in different ways than mothers. In one study, twenty-eight fathers whose babies died unexpectedly felt a necessity to keep busy with increased work. They reported diminished feelings of self-worth, self-blame, and limited ability to ask for help.

For both parents, mourning is difficult because there is, as one psychologist observes, "so little concrete evidence of the child's existence." That is why parents often find it helpful in the long run—although exquisitely painful in the short term—to be with a baby at its hour of death or to view and hold the body.

Typically, parents search for answers and look for a reason why their child died. They may blame themselves, each other, or their caregivers. Not uncommonly, dreams and hallucinatory images of the child persist for weeks or months. They may be part of the grieving process, a way of letting go. Yet they may be so real and so intense that many parents fear they are going crazy. Anger is common, and often doctors, nurses, and the hospital are the primary targets. Some women find themselves feeling angry and resentful of new mothers.

After the intensity of the first emotional reactions fades, parents sink into a depression. They feel sad, tired, disoriented, helpless. They find it hard to get back "into the swing" of things. Many experience physical symptoms, such as aches and pains, a tight feeling in the chest and throat, heart flutters, loss of appetite, insomnia, headaches, fatigue, difficulty concentrating, and problems thinking and making decisions.

The loss of a child can create marital problems for couples, particularly if they have trouble communicating and expressing their feelings honestly. One woman resented the fact that her husband spent all his spare time running and working out until she realized that was his way of releasing his anger and sorrow. Both partners may find it difficult to resume lovemaking or the activities they used to enjoy together. More than ever before, they need patience, tenderness, and reassurance.

Grief knows no schedule. Most parents come to terms with a loss within eighteen months, although anniversaries—the day of death, the baby's birthday, the due date for a preemie—bring a resurgence of sorrow. Among the signs of healing are an ability to laugh without guilt, paying attention to personal appearance, enjoyment of other people's company, a revival of sexual desire, interest in current events, and a diminished preoccupation with the dead child.

Yet the memory of the child never completely dies. Many years after a loss, parents may find themselves recalling the age a child would have been and feeling echoes of the old pain. Some parents never fully recover from a baby's death, even though they mourn and return to more-or-less-normal functioning. A "shadow" grief persists in the form of a sadness that may come and go throughout their life but never entirely lifts.

What Helps

Health-care professionals have learned how deep and significant the loss of a child is. Many medical centers now have bereavement counselors and support groups for parents whose babies die before, at, or shortly after birth. While nothing cushions the awful blow of loss, parents can cope better by relying on certain strategies and supports, including:

• Honest, forthright information from caregivers. Parents should always expect complete answers to their questions and realistic appraisals, however bleak, of their baby's condition.

"We knew from the start that the odds were against him. I remember telling myself that I wouldn't let myself get too attached, but the moment I touched his tiny hand, I felt this surge of love. I was his mommy, and it didn't matter how long he lived or how many problems he had. I loved him with all my heart."

• Talking, rather than bottling up or censoring your feelings. Parents need to "process" the experience of losing a baby, to relive it again and again until they can accept the reality. Sharing memories of the baby—the ears that looked so much like Uncle Joe's; the wisps of reddish hair; the tiny, perfect fingers—also helps focus grief.

• Time alone with the infant so they can see and touch the child. As agonizing as the experience seems at the moment, many parents, looking back from the perspective of time, feel especially comforted if they could be with their babies when they died. "We were with her as her life began and as it ended," one mother explains. "I'll never forget kissing her good-bye and feeling a sense of peace come over her."

• Involvement in making as many choices as possible. Parents, numb with grief, may find it hard to respond to the many decisions they face, but they should never be excluded from the process. The baby, in death as in life, remains theirs.

• Photographs and mementos of the baby, such as crib cards, footprints, a lock of hair, or its tiny stocking cap.

• A memorial or funeral service. Many Christian parents arrange for a baptism before or after death. While the hospital will volunteer to dispose of the body if that is the parents' wish, many couples prefer a formal burial with a gravesite they can visit. Some plant a tree to commemorate the child's brief life.

• Follow-up visits with the perinatal team to explain what happened and, to whatever extent possible, why.

• Dealing with the inevitable worries, anxieties, and confusion of other children in the family. This process may repair a parent's sense of self-esteem and ability to cope.

• Not rushing into another pregnancy. In various studies, the mothers who had the most prolonged grief reactions either had a surviving twin or became pregnant within five months of a loss. In both circumstances, they were unable to resolve their grief. This difficulty can be a problem in bonding with another child. However, once a woman has completed the mourning process, another pregnancy can restore or bolster her sense of self-worth.

• Joining a support group. The company of others who truly understand and appreciate your grief can be an enormous comfort. The appendix lists several organizations that provide programs and support systems for grieving parents.

• Not trying to resume a normal life as if nothing has happened. Something has—something tragic that demands a great deal of energy and time. Parents need to build up their spiritual and emotional strength before they can rebuild their lives.

• Getting professional help. Therapists can help parents work through the painful emotions a child's death brings. Counseling is particularly helpful if parents cannot deal with certain problems alone or physical or emotional difficulties persist for many months, interfering with health, sleep, or day-to-day life.

WHAT THE FUTURE HOLDS

"Will our baby live?" is the first question distraught parents of high-risk babies ask neonatologists. Later comes another painful query: What kind of life will our baby have?

The answer depends on the severity of the baby's problem and the extent and duration of the necessary treatment. Survival rates for high-risk babies, including the very smallest and youngest, are astoundingly good. But even more remarkable is the fact that most "graduates" of newborn intensive care nurseries not only survive but thrive, suffering few, if any, long-term complications.

Only a small percentage—5 to 20 percent of the smallest and sickest babies followed at Johns Hopkins—suffer serious lifelong disabilities, such as blindness, profound mental retardation, or se-

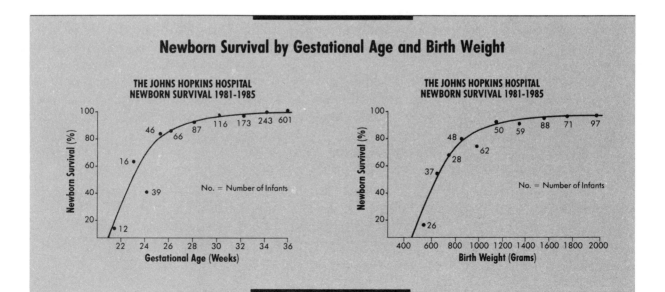

Newborn Survival by Gestational Age and Birth Weight

THE JOHNS HOPKINS HOSPITAL
NEWBORN SURVIVAL 1981-1985

No. = Number of Infants

THE JOHNS HOPKINS HOSPITAL
NEWBORN SURVIVAL 1981-1985

No. = Number of Infants

vere cerebral palsy. About 10 to 15 percent have lesser disabilities: impaired vision or hearing, mild to moderate cerebral palsy, or mild retardation.

By age six, others show evidence of milder difficulties—learning disabilities, behavior disorders, coordination problems, somewhat lower IQs, hyperactivity—and many require extra help in school. (These problems affect about 10 percent of all youngsters, including those who were not premature.)

In general, the most significant predictors of developmental problems at age three are neurologic symptoms, respiratory difficulties, infection, and chronic oxygen deprivation in the womb. Babies who are small for gestational age, have low birth weights, and require extended hospital stays are more likely to have learning problems.

Half of all neurologic handicaps in infants are the result of prematurity. The youngest, smallest babies (under one thousand grams) are at greatest risk of long-term difficulty. Yet the majority of preemies born weighing one thousand five hundred grams (three pounds, five ounces) or more overcome their rocky start in life and grow normally.

In experiments at several medical centers, various early interventions have made a difference. Preemies who had more opportunities to suck on a pacifier between feedings or who were gently rubbed and massaged fared better in both the short and long run. Some medical centers offer special infant programs that combine exercise and oral/motor skills to help preemies catch up.

Before taking your baby home, try to get as clear a picture as possible of the reality of your child's condition and the types of developmental hurdles ahead. Your baby's first caregivers can let you know whether he or she likes to be swaddled (wrapped snugly) or tends to become overaroused easily. In playing or comforting your baby, pay attention to individual likes or dislikes, and tailor your behavior to them. If your child's response baffles you, be sure to ask about it.

Be realistic about the problems of coping with a child with a handicap or developmental disorder. Older children may feel neglected or scapegoated. One partner may feel pushed aside or denied attention. Spouses or siblings may resent the huge investment of money and energy into the support of one child's needs. These are problems that defy quick, easy, work-for-all solutions. But parents can find support. Often medical centers or community organizations sponsor groups for parents of children with various problems.

CHAPTER 15

After Birth

"We took her home, and I got into bed, and my husband sat down next to me, and we just stared at her. We stayed there, the three of us, just looking, until the light faded and the day turned into night."

Your baby has been born. The pregnancy that you may have felt would never end is over. The time has come when all new parents look at each other and ask: What now?

The first days after a baby's birth are a time of enormous adjustment—physically and psychologically. Mothers and fathers find their whole world turned upside down as they add a new member—or members—to the family. Just as anticipating and preparing for the labor helps couples through childbirth, understanding the changes that parenthood brings can ease your way through the "fourth trimester"—the first few weeks of your baby's life.

The postpartum days are a mix of highs and lows. Joy alternates with inexplicable sadness; wonder, with apprehension. You cry for what you lost as pregnancy ended and what you gained when your child's life began. Like all new parents, you grope your way toward confidence and competence. And in the middle of the sea-changes in your life is the baby—precious, sweet, utterly fascinating, and *yours*.

GETTING TO KNOW YOUR BABY

Even babies born at term and in good health face an enormous challenge as they leave behind the only world they've ever known. For the first time, they must fill their lungs with air. Their hearts must take over full responsibility for pumping blood through their bodies.

Their muscles must move in novel ways. Their senses must react to an overwhelming blitz of new sounds, sights, tastes, sensations. Their job is to learn everything. Yours is easier: learning about them.

The Newborn's Body

Months before birth a baby's chest begins "working" in the fluid-filled womb, practicing for its first breath of air. As the baby passes through the birth canal, its chest is compressed, and some of the fluid in its lungs is squeezed out. Most babies can clear the remaining fluid from their lungs on their own. Sometimes the birth attendant will suction mucus and fluid from the baby's mouth and throat to allow easier breathing.

With its first inhalation, the tiny sacs or alveoli within the lungs begin to open, pushing out the rest of the fluid. The lungs expand with each successive breath, as more of the air sacs open. Newborns take about thirty to fifty breaths each minute and inhale through the nose (which is why it's important to keep it clear).

Some babies do not establish a regular breathing pattern immediately, and skip breaths periodically, particularly when sleeping, sucking, or crying. This usually is not dangerous in a healthy infant. If the baby is at risk, the intensive care nursery staff will monitor its breathing to make sure the baby is taking at least thirty breaths a minute.

At birth an infant can digest simple carbohydrates, proteins, and fats. Gradually more enzymes are produced to aid in the breakdown of foods. The baby's stomach empties intermittently, starting within a few minutes of a feeding. Its control of the muscles in the stomach is immature so some feedings may be spit up, or regurgitated.

Full-term babies have their first bowel movements within twelve to forty-eight hours after birth. Usually the stools consist of meconium, thick, tarry, dark green waste material formed before birth. Subsequent bowel movements tend to be green or yellow and liquidy if the baby is breastfeeding and paler in color if the baby is on formula. Some babies have several bowel movements a day; others have one every few days.

Most newborns begin urinating at birth or shortly thereafter. Normal urine in early infancy is straw-colored and almost odorless. Mothers may notice blood on the diapers of baby girls. This "pseudomenstruation," or false menstrual bleeding, is the result of the withdrawal of the mother's sex hormones from the baby's body.

During their first month of life, babies tend to curl up, regardless of the position they're put in. The main reason is that their heads are very large in relation to the rest of their bodies, and their neck muscles are too weak to support the heavy load. By the end of the fourth week, most babies can lift their heads for at least a few moments.

The Newborn's Behavior

Babies spend their first month in two states: asleep and alert. With no sense of day or night, newborns sleep as much as they need—which can be up to sixteen hours a day. Infants often drift into sleep randomly throughout a twenty-four-hour period, even while sucking on breast or bottle. It takes several months for them to "learn" a sleep-wake schedule.

Pediatricians break down the "alert" stages into four different categories: drowsy or semidozing, wide awake, active awake, and crying. Crying serves many purposes. It may distract the baby from hunger and pain (and make the caregiver aware of these problems) and it may help the baby discharge energy and reorganize behavior.

All of a baby's senses are operating from the moment of birth, if not earlier, but each infant has to learn how to use the information the senses provide. While newborns can see, they are nearsighted, focusing on objects about eight to ten inches from their faces. Even at the earliest stages, babies like to look at faces and will look at a face longer than an object or picture.

Long before birth, babies can hear sounds outside the womb. While loud noises startle newborns, recordings of a heartbeat—the sound a fetus lives with in the womb—may soothe them. By the end of their first month, infants can recognize the voices of those who matter most in their lives. Although they may not understand words, they respond quickly to the speaker's tone, crying if their caretakers shout or calming down when their mothers croon softly to them.

Babies are born with built-in "tastes." Given something bitter, acid, or sour, they turn away or cry. Offered some slightly sweetened water, they suck longer and harder. They also respond to touch. When stroked on the cheek, they will turn their heads in that direction. They like warm, soft pressure and motion, whether they're "riding" in a mother's arms, a stroller, or a car seat.

During their first months, babies live totally in the moment. They forget immediately about objects they cannot see. They do not reach for something bright and shining, although they may kick with pleasure when such an object appears within their limited range of vision.

Term babies are born with certain reflexes that they lose and re-learn months later. If placed on their stomachs, they flex their arms and legs as if they're about to crawl. They grip their fingers tightly around anything placed in their hands. If held up on a firm surface, they will take steps, as if they were walking. If startled or handled roughly, they throw out their arms and legs, instinctively seeking support.

Premature babies are biologically incapable of responding the way term babies do. Shortchanged of crucial weeks or months for development within the womb, they are unprepared for life in the world. Often they cannot hold their heads up even for a few seconds, and they may be unable to make or maintain eye contact with their parents. Preemies also startle more, their tiny bodies quivering from head to toe.

Preemies are hypersensitive because their neurological systems are not fully developed. Even the texture of their clothing can upset them. They may be more difficult to feed, console, care for. When eager parents try to interact, they may stiffen and push away. When mothers attempt nursing, they may be unable to suck for more than a few seconds.

Unless parents realize that preemies respond differently from full-term babies, they may assume they're doing something wrong or that the baby doesn't like them. Parents of preemies may find that they have to work harder to get their babies to respond, and then the infants quickly become overaroused. They have to learn the fine line between providing too little and too much stimulation. Often talking to professionals about what to expect helps parents accept their children on their own terms.

RECOVERY: GETTING YOUR BODY BACK

The first days after delivery may not be comfortable. Your body is reacting to the tremendous upheaval of pregnancy and birth. Cramps and bleeding persist. Episiotomy stitches sting. If you're nursing, your breasts become engorged as they fill with milk. Many women tumble from the exhilaration of delivery into a brief depression.

While most women feel much better fairly quickly, during the next few weeks, they continue to experience dramatic changes—inside as well as out. The uterus, stretched bigger than a watermelon, shrinks to the size of a large grapefruit. This process, called "involution," can cause cramps or afterpains that range from mild to severe for up to two weeks, particularly in women who've had other children. Peaking in the first two or three days after delivery, they feel sharpest while you're breastfeeding because nursing releases a hormone called oxytocin that intensifies contractions. The relaxation and deep-breathing exercises used for childbirth can ease the pain.

Your body sheds the by-products of pregnancy in lochia, a vaginal discharge that starts off dark red and may contain clots as big as quarters, turns pinkish-brown after two or three days, then creamy or yellow, and continues for four to eight weeks after delivery. Because your cervix remains open, providing a passageway for bacteria to enter your healing uterus, use sanitary napkins, not tampons, to absorb the flow.

Since your body must eliminate the extra fluids that accumulated during pregnancy, you'll perspire heavily and urinate often. Irritation and pressure on the urethra and bladder during delivery may lead to some temporary tingling during urination.

What Can You Do

Often simple self-care techniques can make you feel better:

• If your perineum (the area between your vagina and rectum) is sore or episiotomy stitches sting, an ice pack will reduce swelling and discomfort. Squirting warm water over the region from a plastic squeeze bottle helps, as does dry heat from a lamp or hair dryer. For added comfort, try a cool "sitz bath"—sitting in a shallow tub of water to which you add ice cubes.

• If you develop hemorrhoids as a result of pressure on the rectum during delivery, try lying on your side with a soft pillow under your bottom. Apply witch-hazel compresses and anesthetic ointments; rectal suppositories may help. Drink lots of fluids and eat high-fiber foods to prevent constipation. Your doctor may prescribe a stool softener so you don't strain during bowel movements.

• For engorged (hard, painful, full, warm) breasts, express some milk to relieve the pressure. If you're waiting for your milk supply to dry up naturally (a process that takes a few days), wear a snug bra or wrap a bath towel tightly around your chest. Ice packs or warm, moist cloths also are soothing. Avoid any breast stimulation.

• Sleep is what you need most. If you don't get the rest you need, exhaustion can reduce milk flow, slow recovery, and make psychological adjustment harder. Nap in the morning and the afternoon for the first two weeks and continue to take one daily nap as long as you can. While you may be tempted to do chores when the baby naps, take advantage of this quiet time to rest.

Take the phone off the hook or ask visitors to return later. Darken the room, play soft music, and get under the covers. To get a longer period of solid sleep, turn over one night feeding to your husband. (If you're nursing, you may want to wait two weeks and then pump your breasts and prepare a bottle before going to bed.)

• Continue to eat for two if you're breastfeeding. You'll need about five hundred to six hundred extra calories and at least eight glasses of fluids a day. Nursing increases your calcium needs by 50 percent over normal. You also need twenty grams of additional protein—about one three-ounce serving of meat—for producing lactalbumin, the major protein in breast milk. Eat extra servings of citrus fruits, whole-grain cereals, legumes (dried peas, beans, peanuts), and vegetables (particularly green and yellow ones) for vitamins B_6, C, E, and folic acid—all important for healing. Get in the habit of drinking water, juice, or milk every time you nurse. If you're on the run, keep nutritious finger foods—cheese squares, yogurt drinks, fruit, carrots—handy.

• Don't worry about your weight—yet. You'll drop ten to twelve pounds after delivery and another five in the first month. Most women lose a total of twenty-five to thirty pounds within two months. If you're nursing, don't restrict your food intake. If not, you no longer need the three hundred extra calories you added to your daily diet during pregnancy. But you do need adequate protein and vitamins for healing, so don't cut back any more for several weeks.

• Exercise is the best way to restore your figure, but start slow and build up gradually. Within hours of delivery, you can begin Kegel exercises—tightening and releasing the muscles that control urination. If you've had a vaginal delivery, start some simple exercises, such as lying on your back and trying to raise your chin to your chest, the next day. Gradually increase repetitions and add leg lifts and modified curl-ups. Tightening your abdominal muscles as you walk or stand will tone and strengthen them. Walking, another excellent postpartum exercise, prevents blood clots and constipation and firms muscles.

Because your joints may still be loose from hormones produced in pregnancy, avoid activities that involve jumping, bouncing, or sudden changes in direction and exercises like deep knee bends, touching your toes, or squatting. Stop exercising if you develop pain, shortness of breath, or dizziness.

Don't forget that your body is healing, and excess activity can interfere with that process. One immediate signal of overexertion is a change in lochia from pink or clear to bright red, the result of fresh bleeding from the site where the placenta was attached to your uterus.

While you may be eager to get back in shape, be sure you ease into an exercise program. Avoid any aerobic activity (running, cycling, fast-paced calisthenics) for at least two weeks. If it takes you a long time to recover after working out, you probably did too much.

• Mothering is a full-time job, and you'll be better at it—and feel better about it—if you baby yourself too. Especially during the first two weeks, your only priorities should be your baby and your body. Even in the frantic first days, savor some minor indulgences: a long shower, a few minutes alone in the sunshine, a brief stroll. If only by telephone, talking to other women—especially other mothers—can be enormously helpful. Some special moments with your husband also can make a big difference.

> "I was so used to thinking of myself as this competent professional, and suddenly I was doing what I thought had to be the simplest job on earth—taking care of a tiny baby—and I felt completely inadequate. What good is an MBA when your kid has colic?"

Danger Signs

Your body will provide clues if something's amiss. Among the warning signals to bring to your doctor's attention:

• A temperature of 100 degrees or higher, which, after the first twenty-four hours, could indicate infection.

• Change in the lochia—foul smell, large clots, a return to bright red bleeding—that might be caused by retained fragments of the placenta, infection, or overexertion.

• Breast tenderness or redness, which could be the result of a clogged milk duct (massage may relieve it) or infection.

• Calf pain or tenderness, possibly caused by a blood clot.

• Urgency, frequency, or burning during urination, signals of a urinary tract infection.

Just as in pregnancy, you shouldn't hesitate to call your perinatal caregivers if something seems suspicious. Prompt treatment could prevent a bigger problem.

If You've Had a Cesarean

You're recovering from major surgery as well as childbirth. Initially, your incision may be painful, especially when you move or go to the bathroom. Once you're allowed to shower, the warm water will be soothing. Get out of bed by rolling to your side and elevating yourself with one arm. With the nurse's help, try to take a few steps as soon as possible; walking decreases the likelihood of blood clots, eases intestinal gas pains, and prevents constipation. If you're breastfeeding, try different ways of holding your baby. Propping a pillow on your stomach may help. Or you can try lying on your side with the baby on the bed.

Once you return home, limit climbing stairs, and don't lift anything heavier than your baby. Don't attempt abdominal exercises for several weeks. Because surgery drains energy and stamina, you may tire easily. Schedule several naps; put your feet up or lie on your side whenever you can. Remember than you'll recover faster if you don't rush it.

LIFE WITH BABY

Finding a Pediatrician

Just as you may have visited an obstetrician before you conceived, you should visit a pediatrician before you give birth. In fact, you may want to visit several. Many practice in a group with a pediatric nurse practitioner, who can handle many of your questions and needs. However, because of the aftereffects of some high-risk pregnancies, your baby may need a specialist.

When you interview pediatricians, find out how they handle routine checkups as well as emergency care. Can you call for advice or reassurance? What if you feel your baby should be seen immediately? Do they set aside a certain time every day for "walk-in" visits? You should feel comfortable with them, their way of handling your questions and concerns, and the hospital they use if a baby requires hospitalization. You also should discuss the possible impact of your high-risk pregnancy and who would care for your baby if he or she requires special care after birth. You and your pediatrician should arrange for an initial evaluation in the hospital as soon after your baby's birth as possible.

Breastfeeding

Breastfed babies have fewer illnesses and a much lower hospitalization rate. Their mortality rate is lower. Breast milk seems not only to prevent or lessen disease but also to help bring infection under control, perhaps because it passes the mother's immunities to the baby. Breastfed infants are less likely to become obese or develop allergies. Another benefit of breastfeeding is psychological. The process of nursing may reinforce the bond between mother and child.

Even when no complications develop before or after birth, nursing is not always easy. According to the American Council on Science and Health, at least 20 percent of women are unable to breastfeed after their first deliveries; 50 percent of new mothers encounter some difficulties in nursing, such as inflammation of a milk gland. Usually such problems can be overcome.

Most mothers who were at risk during pregnancy can and do nurse successfully. You may want to discuss your specific situation with your caregivers before delivery. If you are taking medications that could be transmitted through breast milk, you may have to pump your breasts and discard the milk. You also may have to pump if your baby is too small or too premature to be able to suck. Generally breast milk is fed to a premature or low-birth-weight baby through a tube.

The breast milk of women who deliver early seems especially nutritious for their premature babies because it contains a higher concentration of protein and fatty acids and two to four times the amount of thyroid hormone found in the milk of mothers of term babies. Preemies need extra protein and thyroid hormones, as well as fatty acids for brain growth. The milk of preemies' mothers also contains less lactose, which makes it easier to digest.

Doctors encourage women who are diabetic or who developed gestational diabetes to breastfeed. Because insulin levels change rapidly after delivery, you may have to monitor your blood sugar frequently. Most women who had gestational diabetes or were non-insulin-dependent diabetics before pregnancy can again control blood-sugar levels with diet alone. After delivery, some insulin-dependent diabetics experience a temporary remission. However, because of the increased nutritional demands of breastfeeding, most require more insulin.

Postmature babies benefit from breastfeeding, because it helps their metabolic control. However, they may not suck well initially and often need considerable prodding before settling into a healthy nursing routine. Babies with certain birth defects, such as cleft lip or palate, may not be able to nurse, but can receive breast milk through a tube or dropper. Special nipples and nipple shields also are available. Babies who develop fevers, jaundice, or other brief illnesses tend to do better with continued breastfeeding.

"I had been robbed of so many things—of carrying my baby to term, of having a vaginal delivery, of being with him right from the start. I was determined that nothing and no one would rob me of the experience of breastfeeding. I'm so glad I didn't give up."

Some babies fed with bottles (containing breast milk or formula) for an extended period may not "take" the breast afterward. Patience and perseverance often help overcome this difficulty. If you aren't able to breastfeed, keep in mind that bottlefed babies grow up just as healthy and happy as breastfed ones. Infants do not live on milk alone. Your love and care matter far more in the long run.

Postpartum Depression

In many normal pregnancies, the high of delivery can lead to an emotional low, called the baby blues, or in more serious cases, to postpartum depression. Fatigue, moodiness, sensitivity, and anxiety plague 80 to 85 percent of new mothers. Many simply find themselves crying but can't explain why, even to themselves. The tears may not indicate disappointment or sadness, but may reflect feelings of low self-esteem, loneliness, or irritability. Women facing extra pressure—including those who've had twins, premature babies, or infants with birth defects—are especially likely to feel overwhelmed.

Postpartum Support International, a national network focusing on mental health after delivery, estimates that four hundred thousand women in the United States—about 10 percent of new mothers—develop postpartum depression every year. They feel sad, discouraged, irritable, lose interest in eating or sex, have problems concentrating, and develop vague physical complaints. Among the factors that put a mother at risk are:
- previous postpartum depression
- history of depression or anxiety
- family history of depression
- childhood trauma
- unwanted pregnancy
- long, difficult, complicated, or unsupported labor
- a baby who's premature or has a birth defect.

About one in every thousand new mothers experiences a postpartum psychosis in which she loses touch with reality and may hear voices, believe in delusions (such as thinking the baby is Christ and must die to be reborn), or become agitated or violent. At its most extreme, postpartum psychosis can lead to the mother's killing herself or her infant. Women with previous severe psychiatric problems, such as manic depression, or a family history of psychosis are at highest risk.

Most women with postpartum depression start feeling better

when they get a combination of supportive psychotherapy, practical information, and help in reducing stress. The greatest help often comes from other mothers. In the last few years, support groups—linked by Postpartum Support International—have spread across the country. In more serious cases, psychiatrists report success with antidepressant medication and sometimes hospitalization. Some women who've had a previous bout with depression after delivery may receive preventive injections of progesterone.

Fathers, too, may suffer postpartum blues. If they were actively involved in childbirth preparation and in the delivery, they may feel left out afterward. The full impact of having another family members hits them for the first time, and they—just like new mothers—must adjust to the often unsettling realities of life with a newborn.

After a high-risk pregnancy, both parents may feel they have no right to be depressed. In most cases, they get exactly what they'd been hoping and praying for: a healthy, normal baby. Yet the emotional letdown may be particularly acute.

For the first time in months, they may finally dare to admit their fears and feelings. And their baby—unlike the perfect angel who lived in their imagination for months—cries and wets and keeps them up nights. When they, in their weariness, fondly recall the quiet nights before the baby's birth, they may feel guilty, even though their responses are completely normal.

> "Everyone jokes about not getting any sleep, but you just can't imagine how tired you're going to be. At times, I'd hear the baby cry, an I'd think, 'Kid, I'll give you five hundred dollars if you just let me sleep ten more minutes.' Then I'd remember how we'd yearned and prayed for a healthy baby and I'd feel guilty."

AFTER A HIGH-RISK PREGNANCY

Some risk factors end once pregnancy ends; others take longer and require continued close monitoring. Among those women who may continue to need special attention after delivery are:

• Diabetic women, whose blood-sugar levels may fluctuate during and after delivery. Many enter a "honeymoon" period after delivery when their blood-sugar levels are low and they require little insulin, if any.

• Women with hypertensive disorders of pregnancy. Delivery "cures" these problems, and unless they have chronic hypertension, blood pressure generally returns to normal within several days or, occasionally, weeks.

• Women with heart disease. Within a few weeks, their hearts should return to normal size, position, and functioning, but the time required for complete recovery depends on the severity of the heart problem. With proper care before, during, and after delivery, most

"You spend months
worrying and thinking
about nothing else, and
then all of a sudden,
you're a parent. And even
though the doctors say the
baby's fine, you can't quite
believe it. It takes a long
time to convince
yourself."

women do not sustain any heart damage or long-term impairment.

• Women with seizure disorders, whose anticonvulsant levels must be monitored often after delivery because of rapid physiological changes. After birth their babies may be given vitamin K to prevent blood clots.

Hospital stays need not be longer for high-risk women. But even more so than most new mothers, you need to take whatever time you need to recover. When you return home, arrange for help from friends, relatives, or neighbors so you're not overwhelmed with household chores.

The Emotional Aftereffects

Many parents may feel contradictory emotions after a high-risk pregnancy ends. Some, still weighed down by the burden of anticipatory grief, are hesitant about connecting with a baby whom they once feared would or could not survive. Others, whose babies do indeed have problems after birth, plunge from one high-stress situation into another.

Even parents who take home sturdy, full-term babies may feel unprepared to care for them. Many women feel frustrated and incompetent if they cannot tell why their babies are crying or are unable to quiet them or get them to sleep. They may find it difficult to relax and enjoy their babies.

Many parents find themselves hovering over a baby, listening for the reassuring sound of its breathing, stiffening in anxiety at each sniffle, waiting for something to go wrong. "I'd become so accustomed to worrying about the baby that I couldn't let her out of my sight," one woman recalls. "When she fell asleep, I'd listen for her breathing. When she was awake, I was always checking if she was cold or wet."

This sense of danger can take months to dispel, especially if the baby does indeed have problems or if the parents had lost another child. "Other parents have no reason to expect the worse," reflects a woman whose twin boys died a few weeks after their premature birth. "We've lost our innocence. Fortunately, when I got pregnant again, it was just one baby, and it was a girl. But even though she was big and beautiful and healthy right from the start, I felt on guard the whole first year."

Many parents find support groups especially helpful in putting a high-risk pregnancy behind them. Other couples who've been through the experience can offer practical advice, such as how to cope with complex care instructions or how to find supportive pediatricians.

A network of supportive people also helps. Women who report high levels of support from spouses, parents, or friends generally feel less depressed and more confident three months after delivery.

A New Beginning

In time, parents settle into their new roles. You will too. You'll feel safer and more confident as each month goes by. For months, even years, your memory may take you back, again and again, to the events of your pregnancy. Processing these memories—by talking, writing, drawing, taping, or any other form of expression—is essential.

In time and in its own special ways, the baby—the wondrous star of the drama of birth—does its part in forming a family. As pediatrician T. Berry Brazelton notes, "The work of attachment does not have to be carried out singlehandedly by parents: the newborn is programmed with a great variety of abilities and responsibilities that reach out to his mother and father. He meets them at least halfway." The baby responds to parents' attention and love; they respond to their child's growing awareness of them. And in these moments of connection and mutual awe, something special is born: a family.

GLOSSARY

abortion. The termination, spontaneous or induced, of pregnancy at any time before the fetus has attained a stage of viability, i.e., before it is capable of extrauterine existence.

abruptio placenta. Premature separation of normally implanted placenta.

alpha fetoprotein (AFP). A protein manufactured mainly in the liver of a fetus and released into the amniotic fluid when the fetus urinates.

amniocentesis. Prenatal diagnostic test; sampling of the amniotic fluid that surrounds a fetus in order to obtain information about its well-being.

amniotic sac. The "bag of waters" containing the fetus before delivery.

amniotomy. Artificial rupture of the membranes to induce labor.

analgesic. Drug that relieves pain, used during labor.

anencephaly. Absence of a brain.

anomaly. Malformation.

anoxia. Oxygen deficiency

antenatal. Occurring or formed before birth.

antibody. A protein manufactured by the body's protective immune system that reacts specifically against the foreign substance that initially triggered its production.

asphyxia. Anoxia and carbon dioxide retention resulting from failure of respiration.

bag of waters. The membranes that enclose the amniotic fluid.

Braxton-Hicks. Painless uterine contractions occurring periodically throughout pregnancy.

breech delivery. Labor and delivery marked by breech presentations (buttocks- or feet-first).

cephalic. Belonging to the head.

cephalic presentation. Presentation of any part of the fetal head in labor.

cephalo-pelvic disproportion. A complication of labor in which the baby's head is too large to pass through the birth canal.

cerclage. A suture placed around an "incompetent" cervix to prevent a miscarriage.

cervix. The lower and narrow end of the uterus.

cesarean. Surgical delivery of a baby through the uterus and abdomen.

chorionic villus sampling (CVS). A prenatal test for genetic defects, performed between the eighth and twelfth weeks of pregnancy, in which a physician removes a small sample of the chorionic villus, the tissue surrounding the early placenta, through a syringe or hollow tube.

chromosome. One of several small, dark-staining, and more or less rod-shaped bodies that appear in the nucleus of the cell at the time of cell division.

colostrum. A substance in the first breast milk after delivery, that gives it a yellowish color.

conception. The impregnation of the female ovum by the sperm of the male, resulting in a new being.

condyloma. (*pl.* condylomata) A wartlike growth near the anus or the vulva.

congenital. Born with the person; existing from or before birth, as, for example, congenital disease originating in the fetus before birth.

contraction stress testing (CST). Measurement of fetal heart rate during contractions induced by stimulation of the mother's nipples or IV administration of oxytocin.

corpus luteum. The yellow mass found in the ovary after the ovum has been expelled.

delivery. The expulsion of a child by the mother or its extraction by the obstetric practitioner.

dizygotic. Pertaining to or proceeding from two zygotes (two eggs or ova).

eclampsia. Once called acute "toxemia of pregnancy"; characterized by convulsions and coma that may occur during pregnancy or labor.

ectopic. Out of place.

ectopic pregnancy. Gestation in which the fetus is out of its normal place in the cavity of the uterus. It includes gestation in the fallopian tube or in a rudimentary horn of the uterus (cornual pregnancy), cervical pregnancy, and abdominal and ovarian pregnancy.

effacement. Thinning and shortening of the cervix.

ejaculation. The expulsion of semen.

electronic fetal monitoring. A method of checking a baby's well-being before or during labor by checking its heart rate and response to contractions.

embryo. The product of conception in utero from the third through the fifth week of gestation; after that length of time, it is called the fetus.

endometrium. The mucous membrane that lines the uterus.

engagement. In obstetrics, the entrance of the presenting part into the superior pelvic strait and the beginning of the descent through the pelvic canal.

episiotomy. Surgical incision of the vaginal orifice for delivery of a baby.

erythroblastosis fetalis. A severe disease of the newborn, due to Rh incompatibility.

estriol. The form of estrogen that increases most dramatically in pregnancy.

extracorporeal membrane oxygenation (ECMO). A treatment for high-risk babies with respiratory and circulation problems that carries their blood outside their bodies and through an artificial lung machine, allowing their own fragile lungs to rest and heal.

fertility. The ability to produce offspring; power of reproduction.

fertilization. The fusion of the sperm with the ovum; it marks the beginning of pregnancy.

fetal activity monitoring. A mother-to-be's monitoring of how often her baby moves in a thirty- to sixty-minute period several times a day.

fetal biophysical profile. Prenatal testing, performed with an ultrasound scanner and electronic fetal monitor, that serves as the equivalent of a physical examination in the womb.

fetal echocardiography. A prenatal test, using ultrasound, to detect heart problems or defects in a fetus before birth.

fetus. The baby in utero from the end of the fifth week of gestation until birth.

forceps. Metal devices used to protect a baby's head and guide it through the lower birth canal.

fundus. The upper rounded portion of the uterus

gamete. A sexual cell; an unfertilized egg or a mature sperm cell.

gene. A hereditary factor in the chromosome that carries on a hereditary, transmissible character.

gonad. A gamete-producing gland; an ovary or testis.

hormone. A chemical substance produced in an organ, which, when carried to an associated organ by the bloodstream, stimulates a functional activity.

human chorionic gonadotropin (HCG). Characteristic hormone of early pregnancy.

human placental lactogen (HPL). A protein produced only in pregnancy. HPL levels in the mother's blood generally increase until the thirty-seventh week and then level off.

hydatidiform mole. Proliferation of chorionic villus resembling a bunch of grapes.

hydramnios. An excessive amount of amniotic fluid.

hydrocephalus. Excessive fluid within the skull.

hypoxia. Insufficient oxygen to support normal metabolic requirements.

immune therapy. Treatment of a woman with a history of miscarriage prior to conceiving again with injections or vaginal suppositories of her husband's white blood cells or seminal fluid to trigger an immune response that may prevent another miscarriage.

intrauterine transfusion. Injection of blood cells into a fetus, usually performed for babies with Rh incompatibility.

ketoacidosis. A buildup of weak acids called ketones when the body is deprived of glucose and begins to break down stored fat for energy use.

labor. The series of processes by which the products of conception are expelled from the mother's body.

lactation. The act or period of giving milk; the secretion of milk; the time or period of secreting milk.

lanugo. The fine hair on the body of the fetus.

lecithin/sphingomyelin ratio. A test of fetal lung maturity by measuring the amounts of lecithin, a fat produced by the lungs, and sphingomyelin, a fat produced by the skin.

linea nigra. A dark line appearing on the abdomen and extending from the pubis toward the umbilicus, considered one of the signs of pregnancy.

lochia. The discharge from the genital canal during several days subsequent to delivery.

meconium. The dark green or black substance found in the large intestine of the fetus or newly born infant.

menarche. The establishment or the beginning of the menstrual function.

menopause. The period at which menstruation ceases; the "change of life."

miscarriage. Death of a fetus prior to the twentieth week of gestation; spontaneous abortion.

molding. The shaping of the baby's head so as to adjust itself to the size and shape of the birth canal.

monozygotic. Pertaining to or derived from one zygote, or one egg or ovum.

multigravida. A woman who has been pregnant several times or many times.

multipara. A woman who has borne several children.

neonatal. Pertaining to the newborn, usually for the first four weeks of life.

neonatology. Subspecialty of pediatrics dedicated to caring for sick babies in their first days of life.

nonstress testing (NST). A method of assessing fetal well-being by monitoring its heart rate and response to spontaneous movements or contractions.

nullipara. A woman who has not borne children.

ovary. The sexual gland of the female in which the ova are developed. There are two ovaries, one at each side of the pelvis.

ovulation. The release of an ovum from the ovary.

ovum. The female reproductive cell. The human ovum is a round cell about 1/120 of an inch in diameter, developed in the ovary.

oxytocin. One of the two hormones secreted by the pituitary; it induces contractions of the uterus.

parity. The condition of a woman with respect to her having borne children.

percutaneous umbilical blood sampling (PUBS). A procedure for obtaining a sample of blood from the umbilical cord of an unborn baby or administering blood transfusions or medications.

perinatal. Before, during, and immediately after birth.

perinatology. Subspecialty of obstetrics dedicated to care of high-risk mothers and their unborn babies; also called maternal-fetal medicine.

perineum. The area between the vagina and the rectum.

Pitocin. A synthetic solution of oxytocin.

placenta. The circular flat, vascular structure in the impregnated uterus forming the principal medium of communication between the mother and the fetus.

placenta previa. A placenta that is implanted in the lower uterine segment so that it adjoins or covers the cervix.

placental abruption. Premature separation of the normally implanted placenta.

postmaturity. A condition that occurs in some pregnancies that continue beyond the forty-week term, when the placenta can no longer supply adequate nutrients to the fetus.

postnatal. Occurring after birth.

postpartal. After delivery or childbirth.

presentation. Term used to designate the position of the fetus as felt by the physician's examining finger when introduced into the cervix.

preterm labor. Onset of rhythmic contractions after the twentieth and before the thirty-seventh week of pregnancy.

primigravida. A woman who is pregnant for the first time.

progesterone. The pure hormone whose function is to prepare the endometrium for the reception and development of the fertilized ovum; it also helps to maintain the pregnancy.

proteinuria. High levels of protein in urine.

puerperium. The period elapsing between the termination of labor and the return of the uterus to its normal condition, about six weeks.

quickening. The mother's first perception of the movements of the fetus.

Rh. Abbreviation for Rhesus, a type of monkey. This term is used for a property of human blood cells, because of its relationship to a similar property in the blood cells of Rhesus monkeys.

RhoGAM. A substance containing anti-RH antibodies given to Rh-negative women after delivery, abortion, or miscarriage to prevent the production of these antibodies, which could threaten any Rh-positive babies these women might conceive in the future.

rubella. German measles.

scalp sampling. A test of a baby's condition during labor by obtaining a sample of blood from a blood vessel on its scalp. The physician uses an amnioscope (a cone-shaped device with an attached light source) to view the baby and a scalpel to prick its blood vessel.

small for gestational age (SGA). A baby who weighs less than do 90 percent of babies at the same stage of pregnancy or at delivery.

stillborn. Born without life.

stress testing. A method of assessing fetal well-being by monitoring fetal heart rate and its response to contractions induced by oxytocin.

teratogen. Any substance that causes deformities in an unborn baby.

tocodynamometer. A monitor that measures uterine activity in pregnancy to determine the risk or presence of prenatal labor.

ultrasound (sonography). High-frequency sound waves used to evaluate fetal well-being and diagnose structural defects.

uterus. The hollow muscular organ in the female designed for the lodgment and nourishment of the fetus during its development until birth.

vagina. The canal in the female extending from the vulva to the cervix of the uterus.

version. The act of turning; specifically, a turning of the fetus in the uterus so as to change the presenting part and bring it into more favorable position for delivery.

vertex. In anatomy, the top or crown of the head.

viable. A term in medical jurisprudence signifying "able or likely to live"; applied to the condition of the child at birth.

zygote. A cell resulting from the fusion of two gametes.

SELECTED BIBLIOGRAPHY

BOOKS

Armstrong, Penny, and Sheryl Feldman. A *Midwife's Story*. New York: Arbor House, 1986.

Borg, Susan, and Judith Lasker. *When Pregnancy Fails*. Boston: Beacon Press, 1980.

Filkins, Karen, and Joseph F. Russo. *Human Prenatal Diagnosis*. New York: Marcel Dekker, Inc.

Freeman, Roger F., and Susan C. Pescar. *Safe Delivery*. New York: Facts on File, 1982.

Friedman, Rochelle, and Bonnie Gradstein. *Surviving Pregnancy Loss*. Boston: Little Brown, 1982.

Gabbe, Steven G., Jennifer R. Niebyl, and Joe Leigh Simpson. *Obstetrics: Normal and Problem Pregnancies*. New York: Churchill Livingstone, 1986.

Hales, Dianne. *Pregnancy and Birth*. New York: Chelsea House Publishers, 1989.

Harrison, Helen. *The Premature Baby Book*. New York: St. Martin's Press, 1983.

Katz, Michael, Pamela Gill, and Juith Turiel. *Preventing Preterm Birth: A Parent's Guide*. Health Publishing Company, 1988.

Novotny, Pamela. *The Joy of Twins*. New York: Crown Publishers, 1988.

Olds, Sally B., Marcia L. London, and Patricia A. Ladewig. *Maternal Newborn Nursing*. Menlo Park, Cal.: Addison-Wesley, 1988.

Papiernik, Emile, et al. *Effective Prevention of Preterm Birth: The French Experience Measured at Haguenau*. White Plains, N.Y.: March of Dimes Birth Defects Foundation, 1989.

Pizer, Hank, and Christine O'Brien Palinski. *Coping with a Miscarriage*. New York: Dial Press, 1980.

Rinzler, Carol Ann. *The Safe Pregnancy Book*. New York: New American Library, 1984.

Romero, Roberto, et al. *Prenatal Diagnosis of Congenital Anomalies*. Norwalk, Conn: Appleton and Lange, 1988.

Rothman, Barbara Katz. *The Tentative Pregnancy*. New York: Viking, 1986.

Schrotenboer, Kathryn, and Joan Solomon Wiss. *Dr. Kathryn Schrotenboer's Guide to Pregnancy over 35*. New York: Ballantine Books, 1985.

Schwartz, Susan. "Bed—and Bored." Oakland, Ca.: Birthways.

Wilson, Josleen. *The Pregnancy Planner*. New York: Doubleday, 1986.

JOURNALS AND PERIODICALS

1. The High-Risk Pregnancy

American College of Obstetricians and Gynecologists, "High-Risk Pregnancy," August, 1986.

2. Are You at Risk?

Brody, Jane. "Personal Health: The Proper Care of Future Mothers Can Help Produce Healthy Babies," *New York Times,* August 4, 1988.

Carey, Benedict, and Lisa Davis. "PKU Babies: The Next Generation," *Hippocrates,* November/December 1988.

Chasnoff, Ira, et al. "Temporal Patterns of Cocaine Use in Pregnancy," *Journal of the American Medical Association,* vol. 261, no. 12, March 24/31, 1989.

Goldsmith, Marsha. "Pregnancy Dx? Rx May Now Include Condoms," *Journal of the American Medical Association,* vol. 261, no. 5, February 3, 1989.

Goleman, Daniel. "Lasting Costs for Child Are Found from a Few Early Drinks," *New York Times,* February 16, 1989.

Kolata, Gina. "Vitamins May Cut Birth Defect Risk," *New York Times,* December 3, 1988.

Lemire, Ronald J. "Neural Tube Defects," *Journal of the American Medical Association,* vol. 259, no. 4, January 22/29, 1988.

Moos, Merry K., and Robert C. Cefalo. "Preconceptional Health Promotion: A Focus for Obstetric Care," *American Journal of Perinatology,* vol. 4, no. 1, January 1987.

Squires, Sally. "The Ethics of Genetic Counseling," *Washington Post Health,* November 25, 1986.

Starr, Douglas. "The 12-Month Pregnancy," *American Health,* June 1987.

3. If You're over Thirty-five

Berman, Alice. "More and More Women Giving Birth After 30," *Genesis,* vol. 7., no. 3, June/July 1985.

Blakeslee, Sandra. "Genetic Discoveries Raise Painful Questions," *New York Times,* April 21, 1987.

Friede, Andrew, et al. "Older Maternal Age and Infant Mortality in the United States," *Obstetrics and Gynecology,* vol. 72, no. 2, August 1988.

"Late Pregnancies," *NIH News and Features,* 1988.

Smilgis, Martha. "Older Parents: Good for Kids?" *Time,* October 10, 1988.

4. What to Expect

Barry, Michele, and Frank Bia. "Pregnancy and Travel," *Journal of the American Medical Association,* vol. 261, no. 5, pp. 728–31.

Chasnoff, Ira et al. "Temporal Patterns of Cocaine Use in Pregnancy," *Journal of the American Medical Association,* vol. 261, no. 12, March 24/31, 1989.

Folkenberg, Judy. "A Bright Side to Morning Sickness?" *American Health,* October 1986.

Kolata, Gina. "Study Ties Drugs to Impaired Fetuses," *New York Times,* March 23, 1989.

Krucoff, Carol. "The Nine-Month Workout," *Washington Post Health,* January 30, 1985.

McCarthy, Paul. "Strong Coffee, Weak Babies," *American Health,* October 1986.

Stockton, William. "Researchers Study Effects of Exercise During Pregnancy," *New York Times,* March 27, 1989.

Wagner, Elaine. "Costs of a Normal Birth," Metropolitan Life and Affiliated Companies, September 14, 1988.

Winick, Myron. "Search for the Perfect Pregnancy," *American Health,* October 1985.

Wyngaarden, James. "Effects of Moderate Alcohol Use during Pregnancy," *Journal of American Medical Association,* vol. 259, no. 1, January 1, 1988.

5. Prenatal Testing

Burton, Barbara K. "Outcome of Pregnancy in Patients with Unexplained Elevated or Low Levels of Maternal Serum Alpha-Fetoprotein," *Obstetrics & Gynecology,* vol. 72, no. 5, November 1988.

Goldsmith, Marcia. "Trial Appears to Confirm Safety of Chorionic Villus Sampling Procedure," *Journal of the American Medical Association,"* vol. 259, no. 24, June 24, 1988.

Johnson, Timothy R. B., Richard E. Besinger, and Ronald L. Thomas. "New Clues to Fetal Behavior and Well-being," *Contemporary Obstetrics and Gynecology,* May 1988.

Kolata, Gina. "New Method Allows Very Early Diagnosis of Fetal Problems," *New York Times,* December 29, 1988.

Kolata, Gina. "New Tests to Provide Safer Screening for Down's Syndrome," *New York Times,* October 13, 1988.

Niebyl, Jennifer. "Update on Alpha-Fetoprotein," *Postgraduate Obstetrics and Gynecology,* vol. 6, no. 13, June 1986.

Paine, Lisa L., Ruth G. Payton, and Timothy R. B. Johnson. "Ausculated Fetal Heart Accelerations," *Journal of Nurse-Midwifery,* vol. 31, no. 2, March/April 1986.

Seeds, John W. "PUBS: Important New Aid for Diagnosis," *Contemporary Obstetric and Gynecology,* February 1988.

Spencer, John W., and David N. Cox. "A Comparison of Chorionic Villi Sampling and Amniocentesis: Acceptability of Procedure and Maternal Attachment to Pregnancy," *Obstetrics & Gynecology,* vol. 72, no. 5, November 1988.

6. Coping

Bailey, Leisa A., and B. Jo Hailey. "The Psychological Experience of Pregnancy," *International Journal of Psychiatry,* vol. 16, no. 3, 1986–87.

Brown, M. A. "Social Support, Stress and Health: A Comparison of Expectant Mothers and Fathers," *Nursing Research,* vol. 35, no. 2, 1986.

Chalmers, B. "Psychological Aspects of Pregnancy," *Social Science and Medicine,* vol. 16, 1982.

Kaplan, Barbara. "A Psychobiological Review of Depression during Pregnancy," *Psychology of Women Quarterly,* vol. 10, 1986.

Margolis, Marya. "Coping Strategies for a 'Touchy' Pregnancy," *Genesis,* June/July 1985.

Penticuff, Joy Hinson. "Psychological Implications in High-Risk Pregnancy," *Symposium on Maternal and Newborn Nursing,* vol. 17, no. 1, March 1982.

Powers, Pauline, et al. "Psychiatric Disorders in High-Risk Pregnancy," *Comprehensive Psychiatry,* vol. 27. no. 2, March/April 1986.

Wohlreich, M. "Psychiatric Aspects of High-Risk Pregnancy," *Psychiatric Clinics of North America,* vol. 10, no. 1, March 1986.

7. Bedrest

Crowley, Carolyn Hughes. "The Bed Rest Prescription," *Washington Post Health,* February 16, 1988.

Hales, Dianne. "How to Sleep like a Baby." New York: Ballantine Books, 1987.

Kelly, Marguerite. "Bedridden and Expecting a Baby," *Washington Post,* February 25, 1988.

Mills, Deanie Francis. "When Mom Is Sick in Bed," *Parents,* May 1988.

Schwartz, Susan. "Bed—and Bored." Oakland, Cal.: Birthways.

8. Chronic Health Problems and Pregnancy

"Combing Diabetes' Teratogenic 'Suspect List,'" *Journal of the American Medical Association,* vol. 259, no. 3, January 15, 1988.

"Early Care in Diabetic Women's Pregnancies Reduces Birth Defects," *Diabetes and Heart Facts,* vol. 2, no. 1, June 1988.

Kanaan, Camille, and Leon Speroff. "Diabetes Mellitus in Pregnancy," *Postgraduate Obstetrics & Gynecology,* vol. 8, no. 2, January 1988.

Nelson, Lorene, et al. "Risk of Multiple Sclerosis Exacerbation during Pregnancy and Breastfeeding," *Journal of the American Medical Association,* vol. 259, no. 23, June 17, 1988.

Petri, Michelle. "Outcomes Encouraging in Mothers with Lupus." *Contemporary OB/GYN,* March 1988.

Rovner, Sandy. "MS and Pregnancy: How Safe?" *Washington Post Health,* March 31, 1987.

9. Medical Problems That Can Develop in Pregnancy

Brown, Zane A., et al. "Effects on Infants of a First Episode of Genital Herpes during Pregnancy," *New England Journal of Medicine*, vol. 317, no. 20, November 19, 1987.

Koonin, Lisa M., et al. "Pregnancy Related Deaths due to AIDS in the United States," *Journal of the American Medical Association*, vol. 261, no. 9, March 3, 1989.

Landesman, Sheldon H., and Anne Willoughby. "HIV Disease in Reproductive Age Women: A Problem of the Present," *Journal of the American Medical Association*, vol. 261, no. 9, March 3, 1989.

Prober, Charles G., et al. "Use of Routine Viral Cultures at Delivery to Identify Neonates Exposed to Herpes Simplex Virus," *New England Journal of Medicine*, vol. 318, no. 14, April 7, 1988.

"Risks Associated with Fifth Disease," Maryland Department of Health and Mental Hygiene, 1989.

Selwyn, Peter A., et al. "Prospective Study of Human Immunodeficiency Virus Infection and Pregnancy Outcome in Intravenous Drug Users," *Journal of the American Medical Association*, vol. 261, no. 9, March 3, 1989.

Sever, John L., et al. "Toxoplasmosis: Maternal and Pediatric Findings in 23,000 Pregnancies," *Pediatrics*, vol. 82, no. 2, August 1988.

10. Complications of Pregnancy

Adler, Jerry. "Every Parent's Nightmare," *Newsweek*, March 16, 1987.

American Academy of Pediatrics Committee on Bioethics, "Fetal Therapy: Ethical Considerations," *Pediatrics*, vol. 81, no. 6, June 1988.

Crooks, Cheryl. "Healing the Unborn," *Parents*, June 1988.

Eden, Robert D., et al. "Postdate Pregnancies: A Review of 46 Perinatal Deaths," *American Journal of Perinatology*, vol. 4, no. 4, October 1987.

Gregory, P. Baras, and D. Rush. "Iatrogenic Caloric Restriction in Pregnancy and Birthweight," *American Journal of Perinatology*, vol. 4, no. 4, October 1987.

"Multiple Births: An Upward Trend in the United States," *Statistical Bulletin of Metropolitan Life*, vol. 69, no. 1, January/March 1988.

Ron-el, Raphael, et al. "Triplet and Quadruplet Pregnancies and Management," *Obstetrics & Gynecology*, vol. 57, no. 4, April 1981.

Touloukian, Robert. "What's New in Pediatric Surgery," *Pediatrics*, vol. 81, no. 5, May 1988.

Witter, Frank R., and Claire M. Weitz. "A Randomized Trial of Induction at 42 Weeks Gestation versus Expectant Management for Postdates Pregnancies," *American Journal of Perinatology*, vol. 4, no. 3, July 1987.

11. Preterm Labor

Berman, Alice. "Preventing Preterm Birth," *Genesis,* October/November 1985, vol. 7, no. 5.

Brown, Elizabeth. "Home Monitor System Helps Preterm Labor," *American Medical News,* October 14, 1988.

Creasy, Robert K. "Ways of Preventing Preterm Birth," *Contemporary Ob/ Gyn,* October 1988.

Ernest, Joseph M., et al. "Elevated Vaginal pH—A Marker for Preterm PROM?" Presentation, Society of Perinatal Obstetrics Annual Meeting, Las Vegas, February 1988.

Hales, Dianne. "Will Your Baby Wait 9 Months?" *Self,* May 1983.

Lam, Fung, et al. "Use of the Subcutaneous Pump for Long-Term Tocolysis," *Obstetrics & Gynecology,* vol. 72, no. 5, November 1988.

Lieberman, Ellice, et al. "Risk Factors Accounting for Racial Differences in the Rate of Premature Birth," *New England Journal of Medicine,* vol. 317, no. 12, September 17, 1987.

Main, Denise M., et al. "Intermittent Weekly Contraction Monitoring to Predict Preterm Labor in Low-Risk Women: A Blinded Study," *Obstetrics & Gynecology,* vol. 72, no. 5, November 1988.

Monmaney, Terence. "Preventing Early Births," *Newsweek,* May 16, 1988.

Omer, Haim, and George S. Everly, Jr. "Psychological Factors in Preterm Labor: Critical Review and Theoretical Synthesis," *American Journal of Psychiatry,* vol. 145, no, 12. December 1988.

12. Pregnancy Losses

American College of Obstetricians and Gynecologists, "Grieving: A Way to Heal," January 1988.

Beck, Melinda. "A Medical Mystery," *Newsweek,* August 15, 1988.

Beck, Melinda. "Miscarriages," *Newsweek,* August 15, 1988.

Blakeslee, Sandra. "New Groups Aim to Help Parents Face Grief When a Newborn Dies," *New York Times,* September 8, 1988.

Cole, Diane. "It Might Have Been: Mourning the Unborn," *Psychology Today,* July 1987.

Damewood, Marian D., and Edward E. Wallach. "Ectopic Pregnancy: A Different Disease in the 1980s?" *Postgraduate Obstetrics & Gynecology,* vol. 5, no. 20, September 1985.

"Ectopic Pregnancy—United States, 1984 and 1985," *Journal of the American Medical Association,* vol. 260, no. 18, November 11, 1988.

Hillard, Paula. "Stillbirth," *Parents,* July 1987.

Ilse, Sherokee. "The Baby Blues and No Baby," *International Journal of Childbirth Education,* November 1987.

Knapp, Ronald J. "When a Child Dies," *Psychology Today,* July 1987.

Kolata, Gina. "New Treatments May Aid Women Who Have Repeated Miscarriages," *New York Times,* January 5, 1988.

Leon, Irving G. "Psychodynamics of Perinatal Loss," *Psychiatry,* vol. 49, November 1986.

Maryland State Department of Health and Mental Hygiene. "Questions, Answers and Help for Parents after Stillbirth or Infant Death."

Rose, Julie. "Mourning a Miscarriage," *Newsweek,* August 3, 1987.

Scott, James R., et al. "Immunologic Aspects of Recurrent Abortion and Fetal Death," *Obstetrics & Gynecology,* vol. 70, no. 4, October 1987.

Simpson, Joe Leigh, et al. "Low Fetal Loss Rates after Ultrasound-Proved Viability in Early Pregnancy," *Journal of the American Medical Association,* vol. 258, no. 18, November 13, 1987.

Warburton, Dorothy. "Reproductive Loss: How Much Is Preventable?" *New England Journal of Medicine,* vol. 316, no. 3, January 15, 1987.

Wiley, Kim Wright. "After Miscarriage: Healing the Hurt," *Health,* May 1987.

13. The High-Risk Birth

Gregory, Josephine. "Twenty-five Years of Lamaze Childbirth," *Baby Talk,* October 1985.

Hales, Dianne. "It's Time," *Pre-Parent Adviser: A Guide to Getting Ready for Birth 1989–1990.* Knoxville: Whittle Commonications, 1989.

Hutter, Jeanette. "Special Deliveries," *New Parent Adviser,* 1987–88.

Kolata, Gina. "Cesarean Birth: Why More? Why Now?" *Washington Post Health,* December 9, 1986.

Leveno, Kenneth, et al. "A Prospective Comparison of Selective and Universal Electronic Fetal Monitoring in 54,995 Pregnancies," *New England Journal of Medicine,* vol. 315, no 10, September 4, 1986.

Notzon, Francis C., et al. "Comparisons of National Cesarean Rates," *New England Journal of Medicine,* vol. 316, no. 7, February 12, 1987.

O'Brien, Carol. "Business, Blues Clamping Down on High Rates of C-Sections," *American Medical News,* March 25, 1988.

Pederson, David R., et al. "Maternal Emotional Responses to Preterm Birth," *American Journal of Orthopsychiatry,* vol. 57, January 1987.

14. The High-Risk Baby

Adler, Jerry. "Waking Sleeping Souls," *Newsweek,* March 28, 1988.

Blakeslee, Sandra. "New Groups Aim to Help Parents Face Grief When a Newborn Dies," *New York Times,* September 8, 1988.

Caldwell, Jean. "Unexpected Outcomes," *New Parent Adviser,* 1987–88.

Collaborative European Multicenter Study Group, "Surfactant Replacement Therapy for Severe Neonatal Respiratory Distress Syndrome: An International Randomized Clinical Trial," *Pediatrics,* vol. 82, no. 5, November 1988.

Goleman, Daniel. "Compensations Detected for Smaller of Twins," *New York Times,* August 18, 1988.

Kantrowitz, Barbara. "Preemies," *Newsweek,* May 16, 1988.

Kantrowitz, Barbara. "Two Babies on the Brink of Life," *Newsweek,* May 16, 1988.

Kendig, James W., and Donald L. Shapiro. "Surfactant Therapy in the Newborn," *Pediatric Annals,* vol. 17, no. 8, August 1988.

Klass, Perri. "Baby, Be Good," *Discover,* September 1988.

Kolata, Gina. "The Mystery of Infant Blindness," *Washington Post Health,* January 8, 1986.

McCormick, Marie C. "Long-Term Follow-Up of Infants Discharged from Neonatal Intensive Care Units," *Journal of the American Medical Association,* vol. 261, no. 12, March 24/31, 1989.

Melilio, Wendy. "Giving Tiny Lungs a Chance to Rest," *Washington Post Health,* March 31, 1987.

Ozminkowski, Ronald, et al. "Evaluating the Effectiveness of Neonatal Intensive Care," *American Journal of Perinatology,* vol. 4, no. 4, October 1987.

Short, Billie Lou, and Andrea Lotze. "Extrcorporeal Membrane Oxygenator Therapy," *Pediatric Annals,* vol. 17, no. 8, August 1988.

Stahlman, Mildred. "Implications of Research and High Technology for Neonatal Intensive Care," *Journal of the American Medical Association,* vol. 261, no. 12, March 24/31, 1989.

15. After Birth

Dimitrovsky, Lilly, et al. "Depression During and Following Pregnancy: Quality of Family Relationships," *Journal of Psychology,* vol. 12, no. 3, 1987.

Fishel, Elizabeth. "Baby Makes Three," *Parents,* September 1987.

Hales, Dianne. "This Way to Recovery," *New Parent Adviser,* 1988–89.

Hunt, Jane, et al. "Very Low Birth Weight Infants at 8 and 11 Years of Age: Role of Neonatal Illness and Family Status," *Pediatrics,* vol. 82, no. 4, October 1988.

Lindahl, Elina, et al. "Neonatal Risk Factors and Later Neurodevelopmental Disturbances," *Developmental Medicine and Child Neurology,* vol. 30, 1988.

Lippert, Joan. "Breast, Bottle, and Both," *Pre-Parent Adviser: A Guide to Getting Ready for Birth 1989–1990.*

Roberts, Marjory. "A Parent is Born," *Psychology Today,* December 1986.

Small, Elisabeth. "Postpartum Emotional Responses," *The Problem-Oriented Medical Record for High-Risk Obstetrics,* New York: Plenum Publishing Corp., 1984.

Williams, Lynda. "And Baby Makes Three," *International Journal of Childbirth Education,* November 1987.

RESOURCES: WHERE TO TURN

BIRTH DEFECTS

**American Cleft Palate
  Association**
331 Salk Hall
Pittsburgh, PA 15261
(412) 681-9620

Cystic Fibrosis Foundation
1655 Tullie Circle, Suite 111
Atlanta, GA 30329
(404) 325-6973

**Institutes for the Achievement
  of Human Potential**
8801 Stenton Avenue
Philadelphia, PA 19118
(215) 233-2050

**March of Dimes Birth Defects
  Foundation**
Public Health Education Foundation
1275 Mamaroneck Avenue
White Plains, NY 10605
(914) 428-7100

National PKU Project
Children's Hospital
Boston, MA 02115
(617) 735-7945

**Spina Bifida Association of
  America**
1700 Rockville Pike, Suite 540
Rockville, MD 20852
(800) 621-3141

BREASTFEEDING

La Leche League International
9616 Minneapolis Avenue
Franklin, IL 60131
(312) 455-7730

Lact-Aid
P.O. Box 1066
Athens, TN 37303
(615) 744-9090

CESAREAN BIRTHS

**Cesarean Support Education
  and Concern**
22 Forest Road
Framingham, MA 01701
(617) 877-8266

**Cesarean Prevention
  Movement, Inc.**
P.O. Box 152
Syracuse, NY 13210
(315) 424-1942

**VBAC (Vaginal Birth After
  Cesarean)**
10 Great Plain Terrace
Needham, MA 01292

CHILDBIRTH

American College of Nurse Midwives
1522 K. Street NW, Suite 1120
Washington, DC 20005
(202) 347-5445

American College of Obstetricians and Gynecologists
600 Maryland Avenue SW, Suite 300 East
Washington, DC 20024
(202) 638-5577

American Foundation for Maternal and Child Health, Inc.
30 Beekman Place
New York, NY 10022
(212) 759-5510

International Childbirth Education Association
P.O. Box 20048
Minneapolis, MN 55420

National Association of Parents and Professionals for Safe Alternatives in Childbirth (NAPPSAC)
P.O. Box 267
Marble Hill, MO 63764
(314) 238-2010

National Center for Education in Maternal and Child Health
38th and R Streets NW
Washington, DC 20057
(202) 625-8400

National Perinatal Association
101½ South Union Street
Alexandria, VA 22314
(703) 549-5523

National Perinatal Information Center
668 Eddy Street
One Blackstone Place
Providence, RI 02903
(401) 274-0650

CHILDBIRTH EDUCATION/PREPARATION

American Academy of Husband-Coached Childbirth
P.O. Box 5224
Sherman Oaks, CA 91413
(818) 788-6662

American Society for Psychoprophylaxis in Obstetrics
1840 Wilson Boulevard, Suite 204
Arlington, VA 22201
(703) 524-7802

Read Natural Childbirth Foundation, Inc.
P.O. Box 956
San Rafael, CA 94915
(415) 456-8462

DES (DIETHYLSTILBESTROL) EXPOSURE

Department DES
National Cancer Institute
Office of Cancer Communications
Building 31, Room 10A19
Bethesda, MD 20892
(800) 4-CANCER

DES Action/National
Long Island Jewish Hospital—
   Hillside Medical Center
New Hyde Park, NY 11040
(516) 775-3450

DIABETES

**National American Diabetes
   Association**
1660 Duke Street
Alexandria, VA 22314
(703) 549-1500

**Juvenile Diabetes Foundation
   International Hotline**
(800) 223-1138; in New York
   (212) 889-7575

**National Diabetes Information
   Clearinghouse**
Box NDIC
Bethesda, MD 20892
(301) 468-2162

DOWN SYNDROME

**National Association for
   Down's Syndrome (NADS)**
1800 Dempster
Park Ridge, IL 60068-1146
(312) 823-7550

**National Down's Syndrome
   Society Hotline**
141 Fifth Avenue
New York, NY 10010
(800) 221-4602; in New York
   (212) 764-3070

GENETIC DISORDERS

**Alliance of Genetic Support
   Groups**
38th and R Streets NW
Washington, DC 20057
(202) 625-7853

**March of Dimes Birth Defects
   Foundation**
1275 Mamaroneck Avenue
White Plains, NY 10605

**National Clearinghouse for
   Human Genetic Disease**
National Center for Education in
   Maternal and Child Health
38th and R Streets NW
Washington, DC 20057
(202) 625-8400

**National Society of Genetic
    Counselors**
Clinical Genetics Center
Children's Hospital of Philadelphia
34th and Civic Center Boulevard
Philadelphia, PA 19104
(215) 596-9802

**National Organization for Rare
    Disorders**
Box 8923
New Fairfield, CN 06812
(203) 746-6518

INFANT DEATH

Compassionate Friends
P.O. Box 1347
Oak Brook, IL 60521
(312) 990-0010

**SHARE (Source of Help in Airing
and Resolving Experiences)**
c/o St. John's Hospital
800 East Carpenter Street
Springfield, IL 62769
(217) 544-6464

MULTIPLE BIRTH

**Center for the Study of
    Multiple Birth**
333 East Superior Street,
    Suite 463–5
Chicago, IL 60611
(312) 266-9093

**International Twins
    Association**
P.O. Box 77386, Station C
Atlanta, GA 30357

**National Organization of
    Mothers of Twins Clubs, Inc.**
12404 Princess Jeanne, NE
Albuquerque, NM 87112
(505) 275-0955

Triplet Connection
2618 Lucile Avenue
Stockton, CA 95209
(209) 474-3073

Twinline
P.O. Box 10066
Berkeley, CA 94709
(415) 644-0861

The Twins Foundation
P.O. Box 9487
Providence, RI 02940-9487

PARENT SUPPORT GROUPS

Birthways
3127 Telegraph Avenue
Oakland, CA 94609
(415) 653-7300

**COPE (Coping with the Overall
    Pregnancy/Parenting Experience)**
37 Clarendon Street
Boston, MA 02116
(617) 357-5588

Intensive Caring Unlimited (I.C.U.)
910 Bent Lane
Philadelphia, PA 19118
(215) 233-4723

National Council of Guilds for Infant Survival (SIDS support)
P.O. Box 3586
Davenport, IA 52808
(319) 326-4653

Parent Care (for parents with newborns requiring special care)
University of Utah Medical Center
50 North Medical Drive, Room 2A210
Salt Lake City, UT 84132
(801) 581-5323

Parentele (for parents with handicapped children)
5538 North Pennsylvania Street
Indianapolis, IN 46220
(317) 259-1654

Parenthood After Thirty
451 Vermont
Berkeley, CA 94707
(415) 524-6635

Parents Without Partners
8807 Colesville Road
Silver Spring, MD 20910
(301) 588-9354

Pilot Parents Program (parents whose children have developmental disabilities)
3610 Dodge Street
Omaha, NE 68131
(402) 346-5220

PRETERM INFANTS

Parents of Prematures
c/o Houston Organization for Parent Education, Inc.
2990 Richmond, Suite 204
Houston, TX 77098
(713) 524-3089

Parents of Premature and High-Risk Infants International and National Self-Help Clearinghouse
33 West 42nd Street, Room 1222
New York, NY 10036

SUDDEN INFANT DEATH SYNDROME (SIDS)

National Sudden Infant Death Syndrome Foundation
2320 Glenview Road
Glenview, IL 60025
(312) 657-8080

Eiger, Marvin S., and Sally Wendkos Olds. *The Complete Book of Breastfeeding*. New York: Workman, 1987. An updated classic that answers all the questions a nursing mother might ask.

Eisenberg, Arlene, Heidi Eisenberg Murkoff, and Sandee Eisenberg Hathaway. *What to Eat When You're Expecting*. New York: Workman, 1986. Sound advice on eating for two, complete with recipes.

Eisenberg, Arlene, Heidi Eisenberg Murkoff, and Sandee Eisenberg Hathaway. *What to Expect When You're Expecting*. New York: Workman, 1984. A warm, reassuring month-by-month guide.

Kamen, Betty, and Si Kamn. *Total Nutrition for Breastfeeding Mothers*. Boston: Little Brown, 1986. A practical resource for nursing women.

Lubic, Ruth Watson, and Gene R. Hawes. *Childbearing: A Book of Choices*. New York: McGraw-Hill, 1987. An informative manual that can help you weigh the pros and cons of the many decisions you'll face during pregnancy and beyond.

Presser, Janice. *When Two Become Three: The Couple's Book of Pregnancy*. New York: Doubleday, 1984. An insightful look at how pregnancy affects relationships.

Queenan, John T., ed., with Carrie Neher Queenan. *A New Life*. Boston: Little Brown, 1986. A beautifully photographed and illustrated depiction of life from conception to a child's first birthday.

The more any mother-to-be learns, the better prepared she'll be for pregnancy, birth, and life with her child. Following are some of the books and videos that we or the pregnant women with whom we work have found helpful.

SPECIAL CIRCUMSTANCES

Borg, Susan, and Judith Lasker. *When Pregnancy Fails: Families Coping with Miscarriage, Stillbirth and Infant Death*. Boston: Beacon Press, 1980, and Friedman, Rochelle, and Bonnie Gradstein. *Surviving Pregnancy Loss*. Boston: Little Brown, 1982. When the worst happens and words often offer little comfort, these honest, heart-to-heart books can help.

Novotny, Pamela. *The Joy of Twins*. New York: Crown Publishers, 1988. A helpful, heartfelt book that any mother could use and every mother of multiples needs.

Schwartz, Susan. "Bed—and Bored." A helpful pamphlet available from Birthways, 3127 Telegraph Avenue, Oakland, CA 94609.

VIDEOS

The Childbirth Preparation Program, produced by Feeling Fine Programs with the American College of Obstetricians and Gynecologists. Instruction for labor, including relaxation and breathing techniques, plus tape of fourteen actual births. Available at video rental stores or from 800-345-4688.

The Pregnancy Exercise Program, produced by Feeling Fine Programs with the American College of Obstetricians and Gynecologists. Check with your doctor before exercising. Once you get a go-ahead, this tape provides instruction for safe workouts during pregnancy. From video stores or 800-345-4688.

NATIONAL PERINATAL CENTERS

Reprinted from the National Perinatal Information Center, 688 Eddy Street, One Blackstone Place, Providence, RI 02903.

ALABAMA

Baptist Medical Center— Montclair
800 Montclair Road
Birmingham, AL 35213
(205) 592-1000

Brookwood Medical Center
2010 Brookwood Medical Center
   Drive
Birmingham, AL 35259
(205) 877-1000

Cooper Green Hospital
1515 Sixth Avenue, South
Birmingham, AL 35233
(205) 934-7900

St. Vincent's Hospital
P.O. Box 915
Birmingham, AL 35201
(205) 939-7000

University of Alabama Hospitals
619 South 19th Street
Birmingham, AL 35233
(205) 934-4011

Huntsville Hospital
101 Silvey Road
Huntsville, AL 35801
(205) 533-8020

University of South Alabama Medical Center
2451 Fillingim Street
Mobile, AL 36617
(205) 471-7000

Baptist Medical Center
2105 East South Boulevard
Montgomery, AL 36198
(205) 288-2100

Children's Hospital of Alabama
1600 Seventh Avenue
South Birmingham, AL 35233
(205) 939-9100

DCH Regional Medical Center Druid
809 University Boulevard East
Tuscaloosa, AL 35403
(205) 759-7111

ALASKA

Humana Hospital-Alaska
2801 DeBarr Road
Anchorage, AK 99504
(907) 276-1131

Providence Hospital
3200 Providence Drive
Anchorage, AK 99508
(907) 562-2211

Fairbanks Memorial Hospital
1650 Cowles Street
Fairbanks, AK 99701
(907) 452-8181

ARIZONA

Good Samaritan Medical Center
1111 East McDowell Road
Phoenix, AZ 85006
(602) 239-2000

Maricopa Medical Center
P.O. Box 5099
Phoenix, AZ 85010
(602) 267-5011

Phoenix Children's Hospital
1300 N. 12th Street, Suite 404
Phoenix, AZ 85006
(602) 239-5920

St. Joseph's Hospital and Medical Center
350 West Thomas Road
Phoenix, AZ 85013
(602) 285-3000

Tucson Medical Center
5301 East Grant Road
Tucson, AZ 85733
(602) 327-5461

University Hospital
1501 North Campbell Avenue
Tucson, AZ 85724
(602) 626-0111

ARKANSAS

Arkansas Children's Hospital
804 Wolfe Street
Little Rock, AR
(501) 370-1100

Baptist Medical Center
9601 Interstate 630, Exit 7
Little Rock, AR 72205
(501) 227-2000

St. Vincent's Infirmary
Two St. Vincent Circle
Little Rock, AR
(501) 660-3000

University Hospital & Ambulatory Center
4301 West Markham Street
Little Rock, AR 72205
(501) 661-5000

CALIFORNIA

Kaiser Foundation Hospital— Anaheim
441 N. Lakeview Avenue
Anaheim, CA 92807
(714) 978-4000

Martin Luther Hospital Medical Center
1830 West Romneya Drive
Anahaim, CA 92801
(714) 491-5200

Kaiser Foundation Hospital— Bellflower
9400 East Rosecrans Avenue
Bellflower, CA 90706
(213) 920-4321

Humana Hospital—West Hills
7300 Medical Center Drive
Canoga Park, CA 91307
(818) 884-7060

N. T. Enloe Memorial Hospital
Fifth Avenue and Esplanade
Chico, CA 95926
(916) 891-7300

El Centro Community Hospital
1415 Ross Avenue
El Centro, CA 92243
(619) 339-7100

Kaiser Foundation Hospital— Fontana
9961 Sierra Avenue
Fontana, CA 92335
(714) 829-5000

Valley Children's Hospital
3151 North Millbrook
Fresno, CA 93703
(209) 225-3000

Valley Medical Center of Fresno
445 South Cedar Avenue
Fresno, CA 93702
(209) 453-4000

Glendale Adventist Medical Center
1509 Wilson Terrace
Glendale, CA 91206
(818) 240-8000

Kaiser Foundation Hospital— Harbor City
25825 So. Vermont Avenue
Harbor City, CA 90710
(213) 325-5111

Centinela Hospital Medical Center
555 Hardy Street
Inglewood, CA 90301
(213) 673-4660

Daniel Freeman Memorial Hospital
333 North Prairie Avenue
Inglewood, CA 90301
(213) 674-7050

Loma Linda University Medical Center
11234 Anderson Street
Loma Linda, CA 92354
(714) 796-7311

Memorial Medical Center
2801 Atlantic Avenue
Box 1428
Long Beach, CA 90801
(213) 595-2311

St. Mary Medical Center
1050 Linden Avenue
P.O. Box 887
Long Beach, CA 90801
(213) 491-9000

California Hospital Medical Center
1414 South Hope Street
Los Angeles, CA 90015
(213) 748-2411

Cedars-Sinai Medical Center
8700 Beverly Boulevard
Los Angeles, CA 90048
(213) 855-5000

Children's Hospital of Los Angeles
4650 Sunset Boulevard
Los Angeles, CA 90054
(213) 660-2450

Kaiser Foundation Hospital— West Los Angeles
6041 Cadillac Avenue
Los Angeles, CA 90034
(213) 857-2000

Kaiser Foundation Hospital— Sunset
4867 Sunset Boulevard
Los Angeles, CA 90027
(213) 667-4011

LAC-USC Medical Center, Women's Hospital
1200 North State Street
Los Angeles, CA 90033
(213) 226-2345

Martin Luther King, Jr. / Drew Medical Center
12021 South Wilmington Avenue
Los Angeles, CA 90059
(213) 603-4321

Maxicare Medical Center
5525 West Slauson Avenue
Los Angeles, CA 90056
(213) 410-0999

UCLA Medical Center
10833 Le Conte Avenue
Los Angeles, CA 90024
(213) 533-2101

White Memorial Medical Center
1720 Brooklyn Avenue
Los Angeles, CA 90033
(213) 268-5000

St. Francis Medical Center
3630 East Imperial Highway
Lynwood, CA 90262
(213) 603-6000

Modesto City Hospital
730 17th Street
Modesto, CA 95354
(209) 577-2100

Garfield Medical Center
525 North Garfield Avenue
Monterey Park, CA 91754
(818) 573-2222

Hoag Memorial Hospital— Presbyterian
301 Newport Boulevard
Box Y
Newport Beach, CA 92658-8912
(714) 645-8600

Northridge Hospital Medical Center
18300 Roscoe Boulevard
Northridge, CA 91328
(818) 885-8500

Children's Hospital—Oakland
747 52nd Street
Oakland, CA 94609
(415) 428-3000

Children's Hospital of Orange City
455 South Main Street
Orange, CA 92668
(714) 997-3000

UC—Irvine Medical Center
101 The City Drive
Orange, CA 92668
(714) 634-5678

Kaiser Foundation Hospital— Panorama City
13652 Cantara Street
Panorama City, CA 91402
(818) 908-2000

Huntington Memorial Hospital
100 Congress Street
Pasadena, CA 91105
(818) 440-5000

Pomona Valley Community Hospital
1798 North Garey Avenue
Pomona, CA 91767
(714) 623-8715

Riverside General Hospital / University Medical Center
9851 Magnolia Avenue
Riverside, CA 92503
(714) 351-7100

Sutter Memorial Hospitals
52nd and F Streets
Sacramento, CA 95819
(916) 927-5211

University of California—Davis Medical Center
2315 Stockton Boulevard
Sacramento, CA 95817
(916) 453-3096

San Bernardino County Medical Center
780 East Gilbert Street
San Bernardino, CA 92404
(714) 387-8111

Children's Hospital and Health Center
8001 Frost Street
San Diego, CA 92123
(619) 576-1700

Kaiser Foundation Hospital— San Diego
4647 Zion Avenue
San Diego, CA 92120
(619) 584-5000

Mercy Hospital & Medical Center
4077 Fifth Avenue
San Diego, CA 92103
(619) 294-8111

Children's Hospital of San Francisco
P.O. Box 3805
3700 California Street
San Francisco, CA 94119
(415) 387-8700

Mount Zion Hospital and Medical Center
1600 Divisadero Street
San Francisco, CA 94115
(415) 567-6600

San Francisco General Hospital—Medical Center
1001 Potrero Avenue
San Francisco, CA 94110
(415) 821-8200

St. Luke's Hospital
3555 Army Street
San Francisco, CA 94110
(415) 647-8600

University of California Hospitals & Clinics
San Francisco, CA 94143
(415) 666-1401

Good Samaritan Hospital
2425 Samaritan Drive
San Jose, CA 95124
(408) 559-2011

Santa Clara Valley Medical Center
751 South Bascom Avenue
San Jose, CA 95128
(408) 299-6827

Marin General Hospital
250 Bon Air Road
San Rafael, CA 94912
(415) 461-0100

Western Medical Center
1001 North Tustin Avenue
Santa Ana, CA 92705
(714) 835-3555

Community Hospital
3325 Chanate Road
Santa Rosa, CA 95404
(707) 544-3340

Santa Rosa Memorial Hospital
1165 Mongomery Drive
Box 522
Santa Rosa, CA 95402
(707) 546-3210

Stanford University Hospital
300 Pasteur Drive
Stanford, CA 94305
(415) 723-5222

Ami Tarzana Regional Medical Center
18321 Clark Street
Tarzana, CA 91356
(818) 881-0800

LA County Harbor—UCLA Medical Center
1000 West Carson Street
Torrance, CA 90509
(213) 533-2101

Little Company of Mary Hospital
4101 Torrance Boulevard
Torrance, CA 90503
(213) 540-7676

Valley Presbyterian Hospital
15107 Vanowen Street
Van Nuys, CA 91405
(818) 782-6600

Ventura County Medical Center
3291 Loma Vista Road
Ventura, CA 93003
(805) 652-6000

Kaweah Delta District Hospital
400 West Mineral King Street
Visalia, CA 93291
(209) 625-2211

Queen of the Valley Hospital
1115 South Sunset Avenue
West Covina, CA 91790
(818) 962-4011

**Presbyterian Intercomm
  Hospital**
12401 East Washington Boulevard
Whittier, CA 90602
(213) 698-0811

COLORADO

Memorial Hospital
1400 East Boulder Street
Colorado Springs, CO 80909
(303) 475-5011

Children's Hospital
1056 East 19th Avenue
Denver, CO 80218
(303) 861-8888

Denver Health and Hospitals
777 Bannock Street
Denver, CO 80204
(303) 893-6000

Rose Medical Center
4567 East Ninth Avenue
Denver, CO 80220
(303) 320-2121

Saint Joseph Hospital
1835 Franklin Street
Denver, CO 80218
(303) 837-7111

**University Hospital—
  University of Colorado**
4200 East Ninth Avenue
Denver, CO 80262
(303) 394-8446

Mercy Medical Center
375 E. Park Avenue
Durango, CO 81301
(303) 247-4311

**St. Mary's Hospital & Medical
  Center**
Seventh Street & Patterson Road
P.O. Box 1628
Grand Junction, CO 81502
(303) 244-2273

**North Colorado Medical
  Center**
1801 16th Street
Greeley, CO 80631
(303) 352-4121

Lutheran Medical Center
8300 West 38th Avenue
Wheat Ridge, CO 80033
(303) 425-4500

CONNECTICUT

Bridgeport Hospital
267 Grant Street
Bridgeport, CT 06610
(203) 384-3000

Danbury Hospital
24 Hospital Avenue
Danbury, CT 06810
(203) 797-7000

**John Dempsey Hospital—
University of Connecticut
Health Center**
Farmington, CT 06032
(203) 674-2000

Hartford Hospital
80 Seymour Street
Hartford, CT 06115
(203) 542-2100

Mount Sinai Hospital
500 Blue Hills Avenue
Hartford, CT 06112
(203) 242-4431

**Saint Francis Hospital &
Medical Center**
114 Woodland Street
Hartford, CT 06105
(203) 548-4000

Yale—New Haven Hospital
20 York Street
New Haven, CT 06504
(203) 785-4242

DELAWARE

Medical Center of Delaware
501 West 14th Street, Box 1668
Wilmington, DE 19899
(302) 428-1212

DISTRICT OF COLUMBIA

**Children's Hospital, National
Medical Center**
111 Michigan Ave., NW
Washington, DC 20010
(202) 745-5400

**Columbia Hospital for Women
Medical Center**
2425 L Street, NW
Washington, DC 20037
(202) 293-6500

**District of Columbia General
Hospital**
19th Street & Massachusetts
Avenue
Washington, DC 20003
(202) 675-5000

**George Washington University
Hospital**
901 23rd Street, NW
Washington, DC 20037
(202) 676-2500

**Georgetown University
Hospital**
3800 Reservoir Road, NW
Washington, DC 20007
(202) 625-7001

Howard University Hospital
2041 Georgia Avenue, NW
Washington, DC 20060
(202) 745-6100

Washington Hospital Center
110 Irving Street, NW
Washington, DC 20010
(202) 541-6101

FLORIDA

Broward General Medical Center
1600 South Andrews Avenue
Fort Lauderdale, FL 33316
(305) 355-4400

Holy Cross Hospital
Box 23460
Fort Lauderdale, FL 33307
(305) 771-8000

Lee Memorial Hospital
2776 Cleveland Avenue
Fort Myers, FL 33902
(813) 332-1111

Shands Hospital
University of Florida
Box J326-JHMHC
Gainesville, FL 32610
(904) 395-0111

Hialeah Hospital
651 East 25th Street
Hialeah, FL 33013
(305) 693-6100

Memorial Hospital
3501 Johnson Street
Hollywood, FL 33021
(305) 987-2000

Baptist Medical Center
800 Prudential Drive
Jacksonville, FL 32207
(904) 393-2000

Memorial Medical Center of Jacksonville
3625 University Boulevard South
Box 16325
Jacksonville, FL 32216
(904) 399-6111

University Hospital
655 West Eighth Street
Jacksonville, FL 32209
(904) 350-6899

James M. Jackson Memorial Hospital
1611 NW 12th Avenue
Miami, FL 33136
(305) 325-7429

Miami Children's Hospital
6125 S.W. 31st Street
Miami, FL 33511
(305) 666-6511

North Shore Medical Center
1100 N.W. 95th Street
Miami, FL 33150
(305) 835-6000

Orlando Regional Medical Center
1414 South Kuhl Avenue
Orlando, FL 32806
(305) 841-5111

Good Samaritan Hospital
Flagler Drive at Palm Beach Lakes
    Boulevard
Palm Beach, FL 33402
(305) 655-5511

Sacred Heart Hospital of Pensacola
5151 North Ninth Avenue
Pensacola, FL 32504
(904) 474-7000

Plantation General Hospital
401 NW 42nd Avenue
Plantation, FL 33317
(305) 587-5010

All Children's Hospital
801 Sixth Street South
St. Petersburg, FL 33701
(813) 898-7451

Bayfront Medical Center
701 Sixth Street South
St. Petersburg, FL 33701
(813) 893-6111

Tallahassee Memorial Regional Hospital
Miccosukee Road
Tallahassee, FL 32308
(904) 681-5380

Humana Women's Hospital— Tampa
3030 West Buffalo Avenue
Tampa, FL 33607
(813) 879-4730

Tampa General Hospital
Davis Islands
Tampa, FL 33606
(813) 253-0711

St. Mary's Hospital
901 45th Street
West Palm Beach, FL 33407
(305) 844-6300

GEORGIA

Phoebe Putney Memorial Hospital
417 Third Avenue
Box 1828
Albany, GA 31703
(912) 883-1800

St. Mary's Hospital
1230 Baxter Street
Athens, GA 30613
(404) 548-7518

Crawford W. Long Memorial Hospital of Emory University
35 Linden Avenue N.E.
Atlanta, GA 30365
(404) 892-4411

Georgia Baptist Medical Center
300 Boulevard N.E.
Atlanta, GA 30312
(404) 653-4000

Grady Memorial Hospital
80 Butler Street S.E.
Atlanta, GA 30335
(404) 588-4307

Henrietta Egleston Hospital
1405 Clifton Road N.E.
Atlanta, GA 30322
(404) 325-6000

Northside Hospital
1000 Johnson Ferry Road N.E.
Atlanta, GA 30042
(404) 851-8000

Scottish Rite Children's Hospital
1001 Johnson Ferry Road N.E.
Atlanta, GA 30363
(404) 256-5252

Medical College of Georgia Hospital and Clinics
1120 15th Street
Augusta, GA 30912
(404) 828-0211

University Hospital
1350 Walton Way
Augusta, GA 30910
(404) 722-9011

The Medical Center, Inc.
710 Center Street
Columbus, GA 31901
(404) 571-1000

Hamilton Medical Center
Memorial Drive
Dalton, GA 30720
(404) 278-2105

Dekalb General Hospital
2701 North Decatur Road
Decatur, GA 30033
(404) 297-2700

West Georgia Medical Center
1514 Vernon Road
La Grange, GA 30240
(404) 882-1411

Medical Center of Central Georgia
777 Hemlock Street
Macon, GA 31201
(912) 744-1000

Kennestone Regional Health Care Systems
677 Church Street
Marietta, GA 30060
(404) 426-2000

Floyd Medical Center
Turner McCall Boulevard
P.O. Box 233
Rome, GA 30161
(404) 295-5500

Memorial Medical Center
4700 Waters Avenue
Savannah, GA 31404
(912) 356-8496

Memorial Hospital
410 Darling Avenue
Waycross, GA 31502
(912) 283-3030

GUAM

Guam Memorial Hospital
850 Governor Carlos G. Camacho Road
Tamuning, GM 96911
(671) 646-5801

HAWAII

Kapiolani Women's & Children's Medical Center
1319 Punahou Street
Honolulu, HI 96826
(808) 947-8511

IDAHO

St. Luke's Regional Medical Center
190 East Bannock Street
Boise, ID 83712
(208) 386-2222

Bannock Regional Medical Center
Memorial Drive
Pocatello, ID 83201
(208) 232-6150

Magic Valley Regional Medical Center
650 Addison Avenue West
P.O. Box 409
Twin Falls, ID 83303-0409
(208) 737-2000

ILLINOIS

Children's Memorial Hospital
2300 Children's Plaza
Chicago, IL 60614
(312) 880-4000

Cook County Hospital
1835 West Harrison Street
Chicago, IL 60612
(312) 633-6000

**Michael Reese Hospital &
Medical Center**
Lake Shore Drive at 31st Street
Chicago, IL 60616
(312) 791-2000

**Mount Sinai Hospital Medical
Center**
California Avenue
Chicago, IL 60608
(312) 542-2000

**Northwestern Memorial
Hospital**
Superior Street and Fairbanks
Court
Chicago, IL 60611
(312) 649-2000

**Rush-Presbyterian-St. Luke's
Medical Center**
1753 West Congress Parkway
Chicago, IL 60612
(312) 942-5488

**University of Chicago Hospital
& Clinics**
5841 South Maryland
Chicago, IL 60637
(312) 947-1000

**University of Illinois
Hospital**
1740 West Taylor Street
Chicago, IL 60612
(312) 996-3000

Evanston Hospital
2650 Ridge Avenue
Evanston, IL 60201
(312) 492-2000

**Little Company of Mary
Hospital**
2800 West 95th Street
Evergreen Park, IL 60642
(312) 422-6200

**F. G. McGaw Hospital—Loyola
University**
2160 South First Avenue
Maywood, IL 60153
(312) 531-3000

Christ Hospital
4440 West 95th Street
Oak Lawn, IL 60453
(312) 425-8000

Lutheran General Hospital
1775 Dempster Street
Park Ridge, IL 60068
(312) 696-2210

Saint Francis Medical Center
530 NE Glen Oak Avenue
Peoria, IL 61637
(309) 655-2000

Rockford Memorial Hospital
2400 North Rockton Avenue
Rockford, IL 61103
(815) 968-6861

St. John's Hospital
800 East Carpenter Street
Springfield, IL 62769
(217) 544-6464

Carle Foundation Hospital
611 West Park Street
Urbana, IL 61810
(217) 337-3311

INDIANA

St. Francis Hospital Center
1600 Albany Street
Beech Grove, IN 46107
(317) 787-3311

St. Mary's Medical Center
3700 Washington Avenue
Evansville, IN 47750
(812) 479-4000

Welborn Memorial Baptist Hospital
410 SE Sixth Street
Evansville, IN 47713
(812) 426-8000

Lutheran Hospital of Fort Wayne, Inc.
3024 Fairfield Avenue
Fort Wayne, IN 46807
(219) 458-2001

Parkview Memorial Hospital
2200 Randallia Drive
Fort Wayne, IN 46805
(219) 484-6636

St. Margaret's Hospital
5454 Hohman Avenue
Hammond, IN 45320
(219) 932-2300

Indiana University Hospitals
1100 West Michigan Street
Indianapolis, IN 46223
(317) 447-6811

Methodist Hospital of Indiana, Inc.
1701 North Senate Boulevard
Indianapolis, IN 46202
(317) 924-6411

St. Vincent Hospital and Health Care Center
Box 40970
Indianapolis, IN 46240
(317) 871-2345

William N. Wishard Memorial Hospital
1001 West Tenth Street
Indianapolis, IN 46202
(317) 639-6671

Lafayette Home Hospital
2400 South Street
Lafayette, IN 47904
(317) 447-6811

Ball Memorial Hospital
2401 University Avenue
Muncie, IN 47303
(317) 747-3111

Memorial Hospital of South Bend
615 North Michigan Street
South Bend, IN 46601
(219) 234-9041

Union Hospital
1606 North Seventh Street
Terre Haute, IN 47804
(812) 238-7000

IOWA

Mary Greeley Medical Center
117 11th Street
Ames, IA 50010
(515) 239-2011

Burlington Medical Center
602 North Third Street
Burlington, IA 52601
(319) 753-3011

St. Luke's Methodist Hospital
1026 A Avenue NE
Cedar Rapids, IA 52402
(319) 369-7211

St. Luke's Hospital
1227 Rusholme Street
Davenport, IA 52803
(319) 326-6512

Iowa Methodist Medical Center
1200 Pleasant Street
Des Moines, IA 50308
(515) 283-6212

Mercy Health Center
Mercy Drive
Dubuque, IA 52001
(319) 589-8000

Mercy Hospital
500 Market Street
Iowa City, IA 52240
(319) 337-0500

**University of Iowa Hospitals
and Clinics**
650 Newton Road
Iowa City, IA 52242
(319) 356-1616

St. Joseph Mercy Hospital
84 Beaumont Drive
Mason City, IA 50401
(515) 424-7211

**St. Luke's Regional Medical
Center**
2720 Stone Park Boulevard
Sioux City, IA 51104
(712) 279-3500

Covenant Medical Center
3421 West Ninth Street
Waterloo, IA 50702
(319) 236-4111

KANSAS

Mercy Hospital
821 Burke Street
Fort Scott, KS 66701
(316) 223-2200

St. Catherine Hospital
608 North Fifth Street
Garden City, KS 67846
(316) 275-6111

**University of Kansas College
of Health Sciences and
Bell Memorial Hospital**
39th Street and Rainbow
Kansas City, KS 66103
(913) 588-5000

**Humana Hospital—Overland
Park**
10500 Quivira Road
P.O. Box 15959
Overland Park, KS 66215
(913) 541-5000

Asbury Hospital
400 South Santa Fe Avenue
Salina, KS 67402
(913) 827-4411

**Stormont-Vail Regional
Medical Center**
1500 West Tenth Street
Topeka, KS 66606
(913) 354-6000

**St. Francis Regional Medical
Center**
929 North St. Francis Avenue
Wichita, KS 67214
(316) 268-5000

St. Joseph Medical Center
3600 East Harry Street
Wichita, KS 67218
(316) 689-5300

Wesley Medical Center
550 North Hillside Avenue
Wichita, KS 67214
(316) 688-2468

KENTUCKY

**T. J. Samson Community
Hospital**
North Jackson Highway
Glasgow, Ky 42141
(502) 651-6171

**Community Methodist
Hospital**
1305 North Elm Street
Henderson, KY 42420
(502) 826-6251

University Hospital
800 Rose Street
Lexington, KY 40536
(606) 233-5000

**Humana Hospital—University
of Louisville**
530 South Jackson Street
Louisville, KY 40202
(502) 562-3000

NKC Hospitals
200 East Chestnut Street
Louisville, KY 40402
(502) 562-8025

LOUISIANA

St. Frances Cabrini
3330 Masonic Drive
Alexandria, LA 71301
(318) 487-1122

**Earl K. Long Memorial
Hospital**
5825 Airline Highway
Baton Rouge, LA 70805
(504) 356-3361

Woman's Hospital
Goodwood at Airline
P.O. Box 95005
Baton Rouge, LA 70815-9009
(504) 927-1300

**South Louisiana Medical
Center**
1978 Industrial Boulevard
Houma, LA 70360
(504) 868-8140

Lafayette General Hospital
1214 Collidge Avenue
Lafayette, LA 70505
(318) 261-7991

Women's Hospital of Acadiana
4600 Ambassador Caffery Parkway
Lafayette, LA 70508
(318) 981-9100

St. Patrick Hospital
524 South Ryan Street
Lake Charles, LA 70601
(318) 436-2511

East Jefferson General Hospital
4200 Houma Boulevard
Metairie, LA 70011
(504) 454-4000

Lakeside Hospital
4700 I-10 Service Road
Metairie, LA 70001
(504) 885-3333

St. Francis Medical Center
309 Jackson Street
Monroe, LA 71201
(318) 362-4000

Charity Hospital of Louisiana
1532 Tulane Avenue
New Orleans, LA 70140
(504) 568-2311

**Humana Women's Hospital—
E. Orleans**
P.O. Box 29504
New Orleans, LA 70189
(504) 241-6335

Ochsner Foundation Hospital
1516 Jefferson Highway
New Orleans, LA 71021
(504) 838-3100

Southern Baptist Hospital
2700 Napoleon Avenue
New Orleans, LA 70115
(504) 899-9311

**Tulane Medical Center
Hospital & Clinics**
1415 Tulane Avenue
New Orleans, LA 70112
(504) 588–5471

**Louisiana State University
Hospital**
1541 Kings Highway, Box 33932
Shreveport, LA 71130
(318) 674-5000

Schumpert Medical Center
915 Margaret Place
Shreveport, LA 71120
(318) 227-4500

**Willis-Knighton Medical
Center**
2600 Greenwood Road
Shreveport, LA 71103
(318) 632-4600

MAINE

Eastern Maine Medical Center
489 State Street
Bangor, ME 04401
(207) 947-3711

Central Maine Medical Center
300 Main Street
Lewiston, ME 04240
(207) 795-0111

Maine Medical Center
22 Bramhall Street
Portland, ME 04102
(207) 871-0111

MARYLAND

**Francis Scott Key Medical
Center**
4940 Eastern Avenue
Baltimore, MD 21224
(301) 955-0100

**Greater Baltimore Medical
Center**
6701 North Charles Street
Baltimore, MD 21204
(301) 828-2000

Johns Hopkins Hospital
600 North Wolfe Street
Baltimore, MD 21205
(301) 955-5000

Mercy Hospital
301 St. Paul Place
Baltimore, MD 21202
(301) 332-9000

Sinai Hospital of Baltimore
Belvedere Avenue at Greenspring
Baltimore, MD 21215
(301) 578-5678

St. Agnes Hospital
900 South Caton Avenue
Baltimore, MD 21229
(301) 368-6000

**University of Maryland
  Medical System**
22 South Greene Street
Baltimore, MD 21201
(301) 528-6294

MASSACHUSETTS

Beth Israel Hospital
330 Brookline Avenue
Boston, MA 02215
(617) 735-2000

Boston City Hospital
818 Harrison Avenue
Boston, MA 02118
(617) 424-5000

Brigham & Women's Hospital
75 Francis Street
Boston, MA 02115
(617) 732-5500

Children's Hospital
300 Longwood Avenue
Boston, MA 02115
(617) 735-6000

**Massachusetts General
  Hospital**
32 Fruit Street
Boston, MA 02114
(617) 726-2000

**New England Medical Center
  Hospitals**
171 Harrison Avenue
Boston, MA 02111
(617) 956-5000

**St. Margaret's Hospital for
  Women**
90 Cushing Avenue
Boston, MA 02125
(617) 436-8600

Charlton Memorial Hospital
363 Highland Avenue
Fall River MA 02720
(617) 679-3131

Berkshire Medical Center
725 North Street
Pittsfield, MA 01201
(413) 499-4161

Baystate Medical Center
759 Chestnut Street
Springfield, MA 01199
(415) 787-2500

Worcester Memorial Hospital
119 Belmont Street
Worcester, MA 01605
(617) 793-6611

MICHIGAN

University of Michigan Hospitals
300 North Ingles Street
Ann Arbor, MI 48109-0472
(313) 763-3100

Oakwood Hospital
18101 Oakwood Boulevard
Dearborn, MI 48124
(313) 593-7000

Children's Hospital of Michigan
3901 Beaubien
Detroit, MI 48201
(313) 745-5301

Henry Ford Hospital
2799 West Grand Boulevard
Detroit, MI 48202
(313) 876-2600

Hutzel Hospital
4707 St. Antoine Boulevard
Detroit, MI 48201
(313) 745-7171

Sinai Hospital of Detroit
6767 West Outer Drive
Detroit, MI 48235
(313) 493-6824

St. John Hospital
22101 Moross Road
Detroit, MI 48236
(313) 343-4000

Hurley Medical Center
One Hurley Plaza
Flint, MI 48502
(313) 257-9000

Blodgett Memorial Medical Center
1840 Wealthy Street, S.E.
Grand Rapids, MI 49506
(616) 774-7444

Butterworth Hospital
100 Michigan Street, N.E.
Grand Rapids, MI 49503
(616) 774-1774

Bronson Methodist Hospital
252 East Lovell Street
Kalamazoo, MI 49007
(616) 383-7654

Edward W. Sparrow Hospital
1215 Michigan Avenue
P.O. Box 30480
Lansing, MI 48909
(517) 483-2501

Marquette General Hospital
420 West Magnetic Street
Marquette, MI 49855
(906) 228-9440

Northern Michigan Hospital
416 Connable Street
Petoskey, MI 49770
(616) 348-4000

Pontiac General Hospital
Seminole at West Huron Street
Pontiac, MI 48053
(313) 857-7200

Port Huron Hospital
1001 Kearney Street
Port Huron, MI 48060
(313) 987-7500

William Beaumont Hospital
3601 West Thirteen Mile Road
Royal Oak, MI 48072
(313) 424-3000

Saginaw General Hospital
1447 North Harrison Street
Saginaw, MI 48602
(517) 771-4000

Providence Hospital
16001 West Nine Mile Road
P.O. Box 2043
Southfield, MI 48037
(313) 424-3000

Munson Medical Center
Sixth and Madison Streets
Traverse, MI 49684
(616) 922-9000

MINNESOTA

St. Mary's Medical Center
407 East Third Street
Duluth, MN 55805
(218) 726-4000

Abbott-Northwestern Hospital
800 East 28th Street
Minneapolis, MN 55407
(612) 874-4000

**Hennepin County Medical
Center**
Center for Perinatal Services
701 Park Avenue South
Minneapolis, MN 55415
(612) 347-2121

**Minneapolis Children's
Medical Center**
2525 Chicago Avenue
Minneapolis, MN 55404
(612) 874-6112

**University of Minnesota
Hospitals & Clinics**
420 Delaware Street, S.E.
Minneapolis, MN 55455
(612) 626-3000

**North Memorial Medical
Center**
3300 Oakdale North
Robbinsdale, MN 55422
(612) 520-5200

**St. Mary's Hospital of
Rochester**
1216 Second Street, S.W.
Rochester, MN 55902
(507) 285-4400

Children's Hospital
345 North South Avenue
St. Paul, MN 55102
(612) 298-8666

**St. Paul—Ramsey Medical
Center**
640 Jackson Street
St. Paul, MN 55101
(612) 221-3456

MISSISSIPPI

**Golden Triangle Regional
Medical Center**
2520 Fifth Street
Box 1307
Columbus, MS 39701
(601) 327-2121

**Forrest County General
Hospital**
400 28th Avenue
Hattiesburg, MS 39401
(601) 264-7000

Hinds General Hospital
1850 Chadwick Drive
Jackson, MS 39204
(601) 376-1000

Mississippi Baptist Medical Center
1225 North State Street
Jackson, MS 39201
(601) 968-1000

University Hospital
2500 North State Street
Jackson, MS 39216
(601) 984-4100

Woman's Hospital
1026 North Flowood Drive
Jackson, MS 39208
(601) 932-1000

Jefferson Davis Memorial Hospital
Seargent S. Prentiss Drive
Natchez, MS 39120
(601) 442-2871

North Mississippi Medical Center
830 South Gloster Street
Tupelo, MS 38801
(601) 841-3000

MISSOURI

Southeast Missouri Hospital
1701 Lacey Street
Cape Girardeau, MO 63701
(314) 334-4822

University of Missouri Hospital & Clinics
One Hospital Drive
Columbia, MO 65212
(314) 882-4141

Freeman Hospital
1102 West 32nd Street
Joplin, MO 64801
(417) 623-2801

Children's Mercy Hospital
24th at Gellham Road
Kansas City, MO 64108
(816) 234-3000

Truman Medical Center—West
2301 Holmes Street
Kansas City, MO 64108
(816) 556-3000

Universitiy of Health Sciences
2105 Independence Boulevard
Kansas City, MO 64124
(816) 283-2000

North Kansas City Memorial Hospital
2800 Hospital Drive North
North Kansas City, MO 64116
(816) 346-7000

Lester E. Cox Medical Center South
3801 South National Street
Springfield, MO 65807
(417) 885-6000

St. John's Regional Health Center
1235 East Cherokee Street
Springfield, MO 65802
(417) 885-2000

Barnes Hospital
Barnes Hospital Plaza
St. Louis, MO 63110
(314) 362-5000

Cardinal Glennon Children's Hospital
1465 South Grand Boulevard
St. Louis, MO 63104
(314) 577-5600

Children's Hospital
400 South Kings Highway
 Boulevard
St. Louis, MO 63110
(314) 454-6000

**St. John's Mercy Medical
 Center**
615 South New Ballas Road
St. Louis, MO 63141
(314) 569-6000

St. Mary's Health Center
6420 Clayton Road
St. Louis, MO 63117
(314) 768-8000

MONTANA

St. Vincent Hospital
1233 North 30th Street
Billings, MT 59107
(406) 657-7000

St. James Community Hospital
400 South Clark Street
Butte, MT 59701
(406) 782-8361

Missoula Community Hospital
2827 Fort Missoula Road
Missoula, MT 59801
(406) 728-4100

NEBRASKA

**Mary Lanning Memorial
 Hospital**
715 North Saint Joseph
Hastings, NE 68901
(402) 463-4521

Good Samaritan Hospital
31st Street and Central Avenue
Kearney, NE 68847
(308) 236-8511

**St. Elizabeth Community
 Health Center**
555 South 70th Street
Lincoln, NE 68510
(402) 489-7181

**Archbishop Bergan Mercy
 Hospital**
7500 Mercy Road
Omaha, NE 68124
(402) 398-6060

**Children's Memorial
 Hospital**
8301 Dodge Street
Omaha, NE 68114
(402) 390-5400

**University Hospital—
 University of Nebraska**
42nd Street and Dewey Avenue
Omaha, NE 68105
(402) 559-4000

St. Joseph Hospital
601 North 30th Street
Omaha, NE 68131
(402) 449-4000

**West Nebraska General
 Hospital**
4021 Avenue B
Scottsbluff, NE 69361
(308) 635-3711

NEVADA

St. Mary's Hospital
235 West Sixth Street
Reno, NV 89520
(702) 323-2041

Washoe Medical Center
77 Pringle Way
Reno, NV 89520
(702) 785-4100

NEW HAMPSHIRE

**Mary Hitchcock Memorial
  Hospital**
2 Maynard Street
Hanover, NH 03756
(603) 646-5000

NEW JERSEY

Atlantic City Medical Center
1925 Pacific Avenue
Atlantic City, NJ 08401
(609) 344-4081

**Cooper Hospital—University
  Medical Center**
One Cooper Plaza
Camden, NJ 08103
(609) 342-2000

**Our Lady of Lourdes Medical
  Center**
1600 Haddon Avenue
Camden, NJ 08103
(609) 757-3500

Hackensack Medical Center
30 Prospect Avenue
Hackensack, NJ 07601
(201) 441-2000

Jersey City Medical Center
50 Baldwin Avenue
Jersey City, NJ 07304
(201) 915-2000

St. Barnabas Medical Center
Old Short Hills Road
Livingston, NJ 07039
(201) 533-5000

Monmouth Medical Center
300 Second Avenue
Long Branch, NJ 07740
(201) 222-5200

Jersey Shore Medical Center
1945 Corlies Avenue
Neptune, NJ 07753
(201) 775-5500

St. Peter's Medical Center
254 Easton Avenue
New Brunswick, NJ 08903
(201) 745-8600

**Children's Hospital of New
  Jersey**
15 South 9th Street
Newark, NJ 07107
(201) 268-8010

**Newark Beth Israel Medical
  Center**
201 Lyons Avenue
Newark, NJ 07112
(201) 926-7000

University of Medicine and Dentistry New Jersey / University Hospital
100 Bergen Street
Newark, NJ 07107
(201) 456-5658

St. Joseph's Hospital and Medical Center
703 Main Street
Paterson, NJ 07503
(201) 977-2000

Overlook Hospital
193 Morris Avenue
Summit, NJ 07901
(201) 522-2000

West Jersey Hospital—Eastern Division
Evesham Road
Voorhees, NJ 08043
(609) 772-5000

NEW MEXICO

Presbyterian Hospital
1100 Central Avenue SE
Albuquerque, NM 87102
(505) 841-1234

University of New Mexico Hospital
2211 Lomas Boulevard NE
Albuquerque, NM 87106
(505) 843-2111

Eastern New Mexico Medical Center
405 West Country Club Road
Roswell, NM 88201
(505) 622-8170

NEW YORK

Albany Medical Center Hospital
New Scotland Avenue
Albany, NY 12208
(581) 445-3125

St. Peter's Hospital
315 South Manning Boulevard
Albany, NY 12208
(518) 454-1550

Bronx Municipal Hospital Center
Pelham Parkway South
Bronx, NY 10461
(212) 430-5000

Bronx-Lebanon Hospital Center
Bronx, NY 10456
(212) 588-7000

Lincoln Medical and Mental Health Center
234 East 149th Street
Bronx, NY 10451
(212) 579-5000

North Central Bronx Hospital
3424 Kossuth Avenue
Bronx, NY 10467
(212) 920-7171

Our Lady of Mercy Medical Center
600 East 233rd Street
Bronx, NY 10466
(212) 920-9000

The Jack D. Weiler Hospital / A Division of Montefiore Medical Center
1825 East Chester Road
Bronx, NY
(212) 904-2000

Brookdale Hospital Medical Center
Linden Boulevard and Brookdale Plaza
Brooklyn, NY 11212
(718) 240-5000

Brooklyn Hospital— Caledonian Hospital
121 DeKalb Avenue
Brooklyn, NY 11201
(718) 403-8000

Maimonides Medical Center
4802 Tenth Avenue
Brooklyn, NY 11219
(718) 270-7679

Methodist Hospital
506 Sixth Street
Brooklyn, NY 11215
(718) 780-3000

University Hospital of Brooklyn
445 Lenox Road
Brooklyn, NY 11203
(718) 270-2401

Children's Hospital of Buffalo
219 Bryant Street
Buffalo, NY 14222
(716) 878-7000

Mercy Hospital
565 Abbott Road
Buffalo, NY 14220
(716) 826-7000

Nassau County Medical Center
2201 Hempstead Turnpike
East Meadow, NY 11554
(516) 542-0123

Arnot-Ogden Memorial Hospital
Roe Avenue and Grove Street
Elmira, NY 14901
(607) 737-4100

City Hospital Center at Elmhurst
79-01 Broadway, Elmhurst Station
Flushing, NY 11373
(718) 830-1515

Flushing Hospital and Medical Center
4500 Parsons Boulevard
Flushing, NY 11355
(718) 670-5000

Queens Hospital Center
82-68 164th Street
Jamaica, NY 11432
(718) 990-3377

United Health Services
33-57 Harrison Street
Johnson City, NY 13790
(607) 773-6140

North Shore University Hospital
300 Community Drive
Manhasset, NY 11030
(516) 562-0100

Winthrop University Hospital
259 First Street
Mineola, NY 11501
(516) 663-0333

Bellevue Hospital Center
First Avenue and 27th Street
New York, NY 10016
(212) 561-4141

Beth Israel Medical Center
First Avenue at 16th Street
New York, NY 10003
(212) 420-2000

Harlem Hospital Center
506 Lenox Avenue
New York, NY 10037
(212) 491-1234

Lenox Hill Hospital
100 East 77th Street
New York, NY 10021
(212) 439-2345

Long Island Jewish Medical Center
270-05 76th Avenue
New York, NY 11042
(718) 470-7000

Metropolitan Hospital Center
1901 First Avenue
New York, NY 10029
(212) 230-6262

Mount Sinai Hospital
One Gustave L. Levy Place
New York, NY 10029
(212) 650-5000

New York University Medical Center
550 First Avenue
New York, NY 10016
(212) 340-5505

Society of the New York Hospital
525 East 68th Street
New York, NY 10021
(212) 472-5454

St. Luke's-Roosevelt Hospital
Amsterdam Avenue and 114th Street
New York, NY 10025
(212) 870-6000

St. Vincent's Hospital & Medical Center
153 West 11th Street
New York, NY 10011
(212) 790-7000

The Presbyterian Hospital in the City of New York
622 West 168th Street
New York, NY 10032
(212) 305-2500

Rochester General Hospital
1425 Portland Avenue
Rochester, NY 14621
(716) 338-4000

Strong Memorial Hospital
601 Elmwood Avenue
Rochester, NY 14642
(716) 275-2644

Bellevue Maternity Hospital
Box 1030
Schenectady, NY 12309
(518) 346-9400

St. Vincent's Medical Center
355 Bard Avenue
Staten Island, NY 10310
(718) 390-1234

Staten Island Hospital
475 Seaview Avenue
Staten Island, NY 10305
(718) 390-9000

University Hospital
State University of New York
Stony Brook, NY 11794
(516) 444-2701

Crouse-Irving Memorial Hospital
736 Irving Avenue
Syracuse, NY 13210
(315) 470-7111

Westchester County Medical Center
Valhalla Campus
Valhalla, NY 10595
(914) 347-7000

House of the Good Samaritan
830 Washington Street
Watertown, NY 13601
(315) 785-4000

NORTH CAROLINA

Memorial Mission Hospital
509 Biltmore Avenue
Asheville, NC 28801
(704) 255-4000

**North Carolina Memorial
Hospital**
Manning Drive
Chapel Hill, NC 27514
(919) 966-4131

Presbyterian Hospital
200 Hawthorne Lane
Charlotte,NC 28203
(704) 371-4000

Duke University Hospital
Erwin Road
Durham, NC 27710
(919) 684-8111

**Moses H. Cone Memorial
Hospital**
1200 North Elm Street
Greensboro, NC 27401
(919) 379-3900

Pitt County Memorial Hospital
200 Statonburg Road
Greenville, NC 27834
(919) 757-4100

Frye Regional Medical Center
420 North Center Street
Hickory, NC 28601
(704) 322-6070

Southeastern General Hospital
West 27th Street, Box 1408
Lumberton, NC 28358
(919) 738-6441

Moore Memorial Hospital
Page Road
Box 3000
Pinehurst, NC 28374
(919) 295-1000

Wake Medical Center
3000 New Bern Avenue
Raleigh, NC 27610
(919) 755-8000

**New Hanover Memorial
Hospital**
2131 South 17th Street
Wilmington, NC 28401
(919) 343-7000

Forsyth Memorial Hospital
3333 Silas Creek Parkway
Winston-Salem, NC 27103
(919) 760-5000

**North Carolina Baptist
Hospital**
300 South Hawthorne Road
Winston-Salem, NC 27103
(919) 748-2011

NORTH DAKOTA

Medcentre One, Inc.
300 North Seventh Street
Bismarck, ND 58502
(701) 224-6000

St. Alexius Medical Center
900 East Broadway
Bismarck, ND 58501
(701) 224-7000

St. Luke's Hospitals
Fifth Street N and Mills Ave
Fargo, ND 58122
(701) 280-5000

United Hospitals
1200 S. Columbia Road
Grand Forks, ND 58201
(701) 780-5000

Trinity Medical Center
Burdick Expressway at Main
Minot, ND 58701
(701) 857-5000

OHIO

Akron City Hospital
525 E. Market Street
Akron, OH 44309
(216) 375-3000

**Children's Hospital Medical
  Center**
281 Locust Street
Akron, OH 44308
(216) 379-8200

Aultman Hospital
2600 Sixth Street, SW
Canton, OH 44710
(216) 452-9911

Timken Mercy Medical Center
1320 Timken Mercy Drive NW
Canton, OH 44708
(216) 489-1000

**Children's Hospital Medical
  Center**
Elland and Bethesda Avenues
Cincinnati, OH 45221
(513) 559-4200

Good Samaritan Hospital
3217 Clinton Avenue
Cincinnati, OH 45220
(513) 872-2255

**University of Cincinnati
  Hospital**
234 Goodman Street
Cincinnati, OH 45267
(513) 872-3100

Cuyahoga County Hospitals
3395 Scranton Road
Cleveland, OH 44109
(216) 398-6000

Fairview General Hospital
18101 Lorain Avenue
Cleveland, OH 44111
(216) 476-7000

St. Luke's Hospital
11311 Shaker Boulevard
Cleveland, OH 44104
(216) 368-7000

**University Hospitals of
  Cleveland**
2074 Abington Road
Cleveland, OH 44106
(216) 444-1000

Children's Hospital
700 Children's Drive
Columbus, OH 43205
(614) 461-2000

Doctors Hospital
1087 Dennison Avenue
Columbus, OH 43201
(614) 297-4000

**Ohio State University
  Hospitals**
410 West Tenth Avenue
Columbus, OH 43210
(614) 421-8000

Children's Medical Center
One Children's Plaza
Dayton, OH 45404
(513) 226-8300

Miami Valley Hospital
One Wyoming Street
Dayton, OH 45409
(513) 223-6192

St. Elizabeth Medical Center
601 Edwin C. Moses Boulevard
Dayton, OH 45408
(513) 229-6000

Kettering Medical Center
3535 Southern Boulevard
Kettering, OH 45429
(513) 298-4331

Hillcrest Hospital
6780 Mayfield Road
Mayfield Heights, OH 44124
(216) 449-4500

Riverside Hospital
1600 Superior Street
Toledo, OH 43604
(419) 729-6000

St. Vincent Medical Center
2213 Cherry Street
Toledo, OH 43608
(419) 321-3232

Toledo Hospital
2142 North Cove Boulevard
Toledo, OH 43606
(419) 471-4218

St. Elizabeth Hospital Medical Center
1044 Belmont Avenue
Box 1790
Youngstown, OH 44501
(216) 746-7211

Tod Children's Hospital
500 Gypsy Lane
Youngstown, OH 44501
(216) 747-1444

Youngstown Hospital Association—Tod Children's Hospital
500 Gypsy Lane
Youngstown, OH 44501
(216) 747-1444

OKLAHOMA

Valley View Regional Hospital
430 N. Monta Vista
Ada, OK 74820
(405) 332-2323

Baptist Medical Center of Oklahoma
3300 NW Expressway
Oklahoma City, OK 73112
(405) 949-3011

Mercy Health Center
4300 West Memorial Road
Oklahoma City, OK 73120
(405) 755-1515

Oklahoma Teaching Hospitals
P.O. Box 26307
Oklahoma City, OK 73126
(405) 271-5911

Saint Francis Hospital
6161 South Yale Avenue
Tulsa, OK 74136
(918) 494-2200

St. John Medical Center, Inc.
1923 South Utica Avenue
Tulsa, OK 74104
(918) 744-2180

OREGON

Sacred Heart General Hospital
1255 Hilyard Street
Eugene, OR 07401
(503) 686-7300

Rogue Valley Medical Center
2825 Barnett Road
Medford, OR 97504
(503) 773-6281

Emanuel Hospital
2801 North Gantenbein Avenue
Portland, OR 97227
(503) 280-3200

Oregon Health Sciences
  University Hospital
3181 S.W. Sam Jackson Park Road
Portland, OR 97201
(503) 225-8311

Salem Hospital
665 Winter Street SE
Salem, OR 97301
(503) 370-5200

PENNSYLVANIA

The Allentown Hospital
17th and Chew Streets
Allentown, PA 18102
(215) 778-2204

Altoona Hospital
Howard Avenue and Seventh
Altoona, PA 16603
(814) 946-2011

Bryn Mawr Hospital
Bryn Mawr Avenue
Bryn Mawr, PA 19010
(215) 896-3000

Geisinger Medical Center
North Academy Avenue
Danville, PA 17822
(717) 271-6211

Mercy Catholic Medical Center
Lansdowne Avenue
Darby, PA 19023
(215) 237-4016

DuBois Regional Medical
  Center
Maple Avenue
P.O. Box 447
DuBois, PA 15801
(814) 375-4321

Hamot Medical Center
201 State Street
Erie, PA 16550
(814) 870-6000

St. Vincent Health Center
232 East 25th Street
Erie, PA 16544
(814) 452-5000

Harrisburg Hospital
South Front Street
Harrisburg, PA 17101
(717) 782-3131

Polyclinic Medical Center
Third and Radnor Streets
Harrisburg, PA 17105
(717) 782-4141

University Hospital Milton S.
  Hershey Medical Center of
  the Pennsylvania State
  University
500 University Drive, P.O. Box 850
Hershey, PA 17033
(717) 531-8521

Conemaugh Valley Memorial
  Hospital
1086 Franklin Street
Johnstown, PA 15905
(814) 533-9000

Albert Einstein Medical
  Center—Northern Division
York and Tabor Roads
Philadelphia, PA 19141
(215) 456-7890

Children's Hospital of Philadelphia
34th Street and Civic Center Boulevard
Philadelphia, PA 19104
(215) 596-9100

Episcopal Hospital
Front Street and Lehigh Avenue
Philadelphia, PA 19125
(215) 427-7000

Hahnemann University Hospital
Broad and Vine Streets
Philadelphia, PA 19102
(215) 448-7000

Hospital of the University of Pennsylvania
3400 Spruce Street
Philadelphia, PA 19104
(215) 662-4000

Hospital of the Medical College of Pennsylvania
3300 Henry Avenue
Philadelphia, PA 19129
(215) 842-6000

Pennsylvania Hospital
Eighth and Spruce Streets
Philadelphia, PA 19107
(215) 829-3000

Philadelphia College of Osteopathic Medicine
4150 City Avenue
Philadelphia, PA 19131
(215) 581-6000

St. Christopher's Hospital
5th Street and Lehigh Avenue
Philadelphia, PA 19133
(215) 427-5000

Temple University Hospital
Broad and Ontario Streets
Philadelphia, PA 19140
(215) 221-2000

Thomas Jefferson University Hospital
11th and Walnut Streets
Philadelphia, PA 19107
(215) 928-6000

Allegheny General Hospital
320 East North Avenue
Pittsburgh, PA 15212
(412) 359-3131

Children's Hospital of Pittsburgh
125 DeSoto Street
Pittsburgh, PA 15213
(412) 647-5325

Magee-Women's Hospital
Forbes Avenue & Halket Street
Pittsburg, PA 15213
(412) 647-1000

Mercy Hospital of Pittsburgh
1400 Locust Street
Pittsburgh, PA 15219
(412) 232-8111

Western Pennsylvania Hospital
4800 Friendship Avenue
Pittsburgh, PA 15224
(412) 578-5000

Reading Hospital & Medical Center
Sixth Avenue and Spruce Street
Reading, PA 19603
(215) 378-6000

Community Medical Center
1822 Mulberry Street
Scranton, PA 18510
(717) 969-8000

York Hospital
1001 South George Street
York, PA 17405
(717) 771-2345

PUERTO RICO

Mayaguez Medical Center
Mayaguez, PR 00708
(809) 832-8686

Ponce Regional Hospital
Ponce, PR 00731
(809) 844-0920

Hospital Del Maestro
Domenech Avenue
San Juan, PR 00936
(809) 792-3131

San Juan Municipal Hospital
Puerto Rico Medical Center
San Juan, PR 00935
(809) 765-6728

RHODE ISLAND

Women & Infants' Hospital of Rhode Island
101 Dudley Street
Providence, RI 02905-3218
(401) 274-1100

SOUTH CAROLINA

Medical University Hospital
171 Ashley Avenue
Charleston, SC 29425
(803) 792-3131

**Baptist Medical Center at
Columbia**
Taylor at Marion Street
Columbia, SC 29220
(803) 771-5010

Richland Memorial Hospital
Five Richland Medical Park
Columbia, SC 20203
(803) 765-7011

McLeod Regional Medical Center
555 East Cheves Street
Florence, SC 29501
(803) 667-2000

Greenville Memorial Hospital
701 Grove Road
Greenville, SC 29605
(803) 242-7000

Self Memorial Hospital
Spring Street
Greenwood, SC 29646
(803) 227-4111

Spartanburg General Hospital
101 East Wood Street
Spartanburg, SC 29303
(803) 591-6000

SOUTH DAKOTA

Rapid City Regional Hospital
353 Fairmont Boulevard
Rapid City, SD 57701
(605) 341-1000

McKennan Hospital
800 East 21st Street
Sioux Falls, SD 57117-5045
(605) 339-8000

Sioux Valley Hospital
1100 South Euclid Avenue
P.O. Box 5039
Sioux Falls, SD 57117-5039
(605) 333-1000

Sacred Heart Hospital
501 Summit Street
Yankton, SD 57078
(605) 665-9371

TENNESSEE

Erlanger Medical Center
975 East Third Street
Chattanooga, TN 37403
(615) 778-7000

Johnson City Medical Center Hospital
400 State of Franklin Road
Johnson City, TN 37601
(615) 461-6111

East Tennessee Children's Hospital
2018 Clinch Avenue
Knoxville, TN 37916
(615) 546-7711

University of Tennessee Memorial Research Center Hospital
1924 Alcoa Highway
Knoxville, TN 37920
(615) 544-9000

Baptist Memorial Hospital
899 Madison Avenue
Memphis, TN 38146
(901) 522-5252

Methodist Hospital—Central Unit
1265 Union Avenue
Memphis, TN 38104
(901) 726-7000

Regional Medical Center at Memphis
877 Jefferson Avenue
Memphis, TN 38103
(901) 528-7115

Baptist Hospital
2000 Church Street
Nashville, TN 37236
(615) 329-5555

Hubbard Hospital—Meharry Medical College
1005 D. B. Todd Boulevard
Nashville, TN 37208
(615) 327-6218

Vanderbilt University Hospital
1161 21st Avenue South
Nashville, TN 37232
(615) 322-7311

TEXAS

Amarillo Hospital District
P.O. Box 1110
1200 Wallace Boulevard
Amarillo, TX 79175
(806) 358-9031

Permian General Hospital
Northeast By-Pass
P.O. Box 2108
Andrews, TX 79714
(915) 523-2200

Brackenridge Hospital
601 East 15th Street
Austin, TX 78701
(512) 476-6461

Seton Medical Center
1201 West 38th Street
Austin, TX 78705
(512) 459-2121

St. David's Community Hospital
919 East 32nd Street
Austin, TX 78705
(512) 476-7111

St. Elizabeth Hospital
2830 Calder Avenue
Beaumont, TX 77702
(409) 892-7171

Driscoll Foundation Children's Hospital
3533 South Alameda Street
Corpus Christi, TX 78411
(512) 854-5341

Spohn Hospital
600 Elizabeth Street
Corpus Christi, TX 78404
(512) 881-3000

Baylor University Medical Center
3500 Gaston Avenue
Dallas, TX 75246
(214) 820-0111

Children's Medical Center of Dallas
1935 Amelia Street
Dallas, TX 75235
(214) 920-2000

Dallas County Hospital
5201 Harry Hines Boulevard
Dallas, TX 75235
(214) 637-8000

Methodist Medical Center
301 West Colorado Boulevard
Dallas, TX 75265
(214) 944-8181

Presbyterian Hospital of Dallas
8200 Walnut Hill
Dallas, TX 75231
(214) 369-4111

St. Paul Medical Center
5909 Harry Hines Boulevard
Dallas, TX 75235
(214) 879-1000

Flow Memorial Hospital
1310 Scripture Street
Denton, TX 76201
(817) 387-5861

Providence Memorial Hospital
2001 North Oregon Street
El Paso, TX 79902
(915) 542-6011

R. E. Thomason General Hospital
4815 Alameda Avenue
El Paso, TX 79905
(915) 544-1200

Sierra Medical Center
1625 Medical Center Drive
El Paso, TX 79902
(915) 532-4000

Cook-Fort Worth Children's Medical Center
1400 Cooper Street
Fort Worth, TX 76104
(817) 885-4000

Harris Hospital—Methodist/ Fort Worth, Texas
1325 Pennsylvania Avenue
Fort Worth, TX 76104
(817) 334-6011

Tarrant County Hospital
1500 South Main Street
Fort Worth, TX 76104
(817) 921-3421

University of Texas Medical Branch Hospitals
Eighth and Mechanic Streets
Galveston, TX 77550
(409) 761-1011

Valley Baptist Medical Center
2101 Pease Street
Harlington, TX 78550
(512) 421-1100

Harris County Hospital District
726 Gillettee
Houston, TX 77019
(713) 652-1200

Hermann Hospital
1203 Ross Sterling Avenue
Houston, TX 77030
(713) 797-4011

Memorial City General Hospital
920 Frostwood Drive
Houston, TX 77024
(713) 932-3000

Methodist Hospital
6565 Fannin Street
Houston, TX 77030
(713) 790-3311

Spring Branch Memorial Hospital
8850 Long Point Road
Box 55227
Houston, TX 77055
(713) 467-6555

St. Joseph's Hospital
1919 LaBranch Street
Houston, TX 77002
(713) 757-1000

Texas Children's Hospital
6621 Fannin Street
Houston, TX 77030
(713) 791-2831

Woman's Hospital
7600 Fannin Street
Houston, TX 77054
(713) 790-1234

Lubbock County Hospital District—Lubbock General
602 Indiana Avenue
Lubbock, TX 79417
(806) 942-3111

McAllen Medical Center
301 West Expressway 83
McAllen, TX 78503
(512) 632-4000

Odessa Women's & Children's Hospital
520 East Sixth Street
Box 4859
Odessa, TX 79760
(915) 334-8200

Bexar County Hospital District
4502 Medical Drive
San Antonio, TX 78284
(512) 694-3030

Humana Women's Hospital— South Texas
8109 Fredericksburg Road
San Antonio, TX 78229
(512) 699-8000

Santa Rosa Medical Center
519 West Houston Center
San Antonio, TX 78207
(512) 228-2011

Southwest Texas Methodist Hospital
7700 Floyd Curl Drive
San Antonio, TX 78229
(512) 692-4000

Scott and White Memorial Hospital
2401 South 31st Street
Temple, TX 76508
(817) 774-2111

Wadley Regional Medical Center
Box 1878
Texarkana, TX 75504
(214) 793-4511

UTAH

Logan Regional Hospital
1400 North 500 East
Logan, UT 84321
(801) 752-2050

McKay-Dee Hospital Center
3939 Harrison Boulevard
Ogden, UT 84409
(801) 627-2800

**Utah Valley Regional Medical
Center**
1034 North Fifth West
Provo, UT 84603
(801) 373-7850

LDS Hospital
325 Eighth Avenue
Salt Lake City, UT 84143
(801) 321-1100

**Primary Children's Medical
Center**
320 12th Avenue
Salt Lake City, UT 84103
(801) 521-1221

University of Utah Hospital
50 North Medical Drive
Salt Lake City, UT 84132
(801) 581-2121

VERMONT

Medical Center Hospital of Vermont
Colchester Avenue
Burlington, VT 05401
(802) 656-2345

VIRGINIA

Alexandria Hospital
4320 Seminary Road
Alexandria, VA 22304
(703) 379-3000

University of Virginia Hospitals
Jefferson Park Avenue
Charlottesville, VA 22908
(804) 924-0211

Fairfax Hospital
3300 Gallows Road
Falls Church, VA 22046
(703) 698-1110

Virginia Baptist Hospital
3300 Rivermont Avenue
Lynchburg, VA 24503
(804) 522-4000

Children's Hospital
800 West Olney Road
Norfolk, VA 23507
(804) 628-7000

Norfolk General Hospital
600 Gresham Drive
Norfolk, VA 23507
(804) 628-3000

**Medical College of Virginia
Hospitals**
401 North 12th Street
Box 510, MCV Station
Richmond, VA 23298
(804) 786-9000

Roanoke Memorial Hospital
Belleview at Jefferson Street
Roanoke, VA 24033
(703) 981-7000

Potomac Hospital
2300 Opitz Boulevard
Woodbridge, VA 22191
(703) 670-1313

WASHINGTON

Monticello Medical Center
600 Broadway
Longview, WA 98632
(206) 423-5850

St. Peter's Hospital
413 N. Lilly Road
Olympia, WA 98506
(206) 491-9480

Kadlec Medical Center
888 Swift Boulevard
Richland, WA 99352
(509) 946-4611

**Children's Orthopedic Hospital
& Medical Center**
4800 Sand Point Way, N.E.
Seattle, WA 98105
(206) 526-2000

**Swedish Hospital Medical
Center**
747 Summit Avenue
Seattle, WA 98104
(206) 386-6000

University Hospital
1959 NE Pacific Street
Seattle, WA 98195
(206) 455-3131

**Deaconess Medical Center
Spokane**
800 West Fifth Avenue
Spokane, WA 99210
(509) 458-5800

Sacred Heart Medical Center
West 101 Eighth Avenue
Spokane, WA 99204
(509) 455-3131

Tacoma General Hospital
315 South K Street, Box 5299
Tacoma, WA 98405
(206) 594-1000

St. Mary Medical Center
401 W. Poplar Street
Box 1477
Walla Walla, WA 99362
(509) 525-3320

**Yakima Valley Memorial
Hospital**
2811 Tieton Drive
Yakima, WA 98902
(509) 575-8000

WEST VIRGINIA

Raleigh General Hospital
1710 Harper Road
Beckley, WV 25801
(304) 256-4100

Charleston Area Medical Center
P.O. Box 1547
Charleston, WV 25326
(304) 348-5432

Cabell Huntington Hospital
1340 Hal Greer Boulevard
Huntington, WV 25701
(304) 526-2000

West Virginia University Hospital
Medical Center Box 6401
Morgantown, WV 26506
(304) 293-5233

Ohio Valley General Hospital
2200 Eoff Street
Wheeling, WV 26003
(304) 234-0123

WISCONSIN

Luther Hospital
1221 Whipple Street
Eau Claire, WI 54702
(715) 839-3311

St. Vincent Hospital
835 South Van Buren Street
P.O. Box 13508
Green Bay, WI 54307-3508
(414) 433-0111

La Crosse Lutheran Hospital
1910 South Avenue
La Cross, WI 54601
(608) 785-0530

St. Francis Medical Center
700 West Avenue South
La Crosse, WI 54601
(608) 785-0940

Madison General Hospital
202 South Park Street
Madison, WI 53715
(608) 267-6000

St. Mary's Hospital Medical Center
707 South Mills Street
Madison, WI 53715
(608) 251-6100

Saint Joseph's Hospital
611 St. Joseph Avenue
Marshfield, WI 54449
(715) 387-1713

Milwaukee County Medical Complex
8700 West Wisconsin Avenue
Milwaukee, WI 53226
(414) 257-5936

Mount Sinai Medical Center
950 North 12th Street
Milwaukee, WI 53233
(414) 289-8200

St. Francis Hospital
3237 South 16th Street
Milwaukee, WI 53215
(414) 647-5000

St. Joseph's Hospital
5000 West Chambers Street
Milwaukee, WI 53210
(414) 447-2000

WYOMING

Memorial Hospital of Laramie County
300 East 23rd Street
Cheyenne, WY 82001
(307) 634-3341

Index